TRAIN

THE EVOLUTION OF RAIL TRAVEL

Memorabilia captions, clockwise from top left:
• Letter by John Backhouse (aged 14) to his sisters, describing his witnessing of the
  opening of the Stockton and Darlington Railway dated 10 October 1825 (p.13).
• French TGV publicity announced that you could now reserve seats on these new
  trains (p.145).
• Wartime poster explains to passengers that when they were delayed, they might not
  be told why the delay had occurred as the information could be useful to the enemy (p.93).
• Fold out TGV timetable and route map showing stations served and travel times (p.145).
• Share certificate is for the Charleroy Railway in France issued in 1863 (p.23).
• Detailed General Arrangement drawing of the streamlined LMS Princess Coronation
  Class (pp.96–7).
• Orient Express poster advises the offices in different countries where seats and
  sleepers on the train could be obtained from (p.85).
• 1879 South Eastern Railway illustrated tourist guide was published to boost
  passenger levels (p.40).
• Leaflet produced by the National Union of Railwaymen in 1962 encouraging railway
  staff to protest against the cuts (p.123).
• Advertising and information leaflet for the Central Vermont Railway (p.68).
• Railway companies used leaflets to illustrate areas of interest such as the history of travel
  on a route, famous landmarks and the people that developed the railway (p.82).

THIS IS AN ANDRÉ DEUTSCH BOOK

This edition published in 2015 by André Deutsch
A division of the Carlton Publishing Group
20 Mortimer Street
London
W1T 3JW

First published in 2011

Text and Design © Carlton Books Limited 2011, 2015

Produced under licence for SCMG Enterprises Ltd. National Railway Museum logo
© SCMG. Every purchase supports the museum. www.nrm.org.uk

The National Railway Museum is the largest railway museum in the world with
exhibitions and collections illustrating over 300 years of British railway history.

Printed in China

A CIP catalogue for this book is available from the British Library

ISBN: 978 0 23300 458 7

TRAIN

THE EVOLUTION OF RAIL TRAVEL

PHILIP MARSH

ANDRE
DEUTSCH

CONTENTS

s is the "Flying Scotchman", Great Northern Railway.

INTRODUCTION

Arguably, a railway could be defined as a guided transport system that uses a purpose-built track containing rails above or below the ground to guide wheeled vehicles with the minimum of effort. Either the rails or wheels will be flanged.

This was not always the case – thousands of years ago, the ruts that resulted from constant use of a path or track by a hand- or animal-drawn cart or wagon, may have literally guided early miners or hauliers to dig grooves to make operations easier.

In the same way that the development of the wheel revolutionized ancient society and its working methods, so the railways transformed society, arguably bringing the biggest change that the human race has ever seen by creating wealth, and unifying countries and continents.

There are several aspects to this transformation. Until the 1830s, 99 per cent of the population was largely static, with family units living in close proximity to each other and working close to home.

Travelling any distance for a family holiday or short break was as impractical as it was unthinkable! This was largely because, until the mid-1650s, roads were rough and carriages the preserve of a rich few travelling at walking speed.

In the 1750s, an advertisement appeared for a "Flying Coach" linking London and Manchester, and taking four and a half days. The revenue from turnpikes paid for better, faster roads – up to 19 kph (12 mph). London to Portsmouth took about eight hours, Birmingham ten hours and Edinburgh around 48 hours.

This was the actual travel time and does not include overnight, refreshment and comfort stops. For those without a plodding farm horse at their disposal, walking was the most popular transport choice at this time! People travelled because they had to, not because they wanted to – it was an ordeal to be endured rather than an enjoyable pursuit.

Canals produced huge industrial efficiencies so far as transporting goods was concerned, but like horse-drawn carriages they did not trigger the travel and social mobility explosion that the railways brought about. Horse-drawn omnibuses made a brief appearance in Paris in 1662, not to reappear until 1827 – two years prior to London's omnibus drawn by three horses and the cause of much congestion!

The advent of flight and the motor car nearly resulted in the downfall of the railways, but in this book we explain how railways not only survived but developed into and why millions of people continue to be fascinated by them today.

(LMR) held a competition at Rainhill in 1829 to see which locomotive was suitable for the route, opened the following year. These "Rainhill Trials" were won by Robert Stephenson's Rocket, running at over 48 kmph (30 mph).

In May 1830, the Canterbury & Whitstable Railway opened, becoming the first railway to regularly use a steam locomotive and to issue a season ticket! Four months later, the first railway fatality occurred when William Huskisson MP was hit by Rocket on the opening-day ceremony on the Liverpool and Manchester Railway.

Railway construction led to confrontations such as in 1605 at Broseley when two lines were built from the same mine by rival coal owners. Each owner ripped up the other's rails several times while disputing a Right of Way, and eventually the dispute was settled in court.

Perhaps the most notable incident was the "Battle of Wolverton" on 23 December 1834 between the Grand Union Canal company and the London and Birmingham Railway (LBR), which needed to build a bridge over the Grand Union Canal at Wolverton. The parties could not reach agreement over the bridge so LBR Engineer Robert Stephenson surprised the canal company, building the bridge by torchlight on 23 December using artisans and navvies, being completed by noon on Christmas Day.

A week later the infuriated canal company demolished the bridge but the LBR won a court injunction against the canal company. Thus ended sabotage and pitched battles, allowing the first long-distance UK railway from London to open in 1838 between Euston and Birmingham.

The railway age and a transport revolution had arrived!

PHILIP MARSH

RUTS TO RAILS

(2000 BC TO AD 1800)

Railways of a sort have existed for at least 4,000 years. They were used by Ancient Greeks and Romans, who may have enhanced grooves in stone roads to guide the wheels of animal-drawn carts, possibly defining today's railway gauge. Standardizing the space between chariot wheels or cart shafts allowed an animal to pull loads more easily, as it could avoid uneven surfaces by using ruts worn or deliberately cut into the road.

The first recorded example of a guided transport system using ruts – about 1.5 metres (5 feet) apart – is the 8-kilometre (5-mile) stretch of paved stone track on the Diolkos in Greece, which was once used to transport heavy goods between ports. It dates from around 600 BC, with the Corinth Canal following the same route from AD 67. Around the same time, there was a similar operation in Malta whereby loaded mineral wagons ran downhill using gravity and animals hauled the empty wagons back uphill. An early mine rut-way, dating from AD 200, was found in Portugal at the Três Minas gold mine. Here, ruts 1.2 metres (4 feet) wide were cut into the rock floor to aid wagon operations.

As the mining industry expanded throughout Europe from the 1500s, there was an increase in the volume of minerals extracted from the ground and they were transported over longer distances. Miners discovered that this could be done more efficiently by laying rails to link mines with ports or factories. The first recorded example of a railway line in Britain, using wooden rails, dates from 1604. It was constructed between the Wollaton and Strelley coal pits near Nottingham, with 3 kilometres (2 miles) of rails.

Such wooden ways greatly improved the cost and speed – of transporting bulk goods, and the demand for them, especially in hilly or rocky areas – became more urgent as the importance and benefits became more apparent. Mining companies using wooden railways were soon in competition with each other, prompting confrontations such as that in 1605 at Broseley, near Ironbridge, in the English Midlands at the heart of the Industrial Revolution. Two lines, owned by rival coal businesses, were built from the same mine but each owner ripped up the other's rails several times while disputing a right of way. The matter was eventually settled in court.

Many wagonways were laid in the industrial northeast of England. The famous "Tanfield Waggonway" opened near Newcastle in 1725 (part of it is still open today), incorporating the world's longest single-span bridge at the time – the Tanfield or Causey Arch – and now the world's oldest railway bridge. To give some idea of how busy it was, shortly after opening the Waggonway carried an average of 930 wagons every day. Other famous tracks included Wylam, laid in 1748, and Killingworth 15 years later – mainly linking the staithes on the River Tyne. By 1800, this local railway network alone stretched over 241 kilometres (150 miles) in length, with the longest line more than 16 kilometres (10 miles) long.

Other industrial areas – such as the Forest of Dean in Gloucestershire, and Merthyr Tydfil and Blaenavon in South Wales – also hosted a dramatic growth in early railways. From the 1700s, they carried coal and iron, linking mines to the River Severn and foundries respectively. This was the start of local transport economics driving railway expansion in mining areas.

As the Industrial Revolution gathered pace, iron replaced wooden rails and wheels. Iron wheels were introduced in 1732 and wooden rails were capped with iron near Ironbridge from 1767. It was another 20 years before the first 100 per cent cast iron rails – 0.9 or 1.2 metres (3 or 4 feet) long – were laid in the industrial powerhouses of Merthyr Tydfil and Blaenavon.

It was soon clear that railways were a matter of national importance, and Parliament had to sanction each one before construction. The first Railway Act was in 1662 for the private Stour Navigation Railway near Stourbridge. The first public parliamentary Railway Act was prepared in 1800 for the Surrey Iron Railway and it was sanctioned a year later.

BELOW LEFT The Greek Corinth Diolkos. This is one of the world's oldest surviving examples of a guided transport system, dating back to 600 BC. Most of its traffic was taken by the Corinth canal from AD 67.

BELOW Very early railways used wooden tracks from the sixteenth century, providing an easier way of moving wagons than negotiating rough obstacle-strewn paths. Wheels had a rough edge or flange fashioned on them that kept them running on the timbers.

THE ECONOMICS OF ANIMAL-POWERED RAILWAYS

Animal-powered transport was very labour intensive: only one wagon could be pulled by a horse, with a driver required for each load. This meant that while uneven paths – often strewn with rocks and potholes – were used, only limited quantities of minerals or wood could be slowly transported on each trip.

Gravity and inclines had a large effect on early transport and the steeper the incline, the smaller the load that could be carried. When descending, the driver had to apply a crude handbrake to ensure the cart or wagon did not run over the horse.

The introduction of rut-ways, then rails, brought a huge improvement over previous transport methods, making it possible to move heavier loads faster over greater distances. It even sometimes allowed horses to pull more than one wagon at a time, more than doubling efficiency.

BELOW The Tanfield Arch (also known as the Causey Arch) is thought to be the oldest surviving railway bridge in the world. It was built in 1725 and its 30 metre (105 foot) span was the largest in the world when completed.

RAILS TO ROUTES

AND MINERAL TO PASSENGER TRAINS

As the Industrial Revolution increased demand for heavy commodities, new mines opened further away from factories and canals, so longer railways were needed. Traffic also became more frequent and heavier.

The increase in traffic meant that wooden rails and wheels quickly wore out, so cast iron rails and wheels were introduced. But these 0.9 or 1.2 metre (3 or 4 foot) rails were very brittle, frequently fracturing where locomotives were used. From 1820, the problem was resolved by John Birkinshaw in Bedlington, using rolled iron rails up to 6 metres (20 feet) long.

Originally, flanges on the rails were used to guide wheels, but engineers soon realized it was preferable to fix them on the wheels. The gauge (the distance between the rails) became more uniform and rails, initially fixed to timbers for stability, were spiked on to stone blocks as loads became heavier. Ash and spoil were now used to help create a supporting and level track foundation.

Despite these improvements, it was still only possible for an animal and its driver to haul one 3 ton wagon at 6 kph (4 mph), making longer-distance haulage uneconomic. Thomas Newcomen pondered how to replace animals with steam power (and is acknowledged as the inventor of the first successful steam engine, pumping water from a mine, in 1711; he and fellow Devonian Thomas Savery, who had patented his steam engine design a decade earlier, made significant improvements to steam engine technology and efficiency). But it was a Frenchman who invented the first steam engine capable of moving itself and a load. In 1769, Nicolas Cugnot designed and built a steam-powered road carriage in Paris. This was originally created as a self-propelled gun carriage, which he tried but failed to sell to the French army – possibly because steering was nearly impossible!

ABOVE Cugnot's cumbersome steam car is depicted in this 1770 engraving as having just crashed into a wall. Its steering capability seems to have been, at best, somewhat vague.

TOP Thomas Newcomen's 1712 stationary steam engine was the first steam-driven machine to replace animals pumping water from mines. It used a combination of atmospheric pressure and steam, creating a vacuum to pump the water.

ABOVE Trevithic's *Pen-y-Darren*, the world's first locomotive, is portrayed in this Terrence Cuneo painting pulling the first-ever steam train in South Wales. The rough brittle track can clearly be seen.

ABOVE Trevithick brought the first steam train to London in 1808, as depicted in this drawing. Huge crowds viewed and travelled on the circular track in what was billed as a "steam circus" rather than a railway.

James Watt and Matthew Boulton further improved this technology in the mid-1780s, using steam to move wagons up steep inclines for the first time – one of the many "world firsts" in railway history. Their double-acting, push-pull motion enabled a steam engine to drive cranks or connecting rods for the first time. When used in conjunction with a winding drum, steam could now drive machinery and move wagons up steep inclines in mines using ropes. Boulton and Watt made a fortune manufacturing and operating stationary engines in mines around the UK. They employed a Scotsman, William Murdock, who made a working model of the first road steam carriage. His employers did not develop the idea but patented their own version, so his place in history has been somewhat obscured. But he is recognized as having made huge improvements to mine engines and their profitability.

In the late 1790s, Cornishman Richard Trevithick built several road steam carriages, which were soon adapted for railway use. The resulting *Pen-y-Darren* pulled the world's first steam train on 13 February 1804. This was a private test train pulling wagons over 14 kilometres (9 miles) on the private Merthyr tramroad, and was repeated in public eight days later. Seventy spectators jumped on the five wagons (each carrying 2 tons of iron), becoming the first-ever steam railway passengers! The journey took four hours with a top speed of 8 kph (5 mph), and this event is acknowledged as the starting point of the world's passenger railways.

Because of the problematic fracturing of the cast iron rails at that time, Trevithick only built a few more locomotives but he did provide a glimpse of the future to Londoners in 1808. He built a circular railway offering public rides "designed to be for the education of the public" at 13 kph (8 mph). Tickets cost one shilling, thus creating the first fare-paying steam railway. This was advertised as the "Catch Me Who Can" ride, located yards away from where Euston station was opened less than 30 years later.

In 1812, Trevithick devised a rack-and-cog-rail steam-propulsion system at the Middleton Railway, Leeds (in continuous operation since 1755). After a successful test run pulling eight 3 ton coal wagons with 50 passengers aboard for the 23 minute ride covering 2 kilometres (1½ miles),

three more engines were built for the line. Trevithick devised this system thinking that iron-wheeled locomotives would not provide enough grip on the track to pull a train. Despite early success, the system was short lived, as rolled iron rails allowed locomotives to pull trains using wheels alone for adhesion and propulsion. Trevithick died a pauper in 1833 – he was a brilliant engineer but not a businessman.

The world's first public route opened in 1803, linking the River Thames at Wandsworth Wharf with Croydon. The Surrey Iron Railway, as it was known, had two tracks so traffic could flow in both directions and horses pulled several wagons at a time, creating the first real train and railway system. However, the world's first regular public passenger railway

opened three years later – the 1.6 kilometre (1 mile) long Oystermouth tramway near Swansea, again using horse-drawn wagons.

A century after the first steam engine was built by Thomas Newcomen, the northeast railway heartland produced three lesser-known but outstanding locomotive engineers: William Hedley (an early Stephenson rival), Timothy Hackworth and the mainly unknown Newcastle engineer, William Chapman (granted Patent No. 3632 in 1812, describing the first locomotive design).

The owner of Wylam Colliery wanted a steam locomotive to run on the 8 kilometre (5 mile) railway from the coal mine to Lemington on the River Tyne. Trevithick turned down this

OPPOSITION TO THE EARLY RAILWAYS

The introduction of surfaced roads by Thomas Telford and John Macadam brought with it the golden age of stagecoaches in the first quarter of the nineteenth century. This form of transport had developed rapidly after the first Royal Mail express stagecoach ran between London and Bath in 1784. Road users had to pay tolls on the growing network at turnpikes along the way. The tariff varied according to whether you were on foot, on horseback or in a carriage, and carrying goods or passengers. A few wealthy people used their private carriages to indulge in a limited amount of leisure travel. Public services also operated, hiring coachmen (horse drivers) and "cads" (the nickname given to the conductors) and thereby creating a new line of employment.

The advent of railways, where speeds reached considerably more than 19 kph (12 mph) – the maximum allowed on roads – over longer and increasing distances with heavier loads, seriously threatened the road industry. On the first railways, some horse-drawn carriages with their owners still

aboard were placed on flat wagons within a train. Turnpike operators, coachmen and cads vehemently objected to all railway schemes, saying their livelihood was at stake. The battle was on!

Landowners varied their approach to railways. Some vehemently opposed them while others welcomed them. In the mid-1840s, the Earl of Shugborough was paid compensation and also insisted that the railway was to be built out of sight of his estate near Rugeley, 200 kilometres (125 miles) from Euston. The railway was buried in a tunnel at Shugborough decorated with ornate portals to blend in with estate buildings. Those who flatly refused to allow the London to Birmingham railway to cross their land included landowners around Northampton. The London & Birmingham Railway had to route its line via Weedon and the troublesome 2.4 kilometre (1½ mile) Kilsby Tunnel just south of Rugby. The Northampton objectors eventually realized that they had made a bad mistake and their town was linked to the main line in 1875.

OPPOSITE RIGHT Matthew Boulton, the early English steam pioneer, set up a factory near Birmingham making steam engines in partnership with Watt. By the early nineteenth century over 500 of these engines were in use across the UK.

ABOVE A very early photograph taken in 1862 of Hedley's *Wylam Dilly* at Wylam Colliery when the engine finished its working life. It had worked for nearly half a century and the engine was preserved.

WHO WAS THE GREATEST — ROBERT STEPHENSON OR BRUNEL?

This debate has raged for over 150 years as both engineers designed, built and operated world-class railways.

Brunel (right, top) designed and built the Paddington to Bristol GWR – now a proposed World Heritage Site – to be as level and straight as possible. Robert Stephenson (right, bottom) designed and built the London & Birmingham Railway with torturous curves, deep tunnels, long cuttings and arduous gradients. A popular story says that Brunel's famous Box Tunnel was designed so that sunrise could be seen through it on around 9 April each year – Brunel's birthday. Was this the mark of a genius, or a self-publicist?

Brunel built steamships, huge bridges and viaducts, while Stephenson built *Rocket* and set up the first locomotive works to supply the world.

Brunel made several expensive errors convincing the GWR directors that his "broad gauge" would provide faster and more comfortable rides and that his atmospheric railway would remove the need to buy Stephenson's locomotives.

Stephenson designed all his railways and locomotives ensuring they would be compatible and built to his preferred "narrow gauge", which was uniformly adopted as standard from 1846. So, was Stephenson a genius or a cartel operator?

opportunity, allowing Hedley (the Wylam Mine engineer) and Hackworth (the Wylam Mine foreman blacksmith) to join forces in building their first (unsuccessful) engine in 1813. In 1814 they supplied the successful *Puffing Billy*, followed by *Wylam Dilly* in 1815. After a dispute, Hackworth left Wylam in 1816 and re-emerged eight years later supervising locomotive construction for the Stockton & Darlington Railway (SDR). He is credited with major mechanical innovations in steam engines.

George Stephenson (also from the Wylam area) designed and built his first locomotive, *My Lord*, in 1814 after working on engines at Killingworth Colliery near Newcastle. His

second engine was named *Blucher* (Northumbrian slang for a heavy unwieldy instrument). Although not overly successful, he persevered and, working with Killingworth Mine engineer Ralph Dodds, made significant improvements redesigning the engines and track within two years. From 1822, these modifications were incorporated into the construction of the SDR, bringing Stephenson and Dodds widespread fame when it opened in 1825, as they also supplied *Locomotion No. 1*. In 1823, Stephenson and his son, Robert, opened the world's first locomotive factory – Robert Stephenson & Co. – in Newcastle, cementing the area's indisputable place in railway history.

BELOW The world's first passenger railway, the Swansea and Mumbles Railway, started operations using horses and also experimented with sails. The line linked Swansea with the seaside village of Mumbles a mile away.

OPPOSITE There are very few contemporary accounts written about the early railways not written by those involved. This is a fascinating letter dated 10 October 1825 by John Backhouse aged 14, to his sisters describing his witnessing of the opening of the Stockton and Darlington Railway.

John Church Backhouse's Account
of the Opening of the Stockton & Darlington
Railway.
Eld. Meskin's death, by Ann Backhouse.

From the Bank.
10 mo 1825.
Railway opened 27/9/25

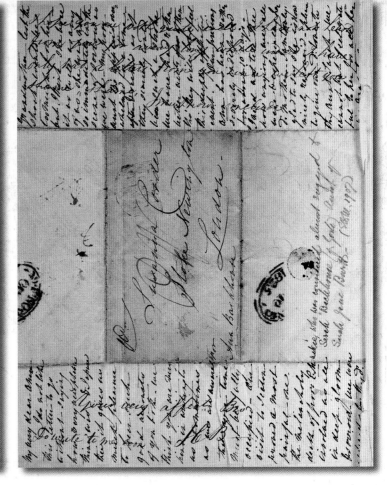

My Dear Sisters;

Perhaps you may not under-
stand what that drawing at the top means,
it is meant to represent the opening of
the Stockton & Darlington railway
which took place on the 27 of September
1825. Fig 26. represents the Locomotive steam engine

     1.2.3.4.5 —— waggons

     22 . is an elegant coach called the Experiment

     21 &c & also waggons for visitors &c to ride in

     24 a flag on Periculum privatum et Publicum
                                        Bonum

23 is an other "May the Stockton & Darlington
Railway give Public Satisfaction &
reward its Spirited Promoters.

25 had a painting or drawing of the L Engine
& waggons —

I have only drawn 21. waggons but there
were 17. more+. It was a very grand sight
to see such a mass of people moving on the
road from D to S. 600 people were said to be in
on & about the waggons & coaches! & the engine
drew not less than 90 tons!!!!!! There was
an excellent dinner prepared &c at Stockton.

+ making in all 38

for the Railway gentry &c &c &c I could tell you
a great many more particulars but I suppose
that you are tired of it by this time

I lodge now at West Lodge & am very comfortable
here. My Grandmother desires her very dear
love, that is to say to Ann to thee, & was much obliged to thee for thy
letter to her as also is my Aunt Ann & she who
says she intends to answer thy letter by & by
when she has time & she & I believe my Aunt Jane
desire their very dear love to you. My father
& mother are either at Sunderland or at least the
do not know which, they talk of something of
returning home to morrow; but I believe it is not
certain. Little Anne as I suppose you have
said has been very poorly indeed with a bilious attack
as well as all & my Aunt Jane was very uneasy about her,
but she is a great better now, & she came down
stairs to day for the first time.
Please & bride arrives here at 9 oclock last
night. Give my dear love to my U & A Harris &
also to M & J Bevan

My very very very dear love.
Do write to me soon.

I remain your very affect. Bro.
John Backhouse

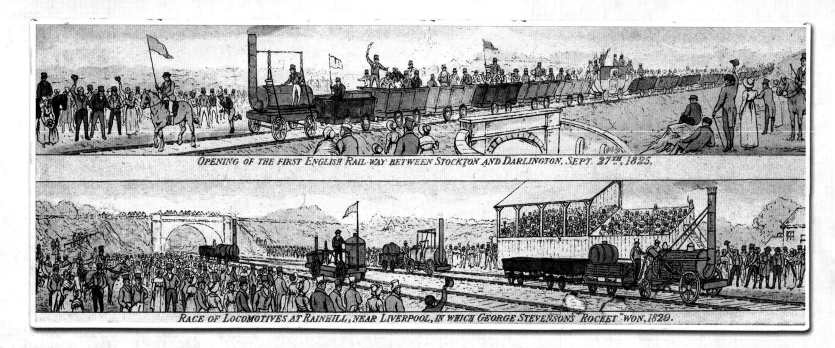

OPENING OF THE FIRST ENGLISH RAIL-WAY BETWEEN STOCKTON AND DARLINGTON, SEPT. 27TH, 1825.

RACE OF LOCOMOTIVES AT RAINHILL, NEAR LIVERPOOL, IN WHICH GEORGE STEVENSON'S ROCKET WON, 1829.

Stockton & Darlington – Canal or Railway?

Businessmen needing a canal or railway to link Stockton with the collieries lodged the first Stockton & Darlington Railway Act, which was defeated in parliament in May 1819. A revision received royal assent in April 1821 and the first rail was laid in May 1822. A third Act sanctioned passenger trains and the use of steam.

George Stephenson built the 26 mile (42 kilometre) line and provided a locomotive, *Locomotion No. 1*, which duly pulled the inaugural train at speeds up to 15 mph (24 kph) on 27 September 1825. It conveyed one passenger coach plus 500 passengers clinging onto 34 empty coal wagons for the 20 miles (32 kilometres) between Stockton and Shildon.

Trains were still hauled by horse and steam power for some years, until it became obvious that steam was the only way forward to cope with ever-increasing traffic.

The Rainhill Trials was a competition held in 1829 with a £500 prize offered by the Liverpool & Manchester Railway (LMR) directors to establish the best locomotive for the line. George and Robert Stephenson's *Rocket* prevailed – defeating, amongst others, Hackworth's *Sans Pareil* and Braithwaite and Ericsson's *Novelty* – thereby assuring their position as early railway barons.

Rocket and *Novelty* both reached around 30 mph, but the former could pull heavier trains further and was a similar design to that of French engineer Marc Seguin. He visited the SDR in 1825 and worked with Robert Stephenson, purchasing two of his locomotives for the St. Etienne to Lyon line that he built in 1826. Although a clear winner, *Rocket* was somewhat unstable with its high cylinders. Nevertheless it marked the creation of the express steam locomotive.

By 1830, several other longer railways were in operation, the Severn & Wye and the Plymouth & Dartmoor Railways –

ABOVE The Rainhill Trials and the opening of the Stockton & Darlington Railway are depicted here in this late-nineteenth-century drawing. Huge crowds were attracted to both events, watching and travelling on the new form of transport.

BELOW John Rastrick was a pioneering locomotive engineer and this is an excerpt from one of his notebooks describing Stephenson's *Rocket*. He was also one of the Judges at The Rainhill Trials at which *Rocket* was deemed to be the winner. These notes describe the design of *Rocket* along with principle dimensions and calculations looking at power output. This could be described as an early General Arrangement drawing.

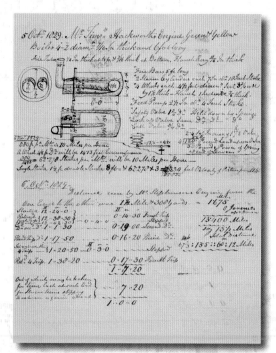

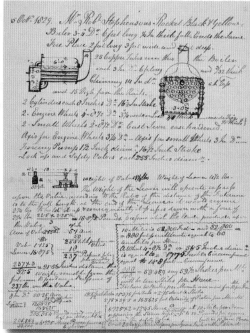

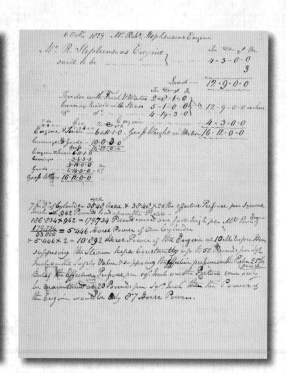

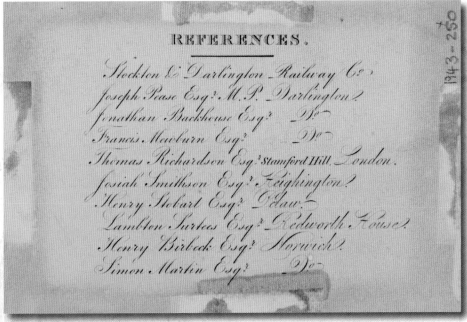

LEFT AND ABOVE Timothy Hackworth was a leading early locomotive engineer and as with all businessmen, carried a business card to give out to potential clients. The card gives says what he can do and where his Works location is. The reverse side lists his existing customers such as the Stockton & Darlington Railway and individuals (see pages 10–15 for further information).

BELOW A print of *Locomotion No.1* clearly illustrating what the engine looked like when new in 1825. The development of the steam locomotive since *Pen-y-Darren* 20 years earlier can clearly be seen.

both over 40 kilometres (25 miles) long. By changing trains between adjoining lines, it was now possible to travel long distances (for the time), such as the 97 kilometres (60 miles) between Newport and Hereford – even if it was in wagons!

William Stephens and Adrian Stephens are little-known engineers, but they invented a vital steam locomotive component – the whistle. As railways developed, a warning device to protect people from the new railway dangers was needed. William Stephens invented a steam boiler whistle in 1826 – when steam escaped, it sounded the whistle and this method was adapted for use in 1835 on the LMR.

A second tranche of famous engineers followed a decade after *Puffing Billy*, such as Isambard Kingdom Brunel, Thomas Brassey, Edward Bury, William Cudworth and Edward Watkin.

French-educated Brunel planned the Great Western Railway (GWR), which opened in 1838 from Paddington to Maidenhead, and to Bristol in 1841. He became a giant in many aspects of engineering but made several errors, such as persuading the GWR to use the 2 metre (7 foot) broad gauge. In 1846, the government's Gauge Commission decreed that the narrower gauge of 1.4 metres (4 feet 8½ inches) was to be used in the UK.

Brunel experimented with an "atmospheric railway" – obviating the need for a locomotive – using pumping stations that sucked air from a tube between the rails, which was linked to the train by a piston. The train was drawn towards the vacuum, pushed by air pressure behind the piston. However, this system failed as the tube was not airtight and the leather seal tended to perish or be eaten by rats.

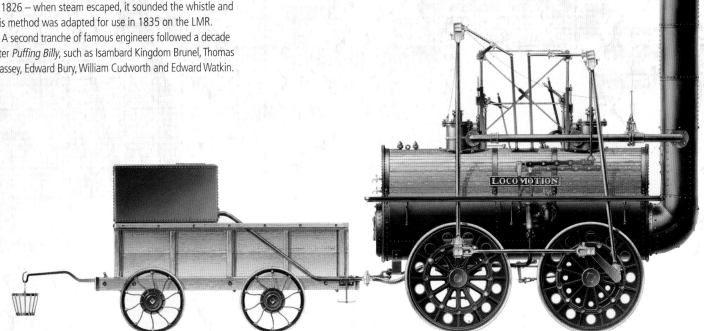

THE RAILWAY AGE BEGINS

/// EARLY RAILWAYS AND EXPANSION 1826–1846

The Stockton & Darlington Railway (SDR), opening in 1825, heralded the advent of the railway age. Soon it was paying large dividends to shareholders, whose shares quickly rose in value.

A year later in 1826, George Stephenson began designing the next major UK line – the Liverpool & Manchester Railway (LMR). He now faced huge opposition from landowners, turnpike operators and the coaching industry, but after several attempts he gained royal assent for the line.

The Canterbury & Whitstable Railway (CWR) opened before the LMR. As with many lines, George and Robert Stephenson had been involved in the construction and provision of its first locomotive, *Invicta*. The CWR's claim to fame is that on opening in May 1830, it became the first line in the world to operate regular passenger services and to issue season tickets.

Robert Stephenson heeded Trevithick's advice when designing *Planet* for the LMR, incorporating insulation and inside cylinders – a concept followed by the Great Western Railway a decade later. This improved steaming efficiency while removing the kind of unstable running previously experienced with *Rocket*.

Burgeoning traffic levels and higher speeds led to accidents, with the first high-profile railway fatality occurring on the LMR's opening day, 15 September 1830. William Huskisson, an MP, died from injuries after descending from the official opening train, only to be hit by a passing locomotive.

Railways were now creating unprecedented economic and social effects. As longer routes opened, and travel became affordable for the masses, railway timetables dictated that time had to be unified across the UK. From the mid-1830s, railways began to spread everywhere and London's first steam railway (to Greenwich) was opened in 1835 – despite fierce opposition by dockworkers and coaching companies who feared for their jobs.

After fierce opposition by landowners, the London & Birmingham Railway (LBR) created the first long-distance route, opening in stages from Euston station in 1837 and to Birmingham in September 1838. The LBR also created Wolverton, the world's first railway town and railway works (then employing 200 people and still open today).

Initially, passengers could only physically endure rail travel for a couple of hours before requiring respite from the rigors involved. Wolverton Station, adjacent to the Grand Union Canal, was a grand affair situated roughly half way between Euston and Birmingham. Locomotives were changed here and passengers allowed just ten minutes to use refreshment and toilet facilities.

RIGHT George Stephenson, born in 1781, was probably the foremost early railway engineer building railways and locomotives. He was in huge demand across Britain's developing railway system, and with his son, Robert, arguably formed the world's foremost railway partnership.

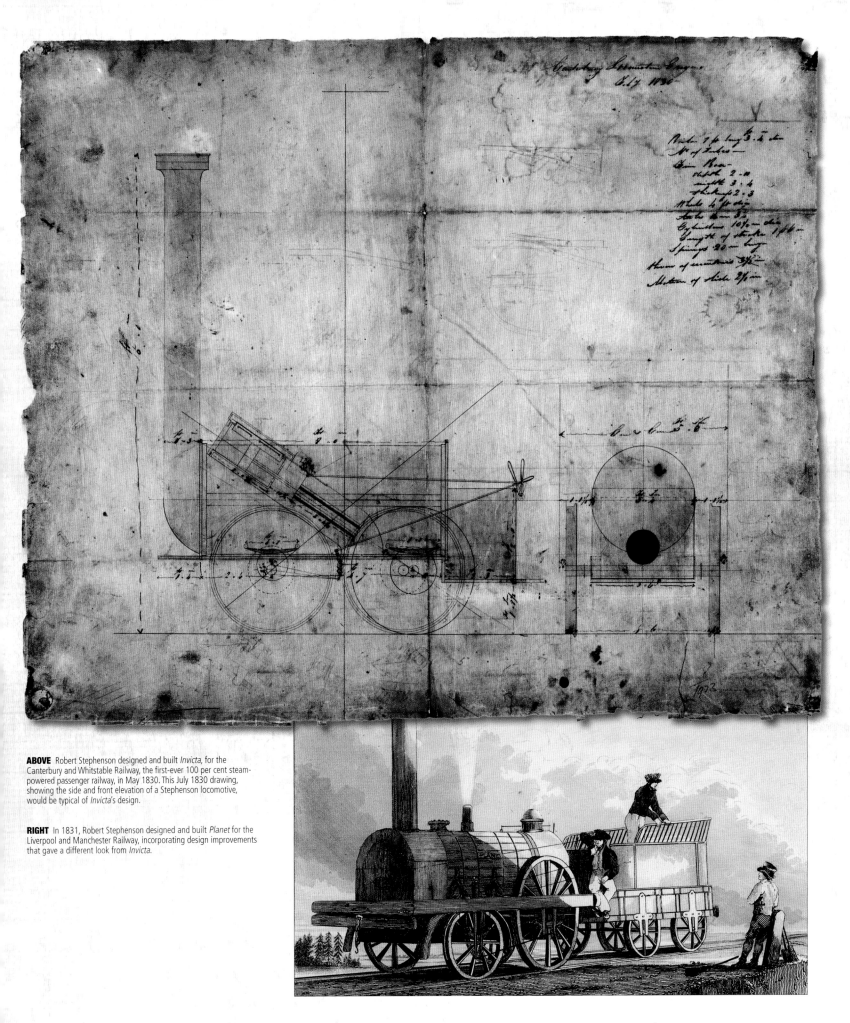

ABOVE Robert Stephenson designed and built *Invicta*, for the Canterbury and Whitstable Railway, the first-ever 100 per cent steam-powered passenger railway, in May 1830. This July 1830 drawing, showing the side and front elevation of a Stephenson locomotive, would be typical of *Invicta*'s design.

RIGHT In 1831, Robert Stephenson designed and built *Planet* for the Liverpool and Manchester Railway, incorporating design improvements that gave a different look from *Invicta*.

FIGHTING THE MANIA – THE ROAD LOBBY OPPOSITION

The early engineers faced a number of battles: the first was advancing technology to keep up with new demands; and then came fierce opposition from the turnpike operators, the landowners, and the coaching and canal industries.

The turnpikes generated profits collecting tolls for their operators and owners, who were often major landowners. The introduction of road steam carriages brought direct competition to the coaching industry and these faced swingeing tolls at turnpikes in an attempt to dissuade them from operating, which quickly succeeded.

The coaching industry was also vehemently against railways as they had created a growing and profitable industry on popular routes, and the drivers and cads understandably wanted to protect their livelihoods.

The landowners were against the first railways as they thought the smoke, noise and speed of trains would scare their livestock and pollute their land. They also stood to lose income from road tolls and have their land dissected by these "dangerous" railway lines.

This was the location of the "Battle of Wolverton" on 23 December 1834, when navvies from the canal company and LBR clashed over a bridge the LBR needed to build across the canal and agreement could not be reached.

Robert Stephenson instructed navvies to build the bridge by torchlight, and it was completed on Christmas Day. A week later, the infuriated canal company demolished the bridge but the LBR later won a court injunction against the canal company, thereby ending the conflict.

The broad-gauge Great Western Railway (GWR) also opened in 1838 between Paddington and Taplow and on to Bristol in 1841, initially using Robert Stephenson's *North Star* locomotive. The GWR was Brunel's masterful creation – he had designed the mainly level and straight route, and persuaded the directors to build the GWR's world-famous Swindon Works, which opened in 1843.

Swindon, unlike Wolverton, was already an established town, but both became railway towns with the railway authorities building houses, schools, churches and hospitals as well as repairing locomotives, carriages and wagons at the two locations.

Queen Victoria gave the royal seal of approval to railways in 1842, travelling from Slough to Paddington on the first royal journey, though not in the lowly style that soon forced the government to pass legislation protecting passengers from the abysmal travelling conditions experienced by regular passengers.

ABOVE The race to open the world's first long-distance railway was won by the London & Birmingham Railway, which opened fully in 1838. Philip Hardwick designed and built the Doric Euston Arch as the imposing gateway to Euston station, flanked by several similar-styled lodges.

OPPOSITE Objectors in Northampton stopped the LBR serving the town and the railway was diverted a few miles westwards. This involved creating Kilsby Tunnel to get through the Chiltern hills but was costly, with 26 lives lost and an outlay of three times the original budget.

RAILWAY MANIA

/// WIDESCALE BUILDING TAKES OFF

The early success of railways like the Stockton & Darlington, Liverpool & Manchester and London & Birmingham led to a speculative frenzy in the 1840s, as investors and promoters sought fame and fortune by opening up new routes. This craze became known as "railway mania", peaking in 1846 when more than 500 bills for new lines were put before Parliament for approval.

Fuelling the mania was a growing economy combined with a cut in interest rates that made government bonds less attractive to investors. Other factors included a growing middle class with savings to invest, booming newspaper circulations that provided a wide audience for promoters, and the birth of the modern stock market, which made share-dealing much easier. All of these elements together meant that promoters were able to offer railway schemes as supposedly foolproof investments to a large number of potential backers.

For each proposed railway line, a parliamentary bill was required to give rights to acquire land – in effect approving the route. Some landowners and rival railway companies raised objections, but as many MPs were themselves investors, most bills were passed without too much opposition. There was little to prevent anyone from forming a company and presenting a bill to Parliament as there were no real checks on who they were or their financial status. So this system was open to abuse, and indeed more than half of all approved routes were never actually built – through financial failure, takeover by a rival or, in some cases, fraud.

One figure who personified railway mania in the 1840s was George Hudson. The son of a farmer, he was a draper by trade, but a £30,000 legacy allowed him to invest in railways, and his strength of character and determination eventually earned him a place on the board of numerous railway companies. This gave him control over thousands of miles of railway from Bristol to Edinburgh and earned him the title "The Railway King". His position eventually collapsed, however, when he was judged to have abused his position of power for his own interests, committing fraud and bribery.

Before his downfall Hudson was responsible for many success stories, including the formation of the Midland Railway in 1844 from three of his companies. He was also instrumental in setting up the Railway Clearing House (RCH), the organization that apportioned any shared revenue between the various rail companies: as the railway network spread, and through journeys became possible using the trains of more than one company, it had become necessary to devise a way of sharing out revenues for both passenger and goods traffic. The RCH began operations on 2 January 1842 with an initial membership of nine railway companies, although more joined over time. The neutrality of the RCH meant that it also became a place to discuss general railway matters and to set standards for railway

ABOVE George Hudson was a hero and villain of the railway mania. He made a fortune developing railways but became heavily involved in fraud and bribery. He lost his own and his investors' money, spending the latter part of his life abroad, relying on friends for support.

ABOVE Built in 1851, the Crystal Palace housed the Great Exhibition in Hyde Park in central London, demonstrating the industrially rampant Britain of the time. The railways carried millions of people to the event. Afterwards the building was moved to the suburbs of southeast London.

RIGHT Rail enthusiasts cannot agree who was the top railway engineer, Brunel or one of the Stephensons. Brunel, to many enthusiasts, was the Great Western Railway. He designed many iconic stations, bridges and viaducts and the 1846 Bristol broad-gauge station was a typical example of his work.

technology, performance and safety. For example, in 1847, the RCH recommended that all of Britain's railways adopt Greenwich Mean Time as a standard, thus unifying the country in the same time zone; some years later, the recommendation was taken up.

Like other financial frenzies before and after, the railway mania bubble eventually burst, in the late 1840s, as proposed schemes became more and more unrealistic and expensive. But at least there was now a decent network, and lines authorized in the mid-1840s produced more than 9,600 route kilometres (6,000 miles) of actual railway – more than half the size of Britain's network today. The scale of the 1840s railway mania was never seen again. This was partly because many of the most lucrative routes had already been built or authorized. But it was also because many investors had got their financial fingers burnt and lost money. There was, however, a continual expansion, plus other smaller surges in the 1850s and 1860s. The network eventually peaked just before World War I at more than 37,000 route kilometres (23,000 miles).

After the mania, the larger railway companies, like the London & North Western, Great Western and the newly created Midland, set about expanding by buying up smaller, struggling lines. Investors in these smaller railways had little option but to sell cheaply or else lose everything through bankruptcy. This pattern of acquisitions and mergers continued on into the early twentieth century.

As the railways expanded to form networks, long-distance passenger journeys became possible for the first time. Seaside resorts developed as factory workers were able to travel en masse during their holidays, and demand started to grow for whole trains to serve this purpose. In July 1841, Thomas Cook chartered his first train to take a party of 1,000 temperance supporters from Leicester to Loughborough. He went on to expand his excursion business, and by 1855 had begun organizing holidays to Continental Europe.

London's Great Exhibition of 1851 was one of the first events to experience large-scale movement of passengers by rail. A million people a month visited the exhibition, with many travelling to London by rail from all parts of the country. Rail played a similar role for the 1867 International Exhibition in Paris, for which Thomas Cook organized cheap excursion fares that allowed working men and their families to attend.

Railway companies soon latched on to the financial benefits of mass passenger travel, and by 1880 more than a third of their income was coming from third-class ticket sales – despite third-class travel still being relatively basic. Rail travel was not only offering recreation, but also a way for working- and middle-class people to get to work, thus bringing about the birth of the commuter and the growth of suburbs around many towns and cities.

ABOVE The Ivybridge viaduct on Brunel's South Devon Railway is just one example of his famous west of England viaducts. This particular one was built in the mid-1840s and spanned a deep valley on the southern edge of Dartmoor.

RIGHT Railways were built using various fund raising schemes. Shares were a popular way of securing finance with the promise of future dividends an increase in the value of the share itself. This example of a share certificate is for the Charleroy Railway in France issued in 1863.

RAILWAY MANIA SPREADS BESIDE THE SEA

Coastal railways faced many a challenge, especially in negotiating river mouths and irregular terrain. In the days before bridges, boats were used to carry goods wagons across rivers: in northeast England, coal wagons were carried by boat from 1842, while ferries were in use for wagons across the Scottish Firth of Forth from 1850 and the Firth of Tay the following year. Gradually bridges and tunnels were built over or under the largest rivers but not across the widest estuaries and inlets. It was not until 1890 that the famous Forth and Tay bridges opened, achieving what were effectively the railways' first successful sea crossings.

Seaside railways also had the task of serving resorts. These became popular but sometimes the station was situated on a cliff high above the promenade and hotels. How could tourists be transported between a railway station and where they wanted to go? The answer was via a cliff railway – a funicular – and nowhere was this better demonstrated than at Scarborough, Yorkshire. The first of five cliff railways built there, introducing such systems to Britain, was a double-track line opened in 1875. Each car carried 14 passengers at an incline of 1 in 1.75, balanced by the car travelling in the opposite direction. Seeing the potential profits to be made from such a venture, a local hotel owner paid for the railway.

ABOVE The railways brought the south coast resorts within easy range for day trips on high days and holidays. The Southern Railway's London termini were the gateway for millions of day trippers, such as these waiting for a Margate train at Victoria between the wars before road transport gained the advantage.

LEFT A French postcard from 1910 depicting French seaside holidaymakers sending greetings from Saint Brieuc, on the northwest coast of Brittany.

The scale of railway development began to reshape the country by boosting those towns that had stations, while diminishing the importance of those without. Some towns grew out of nowhere simply because of a railway. Middlesbrough, for example, was a just hamlet until the Stockton & Darlington Railway extended there in 1830 and turned it into a thriving port. Other places, such as Swindon, Eastleigh, Wolverton, Crewe and Doncaster, grew to become "railway towns" as either major junctions or the sites of railway works. In 1851, the Great Western Railway (GWR) employed more than 90 per cent of Swindon's working population, while the London & Birmingham Railway accounted for more than 85 per cent of Wolverton's.

One of the greatest names to emerge from this period of railway development was Isambard Kingdom Brunel.

He was responsible for many great feats of engineering, including ships and bridges, but he was also chief engineer of the GWR from 1833 until his death in 1859. During that time, the GWR and its partner companies expanded to connect London with Bristol, Exeter, Plymouth and on into Cornwall. It also ran into South Wales, connecting with the port of Neyland in Pembrokeshire, from where passengers could board transatlantic liners bound for New York. Brunel's many railway legacies today include Paddington station, Box Tunnel in Wiltshire and the Royal Albert Bridge linking Devon and Cornwall. However, his beloved broad gauge eventually lost out to Stephenson's narrower but more widespread standard gauge (although the GWR did not finally complete conversion until 1892 – 33 years after his death).

BELOW The world's first railway town was at Wolverton in central England. It employed over 5,000 people at its height around 1900 and when the workforce left work, it was impossible to walk against the tide of people. The main entrance/exit is seen in this picture.

SERVICE DEVELOPMENT
AND LOCOMOTIVE POWER

Whereas early railways had primarily been built to convey goods in wagons, the introduction of locomotives covering longer distances at higher speeds and conveying ever-growing numbers of passengers quickly led to the need for proper carriages and a better standard of service.

Passengers were initially conveyed in little more than covered goods wagons. Most had to travel in spartan, third-class circumstances – exposed to the weather and cinders from the engine, sometimes with holes bored in the floor to provide drainage. Following several fatalities attributed to these conditions, the Board of Trade introduced new laws in 1844. These made railway companies protect passengers from the weather "while admitting light and air" by providing a train with roof and windows at least once a day on every route, at a minimum speed of 19 kph (12 mph). This boosted passenger numbers and, incredibly, these laws still apply today – such trains are deemed to be "parliamentary services".

These early trains were also without an effective braking system and there were no passenger alarms. As accidents occurred more frequently, safety became a growing concern

and brake development was critical. In 1848, Wolverton's James McConnell patented a design using a chain running from the engine along the length of the train; when pulled, it activated the brakes, but was not a fail-safe system. He also patented important locomotive improvements in 1852, creating better and more efficient use of coal while providing more power.

Three classes of travel had emerged by the 1850s. Derived from stagecoach design, first class was a luxurious affair including padded seats with armrests, curtains and suspension. Second class provided cushioned seats, while third class offered passengers a plank to sit on with slits for windows and maybe a skylight! Carriages were not yet interconnected, so passengers were confined to compartments without sanitation, refreshments, effective lighting or heating. Sanitation began to appear from 1856,

ABOVE The London to Greenwich Railway was the first suburban railway in London, opening in stages from 1836. Initially passengers were carried in railway carriages, or their own horse-drawn ones mounted on a flat railway wagon as depicted here.

TOP As railway travel expanded and encompassed continents, better carriages were required for long overnight journeys. Eventually sleeping cars were introduced and this Canadian example dates from the late 1880s with berths slung from the roof above ordinary seats.

when the infirm Lord Dalhousie travelled from London to Scotland and a water tank was fitted to a carriage, but it was not until the next decade that coaches were generally fitted with sanitation and gas lighting. It took a further decade before the faster and expanding railway network attracted the use of luxurious Pullman carriages (imported from America in 1874), creating an opulent travelling experience for a few.

Progress continued apace. The Great Northern Railway's King's Cross station opened in 1852, and a year later Edinburgh could be reached in eight hours at an average speed of 80 kph (50 mph). The iconic "Stirling Singles" (a locomotive designed by Patrick Stirling) increased this average to 97 kph (60 mph), creating a choice via the East and West Coast routes between London and Scotland. A key development took place in 1873 with the introduction of the first sleeping car with sanitation by the North British Railway on services between London, Glasgow and Edinburgh, running on alternate nights in each direction. These developments created the conditions that would lead to the "Races to the North" (see p. 42) between different companies in 1888 and 1895.

Systems of signalling and timetabling were also developing, especially on the Stockton & Darlington Railway (SDR) and Liverpool & Manchester Railway (LMR). The LMR was the first to advertise timetabled trains and provide passenger facilities. It was also the first to use proper signalling methods, managed by lineside railway police (signalmen), nicknamed "bobbies". They changed points and regulated trains by an agreed interval of time considered long enough to keep trains separate. At this time, wooden semaphore arms on high posts (semaphore signalling) were used to transmit messages across the country, and the system was adopted for railway use in the 1840s. If the arm was horizontal, the train had to stop; if vertical, the train could pass. Lights were displayed by night with a red for danger, white for clear, and green for pass with caution. The SDR had previously only used a basic system of flags in daylight and candle lamps by night. The Great Western Railway (GWR) and London & Birmingham Railway (LBR) experimented with the electric telegraph, which was used universally much later on.

With passenger numbers growing, and heavier and faster trains covering longer distances, from the 1840s locomotive

ABOVE The Great Western Railway had an envious record for speed and comfort using Brunel's broad-gauge track. This was replaced by 1892 after years of use of dual-gauge track, as seen in this c.1890 photograph of a London-bound express service hauled by the *Iron Duke* locomotive.

ABOVE King's Cross was the starting point for two bouts of railway racing to Scotland. The first races in 1888 used locomotives such as the Patrick Stirling-designed express single wheelers like this one just arrived at King's Cross from the north.

OVERLEAF King's Cross station in London was a relative latecomer, opening in 1852. Designed by architect Lewis Cubitt, it is still a magnificent gateway for the east-coast route to Scotland. The roof is said to be designed on similar lines to the Russian Tsar's Moscow riding school of the era.

ABOVE Pullman travel, a concept introduced by American George Pullman in the 1870s, became widespread, providing luxury day and night accommodation. This is a Pullman diner used on the Great Northern Railway from King's Cross in the late 1870s, showing the conditions in which the well-off could travel.

BELOW It was not only individuals who took the train for leisure travel as railways quickly realized there was money to be made chartering whole trains to organizations. These trains could go wherever was required at whatever time was suitable; here, traversing the Redruth Viaduct, is the West Cornwall Teetotal Gala charter train used for an outing.

ABOVE Initially, trains were regulated by railway policemen standing by the track using flags. Fixed signals were then used – operated by "bobbies", as signalmen were, and still are, nicknamed by many railway workers.

PICNIC TRAINS

The ever-growing Victorian prosperity meant it was not only the well-off who could now afford to hire a railway coach for their day trips or longer excursions. Family saloons were built from the 1860s by the major railways, carrying up to 15 people and attached to trains of the family's choice. For example, Wolverton built a fleet of "Picnic Saloons" which had a larder at one end, a central seating area with a longitudinal table taking up most of the carriage, plus a toilet compartment at the other end. Families hired them either for a day trip or for journeying to and from longer holidays.

In ensuing decades, older coaches, rather than being scrapped, were converted into holiday accommodation and taken to resorts where they were advertised as places to stay as an alternative to bed-and-breakfast establishments or hotels. A very few wealthy people had their own luxury carriages – used perhaps for the journey to Scotland for the grouse-shooting season in August, to visit far-flung estates or to ports connecting with ocean liners.

development was a fast-growing industry. On opening in 1838, the GWR had purchased 20 locomotives from several builders, the first being *North Star* from Robert Stephenson. Brunel claimed that only seven were dependable so the GWR directors instructed their locomotive superintendent, Daniel Gooch, to build a "colossal locomotive working with all speed". He designed and built *Great Western* in 13 weeks in Swindon Works during spring 1846, the same year as a Royal Commission decided in favour of the narrow gauge rather than Brunel's broad gauge. By 1850, the GWR was running trains up to an incredible 113 kph (70 mph) – with an *average* speed of 80 kph (50 mph) – while the London & North Western Railway (LNWR) decreed an average of 64 kph (40 mph) was fast enough for their trains. But while, Brunel and Gooch had set the standard for longer, faster and more comfortable trains on their GWR – literally, the race was on between railway companies where routes competed with each other.

In 1846, the LNWR had become the largest railway company in the UK after taking over railways including the LBR and the Grand Junction Railway. It had two locomotive works – at Wolverton and Crewe – and became known as the "Premier Line". At the LBR, Edward Bury had designed

the *Lancashire Witch* locomotive that pulled a 125 ton train at 40 kph (25 mph) in 1828, and had been contracted to build the express locomotive fleet for the LBR in 1838. After a decade, these could not manage the demands of the 180 kilometre (112 mile) route and so James McConnell, the LBR's locomotive superintendent, designed a powerful locomotive, nicknamed the "Wolverton Bloomer", in 1849. The scarlet-liveried "Bloomer" set the standard for express locomotives until railway politics led to Wolverton ceasing production of locomotives in 1862 and Crewe taking over. Arguably Britain's leading works, Crewe built the "Lady of The Lake" class from 1859, featuring the world's first water scoops (see p. 112).

On the south coast, the London & South Western Railway (LSWR), helped by the shipping companies, linked London with Southampton in 1840, thus becoming the second major route to open in Britain. The popular Victorian resort of Brighton joined the network in 1841, with trains taking just 90 minutes from London, pulled by David Joy's "Jenny Lind" locomotives. Gosport and Portsmouth gained their rail connections in 1847, linking the navy yards and (via ferry) the Isle of Wight, made fashionable by Queen Victoria. The LSWR also expanded west, reaching Exeter in 1860 and started to run high-speed trains in competition with GWR services from Paddington. This lasted until 1906 when 24 passengers died on the "Ocean Mail Express" from Plymouth, which derailed while travelling too fast at Salisbury. Joseph Beattie, the LSWR locomotive engineer, designed a smokeless coal-burning engine (to avoid smoke, engines had previously used coke, which was smokeless but much more expensive) and built the first real coal-burning express locomotives, enabling competition in economic and time terms with the GWR.

The expanding railways materially reduced transport costs, further fuelling the UK's industrial growth. They made it economically possible to move not only minerals but also perishable items such as milk, fresh fruit, vegetables, meat and fish quickly from agricultural areas and ports to market. Tens of thousands of purpose-built goods vehicles were made, carrying all types of commodities.

ABOVE The Brighton & South Coast Railway, wanting a fast express engine, invited Wilson & Company to visit and propose an engine design. They duly built the "Jenny Lind" type, which was very successful and was used across Britain on many railways.

BELOW The Great Western Railway purchased its first locomotive fleet from Robert Stephenson, including *North Star*, dating from 1837, before constructing their own from 1840. The engine was originally exported to America but was returned unwanted.

GOING UNDERGROUND

CITY UNDERGROUND RAILWAYS

London was a congested city by the mid–1800s, frequently gridlocked by a mixture of carts, omnibuses, carriages and cabs. The estimated 300,000 passengers a day using the different London terminal stations were often delayed when crossing London by road.

Various railway options were considered to solve London's problems such as transforming the Regent's Canal into a railway, or digging an underground line below houses and sewers (rejected as it would have been prohibitively expensive to ventilate and to underpin buildings). The eventual option chosen in 1860 was to build a cut-and-cover, sub-surface line, mainly routed under streets.

This first underground route, the Metropolitan Line or "Met", opened between Bishop's Road, Paddington and Farringdon Street in East London in January 1863. Engineered by Sir John Fowler at a cost of £674,751, it carried ten million passengers that year – despite the carriages having no windows, as it was reasoned there was nothing to see in a tunnel! The Great Western Railway was the Met's partner in this dual-gauge line, with Gooch designing the fleet of 12 condensing steam locomotives. After eight months, a dispute ended the partnership and the Met borrowed locomotives from the Great Northern Railway until it bought its own the next year.

Growing steadily, by 1870 the line served Hammersmith, Swiss Cottage, South Kensington and Westminster, carrying 180 million passengers annually. Typically for London, it cut through a variety of streets, highlighting the difference between the Met's treatment of affluent areas and poorer ones; for example, a dummy house was built to replace one demolished over the line in Bayswater, and stations in upmarket areas were ornate affairs with canopies, whereas others in more run-of-the mill parts were purely functional.

Next, the Met extended northwards via its steep 3 kilometre (2 mile) core section – Baker Street to Swiss Cottage – which climbed 72 metres (235 feet) using powerful locomotives. It reached Harrow-on-the-Hill in 1880, running through the Chilterns to Amersham and Aylesbury. At its peak in 1900, the Met extended 80 kilometres (50 miles) into the Buckinghamshire countryside to Verney Junction and Brill.

Steam ruled until an experimental electric shuttle ran between Earl's Court and High Street Kensington from 1900, leading to the introduction of many electric services. Express electric locomotives were used from 1921 between Harrow-on-the-Hill and Baker Street, operating until 1961 when electrification reached Amersham. Steam lingered on until 1971, powering Underground engineers' trains – the last steam locomotives to work in London.

RIGHT The Metropolitan and Circle Underground lines were built using the cut-and-cover method. This involved removing a few houses, but in affluent areas they were replaced with façades, like this one being erected in Bayswater, west London.

AN INSTANT SUCCESS

The first Metropolitan Railway passengers travelled in dark, sulphurous and suffocating conditions in the tunnels. This was in spite of the steam locomotives being fitted with condensing apparatus feeding steam from the chimney back into the engine's water tanks.

On the first day, trains ran every ten minutes carrying 40,000 passengers with carriage and station lighting provided by gas. More and more passengers travelled, adding to the noxious atmosphere, so in 1881 more ventilation shafts were built.

Some relief from these conditions came in 1890 when the City and South London Railway opened. It was the first electric railway and had windowless coaches nicknamed "padded cells". After the Met's experimental electric service in 1900, it electrified its sub-surface lines within five years, making underground travel endurable.

The growing underground routes allowed goods and passenger trains to run through central London in every direction. Trains served the huge Smithfield and Billingsgate markets as well as the Thameside power stations, considerably reducing street level congestion and the cost of the goods carried.

ABOVE Prime Minister William Gladstone opened the Metropolitan Railway in 1863: this was the scene at the grand opening.

BELOW A picture taken around 1868 showing the construction of the Metropolitan and District Line at Blackfriars with St Paul's Cathedral in the background. This stretch of underground, built to link the main railway stations, became the Circle Line.

LEFT Construction of the Paris Métro at Place de l'Opera replicates the engineering methods used in London in the just-sub-surface railway network.

BELOW The Paris Métro started operations in 1900 for the Olympics and World Fair. The ornate station entrance at Place de la Bastille is seen here in the opening year.

OPPOSITE, ABOVE John Betjeman, the Poet Laureate, tried to halt the demolition of the Euston Arch but narrowly failed in 1961. The movement he created did save St Pancras station a few years later when it too was threatened with demolition. His statue is now displayed on the concourse at St Pancras.

OPPOSITE, BELOW The opening of the City and South London Railway: the deep tube line serving Stockwell and the City of London opened in 1890, and was the first electric railway in the world. The first carriages had no windows, creating a claustrophobic travelling atmosphere.

OVERLEAF By 1908, the City and South London Railway had reached Euston and carriages now included windows, making the journey more bearable.

Two Pullman cars, *Galatea* and *Mayflower*, were introduced in 1910 between Aylesbury, Chesham and Aldgate, each with just 19 luxury seats. North of Aylesbury was Waddesdon Manor station, adjacent to the Rothschilds's Waddesdon Manor estate. As a condition of allowing the line to run through their estate, the landowners could demand a Pullman on trains of their choice. But these were the only luxurious elements of London's Underground.

In contrast, the Moscow and Paris metros made more ornate statements of identity. The Moscow authorities decreed that their metro system should be a prestigious affair: built from the 1930s, it boasted huge chandeliers and grand statues populated the ostentatious marble halls. Congestion and the 1900 Paris Olympics and World Fair prompted the grand Art Nouveau Paris Métro construction from 1898, engineered by Fulgence Bienvenüe. The first section – Porte De Vincennes to Porte Maillot – served the Olympics and then the World Fair, which (it was claimed) attracted 50 million visitors. The metro operation for these events was acknowledged as a huge success.

The Metropolitan Line became part of the London Passenger Transport Board in 1933, when the world-famous diagrammatic London Tube map was designed by Harry Beck. This period saw the launch of "Metroland" – when the Met built houses along the line, encouraging commuting. The lines north of Aylesbury were closed by 1936 but immortalized in 1973 by Poet Laureate Sir John Betjeman's *Metroland* film for the BBC.

SOCIAL CHANGE

RAILWAYS RESHAPE THE COUNTRY

It is said that steam railways brought the biggest change the world had seen since Roman times. Before the age of rail travel, time itself varied across the UK, differing by 30 minutes between the North Sea and Atlantic coasts, with local variations in between. Once railways began running long distances to a timetable, from the 1840s, it became obvious that a unified time was required so that passengers and staff could plan. Therefore in 1847, the daily time check was introduced for all stations and was also widely used by others as the official time.

Before railways, people travelled slowly, on foot or on horseback, so long-distance travel was for a privileged, affluent few. The rich "enjoyed" the rigours of stagecoach travel, which was fraught with uncertainty and averaged at best maybe 19 kph (12 mph). The onset of railways and the parliamentary Act of 1846, enshrining third-class travel with basic comfort, created an explosion of passenger mobility.

Trains soon averaged 80 kph (50 mph), allowing passengers to travel long distances in a day, not only cheaply but in relative comfort. For the first time, travel for the masses became common and trains ran over other companies' lines the length and breadth of the UK. In Europe, international services ran thousands of kilometres – linking east and west, north and south – revolutionizing society and business.

In the Victorian age of prosperity, the railways became a huge employer alongside other growing industries, with large railway towns created across the UK. Business centres like London, Birmingham, Leeds and Edinburgh also created commuters who on a daily basis travelled distances that were previously unheard of. By the 1880s, business travellers could make a same day round trip, in comfort and with dining facilities, between London and Manchester.

BELOW The London to Greenwich Railway was built over an already built-up part of London in the 1830s and was constructed mainly on arches. Pedestrians could buy a ticket to walk along the line on Sundays when it was closed.

OPPOSITE This Edwardian-era station scene is typical of daytrippers getting ready to board a train, maybe to the countryside or coast. The passengers' attire suggests it is a Sunday or bank holiday scene.

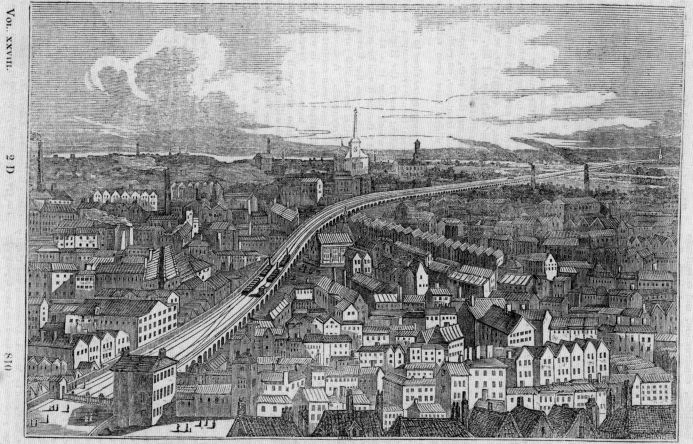

Vol. XXVIII.

2 D

810

No. 810.]

The Mirror
OF
LITERATURE, AMUSEMENT, AND INSTRUCTION.

SATURDAY, DECEMBER 17, 1836.

[Price 2d.

BIRD'S EYE VIEW OF THE LONDON AND GREENWICH RAILWAY.

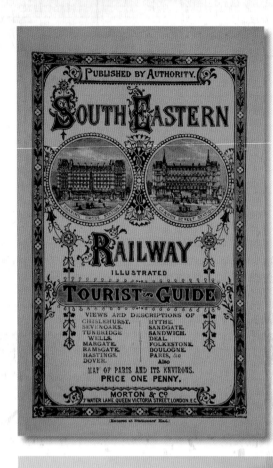

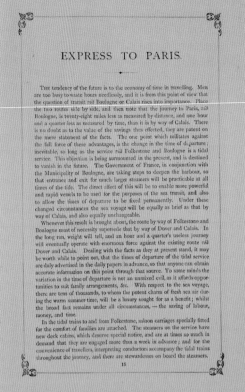

The leisure industry grew as a result of railways, and the Victorians created and promoted many seaside resorts (such as Ventnor and Skegness) as healthy places to visit. As a result, piers, hotels and boarding houses were built in many locations, with ships operating in conjunction with trains. For example, at peak holiday times up to 5,000 passengers an hour used Ryde Pier, with trains running every five minutes. As industrial towns grew, the workforce used trains for their holidays in "wakes weeks" or special outings. The brewing industry in Burton once ran 17 special trains at ten-minute intervals to Blackpool on one day for their employees, and other similar operations were common. The railway companies quickly realized that by running excursions they could attract huge volumes of passengers when trains would otherwise be lying unused in sidings. So trips to popular seaside and country resorts across the UK became commonplace.

Railways also created bulk international travel, providing connections at ports with major shipping lines. Intercontinental journeys were made possible using trains and shipping from London via ports around Britain. Examples were Harwich and Newcastle for Scandinavia, Eastern Europe and Russia, and the Channel ports for Paris, Rome, Athens and Lisbon (where there were further connections with liners to Asia and South America). As a result, the railways were responsible for the growth of ports such as Plymouth and Fishguard, attracting Atlantic shipping for onward movement of mail and passengers by rail. In Edwardian times, the "Cunard Special" took under five hours from Fishguard to Paddington – a reduction in travelling time of up to two days compared with that taken when ships berthed at Southampton or Liverpool (boats took far longer to travel than trains). Manufacturing, too, was boosted by the railway's ability to move heavy, bulky goods as well as raw materials to ports for worldwide export; while domestically, the contents of farms, houses and factories – including animals, plant and machinery – were efficiently transported by trains.

ABOVE AND RIGHT The railway companies boosted passenger levels by producing advertising brochures extolling the virtues of towns and cities served by their railway. This 1879 South Eastern Railway illustrated tourist guide is typical of those published in the boom years of tourist travel.

THE WORLD'S FIRST NEW TOWNS

Railways brought a social revolution by building new towns for the workforce. The first was built at Wolverton in 1837 on a greenfield site alongside the Grand Union Canal midway between London and Birmingham, Oxford and Cambridge. The London & Birmingham Railway (LBR) decided on this location for its engineering headquarters.

The Wolverton Railway Works opened in 1838 and is still open today. It initially employed 200 people, growing to more than 5,000 by 1900. The town was originally named Wolverton Station, reflecting the railway origins, and drew workers from across the UK and overseas. It was built on a grid system around the works, with workers renting rows of terraced cottages from the LBR. This was a prosperous town with full employment and much drunkenness at weekends, centring on "Hell's Kitchen", the nickname for a local pub. The LBR also built a church, school and medical facilities for its highly respected and skilled workforce. This concept was repeated at towns and cities like Swindon, Eastleigh, Doncaster and York, but the crucial difference was that these places were already in existence, whereas Wolverton really was a railway creation.

RIGHT France's leisure travel was no different to Britain's. This 1890s poster, advertising circular excursions and day trips to Normandy and Brittany, is typical of the era.

LEFT Railways created a host of new towns where railway works or headquarters were established. Doncaster built the famous Gresley streamlined record-breaking engines and the workforce lived in terraced houses such as these, built near the works.

BELOW Railways carried vast amounts of freight to and from ports feeding industry. Coal was taken from mines to ports, as here at Barry in South Wales in late Victorian times. Literally millions of wagons were used at this time.

THE QUEST FOR SPEED

/// THE LONDON TO SCOTLAND AND PARIS RAILWAY RACES

By 1880, the railway network reached most extremities of the UK, with established long–distance routes and time–tables. Railway companies now competed, with trains running at speeds of up to 120 kph (75 mph), between major cities served by two or more companies.

There were several key routes where competition was driven by company egos and the need to generate more profits, in turn feeding advertising campaigns. The Anglo-Scottish routes between London, Edinburgh and Aberdeen generated two bouts of "Races to the North", while the start of international travel from London to Paris generated the first cross-Channel competition.

The initial Race to the North took place in 1888 from London's Euston and King's Cross stations to Edinburgh. The Great Northern Railway (GNR) and North Eastern Railway

(NER) combined to compete against the London North Western Railway (LNWR) and Caledonian Railway (CR) over the East Coast Main Line and the West Coast Main Line routes respectively. In November 1887, third-class GNR/NER ticket holders were allowed on the 10 a.m. King's Cross to Edinburgh express, scheduled to take nine hours. Third-class LNWR/CR passengers, already allowed on the Euston to Edinburgh train, which took an hour longer, soon transferred to the King's Cross route, so the LNWR retimed its train to nine hours to compete. The GNR/NER promptly accelerated

OPPOSITE This poster was produced for the London, Chatham & Dover Railway (LC&DR), promoting rail travel to the resorts of Kent and France, showing illustrations of Paris, Canterbury, Ramsgate, Dover, Rochester Castle, Leeds Castle, Maidstone, Calais and Margate.

BELOW The "Flying Scotsman" train is synonymous with speed and comfort travelling in each direction daily between King's Cross and Edinburgh. It is depicted here in 1890.

This is the "Flying Scotchman", Great Northern Railway.

RACES TO PORTSMOUTH

The "Battle of Havant" took place in 1858 as a consequence of the London & South Western Railway (LSWR) and the London, Brighton & South Coast Railway (LBSCR) competing for the lucrative London to Portsmouth business. When the LSWR's direct line opened via Guildford in 1858, saving half an hour, the LBSCR lost its claim to operate the quickest journeys and stood to lose the ocean-liner, navy and leisure traffic.

The battle took place when the LBSCR physically blocked the LSWR's inaugural train near Havant in Hampshire, leaving a locomotive on the junction that joined the railways. Both companies had hired navvies (railway construction workers) to protect their respective trains. After what was recorded as a fierce engagement, the LSWR's gang prevailed, having captured the LBSCR's locomotive and driven it to Godalming, where it was impounded.

The situation was eventually resolved without loss of life but is an example of the lengths railway companies went to get and retain traffic. Tactics included using violence, higher speeds or shorter routes or a combination of all three. These battles were repeated overseas, notably in America where unlike in Britain, gunfire was used.

its train to eight hours and 30 minutes, as then did the LNWR. They achieved this by having the trains convey fewer carriages, and were able to shorten schedules to less than eight hours. Eventually, the King's Cross route prevailed, with a schedule of seven and a half hours – six minutes faster than the Euston route – averaging 52 mph (84 kph) over the 393 miles (632 kilometres).

The second race commenced after the Forth Bridge opened in 1891, reducing the King's Cross to Aberdeen route by 15 minutes. In June 1895, GNR/NER took ten minutes off the Euston to Aberdeen night train's journey time and rescheduled it to arrive within five minutes of the rival LNWR train. A month later, the GNR/NER speeded up the running time by 80 minutes by again reducing the number of carriages. The two routes met at Kinnaber Junction – 61 kilometres (38 miles) from Aberdeen – where the winner was often decided by the signalman (it was rumoured that he was offered bribes to ensure a certain train would be given priority over the other to win the nightly race).

However, passengers were often left behind at intermediate stops when the trains ran early as both companies ignored the timetable – an unsustainable position. On the final night of racing on 22 August, the West Coast train ran the 869 kilometres (540 miles) in 512 minutes, averaging 101 kph (63 mph). After this, it was agreed that eight and a half hours should be the time allowed between London and Aberdeen.

When it came to train travel to France, London to Paris connections were first scheduled from 1849. Sailings first coincided with high tides at the respective ports, enabling ships to berth in undredged quaysides. (In 1865, Charles Dickens, a regular traveller to and from France, was returning to London on a boat train which crashed, killing ten passengers and injuring 49 others. This was due to workers who had been digging up the track being confused by the varying "tidal boat train times".) Once regular sailings had commenced, standard timetables were introduced, with faster times for the Paris mail "Club" train conveying Pullman passengers (this had been running for three years, since 1889). "Boat Expresses", conveying all classes, ran in competition between London Charing Cross and Victoria stations to quayside platforms at Dover and Folkestone for sailings to Calais or Boulogne. There were morning, afternoon and evening departures that connected with direct trains to Paris and, for wealthy passengers on the "Grand Tour" circuit, to fashionable Mediterranean resorts and further afield.

OPPOSITE Rival companies tried to block each other on key routes, such as London to Portsmouth. When the LSWR and the LBSCR clashed at Havant in Hampshire, the LBSCR blocked the line with a locomotive like this, which was commandeered by the LSWR after a pitched battle.

RIGHT Once harbours had overcome the problems of the large English Channel tidal ranges and a regular reliable timetable could be operated, fast services connected with sailings. Services competed in the race between London, Paris and Brussels with the various railways vying for traffic using posters such as this.

BELOW The Staplehurst train crash occurred in Kent on 9 June 1865. The boat train from the Channel to London plunged off a bridge where the track was under repair: ten people were killed and 49 injured. Charles Dickens was among the passengers, but was not injured.

BELGIAN STATE RAILWAYS AND MAIL-STEAMERS

ALFONS MARCHANT.

THE CONTINENT VIA
DOVER-OSTEND
DAILY SERVICES
3 HOURS SEA PASSAGE

For Information and Train Services, apply:
Belgian State Railways, 47, Cannon Street, LONDON, E.C. 4.

FRENCH RAILWAYS

/// HISTORY AND DEVELOPMENT

French railways date back to 5 May 1821 (the date of Napoleon's death), when the first railway application to the government was made. This sought permission to build an 18 kilometre (11 mile) railway, linking the St Etienne coal mines in central France with the River Loire at Andrézieux.

King Louis XVIII granted the concession in February 1823 to the Compagnie du Chemin de Fer de St Etienne à la Loire. The railway opened five years later, initially using horses to pull coal wagons, with passenger trains running from March 1832. The latter were pulled by the first French-designed (by Marc Seguin) steam locomotives, built in Newcastle by Robert Stephenson.

France's second railway – also in St Etienne – opened in February 1833, running to Lyons using horses and steam power. It was another four years before railways reached the capital, when the Compagnie du Chemin de Fer de Paris à Saint-Germain ran trains between Paris and le Pecq.

The first French locomotives – a batch of six – were constructed in 1838 at the Schneider Works in Le Creusot for use on the Paris to Saint Cloud line. Railways were now being built in such diverse places as Mulhouse and Strasbourg, and it could be said that the French railway age had arrived by 1840 with the opening of the Gare d'Orléans in Paris (later renamed Gare d'Austerlitz) on the Paris-Corbeil & Orléans Railway (POR).

OPPOSITE, ABOVE Paris Austerlitz station is today's gateway to the south, including central areas of France. This scene captures the human element of a departure in 1883.

OPPOSITE, BELOW The grand opening of Le Pecq station, 1837.

BELOW The first railway in France, between Lyons and St Etienne, opened in 1829. This tableau illustrates the horse and steam power used on the line as well as the different types of carriages and wagons used.

CHEMIN DE FER DE LYON A St ETIENNE.

ANGLO-FRENCH RAILWAY ENGINEERS

France produced several leading railway engineers who worked with their English colleagues. The pioneering Marc Seguin, who built France's first railway from 1826, had previously worked with Robert Stephenson on locomotive design. Seguin was awarded the *Légion d'honneur* in recognition of his efforts.

Other top engineers working in France included English-born Alfred de Glehn and Gaston du Bousquet, who perfected the compound steam locomotive in the 1880s – something never achieved in Britain. Their engines were so good that the Great Western Railway purchased one to see if they could copy it. Meanwhile William Buddicom and Thomas Crampton left England to work in France, taking their locomotive designs with them. Their locomotives were built in France from the 1840s, many working for 50 years or so.

Every proposed railway required government approval, and, as in Britain, new railways were vigorously opposed by the canal and river transport industry, which was far larger in France. Following the uncontrolled expansion in Britain, the French government passed legislation in 1842 to co-ordinate and pay for most railway planning and construction costs – an early version of privatization. It met the capital costs for bridges, tunnels and trackbeds, leasing these back to the railway companies. This was in exchange for setting maximum public charges, sharing profits and allowing reduced rates for those travelling on government business. Leases were initially for 36 years to the railway companies, which laid tracks, built stations, supplied trains and paid operating costs. A decade later, Emperor Napoleon III (formerly President Louis Napoleon), a keen supporter of railways, extended the leases to 99 years.

The government wanted to link Paris with provincial towns via the "Legrand Star Plan", named after Alexis Legrand, who designed a 2,575-kilometre (1,600-mile) radial network from Paris. The drawback of this plan was that, if travelling between two provincial centres, lengthy detours via the capital were often unavoidable, inflating the cost. The French authorities wanted to protect their military position, something private companies might not do, as evidenced in 1871 when the end of the Franco–Prussian war resulted in the loss of the Alsace-Lorraine network to the Prussians. In 1878 the "Freycinet Plan" ordered 150 rural lines to be built

linking provincial centres with cross-country lines. This was prompted by awareness of the need for a national network after the Prussian war effort had been boosted by their railways, built on a grid system, directly linking many areas.

As the system developed into the twentieth century, five main railway companies emerged, absorbing the smaller ones. Perhaps the most glamorous was the Paris, Lyons and Mediterranean railway (PLM), operating nearly 11,265 route kilometres (7,000 miles) in France, Algeria and Morocco. The PLM goes back to Seguin's Lyons and St Etienne railway, providing a link to the highly lucrative Mediterranean coast destinations. Luxury named trains ran from across Europe, calling at fashionable resorts such as Monte Carlo, Nice and Cannes. Southbound international shipping connections were made at Marseilles, and to the Iberian rail network via Narbonne. The company's image was maintained using the sleek, fashionable and aerodynamic Bugatti Railcar at regular speeds of up to 140 kph (87 mph) between Paris and Lyons, reaching 190 kph (120 mph) under test in October 1934. The PLM also streamlined a steam locomotive which was claimed to have reached 160 kph (100 mph) on a trial between La Roche Migennes and Paris, and introduced a 1,118 kilometre (695 mile) non-stop Pullman service between Paris and Menton, using diesels. These activities justified the PLM's claim of running long-distance, luxury express trains comparable with any in the world.

TOP At the age of 50, in 1878, Charles Freycinet, a prominent French politician, implemented his plan to build a network of lines across France. He appears to be considering progress made in this impression of 1891.

ABOVE Paris Gare de l'Est was the departure point for the east and its grandiose architecture is clear to see in this 1925 picture. Connections ran to Istanbul and Moscow, and Napoleon III was an early traveller from the station in 1849.

OPPOSITE The PLM railway operated over hundreds of miles in North Africa. This is a very representative scene of the era at Oran station in Algeria about 100 years ago.

OVERLEAF Bradshaw published comprehensive railway timetables which were sometimes difficult to visualise without a good geographical knowledge. Therefore, railway maps were published to aid travellers and this is the Bradshaw's Railway map of Europe showing the main railway routes.

BRADSHAW'S RAILWAY MAP OF CENTRAL EUROPE

BY J. BARTHOLOMEW, F.R.G.S.

BRADSHAW'S CONTINENTAL GUIDE. LONDON.

The PLM was linked, via Mulhouse, to the Eastern Railway (ER), whose core route paralleled the River Rhine for 130 kilometres (80 miles). On 2 September 1849, Louis Napoleon had travelled through the Gare de l'Est in Paris to the official inauguration of the railway to Epernay. Although the station was still under construction, he delayed his procession for a few minutes as he surveyed the grand façade. Within five years, two million passengers a year were passing through the station: it linked Paris with Moscow, Vienna, Athens and Istanbul, giving it – and the railway – a level of influence and importance way above their physical size. This was reinforced by the ER's other international credentials, running south-east to Belfort and via Basel to Germany and Switzerland. It also served large industrial areas generating heavy volumes of goods traffic.

Following World War I, in 1918, the railways as a whole were in poor condition and many accidents involving fast trains occurred, resulting in the imposition of a 121 kph (75 mph) speed limit for steam-hauled trains, as in Germany and Belgium. The ER was particularly heavily damaged in the war as the front line crossed it in several locations. Post-war rebuilding and recovery, though hugely expensive, was aided by former German-owned stock and locomotives – provided as part of the reparation agreement – and by 1931 the line was so active that the Gare de l'Est had 33 platforms.

The Northern Railway of France (NRF) was the first to run connections to England, operating from 1845 from Paris via Calais and Dunkirk. Expansion quickly came in 1853 after negotiation of operating rights to Mons, Charleroi and via Liège to Namur in Belgium. The NRF operated the fastest direct routes from France and Belgium to England, plus direct routes to Germany and Holland. It also allowed international services to Scandinavia and Moscow to run over its network. The famed London–Paris "Night Ferry" sleeper service used the NRF from 1936, providing through carriages between London Victoria and Paris Nord stations. Like the PLM, the NRF used large powerful locomotives on heavy, fast but varied long-distance trains. Fish was transported from Boulogne on the Channel coast to the south of France and Switzerland in 20 hours, while the "Indian Mail" travelling post office linked Calais to Brindisi in Italy to connect with P&O steamers.

A fourth company, the State Railways (SR), was created by the Government's 1878 plan, combining minor routes including those from Paris to the important Channel and Bay of Biscay ports. Lucrative ocean-liner and cross-Channel traffic provided links with England and America via Le Havre, Cherbourg and Brest. This traffic increased when the Western Railway of France was absorbed into the SR in 1908, creating stiff competition with the NRF for London traffic. The SR managed St Lazare station in Paris and pioneered cheap sleeper services from there, providing six third-class leather bunks in a compartment. Cheap

FRENCH ENGINEERS

The world-renowned Frenchman André Chapelon joined the POR in 1924 after retiring as chief engineer of the PLM. He introduced huge improvements to steam locomotive performance worldwide and also worked on early TGV ("Train à Grande Vitesse") design principles. He received many awards including the Legion d'honneur.

Anatole Mallett heavily influenced locomotive construction around the world with his unique designs, initially for narrow-gauge railways. These were built in mountainous areas where steep gradients and sharp curves were unavoidable, requiring powerful engines with light axle weights to pull trains. His design was adapted in America for standard-gauge use, leading to the construction of some of the world's largest locomotives.

daytime travel was provided by lightweight, petrol-driven Michelin railcars, each with 16 (pneumatic) wheels.

Other passenger trains also linked the Mediterranean and Channel coasts via the curiously named Paris-Orléans Railway (POR), which also ran to Toulouse and Bordeaux. The POR was the fastest route to the south and Spain for many years, competing against the larger PLM. It also introduced smoking salons and ladies' boudoir carriages in 1909 for "Grand Tour" passengers. In 1934 it absorbed the Midi Railway (MR), becoming the largest French railway company. Twenty years after the first electric railway services ran between Paris, Arpajon and Versailles in 1900, the MR started a huge electrification programme. It then ran "Le Mistral", one of the fastest trains in the world, between Paris and the Mediterranean coast from 1924, followed by ice-cooled carriages in 1932.

The 1930s general Depression brought nationalization to French railways in 1938 when the Société Nationale des Chemins de Fer Français (SNCF) was created, merging the five main railway companies. Nationalization enabled modernization to be planned centrally, but it was not begun until after World War II damage had been repaired. Growing road and air domination could only be fought by developing and running high-speed services. This was demonstrated when a world rail-speed record of 330 kph (205 mph) was set in 1955 between Bordeaux and Dax.

RIGHT The driver's view from a French express steam locomotive taken in around 1930. Note the signals and lack of vision on the right-hand side. Now imagine driving in the dark or fog….

LEFT The Bugatti-designed railcar was a fast, sleek aerodynamic design and a popular way to travel. This was the start of the streamlined railway era across the world. *(See page 98)*

BOTTOM The class 241P "Mountain Class" steam locomotive was one of the best in the world and used on crack long-distance expresses such as "Le Mistral" between Paris and Marseilles. They were built in the late 1940s and remained in service until 1973.

EPIC RAIL JOURNEYS

/// CROSSING CONTINENTS

As railways made it possible to travel across different countries and continents, several epic rail journeys quickly became legendary. Initially a practical means of access to remote regions, today they are more often synonymous with the romance and adventure of travel.

The Trans-Siberian Railway

The Trans-Siberian Railway (TSR) opened up a continent and linked cultures. A century after opening, it still has a mysterious romance attached to it. The Trans-Siberian trains were named *Russia, Baikal* and *Yenisi*, the "Trans-Siberian Express" being only a generic term. The main route runs for 9,300 kilometres (5,800 miles) – 20 per cent in Europe and 80 per cent in Asia – crossing seven time zones and linking Moscow (via Omsk), Krasnoyarsk, Irkutsk and Khabarovsk with Vladivostok in the Russian Far East. The Chinese connection runs for 3,400 kilometres (2,100 miles), from Ulan-Ude (near Irkutsk) to Ulan Bator, Beijing and Shanghai.

Russia's Tsar Nicholas II started construction of the TSR in 1881, and the line was virtually completed by 1905.

However, the quality of the track was poor, leading to most trains being derailed at least once on their 14-day journey. Derailments were caused by flooding, drifting desert sand, fallen rocks and sometimes bandits. The final section was built around Lake Baikal, so that passengers no longer had to use a ferry to cross it in summer or a sledge in winter. European diplomats and businessmen had previously faced a six-week sea voyage to reach embassies in Peking, Shanghai or Tokyo, but the railway cut a month off their journey time during this politically volatile era.

After the Russo–Japanese War (1904–05) the line was upgraded, and by 1912 a twice-weekly sleeping-car train (including a carriage fitted as a Russian Orthodox chapel) was attracting tourists seeking adventure. The train was

advertised as taking 11 days between Moscow and Tokyo (with a final ferry across the Japan Sea), or a further three days to Shanghai. Later, the Russian Revolution and the civil war in Russia (1917–22) intervened, closing the route to foreigners until 1930.

The line was electrified in the 1970s, with trains operating daily in the summer and four times a week in the winter. It was claimed there were 91 stops between Moscow and Vladivostok, the journey taking eight days from beginning to end.

BELOW To understand the tremendous area covered by the Trans-Siberian Railway it is best to look at a map to comprehend the vast distances involved.

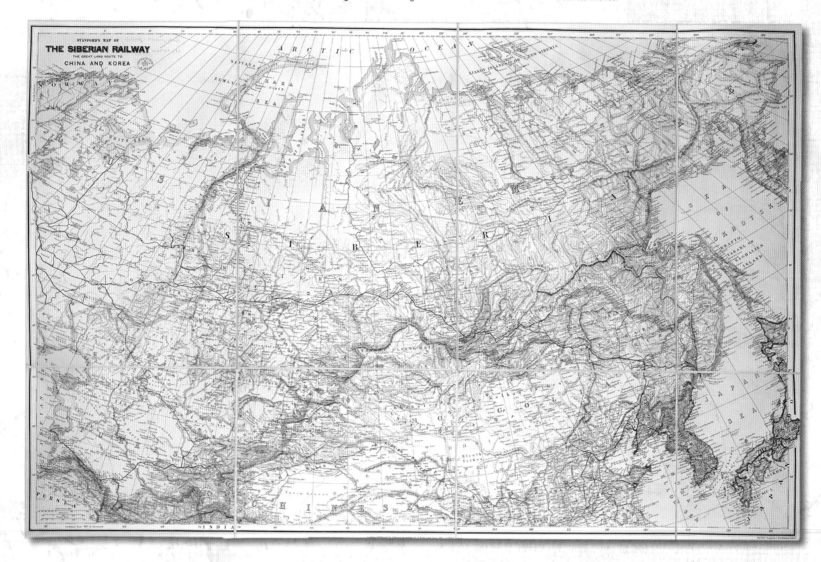

Crossing the Indian Subcontinent

When first introduced, in the 1920s, long-distance trains in India – then part of the British Empire – were often used by government staff or the military, and their names reflected this purpose. They provided excellent travelling conditions for officers and officials (although not for locals), on trains like the "Imperial Mail", inaugurated in 1926.

This was a combined operation by the East Indian and Great Indian Peninsular railways, running roughly east–west between Bombay (now Mumbai) and Howrah near Calcutta (now Kolkata). Some passengers would have travelled from London, Paris or Milan to Brindisi (in Italy) for a ship via the Suez Canal to Bombay. Later renamed the "Calcutta Mails", the "Indian Mail" connected with the P&O steamship *Ranchi* at Bombay's Ballard Pier station.

Running weekly every Friday evening from Bombay, the train averaged 64 kph (40 mph) on the 1,450 kilometre (900 mile) journey, carrying just 32 passengers in five

WILLS'S CIGARETTES

EXPRESS LOCOMOTIVE, BENGAL-NAGPUR RAILWAY, INDIA

TOP The Trans-Siberian Railway covers many different scenes but one constant for much of the year is snow. This picture, taken in 1978, gives a glimpse of the atmosphere in the Communist era and the size of the electric locomotive.

ABOVE A Wills cigarette card from the 1930s depicting a powerful Bengal–Nagpur Railway locomotive built on the de Glehn system.

ABOARD THE TRANS-SIBERIAN RAILWAY

The Trans-Siberian Railway crosses over numerous rivers, and runs through endless forests and mountains and alongside deserts. The route near Yablonovaya climbs to an altitude of 1,800 metres (6,000 feet) and used to require three steam locomotives on the ascent, while sandstorms often stopped trains beside the Gobi desert.

Traditionally, train staff keep stoves burning, providing hot water and for topping up tea. Many passengers purchase food and drink when the train stops, creating a mini-bazaar at stations, where locals also used to buy goods from passengers.

Early trains offered "hard" and "soft" accommodation, and carried Japanese officials, Chinese miners, Russian peasants and the military. It was common for ten people to crowd into one "hard-class" compartment designed for six. Notices on the train used the Russian Cyrillic alphabet, and Western travellers were advised to learn this in order to be sure of when and where to get off, and what to eat!

luxury coaches. One carriage was a restaurant and another was a designated smoking room, separated by a partition and curtained doorway from two sleeping cars containing toilets and bathrooms. The seats were upholstered in blue leather, the window blinds were made of silk and the carriages were painted on the outside in olive-grey with deep blue mouldings that were lined in gold and carried the railway companies' crests. It was an entirely different story for the servants, who travelled with the other train staff and the luggage in a single coach that also served as the kitchen at the back of the train.

The north–south route across India was covered by the "Grand Trunk Express", which ran 3,200 kilometres (2,000 miles) in just under five days from the tip of the country at Dhanushkodi to Peshawar and the Khyber Pass in the north-west. The train passed through cotton- and rice-growing areas, through jungles and into the snowy Himalayan foothills. It was quite a challenge for passengers to keep cool in the south, dry midway and warm in the mountains. This train still runs today, although at faster speeds and over a shorter route.

Coast-to-Coast Across the USA

In North America, railways opened up the continent from the 1820s onwards: the first trans-America line started to operate in 1869, creating a legendary six-day route between the Atlantic and Pacific.

The "20th Century Limited" was a steam-hauled Pullman sleeper train running from 1902 till 1967, covering the 1,550 kilometres (960 miles) between Chicago and New York in 20 hours – four hours less than the previous best train time. The route was mainly level and followed rivers and lakes, giving rise to the advertising slogan "Water level route – you can sleep". This was a jibe at the competing "Pennsylvania Special", which ran between the same cities

but used noisy locomotives to climb the mountainous 80-kilometre- (50-mile-) shorter route. The operators of the "20th Century Limited" had a novel fare strategy: using a previous journey time of 28 hours as a benchmark, they charged a one-dollar premium for every hour saved, but if the train was late, a similar refund was given. Two of the Pullman cars were transferred at Chicago to a Santa Fe service to Los Angeles, providing a luxury coast-to-coast service. In the 1950s, the "20th Century Limited" offered all classes of seating and carried 30 members of staff, but by 1970 competition had put it out of business.

In the heyday of luxury travel, in the mid-twentieth century, trains such as the Union Pacific's streamliners crossed the 5,250 kilometre (3,260 mile) gap between the east and west coasts of America, taking 57 hours to travel between New York and Los Angeles – 30 hours faster than the coast-to-coast steam services had been. The streamliner was a lightweight aluminum train; on this route it had three air-conditioned carriages and travelled at a speed of 145 kph (90 mph) through 22 states at altitudes of up to 2,400 metres (8,000 feet), carrying up to 116 passengers and 11 tons of mail and luggage. The train used New York's Grand Central cathedral-like station, where a red carpet was rolled out along the platform to impress passengers.

Cape to Cairo – An Impossible Dream?

Railwaymen and Africa-based politicians such as Cecil Rhodes dreamt of travelling by rail from the Mediterranean to the southern tip of Africa. But the route was a major challenge, not completed without stretches of boat or road.

The first east–west cross-Africa railway opened in 1931 when the Benguela and Congo railways joined at Dilolo. This created a link from Lobito on the Atlantic Ocean to Beira, 4,750 kilometres (2,950 miles) away on the Indian

ABOVE Many of the early stations on Trans-Siberian routes were basic: when the train arrived, locals sold provisions and flowers to passengers, as at this west Siberian station in the early 1920s.

RIGHT On the Great Indian Peninsula (GIP) railway, the Bhor Ghat pass provided a challenge to railway builders between Bombay and Poona, with an average of a tunnel every kilometre for 26 kilometres (16 miles). This is the view in 1930 from tunnel 26.

OPPOSITE, ABOVE The diesel-hauled Union Pacific and Chicago and North Western railroads' streamlined "City of Los Angeles" passes a steam-hauled train in December 1937. The streamliner ran between Chicago and Los Angeles, was a quarter of a mile long and carried 14 carriages and up to three locomotives, reaching speeds of 177 kph (110 mph).

OPPOSITE, BELOW Railway construction in Africa was difficult: initially everything was imported and transported to the worksite by hand or using animals, including heavy rails, sleepers and machinery. This photo shows the building of the New Congo Railway between Stanley Pool and Matadi, using local porters for transportation.

Ocean, and to Cape Town, 5,800 kilometres (3,600 miles) south. It was mainly built to connect mines in central Africa with sea ports, but there were a few notable passenger services. A weekly sleeper and mail train ran the 2,100 kilometres (1,300 miles) between Lobito and Elisabethville (now Lubumbashi), and also ran as required (not to a timetable) to Delagoa Bay – a journey of 5,600 kilometres (3,500 miles), taking a week or more.

The north–south African railway, served by the "Sunshine Express", started at Alexandria in Egypt and went via Luxor to Aswan. Through services ran just once a week in the winter, connecting with Nile steamers to Wadi Halfa, from where the railway continued to Khartoum. There was then a 1,600 kilometre (1,000 mile) gap until Kampala, where the next tracks linked lakes Victoria and Tanganyika. Beyond Lake Victoria, the railway ran to Cape Town via a circuitous route avoiding mountains, swamps and ravines. It connected with the Benguela Railway at Lubumbashi, and crossed the Zambezi by the spectacular Victoria Falls Bridge It passed through the railway town of Bulawayo, then the historic town of Mafeking, where it divided, with lines to Cape Town and Johannesburg.

The Cape to Cairo dream was never achieved, but the African network spread far and wide, powered by Manchester-built, Beyer-Garratt articulated locomotives and the Glasgow-built North British Locomotive Company's huge engines. These ran over difficult long-distance lines, now electrified and sometimes used by tourist trains following the routes of the classic "Orange Express" and "Blue Train".

THE CAPE-TO-CAIRO ROUTE.
Special Supplement to The Illustrated London News.

COAST-TO-COAST CANADA

The Canadian version of the classic coast-to-coast rail journey is the 4,670 kilometre (2,900 mile) line between Montreal and Vancouver. The first trains to cross Canada from 1886 took eight days – a journey time that was cut in half by 1900. They climbed fearsome gradients as steep as 1 in 23, reaching over 1,600 metres (5,300 feet) at Kicking Horse Pass. The trains used giant Canadian Hudson-built locomotives until the 1950s, when diesels took over and new aluminium American Budd-built trains incorporated a panoramic viewing carriage. Canadian trains such as Canadian Pacific's "Imperial Limited" and "Canadian" linked Vancouver with Montreal and Quebec, travelling through what was claimed to be the most spectacular scenery in the world. The line carried more freight trains than passenger trains and boasted the world's largest freight yard at Winnipeg, containing 480 kilometres (300 miles) of sidings. Today, tourist trains run across Canada, as in the United States, with observation cars and all facilities on board.

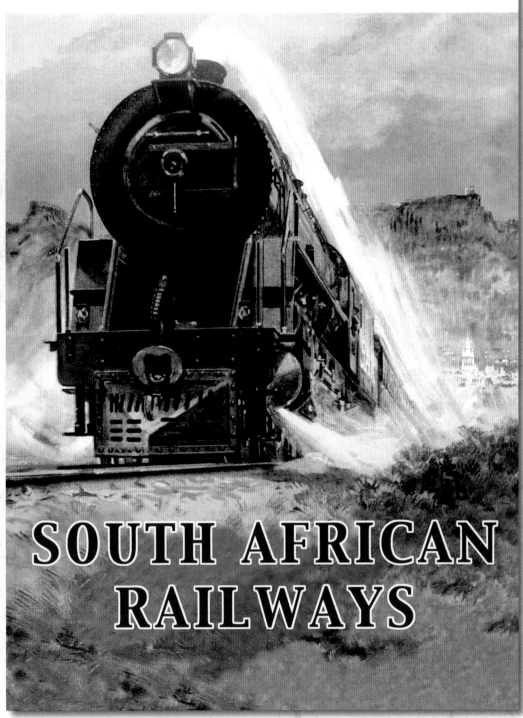

SOUTH AFRICAN RAILWAYS

ABOVE The Cape to Cairo by rail dream was advertised in typical 1930s fashion on this South African Railways poster. Hidden away in the detail was the fact that considerable travel by boat was required!

LEFT Travelling across Canada by train is one of the most spectacular journeys that can be made; this shows the type of scenery to be enjoyed on the mountainous routes. The trains are long and contain observation cars with domes providing all-round views for passengers.

EUROPEAN RAILWAYS

/// NETWORK DEVELOPMENT

Politically, Europe's railways developed in different ways. Some were under government control, while others followed the British example of chaotic, mania-driven expansion. But all quickly realized the importance of forging a network that went beyond national borders.

The French and Belgian authorities decided that railways should be under state control in order to avoid wasting money on competing routes and objectors. The Belgian government passed a Railway Act in 1834, which decreed that railways would be state owned from the outset. Holland's railways, in contrast, expanded – as in Britain – without government constraint. This led to five big railway companies in competition with each other across the country, running to the port of Rotterdam, and

later Hook of Holland and Flushing. Whatever system was used, the level of cooperation between British and European railway engineers cannot be overestimated.

Following their success in Britain, Thomas Brassey and Robert Stephenson were probably the leading engineers to work extensively across Europe. Brassey is said to have planned 75 per cent of all lines in France and 20 per cent of lines around the world, while Stephenson also exported locomotives from his Newcastle Works

around the globe. This is probably the main reason why so many of the world's railways used the UK's track gauge. Cooperation continued, and in 1841, a partnership was launched when railway constructor Joseph Locke invited Brassey to tender for work on the Paris to Rouen line in France. They won the contract, and in 1848 constructed the Barcelona to Mataró railway in Spain, followed by the Turin to Novara line in northern Italy a few years later.

ABOVE Thomas Brassey built railways around the world and employed up to 75,000 people at the peak of his activities. He was introduced to railway engineering by Joseph Locke, who wanted a reliable engineer to join forces with.

ABOVE Another early railway was the Dutch Rhenish Railway serving Rotterdam, which had its origins in the 1830s. Construction was complicated by the international background to the railway and it opened in several stages.

BELOW Germany's first railway was the Nuremburg to Fürth line, opened in 1835 using an English locomotive driver on a Stephenson-built engine named *Adler*. The event attracted huge crowds, as shown in this depiction of the opening train.

Countries with English Channel and North Sea ports were among the first to understand the importance of combined rail and shipping links with Britain, the Industrial Revolution's powerhouse. France, Belgium, Holland, Denmark and Germany started planning railways to their respective ports in order to safeguard and grow their economies. In 1837, railway construction commenced between Cologne and the Belgian border at Aachen, creating Germany's first international railway link. The line opened in 1843, and within three years trains ran to Brussels, Lille and Paris.

Northern Europe

Railway construction proved difficult over much of Holland and Belgium as most of the terrain was low lying and waterlogged. There were also many rivers and canals to be crossed. Engineers concluded that swing bridges should be used to cross these waterways, to avoid obstructing the sails of barges (a potential hazard with normal bridges).

Despite the draw of shipping links, the first lines in continental Europe were far from the sea, in Germany. The track between Nuremberg and Fürth, using a Stephenson "Adler" type locomotive, similar to the Liverpool & Manchester Railway's "Patentee" engine, opened in 1835. Three years later, Germany's first locomotive works opened at Hirschau in Bavaria, run by Joseph von Maffei, thus starting a long tradition – Germany continues to build new steam locomotives today at Meiningen.

The German railway companies were the first to use standard dimensions for their trains, allowing them to run over each other's routes. This agreement was reached in 1850, encouraging international services such as those to Basel seven years later. The first major cross-border route was the Rhenish Railway, created by a company formed in Antwerp but based in Cologne on behalf of industrialists seeking to avoid high tolls charged by the Dutch for using the Rhine. Belgium wanted access to Germany and the Rhine, and the line opened in stages from 1847 to 1856.

Austria's railways were started by Franz Anton, at the government's request. He visited England in 1822 to study railway development before making proposals to his government as to how Austrian railways should be developed. The first line was horse drawn over the long, 129 kilometre (80 mile) route between Linz and Budweis, opening in 1832. The first steam-operated trains arrived five years later between Floridsdorf and Deutsch-Wagram on a line that had the financial backing of the Rothschild family. The Austrian government took a keen interest in the railway network, assuming legislative powers to protect its commercial interests. These powers ensured that there were international railway connections and a national network was built unhindered.

Mountain Routes

The Alps bisect Europe, creating a huge barrier for railway engineers, who had to decide whether to tunnel under them or lay spectacular tracks over mountain passes. In the early years of European rail systems, the mountains of Switzerland and Austria seemingly blocked the continent's northern and southern railways. In 1849, the Swiss Confederation asked Robert Stephenson to plan a national railway system. He wrote a 70-page report, suggesting elimination of competition and only laying track in the valleys. As Europe's railways grew in importance, however, it became obvious that as well as reaching France via Geneva and Germany via Basel, the Swiss network would have to broach the mountain barriers and form more international connections.

After the opening in 1850 of the spectacular Semmering pass linking Austria and Italy, and the building in 1857 of the Mount Cenis tunnel between France and Italy (at the cost of thousands of lives), it was realized that Swiss rail links through the mountains would be possible. These mountain routes required powerful locomotives to get trains over the steep gradients in all weathers. Banking engines pushed from the rear of the train, and engines like the French Mallet-designed articulated tank locomotive – built for Bavarian State Railways in 1914 – epitomized these requirements. This design also offered locomotive crews protection from winter snow, high winds, rain and fierce, high-altitude sun – luxuries not provided 60 years earlier by the Engerth engines used over the Semmering. The conditions in the first Alpine tunnel –

MOUNTAIN RACK RAILWAYS

The establishment of European railways attracted holidaymakers, leading to the opening of mountain tourist lines. These were built as rack railways – climbing the highest Alpine mountains – such as the 32 kilometre (20 mile) Swiss Jungfrau Railway, which opened in 1912 after 19 years in the making. It was operated in three sections from Interlaken, reaching Jungfraujoch station at an altitude of 3,450 metres (11,332 feet). The line has steep gradients of up to 1 in 4, with much of the upper section inside the mountain and "windows" cut into the rock providing stunning views.

Germany followed suit by building the Bavarian Zugspitze Railway up its highest mountain, shared with Austria. This opened in 1930, ending 2,438 metres (8,000 feet) high at Zugspitzplatt station.

ABOVE European railway expansion had to contend with mountain ranges like the Alps, but once technology advanced, tourist railways were built. These eventually reached the highest mountains: the Swiss Jungfrau mountain railway was perhaps the greatest achievement, and generated beautiful artwork used in advertising posters such as this.

LEFT Locomotive construction started in mainland Europe at the Maffei Works near Munich in 1838. The celebration shown here took place in 1864 following completion of their 500th locomotive.

the 13 kilometre (8 mile) Cenis Tunnel between Modane and Bardonecchia – were initially so bad that locomotive crews were issued with breathing apparatus to protect them from the sulphurous atmosphere.

These links provided a fast way to southern Europe, saving weeks of sea travel across the Bay of Biscay and via Gibraltar, so other mountain railways were seen as essential – creating the great international routes through the Alps. From Edwardian times, cheap hydro-electricity brought about the development of electric railways on Alpine routes, improving reliability and conditions for passengers and crews alike.

Mediterranean Europe

Railways in southern Europe developed later than those in the north, and in a more disjointed way. Italy's railways, for example, grew piecemeal – perhaps reflecting the political nature of the region at the time. Italy's first railway was built in Naples in 1839, and was just 8 kilometres (5 miles) long. The country's first long-distance line opened in 1846 between Milan and Venice after pressure from Milan's industrialists, who wanted rail access to Venice and the Adriatic Sea. A railway works was built at Genoa in 1853, specifically to compete with English railway imports. It was founded by the Ansaldo family, whose company is still

ABOVE Before tunnelling expertise had been accumulated, passes were the only way through the mountains. The Semmering railway pass between Austria and Italy epitomized the 1850s engineering achievements, rising several thousand feet through the mountains. This view from that period somewhat "smoothes" the reality of the creation.

BELOW Once tunnelling technology had advanced, the need for difficult mountain passes was somewhat reduced. The St Gotthard tunnel between Switzerland and Italy took a decade to build and was typical of these fantastic achievements. The celebrations surrounding its first train are recorded here.

ABOVE The first major Alpine tunnel, the Mount Cenis Tunnel linking France and Italy opened in 1871, following more than ten years' work. It harnessed water power and used diamond-tipped drills for the first time; having proved their worth here, when the tunnel was completed, the new technologies were used elsewhere.

RIGHT A freight train at Luneville railway station c.1900. The transport of freight around France and indeed the whole of Europe was made so much easier by the introduction of the railways and the later improvements to tunels, viaducts and mountain passes.

TIMETABLES

As railways spread throughout Europe, mass tourism created travel agents who needed timetables. Thomas Cook (an early travel company) published its *Continental Timetable*, designed to be smaller than the voluminous *Bradshaw's Continental Railway Guide*, which was published from the 1840s and included every rail service in Europe. Eventually the Bradshaw guide grew to 1,000 pages while Cook's version, published from 1873, was advertised as a "Cheap, Concise and Simple Guide to All the Principal Lines of Railway, Steamers and Diligences on the Continent of Europe". The Cook's guide carried a cover price of a shilling but was issued free to railway officials and others interested in such publications, for corrections and revisions and to attract advertisements. It was a monthly publication, and is still used universally today.

a major player in the railway industry today. The Italian railways only became unified in the 1870s, after internal fighting within the country ended.

The Iberian rail network was also a latecomer compared to the rest of Europe. It largely developed from the 1850s, with only small sections operating before that date, such as in Barcelona from 1848. Portugal's railways ran from 1856 in Lisbon – the lack of heavy industry and a less dense population may have removed the urgency for railway expansion. Spain and Portugal's lines were joined in 1863, the year before they reached the French border at Irun. The two Iberian countries chose a wider-track gauge than the rest of Europe, which had adopted the British gauge as standard: the Iberian gauge was 20 centimetres (8 inches) wider than that of the rest of the continent, possibly due to a fear of being invaded by France, which would now not be able to use the Iberian railway network or vehicles for military purposes on account of the different track width. It was possible for

some Iberian trains to run through France, but only after they had been fitted with special axles that could be regauged as required to fit either network. Trains had to stop at Irun or Port Bou to have this axle configuration carried out, delaying international goods trains carrying fruit to Europe.

ABOVE Once the mountain passes and tunnels had been built, enabling a spectacular railway network to open, tourists from across Europe flocked to see the scenery. This 1924 poster sums up the period perfectly.

AMERICAN RAILWAYS

/// NETWORK DEVELOPMENT

The first all-American railway came into service on Christmas Day 1830, when the South Carolina Canal & Railroad Company operated a train using an American-built locomotive, New York's West Point Foundry locomotive *Best Friend of Charleston*, to carry 140 passengers 10 kilometres (6 miles). It was a short-lived triumph, however, as the engine exploded the following year, killing the fireman.

From then on, American railways expanded rapidly. Despite suffering heavy damage during the Civil War (1861–65), they proved invaluable for transport of arms and supplies as well troops, and the North benefited from having the better network. The Californian gold rush (1848–55) also demonstrated the need for a rail link to the east coast as it took months to travel coast to coast by wagon or by ship via Panama. The east coast link opened in 1869, when the Union Pacific and Central Pacific lines joined – somewhat bizarrely, after running parallel with each other for over 320 kilometres (200 miles) – at Promontory summit in Utah, completing a project subsidized and specified by the government.

During construction and early operation, there was a constant battle against the elements and the indigenous population – trains used special carriages fitted with narrow windows to protect passengers from ambushes. This led businessmen to conclude that it was safer, as well as a status symbol, to travel and sleep in their own luxury carriages crossing America, rather than staying at wayside hotels and running the risk of attendant dangers. Railway staff, in contrast, had to make do with more basic accommodation on these long-distance journeys – the "caboose", as it was known, was a small compartment at the back of the train for such purposes, most commonly

used on freight trains, providing enough room for several men and a communication link with the driver.

American railroads were built on a huge scale – in every sense – linking all parts of the continent, Mexico and Canada. The railways competed fiercely with each other for coverage, leading to ridiculous situations such as at Richmond in Virginia, where the Chesapeake & Ohio Railroad, Seaboard Air Line and Southern Railway crossed each other on different levels but only the latter called there. There are many spectacular routes, running over high trestle-bridges, round tight curves and up and down steep gradients – often requiring several locomotives on a train. Such long, scenic journeys brought widespread use of observation cars (often with an end balcony), and trains ran into cathedral-like stations, showing off the grandeur of the railway to stockholders and passengers alike.

In keeping with this, America developed and built some of the largest, most powerful steam and diesel locomotives in the world: the legendary steam engines made by Baldwin, the American Locomotive Company (ALCO) and Mallet dwarfed anything used in Britain. The Baldwin locomotive company standardized locomotive design, building narrow-gauge engines as well as massive freight engines weighing over 200 tons, which were exported worldwide and still used in a few countries in the twenty-

BELOW The *Best Friend* was the name given to the very first American-built steam locomotive, here shown in a period illustration of the engine working at the start of its career on a passenger train in January 1831.

OPPOSITE This unusual 1832 Baltimore & Ohio Railroad train comprises double-decker carriages, illustrating the size of even the early American trains. This was the first train to run into Washington DC.

CENTRAL VERMONT RAILWAY

GET ENOUGH REST...
TO BE AT YOUR BEST!

(Go to New York via Central Vermont)

Modern Open Section, Roomette and Bedroom Sleeping Cars

"The Washingtonian"
"The Montrealer"

Vermont - Montreal - Springfield - Hartford
New Haven - New York - Washington

DAYLIGHT SAVING TIME

CENTRAL VERMONT RAILWAY
MONTREAL - VERMONT POINTS - NEW YORK - PHILADELPHIA - WASHINGTON - BOSTON
DAYLIGHT SAVING TIME

Table of southbound and northbound schedules between Montreal, Vermont points, New York, Philadelphia, Washington and Boston. Columns include train numbers 332, 304, 404, 20 (Read Down, Southbound) and 307, 303, 21 (Read Up, Northbound), with Miles and station listings for CN-CV, CV-B&M, NYNH&H, PRR and B&M segments.

SCHEDULES SHOWN HEREIN ARE SUBJECT TO CHANGE WITHOUT NOTICE

CANADIAN NATIONAL RAILWAYS
— Condensed Schedules —
For complete schedule see CNR folder.

Eastern Standard Time unless otherwise indicated.

MONTREAL — QUEBEC

MONTREAL — OTTAWA

MONTREAL — TORONTO — DETROIT — CHICAGO

MONTREAL — WINNIPEG — EDMONTON — JASPER — VANCOUVER

— NOW — TOURIST ROOMETTES ON THE
SUPER CONTINENTAL

Montreal • Ottawa • Toronto • Winnipeg • Saskatoon • Edmonton • Jasper • Vancouver

Enjoy the Privacy and Comfort of day and night enclosed space
– Your own facilities – Picture windows – Air-conditioning.
Economically priced for holders of coach tickets.

Coffee Shop and Tourist Lounge facilities also available
What Could Be Finer!

Schedules shown herein are subject to change without notice.

REFERENCE MARKS

Daylight Saving Time shown except as otherwise indicated.

Reference mark explanations and symbol key.

EQUIPMENT

No. 20 THE WASHINGTONIAN—No. 21 THE MONTREALER
Montreal-New York-Washington

AC Coaches .... Montreal-New York-Washington
AC Sleeping Car (6 8, 6 Rmt.) .... Montreal-Washington
AC Buffet Lounge Car (6 DBR) .... Montreal-New York
AC Sleeping Car (8 S, 6 Rmt. 4 DBR) .... Montreal-Washington
AC Sleeping Car (8 S, 6 Rmt. 4 DBR) .... Montreal-New York
AC Dining Car .... New York-Washington
AC Parlor Car .... New York-Washington

THE VERMONTER
Nos. 304-404-303 — St. Albans-White River Jct.
AC Coach .... St. Albans-White River Jct.

THE AMBASSADOR
Nos. 332 and 307 — Montreal-Boston
Rail Diesel Car. AC. ...... Montreal-White River Jct.-Boston

Nos. 332-76-59 and 66-75-307 — Montreal-New York
Rail Diesel Car. AC. ...... Montreal-Springfield
AC Coaches .... Springfield-New York GCT

WHITE RIVER JCT. - SPRINGFIELD - NEW YORK
No. 20 — AC Sleeping Car (6 S, 6 Rmt. 4 DBR) — White River Jct. to New York Penn. Sta. Ready for occupancy at 10.30 P.M.
No. 21 — AC Sleeping Car (6 S, 6 Rmt. 4 DBR) — New York Penn. Sta. to White River Jct. May be occupied until 8.00 A.M.

CENTRAL VERMONT RAILWAY, INC.
(General Offices—St. Albans, Vt.)
TRAFFIC DEPARTMENT

W. J. Regan .... General Passenger Agent .... St. Albans, Vt.
O. K. Daly .... General Freight Agent .... Boston, Mass.
A. W. Manchester ... Asst. General Freight Agent (Rates) ... St. Albans, Vt.
J. W. Edwards ...... Asst. General Freight Agent (Sales) .. St. Albans, Vt.

CANADIAN NATIONAL RAILWAYS
GRAND TRUNK RAILWAY SYSTEM
TRAFFIC REPRESENTATIVES - PASSENGER AND FREIGHT

Listing of traffic representatives by city: Boston, Buffalo, Chicago, Detroit, Montreal, New Haven, New York, Philadelphia, Washington.

INFORMATION

Time-tables herein are subject to change without notice. They show the times trains and motor coaches should arrive at and depart from stations but their arrivals, departures, or connections at the times stated, are not guaranteed.

Time - Daylight Saving Time. Light-faced type denotes time from 12.01 a.m. (midnight) to 12.00 n.m. (noon) inclusive. Heavy-faced type denotes time from 12.01 p.m. (noon) to 12.00 p.m. (midnight) inclusive.

Stop-overs will be allowed on regular ticket on notice to conductor at all stations where train on which passenger is traveling is scheduled to make regular stop.

Lost Articles. Inquire of Passenger Traffic Dept., St. Albans, Vt.

CUSTOMS AND IMMIGRATION

United States Customs Officers will examine all passengers and their hand baggage, and United States Immigration Officers will examine all passengers entering the United States.

The Canadian Immigration and Customs Officers conduct similar examination of all passengers and baggage entering Canada.

To avoid delay and inconvenience, passengers are requested to cooperate by having their identification papers and hand baggage ready for inspection. It is necessary that passengers be with their baggage when it is examined.

This examination does not apply to checked baggage carried in the baggage car.

NO PASSPORTS REQUIRED TO VISIT CANADA

Insofar as citizens of the United States are concerned they may enter and leave Canada as heretofore, without passports. Regulations do not require passports for United States citizens visiting Canada, although it is desirable that United States citizens have with them means of identification, such as birth certificates, naturalization papers, poll tax receipts or certificates of identity from public officials who can certify American citizenship of the traveler.

HOTELS OF DISTINCTION

The CHARLOTTETOWN
Charlottetown, P. E. I.
J. F. Pellerin, Manager — 110 Rooms

The MACDONALD
Edmonton, Alta.
H. W. Aslin, Manager — 500 Rooms

The NOVA SCOTIAN
Halifax, N. S.
R. S. Pitts, Manager — 327 Rooms

HOTEL VANCOUVER
Vancouver, B. C.
C. C. McCurtney, Manager 560 Rooms

CHATEAU LAURIER
Ottawa, Ont.
C. A. Mann, Manager — 550 Rooms

NEWFOUNDLAND HOTEL
St. John's, Nfld.
W. B. Comforth, Manager 140 Rooms

The FORT GARRY
Winnipeg, Man.
W. G. Foster, Manager — 265 Rooms

The BESSBOROUGH
Saskatoon, Sask.
H. J. Gunning, Manager — 260 Rooms

JASPER PARK LODGE
Jasper Park, Alta.
T. G. Van Dyke, Manager 650 Guests
Open Summer Season

The QUEEN ELIZABETH - Le REINE ELIZABETH
Montreal, Que. 1216 Rooms
Donald M. Mumford, General Manager
(A CNR Hotel operated by Hilton of Canada Limited)

CANADIAN NATIONAL HOTELS

CNR's
Super CONTINENTAL
Fast Daily Schedules East and West
— Serving —

MONTREAL • OTTAWA • TORONTO
WINNIPEG • SASKATOON • EDMONTON
JASPER • VANCOUVER

NO CHANGE ENROUTE

Family Plan Fares

From stations on the Central Vermont Railway to Chicago or Winnipeg or stations beyond, via Montreal.

Good for travel commencing on a Monday, Tuesday, Wednesday or Thursday with return any day within three months.

Head of family pays regular round-trip fare; accompanying parent or children (12-21) pay only one-way fare for the round trip; children under 12 will go for one-half one-way fare and children under 5 go free.

— See Your Local Ticket Agent for Particulars —

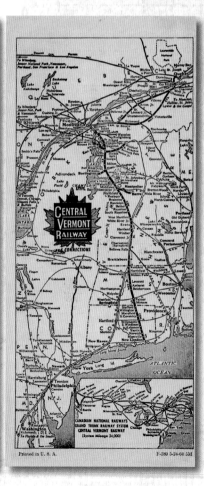

CENTRAL VERMONT RAILWAY AND CONNECTIONS

CANADIAN NATIONAL RAILWAYS
GRAND TRUNK RAILWAY SYSTEM
(System Mileage 24,000)

Printed in U. S. A.

F-280 5-24-60 5M

first century. Some American railroad companies, such as the Union Pacific Railway (UPR) and New York Central, were famous for using massive ALCO "Challenger" and "Big Boy" locomotives. Freight trains up to 3 kilometres (2 miles) long were operated – often using several locomotives – to deliver mass bulk such as raw materials, which were essential for American industry. Finished goods were also transported, including cars on triple-decker wagons – ironically hastening the near-demise of American railroads. Lorries were carried on piggy-back wagons over huge distances.

As the technology modernized, the railways upgraded. The express diesel train "City of Salina" was introduced in 1932 by the UPR. This was followed by the more comfortable services on the Burlington Railroad's "Pioneer Zephyr" and "Rock Island Rocket". The period of changeover from steam to diesel was captured by the photographer O. Winston Link, who used railroad scenes to record social history; nobody has yet matched his legendary black-and-white photography. Steam died out in the early 1960s, and nationalization came in 1971, but despite improved comfort, railway use fell in the face of air and road transport. Today rail is regaining a degree of popularity, mainly on the east coast, with new high-speed trains on the agenda.

OPPOSITE Advertising and information leaflet for the Central Vermont Railway, 1 June 1960.

ABOVE The long scenic routes in America were best viewed from the rear balcony of the train. These tourists were travelling a century ago on a Union Pacific service. Politicians also toured America using these balconies to make speeches from.

RIGHT Heavy American freight trains required powerful locomotives to pull them over thousands of miles. In the steam age, some of the world's most powerful steam locomotives were used on these trains such as this 24-wheeled "Big Boy" locomotive, seen here in Echo Canyon, Utah in the 1940s.

BELOW American railways crossed huge swathes of land where large animals roamed across the tracks. These could derail the engine, so they were fitted with deflectors which quickly became known as "cowcatchers". The introduction of a leading bogie served to "steer" the locomotive, reducing stresses on it.

RAILWAY BOGIES AND COWCATCHERS

Several early American railroads bought locomotives from Robert Stephenson from 1829. These were mainly based on the "Planet" type engine as used in the UK. One of these was Stephenson's *John Bull*, used by the Camden & Amboy Railroad in 1831. *John Bull* was not suited to American railway design, which used tighter curves and lighter track construction than the British, creating stress on rigid locomotive frames so that it was frequently derailed. To prevent this, it was fitted with a front bogie comprising of four wheels that, in effect, steered the locomotive round the curves. It took another 30 years for this system to become widespread in the UK, despite it being invented there in 1812.

Another regular cause of derailments was animals on the unfenced lines, so locomotives were fitted with cowcatchers to deflect animals away from the engine. In this way, a new look was created for the front of a locomotive – soon to be replicated around the world.

AFRICAN RAILWAYS

NETWORK DEVELOPMENT

Africa's railway development was complicated as a result of being administered by various European countries with differing political ambitions. Railways were built to enable the export of vast quantities of mined minerals via seaports and for strategic military purposes. Without a railway, industrial development would have been impossible and military ambitions would have been frustrated by the problems of a varied terrain, coupled with fighting the indigenous population and rampant disease. Initially, all materials and trains had to be imported from manufacturers in Europe, which added to the complexity of the situation.

Railways first appeared in Africa in the 1850s, and by December 1858 Robert Stephenson was able to travel on the Alexandria to Suez Railway he had designed. Days later, the conversation can only be imagined as Stephenson's Christmas lunch guests in Cairo were Isambard Kingdom Brunel and his son.

Far away, in what is now South Africa, a 3 kilometre (2 mile) tramway opened 18 months later in Durban, followed by Cape Town's railway in 1862. The Kimberley "diamond rush" in the 1870s brought railway expansion, with a network of southern lines mainly completed by 1898. Local opposition in Johannesburg had delayed construction, but this was finally overcome in 1890, allowing the city to join the network. The Boer War made the railways strategically vital, and most of the network was subsumed into the Imperial Military Railway in 1900. A decade later, these railways were amalgamated into South African Railways.

BELOW The Cape to Cairo dream was made up of many railway sections: this was the first engine, numbered No. 1, to pull a train on the Umtali to Salisbury section. Note the headboard denoting the aim of a trans-African route, still thought possible when this was taken in 1909.

RIGHT Perhaps the key North African railway was the Suez Canal line, the first in Africa built by Robert Stephenson, opening in 1858. This strategically vital route carried vast amounts of freight and passengers between the desert and the Mediterranean coast.

In the centre of the continent, the west–east, cross-Africa Benguela Railway epitomized the international background of African railways. Funded by a mixture of English private finance and the Portuguese government, it served the Katangan Belgian copper mines. The Benguela was a tough line to build – the 120 kilometre (74 mile) section from Lobito to Catengue took four years, and every drop of water used was transported from the coast. A pivotal moment in African railway history occurred in 1931, when the Benguela and Congo Railways joined at Dilolo, running via Bulawayo to complete the link between the Atlantic and Indian oceans.

Railways in East Africa started operations in 1901, when the Uganda Railway ran from Mombasa in the area of the British Protectorate, using second-hand railway equipment shipped from India under British supervision. This competed with the Tanga Railway of the neighbouring German-run region (started eight years earlier, with all components shipped in from Germany, making it an expensive task). The aim of each railway was to extend its owner's influence to Lake Victoria and the planned Cape to Cairo route.

African railways were mainly narrow gauge due to the long, unrelenting gradients and tight curves, such as on the Kenya and Uganda main line, which reached over 2,740 metres (9,000 feet) above sea level at the Equator. Construction challenges included the Victoria Falls Bridge, which crossed the River Zambezi – 128 metres (420 feet) below – with a single, 152 metre (500 foot) span. Other unusual problems are illustrated by the reputed tale from 1914 of a signal sent by a stationmaster stating, "Lions eating clerk in booking office, kindly advise [what to do]."

RIGHT The Benguela Railway was an incredibly difficult line to construct, with mountainous and desert terrain to be crossed. This picture typifies the topography the railway was constructed across, over deep ravines and through rocky cuttings.

Despite the smaller gauge, carriages and locomotives were larger than in Europe – they were not constrained by a lack of space around and over the railway line. Carriages were up to 0.6 metres (2 feet) wider and higher, providing more spacious and comfortable accommodation than in Britain. They carried blinds and had clerestory roofs (a common British design of the time, which happened to assist ventilation in the hot climate).

Powerful locomotives were required, and these were initially imported from Beyer-Peacock in Manchester and the North British Locomotive Company in Glasgow. Later on, huge Garratt steam locomotives with two tenders were built under licence in Germany and Belgium, and used across Africa. Oil-burning steam locomotives were commonly used, solving two problems: obtaining reliable fuel supplies, and the fire grates often being too large for manual coal firing in the blistering heat.

In post-colonial times, expansion has slowed. The last major African railway to be built was the Tazara Railway in 1976 – financed and equipped by China – linking Dar es Salaam with Tunduma on the Zambian railway network.

ABOVE The Victoria Falls Bridge crossed the River Zambezi on a single-span steel bridge manufactured in Darlington, with the individual parts bolted together. When opened in 1905, it was the highest bridge above water level in the world. During the 18-month construction period, a cableway ran overhead, conveying goods and workmen.

TRANS-SAHARA AND MEDITERRANEAN-NIGER RAILWAYS

Apart from the Cape to Cairo railway plans, there were two other north–south African rail projects. Plans were announced in 1934 to build a Trans-Sahara Railway, but dropped because of the vast distances, lack of water and any economic or military incentive to do so. Construction commenced in 1941 – but was not completed – of the Mediterranean–Niger Railway between the coal mines at Bou Arfa in east Morocco and Oujda in Algeria. This joined the Algerian line opened 30 years earlier, running over 644 kilometres (400 miles) due south to Colomb Bechar. In 1977, one public train a day was still advertised, although the line was mainly used by the French Foreign Legion to transport their troops to their Saharan training grounds.

LEFT A second trans-African railway was planned, crossing the Sahara Desert. Its first train, seen here, ran in 1941 from Algeria while it was under German control, but the line was never completed.

BELOW The powerful Class 25 NC (Non-Condensing) steam locomotive, many of them built in Glasgow, was synonymous with South Africa and its railways. They were used on express services such as the Kimberley to Capetown route, seen here at Orange River in 1968.

ORANJE-RIVIER

ASIAN RAILWAYS

/// NETWORK DEVELOPMENT

Early Asian railways were shaped by the varied political ambitions of European countries, but the nations of the region soon came to rely on their rail networks. In recent decades they have sustained and dramatically modernized their own railways, especially in the densely populated lands of India, China and Japan.

The first railways in India were funded by an investment scheme begun in 1849 by the British Governor-General, Lord Dalhousie, and were designed to expand trade and industry. The British government financially guaranteed railway construction costs, and when the line opened, ownership transferred to the British Government, with services operated by the construction company. The first Indian-owned railway company, the Great Indian Peninsular Line (GIPL), became a huge enterprise, along with the Bombay-Baroda & Central India and Madras & Southern Maharatta railways. India's first rail services started in1853, serving Bombay, and soon expanded to Madras, Calcutta and other major ports and cities.

Initially, every railway component had to be imported from Britain, but in 1862 India's first major railway works opened and started railway repairs at Jamalpur. By 1900, locomotives and carriages were being built in India. These local engineering skills and facilities helped electrification schemes, such as on Calcutta's 32 kilometre (20 mile) tram network in 1902, followed by the Madras and Bombay city networks within five years.

Railway travel soon became a central part of life for many Indians. In 1906 the introduction of new restaurant cars between Bombay and Poona rocked the established sense of social stratification, as they were open to passengers in all classes: officers and officials did not like sharing the open-layout coach, having been used to eating the contents of their tiffin baskets in the privacy of a compartment. This new train introduced Calorex windows, reflecting the sun's heat, and carriages were further insulated with tin under exterior vitreous-enamelled steel sheets.

In the World War I years, from 1914, Indian railways passed to British military control, under which they degraded badly. Post-war reconstruction brought Asia's largest engine shed at Bhusawal, and although regular steam services ended in the 1980s, some are still used on the world-famous Nilgiri Mountain and Darjeeling Himalayan railways.

BELOW The first railways around the world were generally built using imported materials, locomotives and carriages. This provided sights such as elephants carrying and pulling railway materials from the port, as in this 1875 scene of a locomotive being taken to the Madras Railway Company.

British influence extended to neighbouring Burma in 1877, with the first railway running from Rangoon to the River Irrawaddy, a major transport route. A line to China was started from Mandalay; although never completed, the section that was built included the Gokteik viaduct – the longest in the world at the time at 689 metres (2,260 feet) – carrying the line 97.5 metres (320 feet) above the river.

Although an independent nation, Japan also relied on British railway expertise in the beginning – for example, for the Tokyo to Yokohama railway in 1872, the country's first. British businesses helped design, build and operate Japanese railways, meeting the new challenge of earthquakes and associated landslides. Progress was slow until 1890, when railway mania took off. Trains were heavily used, for work, family visits and even pilgrimages to shrines. Nationalized from 1907 to 1987, railways shaped much of life, spawning department stores and towns around terminals. In the 1930s it was decided to electrify the network, and now Japan boasts the world-famous super-efficient Shinkansen network (see p. 148) and gloved platform staff to push passengers on to excessively crowded commuter trains.

China's railways are catching up with Japan's, despite a troubled start. Early lines were again built by British engineers (furthering their business interests), with the first opening in 1876 between Shanghai and Woosung. The full route opening was delayed by riots after a

TOP The Great Indian Peninsular Line (GIPL) reflected the British railways' grandiose ambitions in building lavish stations overseas to make a statement about the railway concerned. This is the palatial Chatrapati Shivaji, formerly the Victoria terminus, of the GIPL in Bombay (now Mumbai).

ABOVE Asian railways faced formidable challenges with the highest mountains in the world to contend with. The long Gokteik viaduct was a classic example of an engineering solution needed to cross a deep mountain valley on the Burma to China Railway.

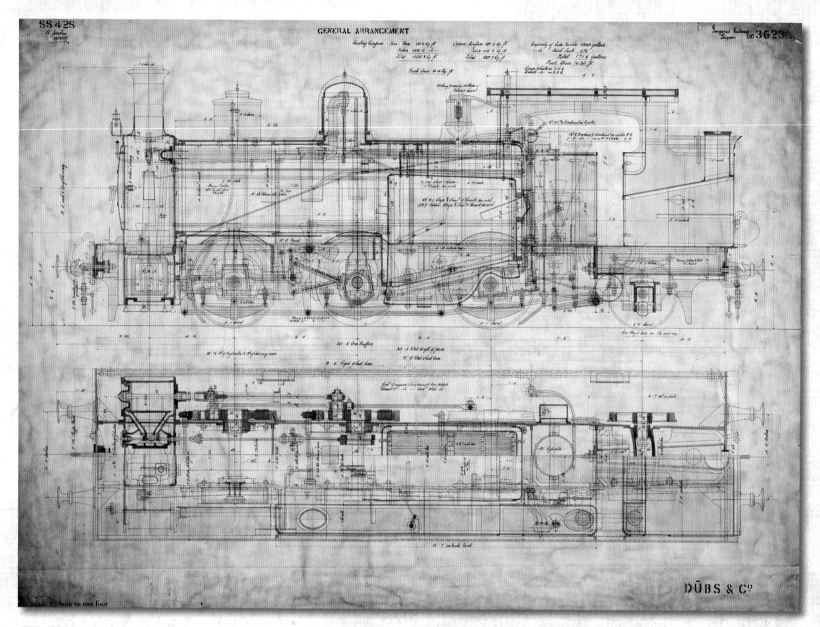

GENERAL ARRANGEMENT

DŪBS & Cº

OPPOSITE This is the General Arrangement (GA) drawing of a steam locomotive built by Dubs, the Glasgow based Locomotive builders, for the Imperial Railways in Japan. These GA drawings show principle dimensions and axle weights which enabled railways to assess if the locomotives would fit and be able to work on the actual lines.

OPPOSITE, BELOW China claimed the world railway speed record for Asia when this ordinary (unmodified) train managed 484 kph (301 mph) on a special test in 2010. According to the Chinese, other trains have gone faster but have been specially adapted, unlike this one.

TURKEY — GATEWAY TO ASIA

Turkey provided the strategic physical link between Europe, Asia and Africa. Recognizing this, France invested £20 million in 1897, financing a railway across the country. Germany quickly followed with its investment, underlining the importance of this development. Russia added to the area's political complexity, once the Trans-Siberian Railway had opened, by building a railway via Tbilisi to Teheran in Iran, Mashad on the Afghan border and Khorramshahr on the Persian Gulf. The more common route to Afghanistan was from the south via the Indian subcontinent and the Khyber Pass (now closed).

War and the mountainous terrain delayed the opening of the Turkish line until 1918. Then it became possible to travel by train from London to Baghdad using the "Orient Express" to Istanbul and the "Taurus Express" from Istanbul's Haydarpasa station, terminating at Basra for ships to India.

local was run over by a train and died. It closed for a few months, re-opened briefly and then was destroyed by anti-railway authorities. It re-opened as part of the Shanghai to Nanking Railway in 1908, followed by the Canton to Kowloon railway in 1911. Chinese railways expanded after World War I, constructed by Westerners using imported locomotives built by Mallet, Baldwin and Stephenson. In the last 20 years, the country's network has undergone continuing expansion and modernization, including a MAGLEV line in Shanghai. The latest high-speed line – through central China – opened in February 2011, with 354 kph (220 mph) trains reducing the travelling time on the 507 kilometre (315 mile) route between Zhengzhou and Xian from six hours to two.

ABOVE LEFT Europe's gateway to the east was via Istanbul's Haydarpasa station on the Asian side of the city, giving connections from London and Paris to the Middle East and beyond. This 1958 picture shows two different trains ready to set off across desert lands.

BELOW Asia boasts the highest railway in the world, the Qinghai–Tibet railway running from China in the north across the Himalayan plateau to the Tibetan capital Lhasa, reaching an altitude of 4,800 metres (16,000 feet). Passengers are provided with oxygen in specially designed carriages.

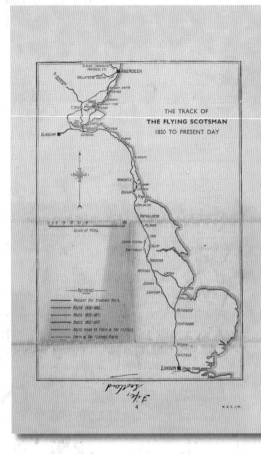

THE 100 MPH STEAM RECORD CHASE

The early railway companies raced each other in an attempt to claim the first-ever 100 mph (161 kph) train, and two unsubstantiated claims were made about this achievement. The first was reportedly accomplished on 15 July 1899 between Liverpool and Southport, but was unsupported by any substantive evidence. The second was made by the GWR on 9 May 1904 when an "Ocean Mail" express from Plymouth Docks to Paddington descended Wellington Bank near Taunton, reaching a maximum speed of 98.8 mph (159 kph).

This run has generated heated debate amongst enthusiasts ever since but is now generally accepted as having just missed the "magic ton". The first authenticated 100 mph (161 kph) run was achieved on 30 November 1934 by the London North Eastern Railway's *Flying Scotsman*, a Gresley A3 class Pacific, named after the famous train.

but perhaps his crowning glory was the prototype locomotive No. 242 A1, operating from May 1946. This took just three minutes to reach 97 kph (60 mph) from a standing start when pulling a train weighing over 600 tons. Despite exceeding what his design had promised, this steam locomotive's future was always doomed since electrification was already well advanced. Maybe because it was more powerful than the new electric locomotives it replaced on trains such as "Le Mistral" between Dijon and Lyons, it was scrapped quietly in 1960 to avoid any embarrassment.

The largest European locomotives were built in Russia. Perhaps the most powerful was the 20 wheeled, 186 ton monster built in 1932, standing 5.2 metres (17 feet) high and used on coal trains between Donitz and Moscow. Germany also produced heavy, hard-working engines, which were built at the Borsig and Henschel Works respectively.

America naturally built huge engines – larger than any in Europe – that pulled lengthy passenger and freight trains over long distances (see p. 66). They were unrestrained by gauge constraints and the American Locomotive Company (ALCO) became famous for the "Hudsons" and "Niagaras" built for the New York Central Railroad. Even larger were the massive "Challengers" and "Big Boys" – arguably its finest examples – that were built for the Union Pacific.

ABOVE *The Flying Scotsman* train epitomised the Golden Age of Steam and the railway companies printed pamphlets to go with their "crack trains". The LNER published this *Flying Scotsman* pamphlet in 1932 and shows that the train was really a moving hotel providing all sorts of ancillary services to passengers. It also makes the point that the train had run since the 1880s at the same time, 10am, and that it was a reliable service in every sense!

In the 1870s, people quickly realized that there was money to be made from offering premium-rate luxury travel in purpose-built carriages travelling behind the new breed of fast, powerful locomotives. American George Pullman had built carriages from the mid-1850s in Detroit, three of which converted into sleeping cars used on the Chicago and Alton Railroad. After the Civil War in 1865, he designed and built a carriage named *Pioneer*, which became the basis for the "Parlor-Sleeper"-car Pullman design. His Pullman Car Company built the "cars" and paid railway companies to use them in their trains while Pullman sold the tickets and retained the revenue. These carriages were introduced into the UK after the Midland Railway signed a 15-year agreement with Pullman in 1873, allowing their Derby Works to assemble the Detroit-built Pullman sections. The first one was named *Victoria* and it marked the start of the century-long Pullman era in Britain. Other companies introducing Pullmans included the London Brighton & South Coast Railway (LBSCR) which used them on the Brighton Pullman service from 1881. This was the forerunner of the 1908 service featuring the "Southern Belle", which became the "Brighton Belle" in 1932 when the line was electrified.

Pullman was seemingly in competition with the French Compagnie Internationale des Wagons-Lits (CIWL), but in practice the two companies' services rarely met. Pullmans were mainly used in Britain and America, while CIWL carriages operated in Europe and further afield. The CIWL's only presence in Britain was overnight between London and Paris or Brussels.

ABOVE The locomotive *Flying Scotsman* pulled the first train authenticated as running at 160 kph (100 mph). This is the engine hard at work accelerating away from a station in its later British Railways career, numbered No. 60103.

RIGHT The Southern Railway ran several prestige trains, one of the most famous being the "Bournemouth Belle", which at the time this advertising poster was produced was an all-Pullman-car service running on Sundays between London Waterloo and Bournemouth.

The CIWL was formed in Brussels by a Belgian, Georges Nagelmackers, in 1876 after he had travelled on the American Pullmans. Using distinctive deep-blue and gold liveried coaches, his company became synonymous with international luxury train travel across continents. These coaches, despite carrying the legend "*voiture-lits*" (bed cars) on the side, ran on daytime services, being convertible for night travel. CIWL built carriages and signed agreements with European railway companies to provide dining- and sleeping-car facilities on their long-distance trains, making their money from supplementary charges and on-board sales. Their services had started in 1872 using a hired-in, four-wheeled coach between Ostend, Paris, Berlin, Munich and Vienna. The profits generated

from these trains provided the funding to form the CIWL in 1876. Dining facilities were introduced in 1880, using a borrowed converted saloon. CIWL-owned dining cars were installed the following year between Marseilles and Nice. Dining on the trains reduced waiting times at stations and hence the overall journey times. On-board cuisine led to the first complete CIWL train running in 1882 from the Gare de l'Est in Paris to Vienna. This was the inaugural run of the "Orient Express".

From 1914, the blue and gold coaches were in use on the Trans-Siberian Railway across Asia (see p. 54), providing an instantly recognizable international brand for travellers. From 1918, CIWL joined forces with travel company Thomas Cook and by 1939 they operated over

Sleeping Cars

fitted with single and double berths, are run on the night Trains between England and Scotland by the East Coast Route . . .

EAST COAST SLEEPING BERTH.

The berths are supplied with hot and cold water, and fitted with **Electric Light** and **Electric Air Fans**, which, combined with their luxurious appointments, and the careful attention of the staff, make the journey a delightful experience of comfortable travelling.

EAST COAST EXPRESS.

LONDON AND SCOTLAND
Via East Coast Route.
MAP OF EAST COAST ROUTE.

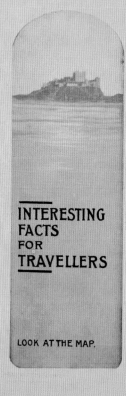

INTERESTING FACTS FOR TRAVELLERS

LOOK AT THE MAP.

A FEW FACTS

1. The **East Coast Route** between London and Edinburgh is the Shortest and Quickest.

2. The **highroad**, known as the "GREAT NORTH ROAD," between London and Scotland was originally constructed by the Romans, whose judgment in roadmaking is too well known to admit of comment. The main direction of that historic road is closely followed by the Railways operating the present-day "East Coast Route," and on the whole length between London (King's Cross Station) (Londonium) and Edinburgh (Waverley Station) (Alata Castra), passing through Peterborough (Castor), Doncaster (Danum), York (Eboracum), Durham (Dunelm), Newcastle-on-Tyne (Novocastrium), there is no gradient greater than 1 in 96.

3. The **Restaurant and Sleeping Cars** run on the East Coast Trains are unsurpassed by any provided on other routes.

4. The **Hotels** of the East Coast Companies adjoin the station at London (King's Cross), Peterborough, York, Newcastle-on-Tyne, Edinburgh (Waverley), Glasgow (Queen Street), and Perth, and are in every respect equal to any in the United Kingdom, and the tariffs are reasonable.

5. **PUNCTUALITY OF SERVICE.** During the three busiest Summer months in 1908 the Flying Scotsman from the Great Northern London Terminus at King's Cross arrived at Edinburgh (Waverley) 67 days out of the 79 at or before time.

6. **Tourists** are allowed practically unlimited facilities for breaking their journey.

7. **Luggage** within the usual limit of weight can be sent **free** in advance between the East Coast Companies' Hotels.

8. The **Waverley Station, Edinburgh,** is the largest in the United Kingdom. It took eight years to complete and cost over £1,400,000. It has an area of 23 acres, the total length of platforms being nearly 2½ miles, and their area 32,520 square yards. The roof is 42 feet high.

9. The **World-renowned Forth Bridge** on the East Coast Route is the greatest triumph of railway engineering, and was opened in 1890 by His Majesty King Edward VII., when Prince of Wales. It is 1½ miles in length, two-thirds of which is over sea water; the two main spans are each 1,710 feet. The summits of the great cantilevers are 361 feet above high water, 50,000 tons of steel being used in the structure. The total cost of the bridge was £3,500,000.

J. AND J. GRAY AND CO., THE ST. JAMES PRESS, EDINBURGH.

EAST COAST ROUTE

FORMED BY THE Great Northern, North Eastern, and North British Railways . .

Via London, King's Cross, York, Berwick, Forth Bridge, and Tay Bridge . . . .

BETWEEN

ENGLAND AND SCOTLAND

Photochrom Co.] THE FIRST LOCOMOTIVE.

S.L.D.R. No 1. 1825.

THE LATEST ATLANTIC TYPE LOCOMOTIVE

Facts—continued.

10. **King Edward Bridge,** the new high-level bridge over the Tyne at Newcastle (opened by His Majesty the King, July 10th, 1906), is an interesting example of engineering *en route*.

11. The **East Coast Route** passes through country richer in Cathedrals, Castles, Abbeys, Battlefields, and Historic Remains, than any other between England and Scotland.

12. The **first passenger train** in the World was run between Stockton and Darlington (now part of the North Eastern Railway, which is the central link of the East Coast Route) on 27th September 1825.

13. **George Stephenson,** who built the first railway locomotive, was born at Wylam, near Newcastle-on-Tyne, where his cottage still stands.

14. This **original locomotive,** No. 1, is now preserved and exhibited at Darlington (Bank Top) Station.

15. **Speed.** Just as the **first** passenger train ran on the North Eastern Railway, so the fastest booked train in the United Kingdom is running on a portion of the East Coast Route, viz., between Darlington and York—44¼ miles in 43 minutes, which is equal to 61·7 miles per hour.

16. **To ensure travelling** with the maximum of comfort combined with economy **be sure** to ask for, **and see that you get,** tickets by the East Coast Route.

For full particulars please write to the
Chief Passenger Agent,
  Great Northern Railway, King's Cross;
Chief Passenger Agent,
  North Eastern Railway, York;
Superintendent of the Line,
  North British Railway, Edinburgh;
or to the various Companies' Agents.

ABOVE The railway companies were always on the lookout for advertising or publicity opportunities. In the pre-internet and television age, printed materials were the only option to reach a mass audience.

800 sleeping cars, 661 dining cars, 133 Pullmans and 138 baggage cars in 24 countries, carrying millions of passengers annually. CIWL ran many famous trains, such as the "Etoile du Nord" between Paris and Brussels and the "Night Ferry" London to Paris and Brussels through service, until 1980.

European *wagon-lits* (sleeper) services were rendered obsolete by a combination of the newly introduced Trans-Europe Expresses and cheap airline travel available from the 1970s. The last Pullman trains for use in Britain were built in 1960. Known as "Blue Pullmans", they were forerunners of the iconic high-speed (diesel) train and were in service between London, Manchester, South Wales and Bristol. They had a short life, being withdrawn in 1973.

PRIVATE LUXURY SALOONS

Pullman and CIWL trains created a market for privately owned luxury carriages. Pullman hired his carriages to anybody for use in any train, but some wealthy passengers travelled in their own private coaches specially designed and built for them. The Duke of Sutherland had a saloon built at Wolverton in 1900, containing two lounges (one for dining), two bedrooms, a kitchen, three lavatories and seats for staff.

This was not as well appointed as the saloon built in 1937 by the Gloucester Railway Carriage and Wagon Company for the Maharaja of Indore. It was fitted with a bedroom, two bathrooms, a drawing room (with a radio-gramophone), a nursery (with beds), servants' quarters and a kitchen with an ice chest for cooling the coach via a water-circulation system. In case heating was required, a charcoal boiler was provided.

BELOW The GWR experimented with streamlining on just two engines, a "King" and a "Castle", for a short period. This is the King No. 6014 *King Henry VII* in its temporary 1935 streamlined guise.

ABOVE Pullman cars were introduced in the 1870s and could be hired by wealthy groups. This is a group of 17 tourists who hired two newly introduced Pullman cars for a 26-day mystery trip around the UK in 1876.

POWER AND LUXURY

TRANS–EUROPEAN GLAMOUR

Among the most luxurious of trains have been those that have served the elite of Europe, linking its most elegant cities. Although limited in their use, they have a unique appeal, which lives on even after the services are no more. The French Wagon–Lits company promoted the first Pullman service between London and Paris in 1889, but lost money and ceased operations after a few years.

The "Golden Arrow"

The "Golden Arrow" reintroduced Pullman travel on this route from 1924, and is still fondly remembered 40 years after its demise. The train was initially advertised as the "Dover Pullman Continental Express", but passengers soon nicknamed it the "White Pullman" because of its livery. The connecting French Pullman at Calais was called "La Flèche d'Or", and the English equivalent ("Golden Arrow") was adopted by the Southern Railway in 1929. Wealthy 1920s socialites boasted about travelling on the fast luxury train and fast ferry *Canterbury*, which was only available to "Golden Arrow" passengers. The train left Victoria at 11a.m., and passengers arrived in Paris less than 6 hours and 40 minutes later. Second-class passengers on separate trains and ferries took much longer!

By 1935, declining traffic dictated economies be made, so a new timetable was introduced along with a 50 per cent reduction in the number of coaches used in France. Southbound services still used Calais but northbound passengers used Boulogne, and a slower ferry was used by all – extending the travelling time.

The service restarted in 1946 using new, powerful Southern Railway "Merchant Navy class" locomotives, adorned with flags and golden arrows. Old flags were used if it was raining, but new ones took pride of place if the weather was sunny. New Pullman cars were introduced in 1951 along with British Rail's flagship

Britannia locomotive. The train and locomotive, which were always spotlessly clean, now used Folkestone rather than Dover, climbing to 1 in 30 on the line from the harbour – a noisy and spectacular ride enjoyed by many.

"Golden Arrow" steam power ended in 1961 in England, and eight years later in France, where the best engines in the world, the Chapelon "Pacifics", were used. The train was electrically operated for three years before becoming a victim to air competition in 1972.

The "Orient Express"

The "Orient Express" is commonly thought to have linked Paris and Istanbul, but throughout its long history it has run over various routes, serving different cities and using different names. The Compagnie Internationale des Wagons-Lits ran the first "Orient Express" in 1883 between Paris, Munich, Vienna and Bucharest, with sea connections to Istanbul via Constanza on the Black Sea.

This was joined from 1919 by the "Simplon-Orient Express" between Paris and Istanbul, routed via Lausanne, Milan and Venice. This train was renamed the "Direct-Orient Express" and ran until 1977 via Venice, Belgrade and Sofia to Istanbul.

There were also several other variants, but all the trains offered romance – the mysterious passengers perhaps carrying secret government papers, taking an escape route or seeking political asylum. This heady mix

was fuelled by wealthy travellers who epitomized the age of luxury and glamorous travel. Adding to the excitement, through carriages were conveyed on part of the journey from Moscow and Athens.

The total journey took three days, crossing over a dozen countries, linking Asia with Eastern and Western Europe, and Istanbul with Athens. Whichever route a passenger took, the mountainous scenery and wide plains provided breathtaking and varied views. The last part of the journey into Istanbul offered a fabulous panorama across the Bosphorus and the ancient city. Passengers could travel onward from these destinations across Turkey to the Middle East or by steamer to India via Suez.

International train travel declined with burgeoning air competition, and in the 1970s the "Orient Express" was little more than an ordinary long-distance pan-European stopping train used by locals, with few people opting to spend more than one night on board. It was no longer luxurious – merely functional – and ceased serving Istanbul in 1997. However, the name lingered on until 2007 for a Paris to Vienna service.

BELOW Luxury trains crossed Europe from early on but not many had the air of mystery, romance and luxury associated with the "Orient Express". This 1883 depiction of the train's early years shows it attracting the attention of farm workers who are taking a good look at a world they were not part of.

RIGHT The Orient Express ran in several versions over different routes but they all had one thing in common. The link from the west to the east and this was depicted by the minarets of the Blue Mosque in Istanbul. This poster also advises the offices in different countries where seats and sleepers on the train could be obtained from, including London.

OVERLEAF The departure gate at Paris in 1946 for a "Golden Arrow" or "Flèche d'Or" service to Paris. The post-war service also carried second-class passengers.

"GOLDEN ARROW" TURNS BLUE IN DEPRESSION

The 1930s Depression forced the decision to carry "Golden Arrow" passengers on one train on both sides of the English Channel. Fares were reduced and the travelling time extended to help keep the service viable. From Calais, "La Flèche d'Or" now included sleeping cars, which were shunted at Paris on to "Le Train Bleu" serving French Riviera destinations between Marseilles and Menton, close to the Italian border. The luxury carriages of the "Golden Arrow" and "Orient Express" continue to be used today in England and mainland Europe on special services that are entirely for leisure purposes. The trains still sometimes use steam power but always provide a glimpse of the heyday of railway travel.

BELOW The Art Deco style of advertising is used to good effect in this 1929 "Golden Arrow" poster advertising the new faster service and boat connections.

LEFT The emblem of the "Compagnie Internationale des Wagons-Lits et des Grands Express Europeens" (the International Company of Sleeping Cars and the Great European Express), on the side of a carriage of the "Orient Express".

ABOVE The "Orient Express" ran over three different routes carrying different names. The "Simplon-Orient Express" was one variation, advertised on this poster routed via Lausanne and the Simplon Pass. This route carried the famous blue *wagon-lit* carriages.

WARTIME RAILWAYS

The history of railways and war has been inextricably linked since 1855 when Briton Thomas Brassey built the 11 kilometre (7 mile) Grand Crimean Central Railway (GCCR) during the Crimean War. In the following decade, during the American Civil War, both sides used the developing railway network to move troops and ammunition.

The GCCR was built as a military supply line from Balaklava to help the Western Allies besieging Russian-held Sevastopol, ensuring supplies got through to the army. It was torn up after the war. The American railways (see p.66), having proved their worth, were expanded.

Forty years later, the British put railways to use during the war in Sudan, where railways were "laid to order" by Edouard Girouard, a Canadian-born Royal Engineer appointed as army railway director by General Kitchener. Starting from scratch, Girouard requested materials and equipment from England in spring 1896 to enable him to rebuild the Sudan Military Railway, an army supply line crossing a hostile desert environment. Kitchener wanted to operate the railway from Wadi Halfa, which had been out of use for a decade.

Progress was slow as finding experienced labour was impossible – an unskilled workforce was often procured from prisons. Some labourers demonstrated an aptitude for railway work and were sent to Girouard's railway school in Wadi Halfa, run by European engineers. The town became the railway's workshop, producing many components which reduced the quantity of imports required. As the line was built, the workforce lived in tents and vital commodities such as coal and water were stored under army guard at stations. All supplies were brought in daily by train, including track components, water, food and luxuries such as whisky and cigarettes. These arrangements made it possible for 5 kilometres (3 miles) of track to be laid on most days and the line was soon operational via

Berber to Khartoum, along with a branch line to Dongola. However, since ancient locomotives and inexperienced drivers were used, there were frequent mishaps. The reopened network transported its own construction materials, soldiers, horses and gunboats (the latter in kit form) – a far cry from desert crossings on foot ten years earlier.

The vitally strategic Hedjaz (military) Railway, linking eastern Turkey with the Middle East and Asia, connected into these African military railways. The Middle Eastern Railway Network was built largely between 1890 and 1920 by the French, German and British governments to provide fast military transit to Asia and East Africa via Suez and the Mediterranean ports.

ABOVE Railways altered the way wars were waged and the Boer War brought armoured trains into daily use. This is such a train on a reconnaissance patrol in around 1900 in the South African war.

OPPOSITE Navy guns were mounted on railway wagons in the Boer War, which were quickly transported over long distances over rough terrain. This is a 1900 picture showing the combining of navy and railway in wartime.

BELOW RIGHT World War I made extensive use of railways in Europe carrying troops and munitions. Troops were often moved from ports such as Ostend, seen here in 1914, to the front line.

The Boer War in South Africa between 1899 and 1902 saw the first widescale use of armoured and ambulance trains. Armoured trains provided an innovative and successful method of waging war as they could fire shells over 8 kilometres (5 miles) using naval guns mounted on wagons, with ammunition stored behind iron platework. Steam locomotives also received armour-plating to protect the crew and boiler, creating what must have been atrocious footplate conditions. This protection did not prevent a famous individual being taken prisoner while on a scouting expedition – Winston Churchill had been commissioned as a war correspondent and was taken captive from an armoured train.

It is a sign of the importance of the railways that many lines were taken over by the Imperial Military Railway (IMR) from 1900, under the direction of Major Girouard. The IMR operated daily travelling post offices, which also provided a mobile basic shopping facility in addition to distributing and collecting mail. The Boer War was the first conflict to rely on railways, providing a sombre foretaste of the two world wars.

RAILWAYS OF DEATH

There are many harrowing reports showing the role of railways in fulfilling inhumane commands during World War II. Germany used cattle trucks on trains to take millions of innocent people to their deaths in concentration camps.

In South-East Asia, the Japanese forced Allied prisoners to work in notoriously savage conditions to build the Thailand to Burma railway. It has been estimated that 15,000 Allied prisoners-of-war and 150,000 others lost their lives during the construction of the 394 kilometre (245 mile) railroad, including the infamous bridge over the River Kwai – this works out to around 675 deaths per 1.6 kilometres (1 mile).

THE GREAT LOCOMOTIVE CHASE

A famous locomotive chase took place in the American Civil War on 12 April 1862 when 22 Union spies stole a train from under the noses of 4,000 Confederate troops near Atlanta. The Union spies were tasked with destroying track and bridges between Chattanooga, on the front line, and a supply base at Atlanta.

They stole a locomotive, *The General*, at Big Shanty (Kennesaw) and raced along the Western and Atlantic Railroad, only stopping to set fire to 11 trestle bridges across the River Chicamaugua, to cut telegraph wires, and to lift track to obstruct the line.

William Fuller, the conductor of the stolen train, gave chase on foot for a few miles then commandeered two locomotives to follow it at speeds of up to 120 kph (74 mph). He had to deal with obstructed and damaged track and bridges while pursuing *The General* for 140 kilometres (87 miles) until it ran out of fuel at Ringgold. A famous film was made about this incident.

BELOW Tanks were developed in the First World War but were slow and cumbersome to drive. They were taken on trains, as with troops, a far more efficient way of moving them to where they were required. This is a German tank and its crew being transported in 1915.

In both World War I and World War II, the British Government took over the running of the railways for a fixed usage fee, calculated to reimburse the railway companies and shareholders for the wartime use, as well as the loss and damage of railway assets. In World War I, the railways were run by an executive committee comprising 13 railway-company general managers with a remit to the Board of Trade to co-ordinate the military and civilian demands on the railway network.

In Britain, railway works played a major part in the war effort of the two world wars, building trains specifically for military and hospital purposes. Ambulance trains were made to carry the wounded at home and abroad while armoured trains patrolled coastal railways – for example, between Dover and Folkestone during both wars. The British Government set up the Rail Operating Department (ROD) in World War I, exporting over 700 locomotives to Europe and the Middle East. Another 250 Belgian locomotives were operated by the ROD and repaired in the UK as required.

Huge, well-equipped railway workshops and skilled workforces also apparently effortlessly turned out a variety of military hardware – not only army wagons, but aircraft bodies and wings, guns, ammunition and tanks. A special train, fitted with a generator, telephones and a locomotive boiler, was built at Wolverton Works for Commander-in-Chief Sir Douglas Haig in April 1917. It was made up of ten vehicles converted from Picnic Saloons, and was sent to France where it served as Haig's living quarters.

RIGHT World War II brought a lot of bomb damage to the railway system, although it was not publicized until after the war. This a graphic illustration of a major station that has been hit, but the railways were so vital to the war effort that they would have been running again in a matter of days.

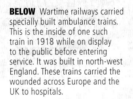

BELOW Wartime railways carried specially built ambulance trains. This is the inside of one such train in 1918 while on display to the public before entering service. It was built in north-west England. These trains carried the wounded across Europe and the UK to hospitals.

In the last few years of World War I, narrow-gauge railways were constructed to order by the army in France. These were relocated as wartime demands dictated, being designed for maximum portability and power rather than speed. Conversely, retreating forces destroyed railway facilities so they could not be used by the opposing troops. In World War I, the Makini river bridge on the Central Railway in German East Africa was blown up by the retreating German army. They then deliberately ran seven trains into the chasm, crashing seven locomotives and an estimated 150 vehicles.

At home, troop and supply trains were given priority over public trains, which were reduced in numbers and run at slower speeds. Hundreds of stations were closed. The first World War I bomb to fall on London was adjacent to Farringdon station, dropped from a Zeppelin.

This brought a taste of what was to come in World War II, when railways the world over would be targeted from the air. Locomotive cabs were sheeted over at night to prevent the fire glow being seen by bombers, and stations had glass removed in case of air raids: damage to stations like St Pancras and Middlesbrough showed why this was necessary. At the start of the air raids in World War II, 79 underground stations in London provided 75,000 people with shelter, and during the Blitz this number was doubled.

Both world wars created chronic manpower shortages, so women were drafted in to carry out tasks previously performed by men, such as locomotive and track work. In Britain in the first 40 months of World War II, women helped to run 160,000 special trains carrying 140 million loads in 600,000 private wagons. The 20,000 British steam locomotives had to pull longer, heavier trains than they had been designed for, and as in World War I, wagons were commandeered by the government, helping to move 4,000,000 tons of coal every week.

In 1939, half a million children were evacuated in four days on 1,450 trains run by the LMS Railway alone,

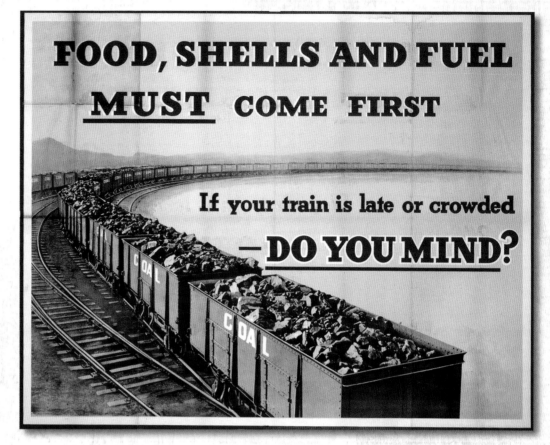

and during the eight days of the Dunkirk evacuation in 1940, 620 trains carrying 300,000 troops in 2,000 carriages ran from seven south-coast ports. By 1942, 5,000 troop and equipment trains ran every month. Between D-Day in 1944 and VE-Day in 1945, 2,840,346 personnel, carried on tens of thousands of troop trains, passed through the Southern Railway's Southampton docks. Later, nearly 600,000 prisoners-of-war were transported in Britain.

ABOVE Adverts were placed exhorting the public not to travel during wartime and that if their train was late, supply trains had taken priority over passenger services. This is one of many similarly themed adverts produced during the war.

BELOW Thousands of troop trains were operated, mostly by the Southern Railway in conjunction with Dunkirk and then the 1944 D-Day invasion. This train is carrying evacuated Dunkirk troops through a Kent station with cheering well-wishers beside the line.

OPPOSITE The railways were a vital asset in wartime and war services took priority over passenger trains. This wartime poster explains to passengers that when they were delayed, they might not be told why the delay had occurred as the information could be useful to the enemy.

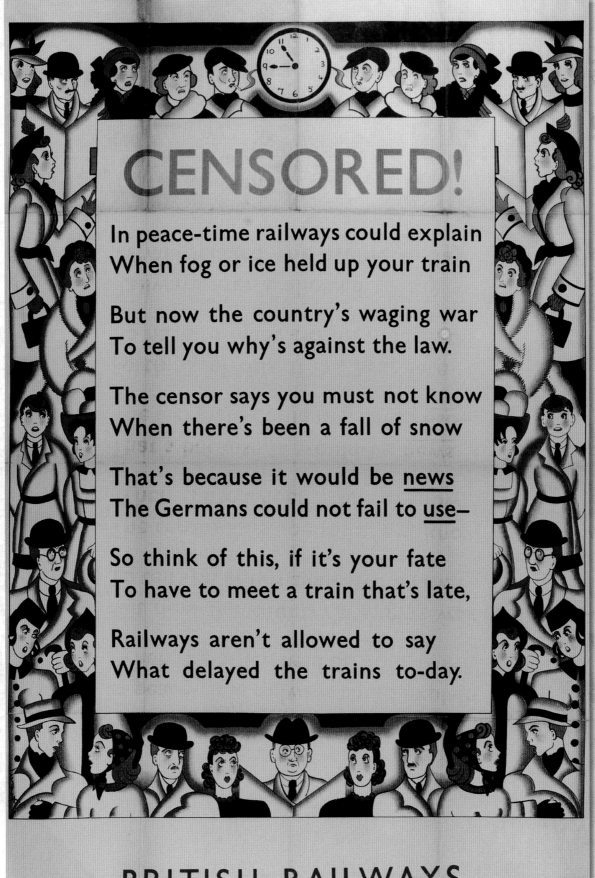

CENSORED!

In peace-time railways could explain
When fog or ice held up your train

But now the country's waging war
To tell you why's against the law.

The censor says you must not know
When there's been a fall of snow

That's because it would be <u>news</u>
The Germans could not fail to <u>use</u>–

So think of this, if it's your fate
To have to meet a train that's late,

Railways aren't allowed to say
What delayed the trains to-day.

BRITISH RAILWAYS

THE GOLDEN AGE
/// STEAM AND STREAMLINERS

When was the golden age of steam? Was it the Victorian and Edwardian Pullman era or was it the streamlined era of the 1930s with its regular 160kph (100mph) high speed running? It is widely considered that the advent of the streamlined era from 1933 was the truly golden age of steam. Curiously, it all started with the short streamlined "Flying Hamburger" diesel service in Germany. The era culminated in England when Gresley's streamlined "Mallard" created the world steam speed record of 126mph in 1938.

Despite the advertising claims, streamlining was only economically beneficial over 120 kph (75 mph), and the reality was that this only regularly occurred on a few headline, steam-hauled express trains in any country.

Streamlining was in two areas, externally creating the highly visual smooth, sleek aerodynamic outline reducing wind resistance and internally where the passage of steam from the boiler to the cylinders was also smoothed The French engineer André Chapelon was the master of the latter and by reducing resistance to the steam on its passage through the engine, he vastly improved performance while reducing operating costs.

The "Flying Hamburger" ran at speeds up to 174 kph (108 mph) between Berlin and Hamburg, with an average scheduled overall speed of 124.6 kph (77.4 mph). This prompted railway companies worldwide to experiment with streamlining, for both operational and advertising reasons.

The first real UK streamlined engine was secretly built by the London & North Eastern Railway (LNER) in 1929 at Darlington, nicknamed the "Hush Hush" engine. It was a high-pressure locomotive which initially worked well but converted to a conventional design after development problems.

In the UK, only the LNER and Southern Railway (SR) persevered with streamlining, while the Great Western Railway (GWR), and London, Midland and Scottish Railway (LMSR) both experimented, but only for a short while.

In 1935, the LNER built the Gresley designed A4s and in 1937,the LMSR built the Stanier-designed "Duchesses" and these two classes led the rivalry in Britain. After the war, the SR constructed the Bulleid-designed "Merchant Navy" and "West Country" classes. which had been called "air-smoothed" rather than streamlined and were introduced from 1945. Many of the latter and all the Stanier engines were "destreamlined" for maintenance and operational reasons.

When the GWR introduced the "King" class in 1927, it was the world's most powerful locomotive and they saw no need for streamlining. However, one was streamlined along with a "Castle" Class for testing but both quickly reverted to their original designs following the test results. This was despite "Castles" hauling the *Cheltenham Flyer* at an average speed of 114.9 kph (71.4 mph) for the 124 kilometres (77 miles)

ABOVE RIGHT The "Flying Hamburger" carried 102 passengers at high speeds made possible by using aerodynamic streamlining and keeping the weight as low as possible, for example only using three axles in total which were under the streamlined exterior.

RIGHT The LNER's 1929 experimental streamlined engine at Haymarket depot in Edinburgh one year after construction. Staff working on the project were sworn to secrecy about it.

SPEED TO THE WEST
CORNWALL DEVON SOMERSET WALES

between Swindon and Paddington, making it the world's fastest train in 1932.

The GWR also ran similar iconic express trains such as the "Bristolian" and "Cornish Riviera Express", using their "King" and "Castle" class engines. A new luxury set of carriages was introduced in 1935 on the "Riviera", which ran 482 kilometres (299.5) miles non-stop on summer Saturdays from Paddington to St Erth in Cornwall. The GWR did not totally abandon streamlining, operating 18 streamlined diesel railcars in 1937 but this was more for their PR department's purposes rather than any functional use!

In the UK, the LMSR and LNER competed for streamlined supremacy on their respective Anglo-Scottish routes. The LNER had run their world-famous flagship train, the *Flying Scotsman*, over the 632 kilometres (393 miles) at 10 a.m. every day between King's Cross and Edinburgh since 1862. The LMSR ran the 645 kilometres (401 miles) between Euston, Glasgow and Edinburgh in similar times but the stakes were raised from May 1928 when the LNER started running their flagship train non-stop using a corridor-fitted

tender, which allowed a crew change to be made en-route. Then from September 1935, 110 years to the day since Locomotion No. 1 first ran, the LNER introduced the Gresley-designed, silver-liveried "Silver Jubilee" between King's Cross and Newcastle. This was Britain's first totally streamlined service (including the carriages) and used the first A4, No. 2509, specially named "Silver Link".

Following this success, Nigel Gresley was awarded a knighthood for his services to locomotive design and he broke new ground again in 1937 when the "Coronation" service between King's Cross and Edinburgh averaged 115.7 kph (72 mph), snatching the UK's fastest train title from the GWR.

The LMSR introduced their streamlined carriages on the "Coronation Scot", pulled by Stanier's streamlined "Duchesses", which with Gresley's A4s, were the iconic highlights of the British streamlined age. The "Duchesses" carried two striking, different liveries – red and blue, with stripes running along the locomotive and the sides of the specially built carriages.

The SR's glamorous trains included the "Atlantic Coast Express" and "Bournemouth Belle", plus many boat trains running as required, often named after the shipping service they connected into such as the "Cunarder" and "Ocean Liner Express". These were pulled by "air-smoothed" engines, so called because the wartime Railway Executive had prohibited construction of streamlined express engines (they were seen as an unnecessary luxury), but by describing them as "air-smoothed mixed traffic engines" Bulleid was duly authorized to build them in 1945.

The British streamliners' swansong was in 1959 when the one-hundredth Gresley Pacific to be built at Doncaster Works – the A4 No. 4498 *Sir Nigel Gresley* – created the world's post-war steam record of 180 kph (112 mph). The driver and fireman are said to have been ready to break Mallard's 203 kph (126 mph) record (achieved in 1938), but the footplate

ABOVE The Golden Age was exemplified by clever advertising campaigns. This Great Western Railway Poster from 1939 is typical of the Art Deco advertising period, creating and emphasizing impressions of speed and luxury train travel.

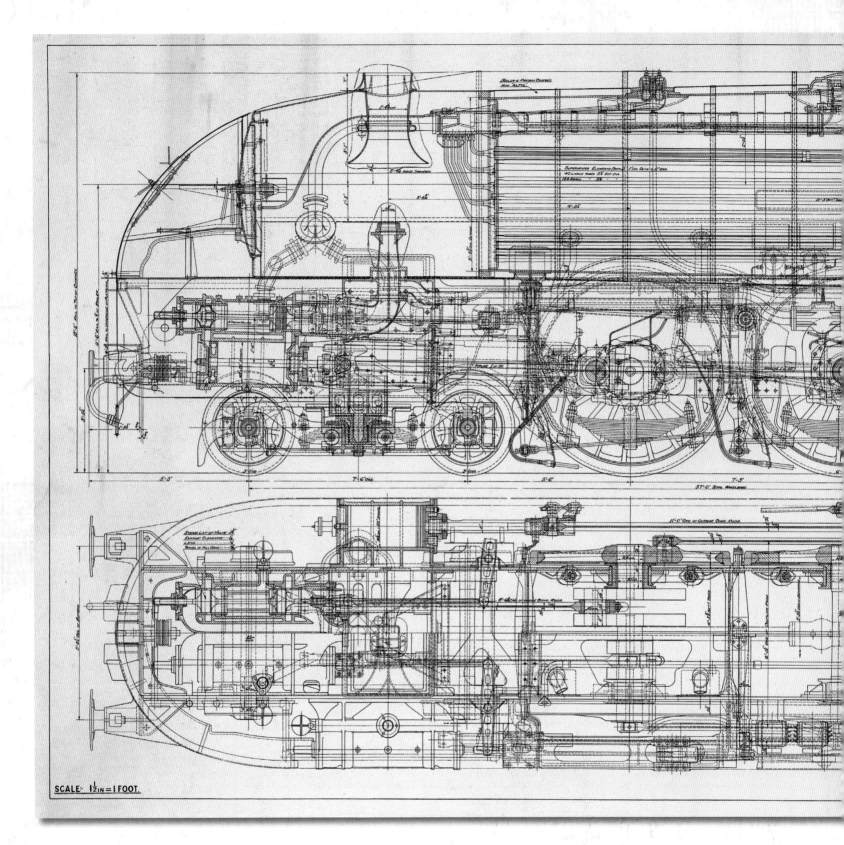

SCALE: 1½ IN = 1 FOOT.

ABOVE The streamlined LMS Princess Coronation Class competed against the LNER A4 streamlined engines between London and Scotland. This is a highly detailed General Arrangement drawing showing two elevations of the engine, the side and more unusually from above.

These plans provide weights and distances of and between axles, overall dimensions plus some internal measurements. The passage of steam from the boiler, via the superheater elements and main steam pipe to the cylinders can also be traced from this plan. Today, these plans are widely used by railway modellers.

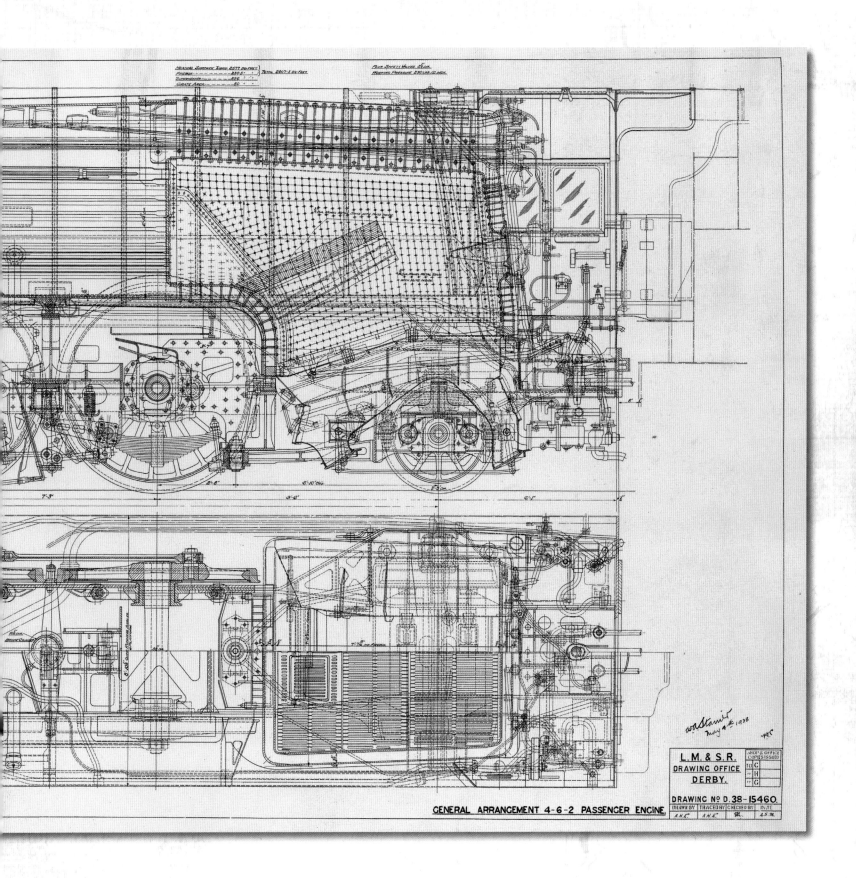

GENERAL ARRANGEMENT 4-6-2 PASSENGER ENGINE

L.M. & S.R.
DRAWING OFFICE
DERBY.

DRAWING No D.38-15460.

inspector told the driver to ease off, in order to avoid embarrassing the authorities who had already announced that express steam traction was coming to an end.

Not all "Duchesses" were streamlined and all had lost their streamlining soon after the war, while "the A4s" retained theirs until withdrawn in 1966.

The LNER also streamlined coaches using two "Beavertail" observation carriages on the "Silver Jubilee". These offered passengers a panoramic view from the rear of the train and were designed in similar fashion to the 1933 French aerodynamic Bugatti designed Railcar.

FRANCE

Bugatti's 1933 designed streamlined French diesel train incorporated streamlining at the end of the last coach which also provided a panoramic view for passengers. This was used by three of the French Railway companies, for example between Paris, Menton and Evian running at scheduled speeds up to 140 kph (87 mph) but had reached 192 Kph (120 mph) on test in October 1934. Initial French streamlining experiments took place in 1899 when the Paris, Lyons and Mediterranean

Railway (PLM) streamlined engines nicknamed "Locomotives à bec" (locos with beaks) and "Coupe-vent" (windcutters).

In 1935, the PLM streamlined a 29-year-old locomotive for tests and also streamlined carriages for the trials. The design was aided by wind tunnel tests on one tenth scale models of the train at the Aerotechnical Institute in St Cyr. Locomotive No. 231.761 was streamlined as a result of these tests which included keeping smoke and steam away from the cab windows. In these experiments, a "vane" running the length of the upper side of the locomotive's boiler aided driver's visibility. Another innovation was the provision of a glassless window for the driver, made possible by deflectors placed above and below the window to displace the air, thereby allowing the driver to see signals without leaning out of the cab.

The final French streamlining development took place in 1949 when the SNCF engineer de Caso designed a Hudson type streamliner to pull the heavy 160 kph (100 mph) Paris, Lille and Brussels expresses and remained in service until 1961.

GERMANY

In Germany, Henschel tried streamlining in 1904 with the

THE WORLD RECORD STREAMLINED RACE

The LMSR was locked in a PR battle with the LNER in the 1930s – almost recreating the Victorian Races to the North – each trying to outperform each other to create publicity for their streamlined Anglo-Scottish express services. The LMSR built the "Duchess" class in 1937, and in May that year No. 6220 *Coronation* touched 183 kph (114 mph), just managing to snatch the LNER's 181 kph (112.5 mph) record to promote their new "Coronation Scot" service.

This record was achieved twice on a "staged" run between Leeds and King's Cross on a four-coach train. The top speed was reached at Little Bytham near Grantham, later the scene for the 203 kph (126 mph) world record run in 1938 by *Mallard*. This was explained away as a run to test the brakes but fortunately just managed to beat the 1936 German record of 200.4 kph (124.5 mph) achieved by their "class 05" engine.

The speed was officially measured using an instrumented dynamometer car linked to the train wheels, creating a trace on a calibrated, continuous roll of graph paper.

THE **Coronation Scot**

EUSTON DEPART 1.30 P.M. | GLASGOW (CENTRAL) DEPART 1.30 P.M.
GLASGOW (CENTRAL) ARRIVE 8.0 P.M. | EUSTON ARRIVE 8.0 P.M.
COMMENCING JULY 5TH (MONDAYS TO FRIDAYS)
6½ HOURS
LONDON MIDLAND & SCOTTISH RAILWAY

driver at the front of the engine and the fireman in the middle, communicating via a "speaking tube." More sensibly, in 1936, they built a "Series 5" tank engine, streamlined at each end designed to run at 160 kph (100 mph) in either direction, and incorporated a clever self-adjusting braking system.

AROUND THE WORLD

Further afield, streamlining was also widely used, nowhere more than in America which produced massive Hudson wheel arrangement locomotives running in gun-metal livery introduced in 1934 to pull the New York Central Lines' "Hiawatha Streamliner Train De Luxe". The first engine was named *Commodore Vanderbilt* and was used on the train of the same name between New York and Chicago, regularly running at up to 160 kph (100 mph).

Other similar, notable services at the time included the Southern Pacific 20-coach long "Coaster" running between Los Angeles and San Francisco. Cleveland and Detroit were linked by the fast, stylish, seven-coach "Mercury Express".

Australia joined the streamlined club in 1934 to celebrate the centenary of the Proclamation of South Australia State. Their engines sported a radiator-type grill on the front of the engine adorned with a set of wings – very much in tune with this Art Deco period with the chimney hidden by a headlight!

So it can be seen why the 1930s are considered to be the true golden age of steam, characterized by these innovative art deco designs and liveries, used across the world on the prestige trains.

BELOW The "Bournemouth Belle" was one of the main Southern Railway expresses and this 1947 picture shows a fairly new streamlined powerful "Merchant Navy" class *Rotterdam Lloyd* at Winchfield on this luxury Pullman service between London Waterloo and Bournemouth.

ABOVE Sir Nigel Gresley is recognized as one of the world's greatest locomotive designers, and his 100th "Pacific" design No. 4498 was named after him. He is with this engine in March 1938 at Doncaster Works, where it was built.

ABOVE The LNER 's Gresley-designed A4 class still holds the world steam record. *Silver Link* was the first of the class and is departing from London's King's Cross station on its trial run on 27 September 1935, when the new silver-liveried train reached 181 kph (112.5 mph).

OPPOSITE Steam's graceful streamlining was to be seen in many countries. This picture of a PLM 221 locomotive taken at Paris Gare de Lyon in 1937 is very representative of the period, with what seems to be a fashionable audience for the French streamlined locomotive.

ROYAL TRAINS

The British royal train is unique in that it has operated continuously for 150 years, being used by senior members of the monarchy and their guests. In other countries, there is nothing to match this long tradition as so-called "royal carriages" were generally only used for one-off royal visits.

Queen Victoria made the first royal train journey between Slough and Paddington in 1842 on a royal saloon built by the Great Western Railway. The importance of the occasion cannot be overstated, with Messrs Brunel and Gooch riding on the locomotive to ensure everything went as planned. In the same year, the London & Birmingham Railway built a carriage for the widow of William IV, Queen Adelaide. This could be converted into a sleeping coach – the railway's first sleeping car. Servants had to use wide footboards outside the coach to gain access to the inside, so while the train was moving they could only get in from the outside, which was highly dangerous.

Other railway companies also built lavishly appointed royal saloons, but in 1861 the definitive royal train was built by the London & North Western Railway (LNWR) at Wolverton, where it has been based ever since. The LNWR proudly issued colour postcards illustrating the train's special carriages.

Queen Victoria's love of Scotland and the Isle of Wight meant she travelled extensively by train across Britain, spending an estimated £10,000 a year on rail travel in the 1880s. She refused to travel over 65 kph (40 mph), so her Scottish journeys took 12 hours in her special sound-proofed, wooden-wheeled sleeper.

She resisted suggestions of a new train, but in 1895 approved the Wolverton conversion plans for her two favourite cork-insulated, six-wheeled carriages (built in 1869) to be combined into one long, 12-wheeled royal saloon.

BELOW Queen Victoria spent a lot of time on the Isle of Wight and was a frequent visitor to Gosport station on the royal train to connect with sailings to the island. This is an impression of a scene in 1846 with Queen Victoria and Prince Albert at Gosport, showing the grandeur of the terminus station.

OPPOSITE Queen Victoria's last living train journey was in November 1900 between Balmoral and Windsor.

LEFT Queen Victoria's carriage, built in 1869, was a luxurious affair as seen in this 1895 picture. It contained day and night rooms plus a small staff room.

BELOW The Royal Train was subject to precise measurements and this depended on which carriages were conveyed. So every time "The Royal" went out, detailed working notices were published so everybody involved knew exactly what could be expected.

Note that the distance from the engine to the Royal Saloon has been measured to the nearest inch so that the stopping place can be determined ensuring the red carpet and reception party would be in the right place.

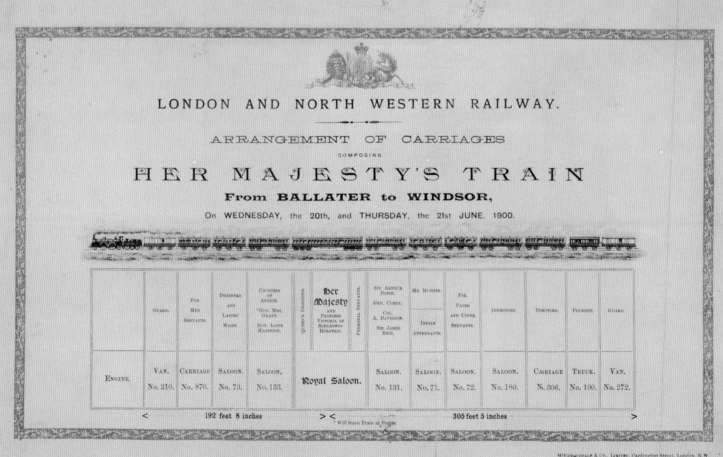

LONDON AND NORTH WESTERN RAILWAY.

ARRANGEMENT OF CARRIAGES

COMPOSING

HER MAJESTY'S TRAIN

From BALLATER to WINDSOR,

On WEDNESDAY, the 20th, and THURSDAY, the 21st JUNE, 1900.

	GUARD.	FOR MEN SERVANTS.	DRESSERS AND LADIES' MAIDS.	COUNTESS OF ANTRIM. HON. MRS. GRANT. HON. ALINE MAJENDIE.	QUEEN'S DRESSERS.	Her Majesty AND PRINCESS VICTORIA OF SCHLESWIG-HOLSTEIN.	PERSONAL SERVANTS.	SIR ARTHUR BIGGE. GEN. CLERK. COL. A. DAVIDSON. SIR JAMES REID.	MR. MUTHER. INDIAN ATTENDANTS.	FOR PAGES AND UPPER SERVANTS.	DIRECTORS.	DIRECTORS.	FOURGON.	GUARD.
ENGINE.	VAN. No. 210.	CARRIAGE No. 870.	SALOON. No. 73.	SALOON. No. 153.		Royal Saloon.		SALOON. No. 131.	SALOON. No. 71.	SALOON. No. 72.	SALOON. No. 180.	CARRIAGE N. 306.	TRUCK. No. 100.	VAN. No. 272.

< 192 feet 8 inches > < 305 feet 5 inches >

* Will leave Train at Perth.

McCORQUODALE & CO., LIMITED, Cardington Street, London, N.W

ABOVE This royal carriage was built for Queen Alexandra and Princess Louise in 1925 and was later used by Queen Mary, who had the interior redecorated to her taste.

RIGHT Since the mid-twentieth century the royal train has only been used by the principal members of the royal family. The Queen and Duke of Edinburgh are about to leave Sunderland in 1954, making full use of the double doors specially designed for the train.

ROYAL PROTOCOLS, PAST AND PRESENT

For 100 years, a locomotive preceded the royal train by ten minutes, ensuring that level-crossing gates and points were in the right position and that there were no obstructions on the line that might cause an accident. A policeman patrolled every bridge, and track staff guarded junctions to make sure nobody crossed the line between the preceding locomotive and the royal train. For added security, tunnels were also checked before the train went through.

Senior railway officials and technicians always travelled on the royal train so if any problems were encountered, there would be someone on hand to rectify them. Today, staff and technicians still travel with the train and are accompanied by police, but they do not patrol bridges and the preceding locomotive no longer runs.

Before setting off, careful measurements are taken; when the train draws into the destination station a railwayman on the platform shows a yellow flag indicating to the driver precisely where to stop – the royal carriage double door has to be exactly adjacent to the red carpet that the royal entourage walks on.

Ironically, the fastest train journey Queen Victoria made was on the funeral train which conveyed her body from Gosport to Victoria at speeds of up to 130 kph (80 mph). It was running late and the operating authorities took the interesting decision to make up for lost time, despite the train conveying many European heads of state.

The end of the Victorian era heralded modernization for the royal train, and King Edward VII requested new carriages, which he decreed should be appointed in the same fashion as the royal yacht. These saloons for Edward and Queen Alexandra became the most used royal carriages ever, serving every monarch for over 50 years, including Queen Elizabeth II.

Bathrooms were added during World War I, as the royal couple used the train for days at a time while touring Britain. World War II brought more new royal saloons, turning the 11-carriage royal train into a self-contained travelling hotel that became the preferred mode of royal rail travel for decades.

The main royal carriages each contained a bedroom, a bathroom and a lounge, plus a bedroom for an aide. Soundproofing and limited air-conditioning was installed, as was a telephone system.

The royal train is sometimes used by visiting heads of state, and in Victorian times it was regularly at the disposal of the Shah of Persia on his visits to Queen Victoria. After one journey from Dover, he is said to have demanded that the driver be executed for travelling at what he considered to be excessive speed. Royal train steam locomotives were often highly decorated and renamed, reflecting the passengers or their country.

Today's royal train was built at Wolverton over a decade from 1976, and is more functional than opulent. Nevertheless, it provides a relaxing method of transport for Queen Elizabeth and Prince Charles. It still carries the distinctive royal claret livery and now has a high level of on-board security, though comments about how luxurious and expensive it is are possibly ill informed.

RAILWAY INFRASTRUCTURE

// TRACKS, TUNNELS, VIADUCTS AND BRIDGES

Railways are the sum of many parts and not just the rails that guide trains to run safely and smoothly. Equally important are the track foundations and the gradients and curves that trains travel along. Curves create "rolling resistance" to wheels, acting like a brake in much the same way as a steep uphill gradient does. Brunel's line between Paddington and Bristol allowed high speeds to be reached, as it was virtually straight and level, but this kind of construction was the exception to the rule. Many lines incorporated magnificent viaducts and bridges, along with deep cuttings, huge embankments and long tunnels.

The London to Birmingham Railway (LBR), for example, toiled from 1838 for many years along Stephenson's preferred route, climbing up a steep incline from Euston then diving into Primrose Hill tunnel; getting through Watford required a curved viaduct followed by a 1.6 kilometre (1 mile) tunnel before traversing the Chiltern Hills – these were negotiated by digging out the long, deep cutting at Tring. Construction of the East Coast Main Line (ECML) from King's Cross during the 1840s–70s was no easier, requiring nine tunnels in the first 37 kilometres (23 miles) plus a 40-arch viaduct at Welwyn. Sea cliffs provided different challenges: for

BELOW The early railways managed fantastic feats of engineering initially just using manpower. The 3 kilometre (2 mile) long Olive Mount cutting near Liverpool on the Liverpool to Manchester Railway was an early demonstration of a railway being blasted through rock. George Stephenson supervised the construction of the line in 1831.

example, at Dawlish in Devon the line runs through numerous tunnels cut through red sandstone outcrops before running along the sea wall, where it is under constant attack from the sea.

The ECML included many iconic structures: in 1850, Queen Victoria opened the 28-arch Royal Border Bridge across the Tweed at Berwick; and the Tyne was crossed in 1906 when King Edward VII opened the bridge of the same name, thereby removing the need for through trains to reverse at Newcastle. Two world-famous Scottish bridges carried the line north towards Aberdeen. The 1.6 kilometre (1 mile) cantilevered Forth Bridge opened just after Britain's most major railway bridge disaster – the Dundee Tay Bridge collapsed a year after opening in 1879 during a violent storm, killing an estimated 75 passengers. Its replacement has been used since 1887 without incident.

ABOVE Railway tunnelling was a hazardous task. This boring machine was used under Mount Cenis in the late 1860s, linking France and Italy.

RIGHT Tracklaying methods have changed from being completely manual to highly automated today. This is a classic scene from 1914 at Bolton, showing gangs of men unloading sleepers and laying a new section of track by hand.

Alongside the grandiose tunnel portals and iconic bridges, similarly styled stations were built, making a statement to the travelling public about the railway company that owned them. The King's Cross, York and Bristol train sheds are examples of magnificent buildings that are still in use and continue to impress passengers today. The classical arch at London's Euston station was demolished in 1961, but half a century later plans are being made to rebuild it.

The introduction of more powerful locomotives allowed steeper routes to be built – such as the Settle to Carlisle line, with its 19 viaducts (including Ribblehead) and 12 tunnels. The West Highland Line was constructed in similar style but included a viaduct across a sea inlet, just east of Beasdale; further inland, at the head of Loch Shiel, the railway crosses the first mass concrete viaduct in the world at Glenfinnan, made more famous as a frequently used Harry Potter film location.

In continental Europe, the most challenging route is probably the spectacular Semmering pass linking Austria and Italy (built in 1850), which uses ten tunnels and 22 viaducts. Alpine tunnels were longer and deeper than the UK's longest, the 6 kilometre (4 mile) Severn Tunnel under the Bristol Channel: starting in the 1850s and under constant construction for over half a century, the Mount Cenis, Lötschberg and Gotthard tunnels were all double the length of the Severn Tunnel, while the Simplon bore (inaugurated in 1906) was 19 kilometres (12 miles) long. In all these cases, construction was only accomplished at the expense of thousands of workers' lives.

WORLD'S HIGHEST RAILWAY

The world's highest railway opened in July 2006, crossing the Tibetan plateau that stretches north of the Himalayas to link the towns of Golmud and Lhasa. Construction had to wait until technology could overcome problems such as laying track on permafrost, the lack of oxygen at over 4,570 metres (15,000 feet) and the large fluctuations in temperature. It took five years and £2.3 billion to build the 1,146 kilometre (712 mile) extension, which has over 40 stations and reaches an altitude of 5,072 metres (16,640 feet) at Mount Tanggula, where the world's highest station is located. High-altitude coaches are specially designed windows with ultra violet filters to keep out the sun's glare, as well as carefully regulated oxygen levels with spare supplies to combat the thin air.

RIGHT The 3.75 kilometre (2.5 mile) long Tring Cutting was opened in 1838 under the supervision of Robert Stephenson, having been dug out by labourers. Horses were used to pull them and wheelbarrows up the embankment sides.

LEFT Advertising posters such as this GWR version dated June 1890 were displayed at stations. This demonstrated that you could use GWR services from the west of England and Wales to connect with trains as far north as Inverness and Aberdeen. This particular poster also highlights the Severn Tunnel which speeded up many services between England and Wales.

ABOVE The Forth Bridge near Edinburgh is still recognized as one of the UK's most famous landmarks. It was opened in 1890 after several years of construction.

RAILWAY PERSONNEL
THE PEOPLE BEHIND THE SCENES

The physical elements of a railway are nothing without people to operate them, and passengers only ever see a small part of the workforce. In the days of steam, train drivers were regarded with awe by youngsters who collected engine numbers and took pictures of their favourite engines.

Locomotive drivers would start their working lives as labourers in engine sheds, shovelling ash from fireboxes and ash pans as well as cleaning locomotives. They were taught to light fires in engines, and once they had progressed to become qualified firemen they were allowed out on the main line. A fireman would only be passed for driving duties after many years of practical assessments and stringent exams on rules and regulations. Today, this may take just a year. Locomotive work was a male domain,

until wartime demands took men away from railways and women acquitted themselves well in unfamiliar roles.

The work was equally rigorous for other railwaymen. Engine sheds were dark, smoky, grimy places, with pits between the rails that enabled labourers to get under the engine to prepare it for its next trip. Preparation involved checking the moving parts (many only accessible from below) and oiling them up. The coal for the engines was stored in huge towers that lifted coal wagons 23 metres

(75 feet) into the air and filled the tenders using a chute. Water was also needed in large quantities, so high-volume water cranes and towers were provided to fill tenders and tanks. Space-saving turntables were used to ensure that locomotives faced the right way for their next job – they were sometimes located in the centre of circular engine sheds called roundhouses.

Away from sheds and stations, water troughs were laid in tracks, allowing engines to replenish water supplies without

GANTRY SIGNALS, RUGBY.

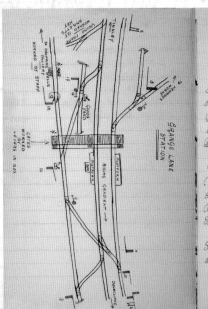

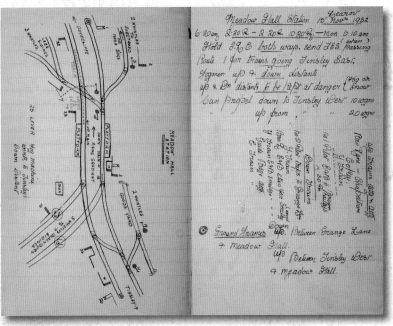

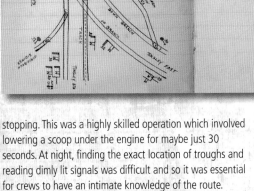

ABOVE AND LEFT Signalmen had a vital job to perform and if they made a mistake, it could cost life and money. Most railway jobs had a relief post which meant that if the regular person was away for whatever reason, a "relief" person took over in their absence. All signal boxes contained a detailed plan of the railway it controlled showing points, signals and any detail important to the safe operation of the railway.

This is an extract from a Sheffield area Relief Signalman's notebook from 1933 with their own plans to jog their memory. Grange Lane station has been long closed but Meadowhall is now a very busy station serving the nearby retail park. Tinsley Yard was a huge freight yard but now virtually unused and much has been redeveloped.

OPPOSITE Reading the signals was a vital skill when driving a locomotive. On a signal gantry such as this one at Rugby, crews had to know which was the correct signal for their train. This was difficult by day, but imagine it by night and in fog!

RIGHT The guard was in charge of the train. They had to make sure everything was safe before a train departed and give a signal to the driver, often using a green flag by day or a green light by night, to indicate it was safe to do so. The whistle was also used to attract attention!

stopping. This was a highly skilled operation which involved lowering a scoop under the engine for maybe just 30 seconds. At night, finding the exact location of troughs and reading dimly lit signals was difficult and so it was essential for crews to have an intimate knowledge of the route.

Footplate crews had to learn how to perform these tasks and understand all about shunting, station work and smoke emissions before they were allowed out on the working railway. Drivers and firemen were required to avoid smoking out a covered station; emission control was important because smoke and steam prevented crews seeing signals and station staff. Also, excessive smoke was a sign that coal was not burning properly – the more smoke emitted, the less heat created. In stations, crews had to look out for humble platform porters, who helped make sure passengers were safely on or off the train before it was allowed to depart. Porters in turn worked closely with the guard of the train, who was in charge of safety: the train only moved off when he had whistled and waved his green flag, giving the "right away" signal to the driver.

The early railways used different signalling systems, leading to confusion where they met and operated trains over each other's routes. Some solved the problem by using an "interval system" which allowed a train to run a set distance over a specific amount of time, and once this had passed another train was allowed to follow. Following the increasing number of accidents up to 1840, a common set of rules and signalling systems was adopted in 1841, based on the Liverpool & Manchester Railway system.

Signalmen controlled signals and points; like footplate work, this could be a very physically demanding job, requiring concentration and in-depth railway knowledge. Their role was to pull large levers attached to wires running for up to 800 metres (½ mile) to operate a distant semaphore signal. Drivers and firemen had to keep a lookout for these, and at major junctions – such as Rugby and Preston – a huge signal gantry would have to be correctly read by crews to ensure a danger signal was not passed.

ABOVE This 1905 view of a locomotive crew shows how little protection from the elements was afforded to them in their spartan cab. This is a very simple engine; bigger engines had far more controls to use and slightly better conditions to work in. Note the oil cans on the drip tray above the fire. This meant the oil flowed freely from the can when required.

OPPOSITE Shunters prepared a train before it entered service – a skilled job. They would also signal to the driver that the train needed to stop, go forward or back, using hand signals or a lamp when it was dark. The long pole is a shunting pole, which was used to uncouple wagons.

RIGHT Wheeltappers are no longer used in many countries but some people will recall the days when they walked alongside the train tapping the wheels, listening for the clang. If the sound was muted, this indicated a possible wheel or axle fault and they had to examine it.

WHEELTAPPERS AND SHUNTERS

Some trains stopped for ten minutes at key stations, and the rhythmic clang of a metal hammer could be heard as a wheel tapper hit the wheels to ensure that they had not developed a flaw – if a crack had formed, the clang became a hollow, ringing sound.

Many trains had coaches added or taken off at key stations, shunted on to or from other services. This required close teamwork between the driver, the guard and the shunter. The latter would go under the train to couple or uncouple carriages, joining or splitting the vacuum brake, steam-heating pipes, and the carriage connections.

FREIGHT, MAIL AND FILM

THE NON-PASSENGER RAILWAY

Freight traffic was the driving force behind the development of railways, but the individual wagonloads that were typical prior to World War II have now been largely replaced by long-distance, bulk rail transportation. Coal traffic has been around for as long as there have been railways — as has mail, which benefited from the faster inter-city connections offered by rail.

Over the years, the nature of rail freight has changed enormously. In the early days, when roads were still little more than dirt tracks, railways were often the only way to move products from one place to another. In Britain and other European countries, the network spread so that nearly every town had a goods facility where various kinds of freight were collected in different wagons, sorted in large marshalling yards and dispatched to their destinations. Railways expanded especially rapidly when it became necessary to move goods further and more quickly than before. Coal transportation had a major impact and many lines were built to link mines to the factories and iron works that powered the Industrial Revolution.

Nowadays, with heavy competition from both road and air, rail freight is typified by bulk movements direct from origin to destination, as well as the movement of some smaller specialist loads. Typical bulk movements include coal from mines or docks to power stations, stone from quarries, and sea containers from ports to local road-distribution depots. In an ironic twist, new cars are often delivered by rail, and long-distance lorries are frequently carried on specially adapted "piggy back" railway wagons. Specialist traffic includes nuclear materials to and from power stations and naval dockyards, refrigerated wagons carrying perishable goods long distances, and varying quantities of mail. In the 1930s, even live fish were transported in water tanks carried within carefully designed wagons.

Railways have always been an important carrier of mail. At first it was a matter of speed, as trains could

RIGHT American freight trains cover thousands of miles and have always been much longer than anything seen in Britain. This is a typical scene of a lengthy freight train crossing the American prairie in the late 1930s. The engine is working hard, as can be seen from the way the smoke is being blasted skywards from the chimney.

OPPOSITE Milk churns were once an everyday sight on platforms. Freshly filled, they were collected from wayside halts in the countryside and taken to towns and cities. This 1923 picture at Paddington shows the vast quantity in use at the time.

BELOW One of the most famous railway crimes was the 1963 Great Train Robbery. This was the scene afterwards; the venue is now known locally as Train Robber Bridge.

THE GREAT TRAIN ROBBERY

One of Britain's most infamous crimes took place on 7 August 1963 at Linslade – just over 48 kilometres (30 miles) north of London. An armed gang of 15 men robbed a Glasgow-to-London mail train. They forced the train to stop by changing the signals to red, and then assaulted the driver.

The robbery occurred in open countryside and the gang had plenty of time to make off with £2.6 million (equivalent to more than £40 million in today's money) from the train. They were all rounded up, but some – most notably Ronnie Biggs – escaped from prison and fled abroad.

This is the car for sorting letters in the Mail Train.

travel more quickly and further than horse-drawn stagecoaches; later sheer volume entered the equation as well, with the railways running dedicated mail trains. The British Parliament passed a law in 1838 that effectively forced railways to carry mail as and when required by the Postmaster General. Such trains, many of which carried postal workers to sort mail along the way and speed up delivery, eventually became known as travelling post offices. Some postal trains were also equipped with apparatus for picking up and setting down letters (wrapped in tight leather pouches) using lineside equipment while on the move. Travelling postal workers had to make sure they were clear of the pouches when these were collected from the lineside as they were catapulted at high speed through a small opening into the carriage. Transporting mail soon proved to be a lucrative business and by the mid-nineteenth century many countries in addition to the UK were running dedicated mail trains. In the USA, for example, travelling post offices spread out to cover more than 321,000 route-kilometres (200,000 miles), but they had all been discontinued by the late 1970s.

Mail by rail has been in general decline over the last few decades, but there are still a few services in regular use. In Britain, for example, a handful of trains still carry pre-sorted mail – but no longer postal workers – using a small fleet of specially built "Class 325" electric trains, while in France the SNCF operates a number of high-speed postal services using specially adapted "Trains à Grande Vitesse" (TGV) sets. These are capable of travelling at 270 kph (168 mph), making them the fastest non-passenger trains in the world.

For half a century in the late Victorian era, special slow-moving, non-passenger trains carried many odd cargoes, including animals (usually for circuses and farms). In 1872, the P. T. Barnum Circus in America had grown so large that it built its own dedicated train of about 60 wagons and carriages to carry everything from tents to elephants. By the end of the century the idea had spread to Britain, where a smaller version was used. Circus trains survive to this day in the USA with the Ringling Bros and Barnum & Bailey circuses. There is a "Blue" and a "Red" train to take two shows around the country, each stretching to more than 1.6 kilometres (1 mile) in length.

ABOVE Railways brought big improvements to the postal system and special postal trains were built for the Royal Mail. These conveyed staff who sorted letters while the train ran, saving time, a system that was adopted worldwide.

One of the strangest train loads ever carried in Britain was a whole farm, which was moved from North Yorkshire to Sussex. Over the course of two days a single train was loaded up, transported overnight and unloaded again the next day, taking all the animals, stores, machinery and personal belongings that made up the farm. The relocation was documented in the 1952 film *Farmer Moving South*, this being one of many examples of the railways recording their activities for promotional purposes.

Among the most famous of documentary films – now a classic – is *Night Mail* (1936). It aimed to show the work done by postal workers on an overnight train from London to Scotland, and was accompanied by a poem specially written by W. H. Auden with music by Benjamin Britten. Railways have fascinated filmmakers since the dawn of moving images. One of the first films made by cinema pioneers the Lumière Brothers, in 1896, was a short documentary, *Arrival of a Train at La Ciotat*. Popular myth has it that the sight of a train heading towards the audience had them running for cover. Since then, trains and railways have featured in a vast range of films across all genres.

A classic in fiction is *Murder on the Orient Express* by Agatha Christie. Set in the 1930s, it features Belgian detective Hercule Poirot solving a murder committed while the luxury "Orient Express" was trapped in a snow drift north of Belgrade. Other notable films include the spy drama *Avalanche Express* (1979) and the classic

BELOW A narrow-gauge railway was built under London by the Post Office for transporting mail between major sorting offices and stations quickly by avoiding street-level congestion. This is a 1950s depiction of this mail railway.

POST OFFICE UNDERGROUND MAIL TRAIN: LONDON

World War II love story *Brief Encounter* (1945), which was filmed at Carnforth station in Lancashire, making use of the enormous station clock there. It had to be filmed away from any large town in case of bombers flying over. Buster Keaton made a silent film, *The General*, in 1927, depicting the great train chase from the American Civil War. Another film set in wartime was *The Train* (1964). A family classic, *The Railway Children* (1970), was shot in Yorkshire, and Alfred Hitchcock's thriller *Strangers on a Train* (1951) still has audiences on the edge of their seats.

More recent times have seen dramas like the runaway train in *Unstoppable* (2010), and the modern series of films using the "Hogwarts Express" in the "Harry Potter" series (from 2001). This train has been based in Carnforth for nearly 15 years and used for filming across England and Scotland, mainly under tight security. The Hogwarts Express is a magical, steam-hauled train that takes student wizard Harry Potter and his friends to and from Hogwarts School each term. The story has it departing from London King's Cross in the morning and arriving into Hogsmeade in the evening. It leaves from "Platform 9¾", which can only be accessed by passing through a brick wall. The success of the films made the London terminus a tourist attraction for fans, leading to the installation of fake signs for "Platform 9¾", and a luggage trolley that appears to be pushed halfway through a wall.

OPPOSITE One of the first films made was of a train arriving at La Ciotat in the south of France. Audiences on the left-hand side of the auditorium were very apprehensive when the train approached them on a big screen. It was a silent film and behind the screen, sound effects were made by a set of bellows being puffed.

OPPOSITE, BELOW Circus trains were common in America, taking the whole show around the country. They were specially decorated to advertise the circus and this is a picture from 1905 of part of the Barnum & Bailey train.

BELOW In Britain animals were transported in ordinary freight trains. These elephants are being persuaded to join a freight carriage at St Botolphs in 1961 to be used in filming *Cleopatra*.

SUPER-SIZE TRAINS

In the past, larger items of heavy manufactured goods would invariably be sent by rail from the factory to where they were required, or to a port for export. It was common practice for an "out-of-gauge" load (such as large turbines for factories) to be carried, and in wartime tanks would be taken on flat wagons to ports for overseas use. When these trains ran, others would not be allowed to pass on adjacent lines, and tracks were sometimes moved to avoid the goods colliding with a bridge. This has not happened for decades because modern railways cannot cope with anything out of the ordinary anymore.

In January 2010, two centuries on from horses pulling one or (at best) two wagons, the American railroad company Union Pacific ran a special test train that was nearly 5.6 kilometres (3½ miles) long. It was formed of 295 wagons, mostly double-stacked with containers. Nine locomotives were used and these were evenly spread throughout the train to reduce the strain on couplings. The train took two days to travel from Texas to California at speeds of up to 105 kph (65 mph). Even travelling at this speed, it affected road traffic by taking at least three minutes to clear a level crossing, and of course at 50 kph (31 mph) it would block crossings for seven minutes! It is thought that such monster trains could be the future for freight.

COMPROMISE AND CHANGE

THE POST-WAR DECADE AND BEECHING

Heavy traffic took its toll on Britain's railways during World War II, and by 1945 the system was in urgent need of repair and investment. Thousands of aging locomotives, carriages and wagons kept the service going, via dilapidated, soot-encrusted stations. Post-war freedom saw leisure travel peak in 1946, with the highest passenger numbers since the 1920s. Trains to coastal resorts were often overcrowded and many passengers were forced to sit on their suitcases in corridors; in any seats near open windows, they became covered in black smuts. The post-war railways were short of labour, money and access to the assets we have today, and were unable to generate the profits needed to modernize.

After the war, the country chose a Labour government, hoping that along with the unions it would implement its ideology of "the people" owning major national assets. Nationalization was the key word, and transport became a big part of this policy – British Railways (BR) was born on 1 January 1948, to be run by the Railway Executive, which was answerable to the British Transport Commission. Little changed at first, but processes and procedures began to be standardized, largely following London Midland & Scottish Railway practices. Locomotive modernization policy came in two parts: 1500V DC (see p.126) electrification was used on the Manchester–Sheffield–Wath and London–Shenfield–Southend routes, while modern steam locomotives handled all traffic on non-electrified lines. New, simple BR standard steam locomotives were designed, with 999 built between 1951 and 1960.

The 1951 Conservative government questioned

SAVE YOUR RAILWAYS

➤ In his first report as Chairman of the British Transport Commission, Dr. Beeching said that most of the passenger stopping trains " . . . should be discontinued as quickly as possible."

➤ What will you do if he has his way?

➤ Take a bus? Ride a bike? Walk? Stay at home?

➤ Why be pushed around?

Do something about it, before it's too late

Protest to your Member of Parliament and to any Soci which you belon

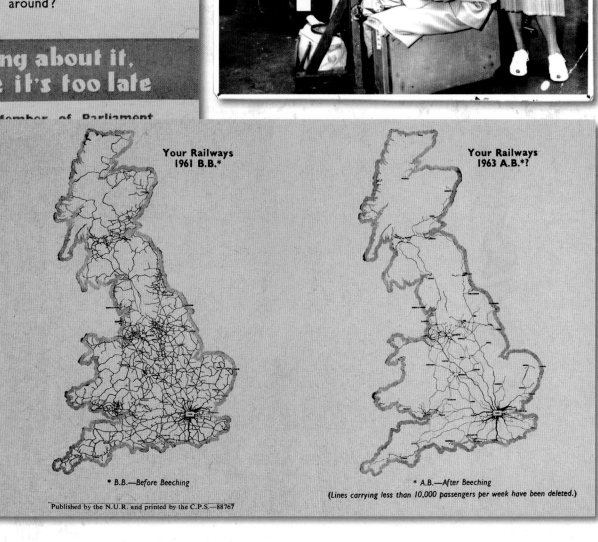

OPPOSITE Post-war rail travel boomed to coastal resorts, and Waterloo was often crowded with holidaymakers. The most popular meeting place was, and still is, under the famous clock, seen here in 1946 with waiting passengers.

ABOVE RIGHT Trains were so crowded that some trains were only available if passengers had reserved a seat in advance. The 09.24hrs train from Waterloo to Bournemouth was one such train that the Walker family were queuing for on the August Bank Holiday in 1953.

ABOVE AND RIGHT The modernisation plan and Beeching brought a massive campaign to save the wholesale proposed closure of many railways. This 1962 leaflet is typical of the time when campaigns were launched against the cuts.

This one entitled, "Save Your Railways" was produced by the National Union of Railwaymen encouraging railway staff to protest against the cuts. This was a graphic demonstration of how the railway network might look if the cuts went through but obviously also designed to try and save union members' jobs!

Your Railways 1961 B.B.*

Your Railways 1963 A.B.*?

* B.B.—Before Beeching

* A.B.—After Beeching
(Lines carrying less than 10,000 passengers per week have been deleted.)

Published by the N.U.R. and printed by the C.P.S.—88767

BEECHING, SAVIOUR OF THE RAILWAYS?

Richard Beeching (1913–85) was a director of ICI with a doctorate in physics. He joined BR in 1961 (on secondment from ICI, to which he returned in 1965) to formulate ways of making the railways pay, and he was soon appointed chairman. His 1963 report, entitled "The Reshaping of British Railways", made many recommendations, including closing all loss-making routes; it met with forceful objections, and gained him a name as the axeman, but in reality most closures were inevitable, following the pattern of closures under BR before the Beeching era.

The Beeching regime introduced better management training, and efficient, merry-go-round coal trains between mines and power stations; it also created a type of modern freight train dubbed the "Freightliner". This carried the new world-standard containers, a huge improvement on BR's small wooden ones. Crucially, it improved the financial management regime so future investment decisions would have a better basis.

BR's locomotive policy and whether diesel and electric locomotives should be used. The 1955 Modernization Plan proposed better facilities and stations, as well as a freight ring route around London linking south-coast ports (via Tonbridge and Reading) to the West Coast Main Line at Bletchley over a curved concrete flyover. This exists today as a rarely used monument to the era, since freight declined due to road competition. BR's plan to use small diesels for shunting and diesel railcars or multiple units for inter-urban and rural lines remained unchanged, and in the decade from 1953 BR gained over 4,000 diesel railcar vehicles. BR ordered some pilot mainline diesel test-designs from UK manufacturers and the ones that performed best were selected for mass production.

Electrification policy changed again, and the 25kV AC system was chosen for the Euston, Liverpool Street and Fenchurch Street routes. It was deemed uneconomical to change the Southern Region's third-rail 660V DC conductor rail system, so the voltage was increased to 750. Politicians now decided to end the steam age as quickly as possible in this part of the world and from 1958 large orders were placed for little-tested diesels. The last BR steam locomotive was built at Swindon – a heavy freight engine, No. 92220 *Evening Star* – at the same time as Swindon's diesel construction was underway. The London, Tilbury & Southend lines, Glasgow suburban routes and the London to Birmingham, Manchester and Liverpool routes were electrified with the 25kV system, while the Southern Region's third-rail network expanded to the Kent main lines. A new diesel "Blue Pullman" service for businessmen ran between London and Birmingham, Bristol and Manchester while the disruptive electrification work was underway.

BR obtained improved diesels in the early 1960s, including the "Deltics" for the East Coast Main Line, and "Westerns" for Paddington services, but the most useful were the mass-produced "Class 37" and "Class 47". New carriages spelled the demise of non-standard trains such as the "Brighton Belle Pullman". However, modernization during the 1950s had not stemmed mounting financial problems, and radical measures were needed, but accounting systems failed to show what caused the worst losses. BR's chairman, Richard Beeching (see box), instigated radical policies that stemmed financial losses, until a new Labour government from 1964 slowed his route closures, resulting in an increased loss. In more recent years, two of BR's chairmen, Sir Peter Parker and the first Sir Bob Reid, reorganized the company so managers understood the financial consequences of their decisions and BR moved towards profitability and privatization.

OPPOSITE These two huge mainline express diesels, No.1000 "Royal Scot" and No. 10001, were the first to be used on Britain's railways. Doubleheading, they have just brought this express from London Euston, over the hills via Beattock, to Elvanfoot on the way to Glasgow in 1958.

RIGHT A British Rail poster from 1961 promoting its three new Pullman diesel services, between London and South Wales, Bristol and Birmingham.

BELOW As the Beeching cuts were made, scenes like this became common when lines closed and the rails were ripped up. This route in London near Crystal Palace was actually closed a few years beofre Beeching's report but is typical of his effect.

ELECTRIFICATION

Electrification is the future of railways, but electric trains have in fact been around longer than trains powered by diesel. In the beginning, electrification was used for urban and underground railways, where the smoke from steam was unacceptable. But over time, electric railways have proved superior for high-intensity, high-speed, or high-power usage where the large infrastructure costs can be justified. Here the advantages include lower running and maintenance costs, faster acceleration, higher top speeds and less pollution. Electrified railways can also cope more effectively with steeper gradients, having more power to hand for the locomotives. Electrification continues to spread in most countries (except perhaps the USA), not least because it does not depend on fossil fuels to generate the power supply and is therefore future-proofed.

There are two main types of railway electrification: third-rail and overhead wire systems. Third-rail (or sometimes fourth-rail) is the more robust system as the current flows through insulated rails at track level and is collected by a "shoe" mounted on one of the train's bogies. It is not suitable for high-speed trains and so tends to be found only on metro systems and urban commuter networks. Overhead wire systems use a thin contact wire suspended from lineside structures above the train from which the current is collected by a pantograph on the train's roof. They are suitable for high-speed use, typically for long-distance, commuting, inter-city and international services.

Third and fourth-rail lines normally use direct current (DC), but overhead wires can use DC or alternating current (AC). Broadly speaking, high-voltage AC requires lower-cost infrastructure but more complicated and expensive locomotives, whereas medium-voltage DC requires more expensive infrastructure, but simpler and cheaper locomotives. The most commonly used DC voltages are 600–750V for third- and fourth-rail systems, and 1,500–3,000V for overhead use. AC voltages are usually 15kV at 16.7Hz or 25kV at 50Hz. The benefit of using high voltage is that much smaller currents flow, which means the energy losses due to resistance are smaller. Some locomotives and electrical multiple units (EMUs) are designed to operate over more than one system – as with Eurostar trains running between London and Paris. Initially, these used third-rail DC on the English side of the Channel Tunnel and high-voltage overhead AC on the French side; since the full opening of the Channel Tunnel Rail Link, 25kV has also been used in England.

The first-known electric locomotive was invented in 1837 by Scotsman Robert Davidson (whereas diesel engine design would not be patented until 1892). It

BELOW This is the first electric locomotive made by Werner Von Siemens in 1879 being demonstrated in Berlin. Siemens are now a huge electric train builder supplying railways around the world.

ABOVE This is the inside of a City & South London Railway carriage in 1890. These electrical trains were the first real "tube" trains in the world and were somewhat claustrophobic for passengers.

was only a model, but by 1842 he had built a full-size machine powered by zinc batteries. This was tested on the Edinburgh to Glasgow line, where it managed a top speed of 6.4 kph (4 mph). The first practical electric railway was demonstrated by Siemens & Halske at the Berlin Exhibition of 1879, where a 2.2kW locomotive pulled three carriages around a 300 metre (984 foot) track at a top speed of 12.9 kph (8 mph). This led to the establishment of a number of small-scale lines, including Volk's Electric Railway – in Brighton, UK – which opened in 1883 and now claims to be the oldest operating electric railway in the world.

It was soon realized that electric trains were ideal for use in tunnels, where steam locomotives could not be used. For example, the City & South London Railway (the world's first deep-level underground railway, which opened in 1890) used electric traction to power its 5.1 kilometre (3.2 mile) line under the Thames. Similar schemes soon followed in Paris and New York.

Italian railways were the first to electrify an entire mainline when the 106 kilometre (66 mile) Valtellina line opened in 1902, using a 3kV AC overhead wire system. A series of speed tests were conducted the following year by Siemens & Halske using an EMU. This reached a record 211 kph (131 mph) between Marienfelde and Zossen in Germany. Switzerland opened its first electric line in 1913 with the Bern–Lötschberg–Simplon (BLS) railway, using a 15kV AC overhead wire system. Many mountain railway sections were electrified because cheap hydro-electricity could be generated locally. France then commissioned the Paris to Tours section of the Orléans railway at 1,500V DC, and in

LEFT The French railways were early users of electric trains. This picture dating from around 1900 shows an electric train on the Invalides Railway passing the Eiffel Tower.

ABOVE The Liverpool Overhead Railway was the world's first elevated electric railway. This is a poster from 1910 extolling the line's virtues of speed and the views afforded by the elevated route.

the final years before World War I, railways in southern Britain were busy expanding their third-rail urban networks at 600V DC. After World War I, more countries began electrifying their main lines, and by 1930 it was possible to travel up to 805 kilometres (500 miles) by electric traction from Geneva to Salzburg (nowadays the electrified Trans-Siberian Railway means it is possible to travel thousands of kilometres). In Britain, the Manchester South Junction & Altrincham Railway was electrified using 1,500V DC overhead. This became the standard in Britain until British Railways followed France and switched to 25kV AC overhead in 1956. Just before World War II, the London & North Eastern Railway (LNER) began electrifying its heavily graded line from Sheffield to Manchester at 1500V DC, but work was interrupted by the war and was not completed until 1956. "Class 76" and "Class 77" locomotives were specially built for the line to work freight and passenger trains respectively.

THE CHANNEL TUNNEL RAIL LINK

Britain's only high-speed line connects London with Paris and Brussels via the Channel Tunnel (see p.138). The tunnel was opened in 1994 and carries a mixture of high-speed Eurostar passenger trains, international freight trains and Eurotunnel vehicle shuttles between Folkestone and Calais. Each service requires its own specially designed motive power. The Eurostar trains are essentially modified TGV sets for use on the British loading gauge. Freight trains are pulled by dual-voltage 5MW (6,700hp) "Class 92" locomotives, while the vehicle shuttles are pulled by 5.8MW (7,700hp) "Class 9" locomotives.

OPPOSITE Demonstrating the size of a Westinghouse Turbine locomotive, the worker is dwarfed by the engine as he works inside the engine in this 1930 picture.

BELOW Electric railways spread quickly after the First World War, especially in hotter climates where water supplies could be unreliable. India's main routes were electrified and the Great Indian Peninsula Railway used electric locomotives like this from the late 1920s.

ABOVE The "Class 92" electric locomotive was introduced in 1993 for use in the UK and through the Channel Tunnel into France. These can work from an AC or DC power supply and are now used on high-speed international freight services between Britain and France.

Modern electric locomotives can be traced back to an important development in 1944 for the BLS in Switzerland. Until then, most electric locomotives were built with a mixture of powered and unpowered axles. However, the BLS locos were "Bo-Bo" types, meaning that all four axles were driven by motors. It was a successful idea taken up by the French and subsequently used elsewhere around the world. Britain acquired its first mainline AC locomotives in the early 1960s, when the so-called "AL1-5s" (later "Classes 81–85") were delivered as part of the west coast route modernization. They could pull heavy trains at up to 160 kph (100 mph) – revolutionizing the line and reducing journey times – and remained in service for nearly 30 years until the early 1990s.

Locomotives capable of hauling passenger services at 200 kph (125 mph) first appeared in Germany and France in the 1960s. Ironically, this was a time in the USA when the use of electric traction was in decline as passenger traffic lost out to airlines and the cost of infrastructure meant that diesels were more economical for long-distance freight transportation. Other countries, however, recognized

that high-speed trains could compete with airlines for inter-city travel. The French developed the "*Train à Grande Vitesse*" (TGV, see p.142) and the Japanese their Shinkansen "bullet" trains (see p.148). Countries such as Spain, Italy and Germany also began building high-speed lines.

Germany's "Inter-City Express" (ICE) trains were introduced from the late 1980s and the ICE network was officially launched in May 1991. It is the flagship service of Deutsche Bahn, travelling across Germany and into Switzerland, Belgium and France at speeds up to 320 kph (200 mph). Trains based on the ICE design also operate in Spain, China and Russia.

Italy opened its first high-speed route from Rome to Florence in 1978 with a top speed of 250 kph (160 mph). Since then, Italy's high-speed network has continued to grow using "Elettro Treno Rapido" type "Pendolino" trains. These use tilting technology acquired from British Rail's aborted 1980s "Advance Passenger Train" project, although some versions do not tilt but can go faster, such as the "ETR500" units.

CURRENT ELECTRIC RECORD HOLDER

The title of the world's fastest conventional electric locomotive is currently held by a "Siemens Eurosprinter ES 64 U4", which set a speed of 357 kph (223 mph) in 2007 during trials near Nuremberg in Germany. It is one of a family of locomotives introduced in 1992 for freight or passenger use across country borders and electrical systems. "ES" refers to "Eurosprinter", "64" to its 6,400kW (8,600hp), "U" to "universal use" for freight or passenger trains, and "4" to the four most commonly used electrical systems in Europe. Variants on the class are used across Europe, China and Korea.

OPPOSITE The Newton-le-Willows-based Vulcan Foundry supplied the world with steam, diesel and electric locomotives. This was the most powerful electric locomotive to be built in Britain when constructed in 1952 for export to Spain. It is shown being inspected by Spanish railway staff and other invited guests.

ABOVE Britain's first modern electric locomotive, the "Class 81" electric, was introduced in 1959 and was tested in the Manchester area, where this shot was taken. The T3 indicates that the engine was on a test run when photographed in 1960.

BELOW The LNER introduced a "Class 76" electric locomotive, designed by Gresley, to pull heavy coal and freight trains through the hills between Wath and Manchester in 1941. The rest of the fleet was built from 1950 and used until the Woodhead route was closed in 1981 when they were no longer required.

OTHER RAILWAY SYSTEMS

/// NARROW GAUGE, TRAMS AND MONORAIL

Railway development over the last 200 years has generated many different ideas, producing a range of different systems. Railways have brought prosperity to the countries they serve, despite the different formats and operating methods used. Apart from standard gauge, there are many other systems around the world that use a gauge of less than 1.435 metres (4 feet 8½ inches) and are therefore commonly described as narrow gauge (there was never any legislation passed to regularize anything other than standard or broad gauge). Narrow-gauge railways have an advantage over standard and broad gauge railways as they are able to negotiate tighter curves and follow the contours of the land more closely. They also require smaller tunnels, bridges, cuttings and embankments, thereby reducing the costs of construction and subsequent maintenance. The gauge chosen depended on the topography of the route to be followed, as well as the traffic the line was intended to carry.

In mountainous areas, narrow-gauge lines provided the only possible railway solution and many different gauges were used. In Britain, the narrow gauge was generally less than 90 centimetres (3 feet), and the dominant narrow gauge evolved at 60 centimetres (2 feet), but elsewhere the minimum used was generally 1 metre (3 feet 3 inches). In 1897, after most UK narrow-gauge lines had been constructed, the Government's war department directed that all new military narrow-gauge lines should be 76 centimetres (2 feet 6 inches). They would then be compatible with the lines in the Empire's colonies, meaning that locomotives, carriages, wagons and spares could be interchangeable – a crucial factor in subsequent wars.

Among British narrow-gauge pioneers were the Ffestiniog Railway (FR) and Welsh Highland Railway (WHR), both in Wales, and both using a 59.7 centimetre (23½ inch) gauge. Both were conceived and engineered by Charles Spooner, who tried unsuccessfully to construct a network of narrow gauge lines in north Wales. Founded by an Act of Parliament in 1832, the 21 kilometre (13 mile) FR linked the port of Porthmadog with the slate mines 300 metres (1,000 feet) up in the mountains at Blaenau Ffestiniog. It used animal power and gravity until 1863 when it purchased two steam locomotives. The following year it became legal to carry passengers on narrow gauge trains. Trains carrying slate descended using gravity, and

the speed was controlled by a brakesman riding on the wagons. The FR closed in 1946 and was taken over by volunteers, who reopened it in stages from 1955 to 1982, when the entire original route was running again.

The FR connected at Porthmadog with the WHR, which ran 43 kilometres (27 miles) northwest through Snowdonia to Caernarfon. WHR construction began in 1873 (replacing earlier, differently gauged tracks that had been laid in various places along the route) and it was subsequently extended,

BELOW This scene, taken in 1880 at Tan-y-Bwlch station on the Ffestiniog Railway, clearly shows the nature of this pioneering narrow-gauge line opened in the 1830s, and is little changed today.

ROUGH SEA OVER ELECTRIC
RAILWAY, KEMPTOWN, BRIGHTON

ABOVE The electric tourist Volk's Railway in Brighton commenced operations in 1883 and is the oldest electric railway in Britain, now operated by Brighton Council. It runs for just over a mile along the beach in the tourist season. The track has been lowered onto the beach since this undated picture was taken.

RIGHT Not all steam locomotives had a fire, so they could work without risk of fire in factories. This one was built in 1876 by Theodore Schaffer for the Crescent City Railroad in New Orleans. It was charged with steam from another engine, using the valve seen at the front on top of the engine.

PROPELLER RAILWAYS

In Germany the Kruckenberg propeller-driven railcar was developed and tested from 1930. It averaged 230 kph (143 mph) on test runs between Berlin and Hamburg over a distance of 10 kilometres (6 miles). The line had to be straight to achieve these speeds, but the train was never put into public service. The idea was further developed on the Railplane Test Line at Milngavie near Glasgow, using a combined monorail and guide rail system above and below the train. This counteracted centrifugal forces on curves, providing what was claimed at the time to be a stable ride. The brakes were said to be four times more efficient than on normal trains, and a constant signal was displayed in the cab so the driver knew how fast he could go. Both propeller trains were powered by internal combustion engines, but the idea did not take off.

traversing the spectacular Aberglaslyn Pass in 1905. Financial difficulties meant that the WHR was not completed until the 1920s. Construction was funded by government loans, which the railway was unable to repay as it did not make enough money. The WHR went into receivership in 1927, but it managed to run trains until 1936. The WHR was reopened in March 2011, and the WHR and FR are running again as one company, although they have encountered some teething problems.

The Leighton Buzzard narrow-gauge railway, 56 kilometres (35 miles) north of London, was probably the first permanent railway in the world to be exclusively worked by internal-combustion motive power. It has operated continuously since 1919, initially using steam locomotives to transport sand from a quarry. These were soon replaced by small, petrol "Simplex" locomotives built by the Motor Rail Company in Bedford and used in large numbers in quarry and industrial complexes. Over 100 similar locomotives worked within 3 kilometres (2 miles) of

Leighton Buzzard's town centre in the boom years of the sand industry. Steam returned to the line when part of it was run by conservationists, and both types of engines are used on the line today.

While narrow-gauge railways were expanding across the world, the monorail system was being developed worldwide with varying success. Monorails started in southwest Ireland in 1888 with the 16 kilometre (10 mile) Listowel and Ballybunion Railway, developed by French engineer Charles Lartigue. His design, running trains on a single rail supported on a trestle, ran for 36 years but was expensive as everything had to be carefully balanced across the one rail. Seven years earlier Lartigue had built a similar, 90 kilometre (56 mile) line in Algeria – using camels instead of locomotives. Meanwhile, in 1886, the American Meigs Monorail had opened in Massachusetts, using a different type of structure which supported the rail high above the streets. Passengers travelled inside a futuristic-looking, cylinder-shaped carriage, but the line only ran until 1894.

OPPOSITE The Meigs Monorail in Massachusetts ran from 1886 above the streets as captured in this fascinating picture. This must have been an amazing experience and sight for everyone who saw or travelled on it.

BELOW The onset of reliable electricity brought many tram systems across the world running on roads in towns and cities. This 1903 picture shows the opening of the London United Electric Tramways system at Teddington, which had attracted a huge crowd of onlookers.

Also in 1894, construction began on a similar railway on the sea floor between Brighton and Rottingdean, with the carriage riding above the waves for 5 kilometres (3 miles). Legally defined as a "tramroad", this so-called "Daddy Longlegs" railway copied the principle of the cable-worked 100 metre (110 yard) line across the harbour at St Malo in northern France, which ran from 1878 to 1916. The Brighton line was built by Magnus Volk at 4.6 metres (15 feet) below the high-tide level and up to 183 metres (600 feet) out to sea. The 83 centimetre (32½ inch) wide track was secured to the chalk seabed and opened in 1896 using a carriage called "Pioneer", which carried 150 passengers as well as lifeboats and lifebelts. The train was driven by a qualified nautical captain, reaching a top speed of 13 kph (8 mph) at low tide and 6 kph (4 mph) at high tide. It was powered by an overhead electric wire and the highlight of its career was carrying the Prince of Wales in 1898. Operation ceased in 1901 after Brighton Council demanded that the track be moved further out to sea, which was financially impossible.

ABOVE Railways served many coastal resorts, but stations were often situated on a clifftop such as at Scarborough. Cliff railways, or funiculars, were built to carry passengers between the beach and the railway. Five of these were built at Scarborough, one of which is seen here and is still working today.

BELOW The main line railway equivalent of a tram was the steam railcar, which was a carriage built with a small steam locomotive permanently attached to it also sharing a set of wheels. These were cheap to operate and kept many lightly used branch lines open for years. This is an undated example from the South East & Chatham Railway.

At the same time another unique tram system – located in Buckinghamshire, nearly as far away from the sea as is possible in the UK – ran the same distance and at the same top speed, carrying thousands of workers every day. This was the steam-hauled rail tram running in the middle of the main road from Deanshanger, via Stony Stratford, to Wolverton's railway works. The rails were buried in the road and the locomotive was streamlined, enclosing the wheels and other moving parts to protect other road users from injury. The Stony Stratford Tramway opened in 1887 and became one of the last steam trams to run, closing in 1926 after the General Strike. Modern versions of these light railways – using modern electric trams – have made a comeback in the UK (for example, in Croydon and Manchester), but are far more common in major European towns and cities. They often run on rails buried in roads – mingling with cars and people – and are powered by overhead electric wires.

Fireless steam locomotives were also widely used to haul hazardous goods in streets running to and from factories and docks – for example, around munitions factories and refineries to bring in or take out raw materials that were deemed to be dangerous if exposed to sparks, glowing ashes and heat from the fire. In essence, these locomotives carried a supply of high-pressure steam taken from a traditional steam locomotive or stationary boiler, thereby avoiding the risk of sparks that could cause an explosion.

TRAIN FERRIES

Railways crossed over or under the largest rivers, but the open sea hindered passengers' journeys across the English Channel and elsewhere, such as the Mediterranean and Baltic Seas. International travellers had to change from the train on to a ferry, with the added inconvenience of having to carry their luggage and a longer journey time. So special ships were built with rails which allowed trains to be shunted on and off at ports, offering passengers and freight customers direct rail services.

The first to operate were in 1907 across the Baltic on the 3 kilometre (2 mile) crossing from Fredericia and the 26 kilometre (16 mile) crossing from Nyborg, both in Denmark, bringing direct trains from Copenhagen, Berlin and Paris. In the UK, train ferries were introduced in World War I for military traffic. Later they were used for freight wagons and passenger carriages. Trains were carried first across the North Sea and then across the English Channel, paving the way for direct services from London to Paris and Brussels.

RIGHT Trams were rendered redundant by cars and buses in Britain by the 1960s and only remained in use at Blackpool as a tourist attraction. This was Britain's first electric tramway when opened in 1885 and today still flourishes on the seafront, running past Blackpool Tower – seen here a few years ago.

THE CHANNEL TUNNEL

A Channel tunnel was first suggested in 1751 by Frenchman Nicholas Desmaret, then in 1802 engineer Albert Mathieu proposed a scheme to Napoleon. He was in favour of a link using horse-drawn vehicles in an upper tunnel lit by oil lamps, with a lower tunnel for drainage. The first real underwater tunnel was built by Brunel, opening in 1842 under the Thames between Wapping and Rotherhithe. Then the technology and knowledge existed but the problem of ventilation and using steam locomotives in a long tunnel remained unsolved.

In 1875, an Act of Parliament authorized the Channel Tunnel Company Ltd to undertake preliminary trials near Dover on the English coast, and further trials took place at Sangatte in France in 1877. Three years later, more English test excavations were carried out in Abbot's Cliff near Dover and a pilot tunnel was scheduled for completion in 1886. The trial tunnelling was carried out using compressed air machines designed by Colonel Fredrick Beaumont, a system said to be three times quicker than using explosives and manual labour. In 1880, Captain Thomas English developed a more powerful boring machine, which could cut 800 metres (½ mile) of tunnel every month. The pilot tunnel was 2.4 kilometres (1½ miles) long and 30.5 metres (100 feet) below the sea floor in 1883 when the project was halted by the military establishment, whose concerns that a tunnel would put England at great risk from invasion were voiced by Lieutenant General Sir Garnet Wolseley. A government commission banned any tunnel to France on military grounds – a decision that was only rescinded in 1955 after modern warfare effectively rendered the ban useless.

Railway electrification from 1900 solved the locomotive smoke ventilation problem. Finance now became the main issue; British and French companies were formed, but

BELOW An 1802 impression of what an invasion of England from across the Channel might look like, intriguingly making use of a Channel tunnel that had just been proposed.

THE CHANNEL TUNNEL.
A MARTIAL NIGHTMARE.

OTHER CROSS-CHANNEL SCHEMES

A railway ferry was suggested in 1870, but probably the most bizarre plan was one put forward in 1875 for a submarine running on rails laid on the Channel floor, and pulled by chains from winches. In 1929, an Anglo-French commission evaluated tunnel, ferry and bridge options. The latter contained over 50 spans of 610 metres (2,000 feet) carrying four lines, at a cost of £75 million. A tunnel system, at an estimated cost of £31 million, consisting of two independent railway tunnels plus a central pilot tunnel, was the preferred plan.

LEFT Dating from around 1880, this depiction of "A Martial Nightmare" shows presumably the chaos that a Channel tunnel would bring to Neptune's kingdom.

BELOW When the Channel Tunnel was eventually built in the late 1980s it used several TBMs, tunnel-boring machines. This is what they looked like: huge rotary cutting machines that bored their way through the ground below the sea.

although they were confident of generating the necessary investment funds, World War I put a stop to the plan. In the 1950s and '60s, the English and French authorities discussed a fixed link across the Channel, leading to the 1971 agreement for a tunnel. It was to follow the same method of construction (using rotary boring machines) and the same route that were eventually used 15 years later. Even the proposed train design – a double-deck passenger and car shuttle – was similar to the ones actually built in 1993. The scheme was formally launched by Prime Minister Heath and President Pompidou in 1973 but abandoned two years later during the fuel crisis.

Eventually, in 1984, the UK and French governments again agreed a scheme and invited plans from the private sector for a fixed link under the Channel. Prime Minister Thatcher and President Mitterand announced in 1986 that the Eurotunnel proposal based on the 1970s scheme (using two rail tunnels and a service tunnel) had been selected. On 29 July 1987, the Treaty of Canterbury was signed by the political leaders and simultaneous tunnel boring commenced from France and England. The two tunnelling teams met in the service tunnel under the Channel on 1 December 1990, 23 kilometres (14 miles) from England and 16 kilometres

(10 miles) from France. The main tunnels were joined in May and June the following year. In December 1993, 46 metres (150 feet) below the seabed, the construction company Trans Manche Link handed the system over to Eurotunnel for fitting out.

The 50 kilometre (31 mile) long "Chunnel", as it was by now widely known, was formally opened by Queen Elizabeth and President Mitterand in May 1994, with international freight trains running from the following month. International passenger services run by Eurostar started six months later between London, Paris and Brussels.

The Chunnel has not been without incident: lorry fires in November 1996 and in September 2008 caused temporary closures. However, there has been no loss of life due to the stringent fire precautions which ensure passenger carriages can withstand fire spreading for 30 minutes. The smoke alarms were tested by sending a French steam locomotive 6 kilometres (4 miles) into the tunnel. Perhaps the biggest hurdle was the debt incurred building the tunnel. It was estimated to cost £5 billion but this figure ultimately doubled and the subsequent debt could not be serviced, bringing about a refinancing of the project in 1998 and again in 2005 following a bankruptcy scare.

LEFT While the Channel Tunnel was being built, an electric narrow-gauge railway was used to transport workers, spoil, tools and equipment. This is the service narrow-gauge railway.

BELOW The Channel Tunnel has a central service tunnel between the two main bores, also for use in an emergency. This picture was taken in 1992 in the service tunnel bore.

OPPOSITE Terence Cueno's painting of the inaugural Eurotunnel Shuttle, May 1994. Cuneo is acknowledged as being a talented and creative painter, whose career spanned the period from the Second World War to the Channel Tunnel opening.

THE TGV

THE TRAIN THAT CHANGED THE WORLD'S RAILWAYS

The French "*Train à Grande Vitesse*" (TGV) transformed rail journeys around the world and has quite possibly saved railways from terminal decline. It has proved that rail can deliver high-speed, comfortable and affordable travel, successfully competing with air and road transport. The train and its many derivatives were designed and built in France by Alstom; it celebrated its thirtieth anniversary in late 2011.

TGVs were designed to run on dedicated, newly built, high-speed lines – "*Lignes à Grande Vitesse*" (LGV) – constructed with steeper gradients than conventional lines. They can also operate on conventional railways, mixing with different trains and using different voltages across Europe. The need for these trains and new lines was brought about by the high volume of rail travel between Paris, Dijon, Lyon and Marseilles in the 1970s: in essence, the existing trains and track could not carry any more traffic. Most of the route was four tracks but there were around 110 kilometres (70 miles) where only two tracks were possible, constraining growth, so the decision was taken to build a new line.

Reaching 319 kph (198 mph) during tests in December 1972, early TGVs were high-speed locomotives powered by gas turbine, but the ensuing fuel crisis made the authorities decide to electrify the new route and not to rely on oil- or diesel-powered locomotives. By 1978, high-speed electric power units used in TGVs had been developed and built at Alstom's Belfort and La Rochelle factories. The TGVs were given an eye-catching orange livery and all TGV components were purchased from companies in France.

On 22 September 1981, the first TGVs to run in commercial service used the newly constructed LGV, known as Paris-Sud-Est, between the Gare de Lyon in Paris, Dijon and Lyon. Trains ran at up to 250 kph (156 mph) on the LGV but travelled at normal speeds on conventional lines. The service only started after rigorous trials with test trains – part of any new line's commissioning procedure to ensure that trains, track and signalling work together safely. During testing on 26 February 1981 – under a project codenamed "TGV 100" (referring to the target speed in metres per second) – the first TGV world rail-speed record, 380 kph (237.5 mph), was created, literally signalling the arrival of the new high-speed railway age. The Paris-Sud-Est line was originally designed to allow a maximum speed of 270 kph (169 mph) but was upgraded in 1996, allowing services to run at a maximum of 300 kph (186 mph).

Once the base services had proved to be reliable and had become successful, their application was extended. A new TGV brand – the "*Neige*" ("Snow") – was introduced for the winter of 1983, running services to Alpine resorts in the daytime, attracting skiers who had traditionally travelled on overnight trains from Paris to places like Modane, Chambéry and Aix-les-Bains. The growing realization that trains could now compete with air services persuaded the French postal authorities to move from air transport to specially designed postal TGVs from 1984: these could carry up to 90 tons of mail – far more than the 32 tons carried by air every day.

TOP This is the "Turbotrain", the gas-turbine-powered precursor of the electric TGV, on a Paris to Cherbourg service in 1970. The fuel crisis a few years later made the authorities decide to make the TGV an electrically powered train.

ABOVE President Mitterrand climbs on to the inaugural TGV service at Paris Gare de Lyon in September 1981.

Speeds were also sustained and extended. The second LGV route, the Atlantique, opened on 24 September 1989, with a maximum speed of 300 kph (186 mph). Again under test conditions, a new world rail-speed record was created by TGV No. 325, leading to the creation of a SNCF master plan for TGV and LGV expansion, which was presented to the French government in 1992. It was a matter of French pride and UK despondency that from November 1994 the "Eurostar"-branded TGVs travelled at 300 kph (186 mph) through France on the Nord-Europe LGV but slowed to 160 kph (100 mph) for the Channel Tunnel and onwards to London. This was a key year for the TGV service as the Lille Europe interchange opened, becoming an important junction for TGV services in all directions.

Passenger volumes rose as the high-speed European network grew, and the large-capacity TGV "Duplex" was developed, carrying 330 more passengers than a Eurostar train. This was a double-decker train powered by triple voltage, and was first used on 2 June 1996. Marketed under the name "Thalys", it operated between Paris, Brussels, Amsterdam and Cologne. These trains were brought into service six months later on the Paris-Sud-Est route.

The year 1998 saw a key development – the introduction of a TGV with a tilt facility on the LGV Sud route. Tilt enables trains to run at higher speeds around curves as it leans into them, in similar fashion to bike riders. Fares were simplified, a revised regular interval timetable was introduced, and passenger numbers subsequently soared.

The ever-expanding LGV network and high operational speeds were good for publicity. A record journey was made on 26 May 2001 when a TGV travelled 1,073 kilometres (667 miles) non-stop from the English Channel to the Mediterranean in under three-and-a-half hours. This was the prelude to the official opening a few weeks later of the 5.6 billion LGV Méditerranée, linking Paris (via Lyons) with Marseilles and Montpellier.

BELOW TGVs operate across France and Europe. This is a TGV at Modane, the frontier station between France and Italy, on a Paris to Milan afternoon service at in 2008. On departure towards Milan, the railway dives under Mount Cenis in the tunnel of the same name.

ABOVE One of the brightly liveried first-generation TGVs running on the Paris-Sud-Est LGV. This train quickly became a national icon after it started running in 1981.

A year later, construction of the East-European LGV linking Paris, Frankfurt, Stuttgart, Luxembourg and eventually Zurich commenced. The first section opened for testing on 13 November 2006, followed a month later by an announcement detailing the "French excellence in very high-speed rail transport programme", which aimed to break the world rail-speed record yet again. On 14 February 2007 an unofficial speed record of 553 kph (346 mph) was recorded, publicizing the opening of the East-European LGV. The record was officially broken when a specially prepared, five-coach TGV "V150" ran on 3 April 2007 under special test conditions. Part of the line was publicly opened on 10 June 2007 and is scheduled for completion in 2015.

A physical barrier to the high-speed European network was the different track gauge used in Spain from the rest of Europe. On 27 January 2011, the new 45 kilometre (28 mile) cross-border rail link between Perpignan and Figueres officially opened (it had operated since the previous month). Costing €280 million, this connected two high-speed

European rail networks for the first time. The line includes the 8 kilometre (5 mile) Perthus tunnel and uses the latest train control systems designed for operation at up to 350 kph (220 mph). This link shortened the journey time between Barcelona and France by an hour, and Barcelona to Figueres now takes just 50 minutes (instead of the 210 minutes previously taken) to travel between Barcelona and Perpignan.

Future scheduled developments are the Nîmes-Montpellier bypass line, which will carry high-speed passenger and freight trains around the two cities as an extension to the LGV Méditerranée. Both cities will be served by new stations as part of the scheme. A further section of LGV – the 192 kilometre (119 mile) Rhin–Rhône line – opened at the end of 2011 between Dijon and Mulhouse, providing high-speed links towards Zurich and Frankfurt and connecting with two other LGVs to the west and south, filling an important gap in the network.

ABOVE Eurostars were meant to operate between Glasgow, Manchester, York and Paris, and a small fleet was specially built for these services. They were never used as planned and are now working on French internal services. This one is at Lille in 2008 alongside a newer grey-liveried internationally used TGV.

BELOW LEFT A derivative of the TGV is the Italian "Eurostar" which entered service in 2009. The train is about to depart from Torino PN for Rome and the guard is checking with the driver that all is ready for departure.

THE TRANS-EUROPE EXPRESS

A decade after World War II, the rail network in Europe had been repaired and large sections electrified, so with the economy recovering, fast, modern, comfortable, international daytime services were required. The "Trans-Europe Express" (TEE) concept was born and initially operated across France, Holland, Germany, Italy and Switzerland, with Belgium soon joining. Services commenced in 1957, paving the way for today's dedicated international European high-speed routes and TGVs. TEE services rapidly expanded across Europe, running on conventional lines at speeds up to 200 kph (125 mph) and offering a stylish and efficient way to travel.

The French TGV network continues to expand rapidly and it appears likely that this expansion will continue for many years to come. Legal formalities for the proposed high-speed line between Montpellier and Perpignan will start by 2015, and construction of the line could start in 2020. Another LGV will link Tours to Bordeaux on the LGV Sud Europe Atlantique. The extension is estimated to cost around €7·8 billion but will reduce the Paris to Bordeaux journey by 50 minutes. To meet this demand, Alstom continues to develop TGV technology and is building 360 kph (225 mph) TGVs (introduced in Italy in 2011). These, plus those produced by the firm for use in Korea and America, will add many more TGV passengers to the 120 million currently carried every year across Europe.

BELOW AND BOTTOM When the record breaking French TGV services were introduced, the accompanying publicity was produced announcing that you could now travel long distances at high speed and in comfort.
These took the form of a certified 260 kph certificate signed by the Commercial Director. The leaflet also announced that you could now reserve seats on these new trains from running from 27 September 1981 at various stations. This is not dissimilar to the style of the Orient Express poster.

RIGHT A fold out TGV timetable and route map showing stations served and travel times was also issued to publicise the growing TGV network which was opened in stages. This also explained how to use the new trains and what facilities were provided on them.

TGV FACTFILE

World rail-speed records achieved

26 February 1981	380 kph (237.5 mph)
18 May 1990	515 kph (322 mph)
3 April 2007	575 kph (359 mph)

World's longest non-stop run

26 May 2001   1,067km (667 miles)
averaging 306 kph (191.5 mph) between Calais
and Marseilles in 209 minutes

Average annual kilometres run by each TGV
450,000 (281,250 miles)

Worlds fastest start-to-stop station-to-station journey

27 Sept 2008 TGV Gare Lorraine and
TGV Gare Champagne
167.6 km (104.05 miles) average speed 277.97 kmph
(172.73 mph) in 36 mins 10 seconds

Seating capacity

Duplex (double decker) 1,100 seats
Non Duplex 770 seats
28 November 2003 billionth TGV passenger carried
(An estimated two billion passengers had been
carried by the end of 2010)

Braking time

When travelling at full speed, an emergency stop
takes 3.6 kilometres (2¼ miles).

ABOVE The official end of the world-record-breaking run on 3 April 2007 when a specially adapted TGV train No. 4402 reached 574.8 kph (359 mph). The run was made on the LGV just before it opened for public service.

RIGHT London St Pancras was reopened in November 2007 by Her Majesty the Queen and other dignitaries as an international station. This marked the completion of the UK's first high-speed rail link into St Pancras, a station nearly closed in the 1960s.

THE SHINKANSEN

HIGH-SPEED RAIL IN JAPAN

The Japanese "bullet" train and the Shinkansen railway network on which it runs have combined to achieve worldwide recognition for quality, punctuality and reliability. These were the first high-speed services in the world when launched in 1964 — but how and why did they achieve such excellence?

In the late 1950s Japan's pre-Shinkansen network had become full to capacity, especially on the Tokyo to Osaka route, and a radical solution was essential if Japan's transport system was to keep going and avoid being dominated by airlines. The choice made was to build a brand-new railway, routed via a much straighter alignment and using a new gauge. The Shinkansen ("new railway") network is built to the "Stephenson gauge" — 1.43 metres (4 feet 8½ inches) — but with a wider loading gauge (the space that has to be kept clear around the railway line) than in other countries. Japan's traditional railways, in contrast, are mostly of 1.07 metres (3 feet 6 inches) gauge.

By the early 1960s, Japanese National Railways had already reached 160 kph (100 mph) on some pre-Shinkansen main lines, notably with "Kodama" express trains (confusingly, the name now refers to the slowest of several types of "bullet" train) on the Tokyo to Osaka run. When the Shinkansen's "bullet" trains — so dubbed, in the West but not in Japan, for their distinctive bullet-shaped noses, although these no longer feature on later models — were introduced, they had a top speed of 210 kph (130 mph). Even this was impressive for the time, and they were soon upgraded to 240 kph (150 mph), creating a world record. This was equalled when French TGV operations between Paris and Lyons began, and today — as with many TGVs worldwide — Shinkansen services have a top speed of 300 kph (186 mph).

In terms of quality, as well as speed, the Shinkansens had a huge advantage in being new and unconstrained by entrenched layouts or rules. Starting afresh allowed a customized design to deliver a service that could manage the anticipated traffic. Timetables could also be created free from historical restraints, so that the track layout and the desired timetable were compatible. Station platforms have been mainly sited on loops off the main line, allowing faster trains to overtake slower or stopping trains, maximizing use of the network. The UK's equivalent line is the Channel Tunnel Rail Link between the Kent coast and St Pancras. Here, similarly, 300 kph (186 mph) Eurostars are scheduled to operate in front of 225 kph (140 mph) "Javelin" trains, the UK's version of the Japanese "bullets".

On busy Shinkansen lines, signals can be closely spaced to allow track occupation to be maximized, and as soon as one section is vacated, another train can follow. Older railways sometimes had up to 32 kilometres (20 miles) between signals – this reduced the number of trains that could run due to the time it took to pass every signal, but with frequent signals an intensive service can be operated. Delays can also be caused by trains changing lines, but when a new railway is built hold-ups can be minimized by using grade-separated or split-level tracks, meaning a train does not have to wait for another train to cross in front of it.

Train design also facilitates punctuality, offering passengers fast access and egress by providing doors wide enough for two passengers to get on or off side-by-side. Easily accessible luggage spaces are provided to avoid causing delays at stations.

SHINKANSEN STAFF

The Japanese Shinkansen network prides itself on being spotlessly presented, and the staff are meticulous in operating these successful, world-famous, high-speed services. This level of care, combined with high-quality and informative bilingual signage, makes it easy for passengers to understand how the system works – for example, where to stand or how to exit from the platform, thus avoiding congestion. This is essential for maintaining punctuality when thousands of passengers travel on trains running every three minutes.

All staff, irrespective of working at a station or on a train, work closely as a team and are acutely aware of what is going on around them at all times. When drivers pass a signal, they have to say the signal colour out loud, even though they are alone in the driving cab. Other staff must ensure nothing they do might cause a delay to the operation.

OPPOSITE A ceremony at Tokyo station marked the launch of the world-famous Shinkansen services in 1964. The inaugural Tokaido Shinkansen line carried passengers to Osaka in four hours.

BELOW A modern-generation "bullet" train rushing through the city above the streets of Tokyo, complementing the Yurakucho Mullion building.

Another key to its success is that the Shinkansen combines seamlessly with other transport modes. For example, Tokyo's busy metro system links into the Shinkansen network at stations such as Ueno on the Tohoku line in the west of the city. It is not just the physical connection that is important – ticketing and reservation systems have their part to play, making it easy for passengers to organize travel well in advance, as well as at the last minute: at metro booking offices like Ueno, passengers can obtain reservations – quickly processed and free of charge – for the next mainline service from the station.

Passengers enter through the wide Shinkansen passenger gate, which has one barrier labelled "paper tickets" (English signs supplement Japanese everywhere). The gate inspector waves customers through, giving a slight nod of respect as they pass. Escalators descend to island platforms 19 and 20 where all westbound and northbound Shinkansen trains stop, and opposite is a similar arrangement for trains to Tokyo Central. Above and across the platforms are wide electronic signs listing

ABOVE The "bullet" trains were carefully designed for maximum comfort and operational efficiency. This is the inside of an early "bullet" train, showing how organized the accommodation was, which speeded up passenger boarding and alighting.

RIGHT A Central Japan Railway Company "bullet" train passing through Odawara station in 2010. The gradient and curvature of the high-speed track is clear to see, as is the length of the train.

the next six trains to call: the train numbers, times and destinations are clearly displayed, as are the different words used to describe the train types. Using the Joetsu line towards Niigata as another example, "Max Toki" (double-decker fast) and "Tanigawa" (stopping) trains are listed. Platform surfaces are marked, showing where each numbered door will stop, with lines indicating where passengers should queue. Above each door position is a small illuminated sign to indicate which door number on the next train will stop there.

Within 15 minutes, six different designs of high-speed "bullet" train – single and double-decker, some with a higher body profile, and of varying lengths between six and 16 cars – go past. The Japanese high-speed trains, despite being made by different manufacturers who have introduced new designs over the years, can all work perfectly when coupled together. For example, a train made up from a combination of a six-car "Type E3" (bound for Akita) and a ten-car "Type E2" (for Hachinohe) stops precisely next to the queue for Door 7, as indicated on the platform. The door

opens into its pocket in the carriage bodyside, giving easy, unhindered access to the seats, which are arranged mainly in airline style. After departure, the train speeds from the urban tunnel, rising on viaducts over the city. A trolley girl appears, offering drinks and snacks, and bows to the passengers as she leaves the carriage.

The Tokaido (between Tokyo and Osaka) was the first Shinkansen line to be constructed. It was begun in 1959 and took five years to complete. Japan's topography is such that long stretches of flat land are rare, so the new railway had to use lengthy tunnels and viaducts to maintain its high-speed course. These included the 8 kilometre (5 mile) Tanna tunnel, the nearly-as-long tunnel at Otoyamaha, and the Fujigawa viaduct at 1,207 metres (3,960 feet). The line opened in 1964, using "bullet" trains distinguished by their bullet-like noses and high driving cabs. They used electric motors placed along the train to give better acceleration from a stop position, thus minimizing journey times.

The Shinkansen spread across Japan, and in 1972 the Tokaido line extended southwest to Hiroshima, Fukuoka

and Hakari. In the north and west, further high-speed lines tunnelled through the mountains, reaching Niigata on the west coast, and Shin-Aomori in the north of Honshu island in 1982. The world's longest railway tunnel links the islands of Honshu and Hokkaido in the north. It is currently used by a conventional railway, but this will eventually be replaced by a Shinkansen line. On the southern island of Kyushu, another Shinkansen opened in 2004. It ran from the south coast and was extended in 2011, connecting with the Sanyo Shinkansen at Hakari.

Shinkansens have revolutionized travel in Japan, with airlines now only carrying a small proportion of domestic travellers. So much traffic runs on the Tokaido line that, among several planned extensions, another railway is being promoted to link Tokyo and Osaka by a more inland route. Although expensive to build, it would open up more towns to the system and provide extra, vitally needed, through capacity. The ongoing success of Japan's Shinkansen has inspired the rest of the world to embrace high-speed rail as the civilized way for future travel.

ABOVE Near the foot of Mount Fuji, a Central Japan Railway Company "bullet" train passes a field of Chinese milk vetch flowers in a colourful scene photographed in 2010.

OPPOSITE, BELOW Shinkansen signalling is controlled from modern signalling centres such as this one in Tokyo. They have a network map displayed on a 21.3 metre (70 foot) electronic panel on the wall showing the location of every train.

RIGHT Japan's iconic Mount Fuji, with a Japanese Central Railways N700 "bullet" train in the foreground – a world-famous railway photographic location for obvious reasons.

THE FUTURE

The railways are more than 200 years old — the blink of an eye in the world's history, but very few inventions have brought so much change. Following 150 years of expansion and consolidation, they fell into steep decline and their very existence was threatened in many countries. However they are now fighting back.

Today's railways are beating road and air competition in a new golden era of expansion across the world. They have a secure future which is likely to see more electric services as oil becomes more expensive and supplies are potentially limited. New railways are under construction in many countries that are normally strangers to this mode of transport, and they are being built for three prime purposes.

Mass transit systems are being created as the only effective transport solution in the expanding major conurbations around the world where road traffic congestion and pollution are a problem.

High-speed rail links will take over from flying on journeys up to about 1,600 kilometres (1,000 miles), but conversely they will probably spell the end of most sleeper services. Longer tunnels and bridges will allow networks to expand across or under mountains and water in a way that the Victorian pioneers could only dream about. The potential speeds on the UK's "High Speed 2" may make it possible to travel between London and Edinburgh in just over two hours – unimaginable in the steam age.

The third area of expansion is heavier and faster freight trains. The Trans-Siberian Railway has been upgraded,

giving quicker freight transit times across Asia. New routes, such as the proposed Trans-Panama Railway linking the Pacific and Atlantic Oceans, will transfer traffic from ships to trains.

There is a fundamental debate over the form of future trains. Conventional high-speed trains can run up to 400 kph (250 mph). But other forms of propulsion are being tried, such as "magnetic levitated" (maglev) trains, to increase speeds even more. Maglev trains are not new. Instead of travelling on rails, they are guided by magnets, so that they hover over a tiny gap above and around a

guide rail and are propelled by magnetic forces. The lack of rail contact means there is no wear on wheels and rails, and this is one reason why they can operate at very high speeds of up to 580 kph (362 mph) – as they have done in tests.

The world's first commercial maglev system was used between Birmingham Airport and Birmingham International railway station in 1984. It was completely automatic and driverless, running for 550 metres (1,800 feet) just over 1.25 centimetres (½ inch) above an elevated concrete section, but was closed in 1995. Japan and Germany have been the main ongoing developers of maglev, while in China today, the Shanghai Maglev uses a German-built "Transrapid" system to take passengers between the metro and the airport at speeds of up to 430 kph (268 mph), and there are intermittent plans to extend the system over much longer distances across the country. However, maglev is far more expensive than a conventional high-speed railway, so how many lines actually come into being, in China or worldwide, remains to be seen.

Whichever rail system(s) are used, new signalling systems will enable more trains to operate on existing track. Over the next 30 years, traditional lineside signals will disappear, being replaced by driving-cab signal displays that control the train's progress. These will depend on how fast the train is travelling, the maximum permissible speed of the track it is on and the position of the nearest train or obstacle in front of it. The driver monitors the equipment and drives as instructed or "authorized" (as it is officially known). If the driver ignores the computer, control of the train will be removed from him until the situation is back to an acceptable standard. This "European Rail Traffic Management System" is being introduced on all railways.

DRIVERLESS TRAINS

Driverless trains were introduced when London Underground's Victoria Line opened in 1967. The trains were the first to run automatically according to signals sent from lineside equipment to the trains' computers. The only human activity required was control of the doors, but since it was felt that the public would not feel safe without a driver, one continued to remain on board.

Perceptions had changed enough by 1984 for the maglev from Birmingham Airport to be driverless, completely automated and used unquestioningly by passengers. The Docklands Light Railway (DLR) in London (below), opened by Queen Elizabeth II in 1987, became the first major driverless rail-based transport system in Britain over any real distance. Today, it carries 70 million passengers a year over a 34 kilometre (21 mile) network serving 40 stations, which just goes to show that passengers are not concerned by the absence of a driver.

OPPOSITE Maglev trains have the kudos of speed and style but cost limits their use. This "Transrapid" maglev train operates in Lathen, north Germany, where a serious accident killed 23 people in 2006.

RIGHT The latest version of the Japanese "bullet" train, the E6 series for use on the Akita Shinkansen, carries the same aerodynamic design as the test maglev train below left.

OVERLEAF A maglev test track is in use at Tsuru in Japan, and is seen here with a trial train demonstrating the system to the US Transport Secretary in 2010.

INDEX

Page numbers in *italic* type refer to pictures or their captions.

AUTHOR ACKNOWLEDGEMENTS

I would like to thank my wife Vicki for her support, encouragement and help while researching and writing this book. I must also apologise to the rest of my family, Adric, Fiona, Stephen, Stewie (and my mother), who were largely ignored while the project was underway!

The book would also not have been possible without the assistance of Paul Bickerdyke and Colin Boocock. Lastly but by no means least, I would like to thank Gemma and Steve at Carlton for their input, guidance and the opportunity to author this book. It has been a fabulous exercise and my railway knowledge has been hugely expanded. I sincerely hope that readers will enjoy the contents as much as I have in writing them!

CREDITS

The publishers would like to thank the following people for their valuable assitance with the preparation of this book:
Wendy Burford, Science Museum Group Enterprises
Tim Procter and all the staff at the National Railway Museum, York

BIBLIOGRAPHY

The Locomotive and Carriage and Wagon Review, published monthly between 1896 and 1959
The Railway Magazine, published monthly continuously from 1897
Railway Wonders of The World, Clarence Winchester 1936
The Pictorial Encyclopedia of Railways, Hamilton Ellis 1985

THE NATIONAL RAILWAY MUSEUM

The National Railway Museum, York is the largest railway museum in the world. Its permanent displays and collections illustrate over 300 years of British railway history, from the Industrial Revolution to the present day. The NRM archive also includes a fabulous collection of railway advertising posters charting the history of rail. Visit nrm.org.uk to find out more.

PICTURE CREDITS

THE
MUSICALS
— OF —
ANDREW
LLOYD WEBBER

THE
MUSICALS
— OF —
ANDREW
LLOYD WEBBER

KEITH RICHMOND

ACKNOWLEDGEMENTS:

I want to thank my publisher, Philip Dodd, for having the idea in the first place and for offering me the project; Carolyn Price, my editor, for her unflagging enthusiasm and attention to detail; and Julia Hanson, my picture researcher, for finding photos we didn't even know existed.

I'd like to thank my mum and dad for putting up with me singing *Joseph and the Amazing Technicolor Dreamcoat* over and over again at the top of my unbroken adolescent voice all the way back from a holiday in Cornwall; and most of all, my wife, Lucy Knox, for all her help and love and support. With a change of gender, you're the 'Last Man In My Life' (from *Song & Dance*). You know what I mean...

First published in Great Britain in 1995
by Virgin Publishing Limited
332 Ladbroke Grove
London W10 5AH

Text © 1995 Keith Richmond

A catalogue record for this book is available
from the British Library

ISBN: 1 85227 557 X

Printed and bound in Great Britain by
Butler & Tanner Ltd

Designed by Peter Crump
For Virgin Publishing: Philip Dodd, Carolyn Price

CONTENTS

PREFACE

Andrew Lloyd Webber is the musical genius with the Midas touch who has, for more than twenty-five years, been the dominant force in musical theatre on both sides of the Atlantic, and indeed around the world.

The story of his success began not in one of the prestigious West End or Broadway theatres but in the assembly hall of a small West London prep school in 1968. The couple of hundred parents who had gathered there for an end-of-term concert were witnessing the birth of a modern musical phenomenon. The engaging pop cantata which their sons were singing - a piece called *Joseph and the Amazing Technicolor Dreamcoat* - had been composed by Andrew Lloyd Webber, still not twenty years old.

Twenty-four years later, the same composer became Sir Andrew when he was knighted by the Queen for services to the arts in June 1992. And in February the following year he was given the ultimate showbiz accolade of a Star on the Hollywood Walk of Fame.

His string of hit musicals are all household names. With Tim Rice providing the lyrics, Lloyd Webber followed up *Joseph* with *Jesus Christ Superstar*, the definitive rock opera, and *Evita*, the story of another charismatic star.

After he and Rice ended their creative partnership, Lloyd Webber went on to create the feline fantasy of *Cats*, the thundering steam-train energy of *Starlight Express*, the Gothic melodrama of *Phantom of the Opera* and the emotional maturity of *Aspects of Love*. His latest musical - the glitzy, glamorous *Sunset Boulevard* - has been another smash hit worldwide.

As well as musicals (and he's only had one flop - *Jeeves*), Lloyd Webber has written two film scores, an Olympic anthem, a moving setting of the Latin Requiem Mass and the pumped-up *Variations* performed by his cellist brother Julian. Songs from the shows have become international standards, including 'Don't Cry For Me Argentina', 'Memory' and 'The Music Of The Night'.

Now the most successful composer in the history of musical theatre, Andrew Lloyd Webber has established his place alongside the other greats: Irving Berlin, George Gershwin, Jerome Kern, Frederick Loewe, Richard Rodgers and Stephen Sondheim.

From the first shows staged in a toy theatre at his parent's home to fame writ large in neon lights, this is the story of one man and his life of music...

EARLY DAYS

When Andrew Lloyd Webber was born in London on 22nd March 1948, music was already in his blood. 'As a boy I was always surrounded by music.'

His father, William Southcombe Lloyd Webber, was professor of theory and composition at the Royal College of Music and his mother, Jean Hermione Johnstone, was a respected and much loved music teacher. He grew up in a home in South Kensington filled with the sounds of music and, from an early age, showed an extraordinary natural talent for a tune.

His parents never forced him to sit at a piano and play; they just encouraged him when he did. But Andrew never found practising his scales or listening to the great composers a chore; it was a pleasure, a joy, and his parents could see that he had a gift not so much for playing as for composing his own songs.

His father, the son of a plumber, was known as plain Bill Webber until he went to study at the Royal College of Music. There was another organ student there called W. Webber, so to distinguish himself he took his third Christian name and began to use it as a second, though never hyphenated, surname. He grew to like it so much he baptized both his boys, Andrew and Julian, Lloyd Webber.

Music ran deep in the family. Andrew's grandfather, William Charles Henry Webber, sang with the George Mitchell Choir and the Black & White Minstrels; while Bill, a child prodigy who began giving organ concerts at the age of ten, was organist and choirmaster at the High Anglican church of

ABOVE, the young
Andrew, second from
left, demonstrated early
artistic skills, but music
was always his first love.
Dedicated followers
of fashion (PREVIOUS
PAGES) - Tim Rice and
Andrew Lloyd Webber
escort Jenny Burbidge
and Ross Hannaman
(singer on their first
released record) to
Ascot in 1967.

All Saints, Margaret Street in Marylebone, and
then at Central Hall, Westminster, a leading
Methodist church. He left the Royal College
of Music to become director of the London
College of Music in 1974. It was a long and
distinguished musical career and he was made
a CBE in 1980.

But in some ways it had been a frustrating
career because what William Lloyd Webber
would most liked to have been was a
composer, an English composer in the tradition
of Edward Elgar, Frederick Delius, Ralph
Vaughan Williams, Gustav Holst, Benjamin
Britten, William Walton and Arnold Bax. 'In
the end,' he admitted in 1980, 'it became
basically a matter of finance. It's very difficult
to make a living out of composition unless you
succeed in the kind of work that Andrew does.'

It was through their shared love of music
that William Lloyd Webber met his wife Jean in

1939; she was a singer and violinist and a
student at the Royal College of Music. They
courted for three years before they married at
All Saints on 3rd October 1942. He was 28,
she was 20. Six years later, they had the first
of their two sons.

Andrew was a difficult child. As a baby
he screamed and yelled so loudly that their
neighbours in Harrington Court near South
Kensington underground station complained.
The only thing that would calm him was music.
Not the Mozart, Puccini or Rachmaninov his
father so admired but the rumbas of bandleader
Edmundo Ros. 'Andrew was a terror,' admitted
William. 'Edmundo Ros was a great favourite
of his and if he couldn't get to sleep we'd play
him some Edmundo Ros records. He'd jump
around to the tunes for a while and then fall
asleep.' Andrew was a hyperactive child, so
much so that his father nicknamed him Bumper

because he was always rushing around and bumping into things.

Just after his third birthday Andrew was given a violin and, soon after, a French horn. However, even at an early age it was evident that he lacked the manual dexterity that marked out his brother Julian, born on 14th April 1951, as a future virtuoso. But it was clear that he had talent and that he enjoyed playing his own music more than the music of others. In formal piano lessons he often surprised his teachers by preferring to play pieces he had written and learned himself rather than the standard practice pieces .

'I was forced to play the violin when I was about three,' said Andrew. 'My mother thought I ought to play the violin and I was given a tiny, baby-sized violin and appeared with it on the cover of *Nursery World*. But I was not to be a young Yehudi. I learned to play the piano as a child but was never any good at it and I learned the French horn as well but was no better than average. I remember an attempt going on to try and make Julian play the trumpet which was very unpleasant but, strangely enough, I do not remember his early attempts at the cello.'

The house, with four pianos, William Lloyd Webber's electronic organ and various assorted record players and radios, was always alive with the sound of music. As well as mum and dad and two children all playing instruments, there were three cats - Perseus, Dmitri (named after the composer Shostakovich) and Sergei (after Prokofiev) - and assorted bohemian musician friends dropping in. 'It was,' admitted Andrew, 'often like bedlam.'

'Life at Harrington Court - the large, run-down, late Victorian, redbrick block of flats just by the South Kensington tube - was chiefly memorable for the astonishing, ear-blowing volume of musical decibels which seemed to burst forth from every room most of the day and night,' wrote Julian in his memoir, *Travels with My Cello*. 'My father's electric organ, mother's piano, grandmother's deafening (she was deaf) television, elder brother's astounding piano and French horn and my own scrapings on the cello and blowings on the trumpet by themselves would have made the cannon and mortar effects of the 1812 Overture seem a bit like the aural equivalent of a wet Sunday morning on Hackney marshes.'

There was never any pressure on Andrew and Julian to do anything they didn't want to do. I was always available if they wanted an opinion but they were both rather determined people and I wouldn't say I influenced them greatly.

WILLIAM LLOYD WEBBER

But Andrew's first passion was architecture, not music 'When I was seven I wanted to be the Chief Inspector of Ancient Monuments. When I was ten I wanted to write historical musicals. And then I progressed to just wanting to write musicals. But I used to read *The Buildings of England* in bed at night.'

It was his mother's vivacious sister Aunt Vi, a successful actress, who turned the young Andrew on to theatre and, especially, musical theatre. She took him to see all the hit musicals

BELOW, with mother, Jean and brother Julian at the opening of Sunset Boulevard in 1993.

in town, starting with *My Fair Lady*, and to films like *Gigi* and *South Pacific*. The young Andrew was enthralled and, with his aunt's encouragement, he built, at the age of eleven, a toy theatre. It was a proper, fully functional little theatre, built of bricks, with an authentic proscenium arch, wings, a fly tower and a revolving stage made from a turntable rescued from an old record player. They spent many happy hours playing with their theatre, giving performances for family and friends, with Julian moving their toy soldiers around the stage while his brother pounded out popular show tunes on their old piano.

Andrew had written his first original composition at the age of seven and been busy writing ever since. He had his first piece of music published in 1957, at the age of nine, when the magazine *Music Teacher* ran excerpts from The Toy Theatre, a suite of six short pieces. 'I have been rather amused at the efforts of my own boy, Andrew, to find his own harmonies for the tunes he composes on his playroom piano,' wrote his father in a note. 'He makes up various incidental music for

plays which he produces in his playroom theatre: it is all quite spontaneous, and this branch of music making is deliberately self taught at the moment. In the six pieces he has composed, the tunes and harmonies are all his own; all I have done is to do the slight editing which is obviously necessary to make them acceptable to players.'

Andrew began his education at Wetherby, an exclusive private elementary school near their home in South Kensington, where his mother taught music. In 1956 he went to Westminster Under School, for boys aged eight to thirteen, and in 1961 to Westminster, one of the most prestigious English public schools. His school reports were mixed. He was, his teachers thought, an able student who did not always appear to apply himself. He excelled at history and music, which he loved, but only just got by in other subjects. He hated games, on which the old fee-paying schools place great emphasis, but he was happy there. 'It has the most relaxed atmosphere of any school I know,' he said. Andrew started buying records by Bobby Vee, Bill Haley and the Comets, Elvis Presley and The Everly Brothers. And he liked to slope off round the concert halls of London with Julian and the pianist John Lill, who Jean had taken under her wing. 'I was very lucky, being at Westminster. I mean, they were quite keen that one didn't have to do all this sport kind of thing. Even if in theory you were supposed to do it, they turned a blind eye if they felt one was doing something constructive. So, with a friend, I used to walk around the streets a lot, armed with our books, looking at great churches and buildings. If I hadn't succeeded in music I'd have been involved somehow with the history of architecture.'

He made his stage début at the age of fourteen at Christmas 1962 with the school pantomime *Cinderella up the Beanstalk and Most Everywhere Else!* Andrew wrote the music with words by an older boy, Robin St Clare Barrow. It was such a success they teamed up again the next year for *Utter Chaos or No Jeans for Venus*, a spoof of Greek mythology also known as *Socrates Swings*. In June 1964 he wrote his third and final show at Westminster called *Play the Fool*. A programme note told the world: 'Ever since Andrew Lloyd Webber came to the school, it was obvious that here was someone

BELOW, Lloyd Webber went up to Magdalen College, Oxford to read history, but left after only one term to study at the Royal College of Music.

*The first two records I ever
heard were The Nutcracker
Suite and Elvis Presley's
'Jailhouse Rock', which is
a pretty fair illustration of
what influenced me.*

ANDREW LLOYD WEBBER

with no ordinary genius for music and the
theatre. Not only is he making quite a stir as a
composer and writer, but as an entertainer in
his own right. "I expect I'll give up writing pop
soon. Then I'll devote myself to composing for
the musical theatre."'

Andrew was already making his way in the
world outside Westminster. At the age of
fourteen he signed a short-lived contract with
the Noel Gay theatrical agency. He had sent
them an idea and some songs for a musical,
with lyrics by Aunt Vi's actress friend Joan
Colmore, and they were impressed. Andrew
also sent a demo tape to Decca Records; they
passed it on to the record producer Charles
Blackwell, a client of the publisher Desmond
Elliott, who, liking what he heard, decided to
take a chance and sign up the young composer.
In 1963 Lloyd Webber wrote and recorded the
song 'Make Believe Love' with Blackwell
although it was never released.

Andrew did not shine academically at
school, but he did well enough for Westminster
to put him forward to take the entrance exam
for Oxford University and in December 1964,
largely on the strength of a brilliant paper on
Victorian architecture, he won an open
exhibition to read history at Magdalen College.
Wetherby, Westminster, Oxford. His parents
were rather pleased. The money they had spent
on their son's education had clearly paid off.
But before he went up to the ancient university
a letter, dated 21st April 1965, dropped on his
doormat from an ambitious young songwriter.
'Dear Andrew,' he read, 'I've been told you're
looking for a "with it" writer of lyrics for your
songs, and as I've been writing pop songs for
a while and particularly enjoy writing the lyrics
I wondered if you consider it worth your while
meeting me.'

Tim Rice was a tall (6ft 4in. in his socks),
beguilingly handsome blond who, after public
school, a brief course at the Sorbonne and an
even briefer stint as a petrol pump attendant on
a garage forecourt in Hertfordshire, wanted to
be a pop singer 'but subtle hints were dropped
that I wouldn't make it' so he'd turned his hand
to writing songs. He'd put pen to paper at the
suggestion of Desmond Elliott, the publisher
much impressed by the maturity of the music
of seventeen-year-old Andrew Lloyd Webber,
who had, quite by coincidence, been asked by
Mrs Rice to help her son fulfil his ambition to
have a hit song.

Andrew was intrigued. He rang Tim and a
couple of days later the aspiring lyricist called
round to see the aspiring composer at
Harrington Court. They hit it off at once.
Although they were superficially different -
Tim was an affable extrovert with a string of
leggy blonde girlfriends, while Andrew was
serious, introverted and really rather shy - they
were, fundamentally, very similar. They were
both public schoolboys from solid middle-class
families with a sense of that something that is
forever England - the church, the cricket square
and the village pub; eggs and bacon for
breakfast, tweed jackets, green fields and
afternoon tea. They were both passionately
interested in music - they knew their Elgar as
well as their Elvis - and they both had
something the other wanted. Andrew was after
a lyricist and Tim - who loved the Romantic
poets, especially Byron and Shelley, and was
fascinated by Rupert Brooke - had a way with
words; while Tim was looking for someone
with an ear for a good tune. They had, they
found, an awful lot in common and clicked
straight away. Andrew warmed to Tim's easy,
sophisticated manner; Tim admired Andrew's
exceptional musical ability. They spent a lot of
time together over the summer, walking and
talking and discussing ideas, although they
didn't actually get round to writing anything
before Andrew went up to Oxford in October.

It didn't take him long to realize he had
made a mistake. He didn't want to study
history. He didn't even want to study music
anymore. He didn't want to write essays - he
wanted to write music. With Tim. Back in
London. At Christmas, after just one term, he
told his parents he was leaving to give it a go.
Most parents would have been furious at the

prospect of one of their children dropping out of one of the world's most prestigious academic institutions, especially after investing a not inconsiderable sum on his private education, but William and Jean were both fully supportive. If that's what you want to do, they said, go ahead and do it.

'Parents have an impossible job, anyway, and like most easy-going parents they probably felt the best thing they could do was to let me get on with it. In fact there came the stage when, against the odds, I got into Oxford and I stuck it out for a term. I then said I wanted to leave because I realised I was wasting my time there in musical terms. I said to my father, "Look, I think really the best thing for me would be to get into the Royal College of Music." And he said, "Well, knowing the sort of music you want to write, it would be better not to be formally trained at all. Pick it up in your own way and do it as a kind of inspired amateur." Whenever he moans at me - and

> *No one, especially within the Beatles' generation, had attempted to do what Tim and I wanted to do, which was to create a different sort of English stage musical, instead of apeing Broadway badly.*
>
> ANDREW LLOYD WEBBER

it's often - he says, "Well, the thing to do is not to let the academic interest in music knock out the basic thing of writing what you feel." He contends that a lot of atonal music is totally academic and only pleases a very few people, and he's right. I studied composition, but you can't teach people to compose; I learned the mechanics of it. All you can do is to say to yourself that other people did it this way. You can't teach people to do what Beethoven did.'

As a sop to his parents, he spent a year studying part-time at the Royal College of Music. 'I didn't complete any course because all I really wanted to know were things like the

techniques of orchestration and there isn't really a great deal you can teach a composer formally. I suppose I was really the odd one out in the family. I'd always been fascinated by pop and really wanted to work in that medium.'

Andrew was pouring all his enormous energy and enthusiasm into working with his new partner who, to make things easier, had moved into Harrington Court. Timothy Miles Bindon Rice was three years older than Andrew. He was born in 1944 in Amersham, Buckinghamshire and enjoyed as impeccably a conventional an upbringing as Andrew. Tim was educated at Lancing, where he was good at games and passed exams without over-exerting himself. 'There's nothing to O levels if you can write English at high speed.' But he ducked out of university, instead spending six months at the Sorbonne in Paris before becoming an articled clerk at the solicitors Pettit & Westlake. 'I worked in law only because it was respectable,' he said. 'I really wanted to be a pop star. But when I did sell my first song I decided to forget about singing and concentrate on writing.'

American rock'n'roll - especially the music of Elvis Presley, Buddy Holly, Chuck Berry and Jerry Lee Lewis - and early 60s British pop - the Beatles, the Rolling Stones, the Kinks and the Who - had been a revelation. He didn't want to be a lawyer. He wanted to be a pop star. And as a start, while still at Pettit & Westlake, he began writing and selling songs. One, called 'That's My Story', was released as a single by the pop group Night Shift. It wasn't a hit. 'Though I've no doubt I might have been perfectly happy as a solicitor', he moved to EMI in May 1966 and worked for the bandleader and record producer Norrie Paramor.

Lloyd Webber and Rice wanted to write a musical and Desmond Elliott suggested as a subject the life of Dr Thomas Barnardo, the Victorian social reformer who set up the children's homes which still carry his name. The book - the spoken dialogue and the story-line - was by another of Elliott's clients, Leslie Thomas, who wrote *The Virgin Soldiers*.

With its nineteenth century orphans, street urchins, thieves and rogues, *The Likes of Us* owed a lot to Lionel Bart's 1960 hit *Oliver!* At first they planned a low-key production in Oxford, a hothouse of acting talent and student theatre, but Elliott had grander ideas. The West End was

his dream and he dangled the bait of a lucrative run under the noses of his two protégés. 'Andrew has written some very colourful tunes,' he announced in the summer of 1966. 'I've every confidence we can get this on in the autumn.' He was wrong. Elliott was a big fish in books, but a minnow in the world of musical theatre. No one was ready to risk investing in a big-budget production of a new musical by a couple of unknowns. And besides, *The Likes of Us* wasn't really very good. It had a decent dramatic structure and a couple of good ideas, but the music was unsophisticated and the lyrics too naïve. But they had managed to write a musical together. The next one, they knew, would be better. And they had learned that in musical theatre, as in most other walks of life, you have to start at the bottom. It would have been better, they realized, to have a small-scale student production in Oxford than to be seduced into believing they could walk straight into the West End and end up with no production at all.

After the disappointment of *The Likes of Us*, they decided to have a crack at the Top Twenty while they cast around for a subject for another musical show. On 23rd June 1967 Ross

Hannaman, a pretty blonde singer with a sexy, smoky voice, released the first joint Tim Rice/Andrew Lloyd Webber composition to make it to the market: 'Down Thru Summer' backed on the B side with 'I'll Give All My Love To Southend'. It didn't make a dent on the charts but on 27th October EMI released her second single, another Rice/Lloyd Webber song called '1969', coupled with 'Probably On Thursday'. This garnered a good deal of radio play, but again failed to chart. But they weren't easily put off. And Rice had a theory. He'd examined what did hit the Top Ten and seen a long list of records which featured an American city or state in the title. That, he reasoned, was the way to the top. So they sat down and wrote a love song called 'Kansas Morning'. The trouble was that Ross Hannaman had married and retired from showbusiness to bring up a family and run a dress shop in Notting Hill, so there was no one willing to record the song.

They weren't sure what to do. Rice wanted to write more pop songs, Lloyd Webber wanted to write another musical. They had tried both, without success. Then they got a call out of the blue from Alan Doggett.

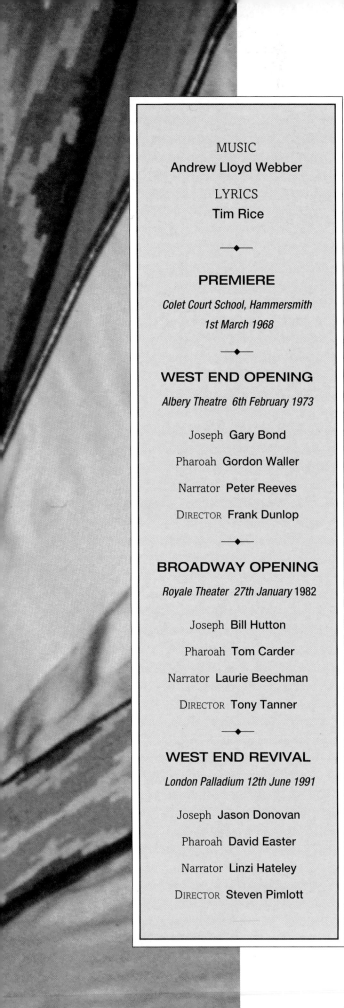

MUSIC
Andrew Lloyd Webber

LYRICS
Tim Rice

◆

PREMIERE

Colet Court School, Hammersmith

1st March 1968

◆

WEST END OPENING

Albery Theatre 6th February 1973

Joseph **Gary Bond**

Pharoah **Gordon Waller**

Narrator **Peter Reeves**

Director **Frank Dunlop**

◆

BROADWAY OPENING

Royale Theater 27th January 1982

Joseph **Bill Hutton**

Pharoah **Tom Carder**

Narrator **Laurie Beechman**

Director **Tony Tanner**

◆

WEST END REVIVAL

London Palladium 12th June 1991

Joseph **Jason Donovan**

Pharoah **David Easter**

Narrator **Linzi Hateley**

Director **Steven Pimlott**

JOSEPH
AND THE AMAZING
TECHNICOLOR DREAMCOAT

───────────◆───────────

Alan Doggett was head of music at Colet

Court, a small preparatory school in west

London for the public school St Paul's. He

knew the Lloyd Webbers well, had taught

Julian at Westminster, and knew that

Andrew was a promising young composer.

Now he wanted something for an end of term concert. Something morally uplifting, he said, would be suitable. Something with a religious theme that the boys could sing under the beady eyes of John Colet, the school's founder and Dean of St Paul's Cathedral, whose portrait looked down sternly on everyone sitting in the old assembly hall.

For inspiration, Lloyd Webber and Rice opened the Old Testament and quickly turned the pages past Adam and Eve, Cain and Abel, Noah, Abraham, Isaac and Esau before stopping at Genesis 37 and the story of Jacob and his eldest son Joseph. Now here was a story they could tell.

It took them two months to turn out a fifteen-minute rock'n'roll version of the biblical story of Joseph and his splendid coat of many colours. With Rice working at EMI and Lloyd Webber studying at the Royal College, they worked in the evenings and at weekends. First they talked about the plot; then Lloyd Webber wrote the melodies; and finally Rice wrote the lyrics to fit. It was the way they would always work and the result was naïve, simple and exuberant; an enchanting blend of pop and pastiche.

ABOVE, Colet Court School was the venue for the first performance of Joseph; the second followed two months later (BELOW). Twenty-five years on, Joseph was still going strong with Darren Day (PREVIOUS PAGES) in the title role.

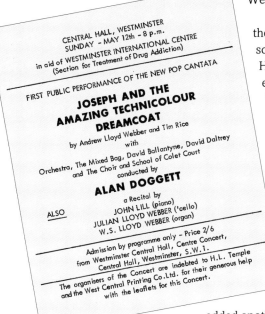

CENTRAL HALL, WESTMINSTER
SUNDAY - MAY 12th - 8 p.m.
in aid of WESTMINSTER INTERNATIONAL CENTRE
(Section for Treatment of Drug Addiction)

FIRST PUBLIC PERFORMANCE OF THE NEW POP CANTATA

**JOSEPH AND THE
AMAZING TECHNICOLOUR
DREAMCOAT**

by Andrew Lloyd Webber and Tim Rice
with
Orchestra, The Mixed Bag, David Ballantyne, David Daltrey
and The Choir and School of Colet Court
conducted by

ALAN DOGGETT

a Recital by
JOHN LILL (piano)
JULIAN LLOYD WEBBER ('cello)
W.S. LLOYD WEBBER (organ)

ALSO

Admission by programme only - Price 2/6
from Westminster Central Hall, Centre Concert,
Central Hall, Westminster, S.W.1.
The organisers of the Concert are indebted to H.L. Temple
and the West Central Printing Co.Ltd. for their generous help
with the leaflets for this Concert.

At the end of the first performance on 1st March 1968 in Colet Court School on the Hammersmith Road, the audience of several hundred parents applauded politely and went home. And that might have been that. Except for the persistence of William Lloyd Webber. He was genuinely impressed and didn't want the work to disappear so he arranged for a second performance - revised, expanded to twenty minutes, and rearranged for a rock group and orchestra - in front of 2,500 people at the Central Hall, Westminster, on 12th May 1968.

One of those in the audience was the jazz critic Derek Jewell, whose son Nicholas was in the chorus. He was so impressed he wrote an effusive review in *The Sunday Times*: 'This new pop oratorio is attractive indeed. On this evidence the pop idiom - beat rhythms and Bacharachian melodies - is capable of being used in extended form. It bristles with wonderfully singable tunes. It entertains. It communicates instantly, as all good pop should. And it is a considerable piece of barrier-breaking by its creators, two men in their early twenties.'

Over the summer they added another ten minutes, bringing in songs such as the vaudeville two-step 'Potiphar' for the first time. Then Norrie Paramor, who had taken Tim Rice with him when he left EMI to form his own company, recorded this 'pop cantata' (as he called it) for Decca, with William Lloyd Webber on organ; Rice as Pharoah; The Mixed Bag, a rock group whose singer David Daltrey was a distant cousin of The Who's Roger Daltrey; and the choir from Colet Court.

They gave one more concert performance, this time at St Paul's Cathedral, on 9th November. 'It was an evening when everything went right and the show was a huge success,' said Lloyd Webber. 'But we felt that *Joseph* had gone about as far as it could and we decided to have a go at writing something else.'

It was the success of that something else - *Jesus Christ Superstar* - which led to the continued growth of *Joseph*. The *Joseph* record, which enjoyed only modest sales in Britain, spent three months in the American charts after an advertising campaign which misleadingly implied that this was the follow-up to *Jesus Christ Superstar*.

But, as Lloyd Webber candidly admitted, 'the work received its biggest boost of all' when Frank Dunlop directed the Young Vic Company in an imaginative 40-minute glam rock version which wowed the critics at the Edinburgh Festival in September 1972. It played to packed houses at the Young Vic itself for two weeks in October before moving in November to the Roundhouse, an innovative arts and music venue in Chalk Farm, north London, where the audience sat on three sides of the floor space - there was no stage - and the atmosphere was satisfyingly intimate.

The music - which now included songs like the burlesque country and western carol 'One More Angel In Heaven' - was upbeat and unpretentious and the lyrics refreshingly colloquial. It fairly rattled along, with Peter Reeves as the narrator dismissing whole decades in a single line, without the old-fashioned stop-start structure of the conventional musical. 'We realised,' said Lloyd Webber, 'that it was possible to put together something continuous without that ghastly moment when the violins are lifted and the dialogue starts.'

The production, full of wit and energy, starred Gary Bond as a charismatic Joseph, Gordon Waller as Pharoah and Ian Charleson, who would go on to star in *Chariots of Fire*. As half of Peter And Gordon, Waller had enjoyed Top Ten hits on both sides of the Atlantic in the mid-60s with 'A World Without Love' by Paul McCartney and cover versions of Buddy Holly's 'True Love Ways' and the Teddy Bears' 'To Know You Is To Love You'. Camping it up in a tight white satin suit, he delivered an affectionate, note perfect, pelvis-wiggling parody of Elvis as a rock'n'roll Pharoah in 'Song Of The King', complete with a wonderful 50s bopshowaddywaddy chorus. 'We found we could switch styles crazily throughout the whole thing,' said Lloyd Webber. 'Mixing musical comedy numbers with calypso, country and western and Elvis Presley.'

> *The keys are all inter-related so it doesn't sound disjointed and the main themes occur again and again.*
>
> ANDREW LLOYD WEBBER

The house full signs outside the Roundhouse each night prompted Robert Stigwood to transfer the show to the Albery Theatre in the heart of the West End. Rice and Lloyd Webber again extended the show - bringing in songs like 'Those Canaan Days' and 'Benjamin Calypso' - but in the rush to get it ready for the first night on 6th February 1973 they invited Ray Galton and Alan Simpson, the comic geniuses behind TV sitcoms like *Hancock's Half Hour* and *Steptoe and Son*, to write a prologue telling the story of Jacob from the row with Esau. Isaac's family became porridge-eating Scots and God an absent-minded Lancastrian who arrives with the heavenly host in tow because 'otherwise nobody ever believes it's really me!' 'Jacob's Journey' sat uneasily with the rest of the show and well before the end of its seven-month run at the Albery it was dropped, with Rice and Lloyd Webber filling out the evening by the simple expedient of reprising several songs.

Three years later, on 30th December 1976, *Joseph* opened at the Brooklyn Academy of Music in New York with David James Carroll in the title role and Cleavon Little, who starred in Mel Brooks' spoof Western, *Blazing Saddles*, as the narrator. It didn't last long. The production was greeted with hostility by the critics and indifference at the box office.

LEFT. 'Come and lie with me, love...' - Gary Bond is led astray by Joan Heal at the Albery Theatre in 1973.

What really sustained the show during the 70s and 80s was its extraordinary success in schools and colleges on both sides of the Atlantic. There can hardly be a child, British or American, who didn't have a Go Go Go at *Joseph* during these years.

A two-act, 90-minute production opened off Broadway at the Entermedia Theater in the East Village on 18th November 1981. It transferred uptown, on the back of the phenomenal New York success of *Evita* with Bill Hutton in the title role, Tom Carder as Pharoah and Laurie Beechman as the narrator, to the Royale Theater on Broadway in the following January. Lloyd Webber's initial wariness, because of the way the show had bombed in New York five years before, evaporated when Tony Tanner's new production was hailed by the critics and ran for 747 performances. An unhappy footnote saw Andy Gibb, younger brother of The Bee Gees, fired for 'erratic behaviour' - he missed twelve

performances in a month - after taking over the lead. He was, he said, devastated by the break-up of his well-publicized romance with Victoria Principal. He was also struggling with the demons of drink and drugs which would lead to his early death in 1988. But he blew a golden opportunity to put his career back on track, a chance seized in Britain by P. J. Proby and in America by David Cassidy.

As well as being an end of term favourite for schools and a popular alternative to pantomime for amateur dramatic societies at Christmas, *Joseph* enjoyed enormous popularity with touring productions in the provinces. One, which opened at the New Theatre, Oxford, on 10th March 1974, starred Leonard Whiting (who shot to fame at seventeen as Franco Zeffirelli's Romeo opposite Olivia Hussey's Juliet) and Tim Rice in a black wig, with an outrageous rockabilly quiff and DA, as Pharoah. 'I'm a bit nervous as I'm really a behind-the-scenes man,' said Rice

BELOW, Andy Gibb during his short run as Joseph on Broadway, with Tanya Tucker, Patrick Cassidy and Maureen McGovern.

before the curtain went up on his professional stage début, 'but I think I can remember the words, because I wrote them!' Former Manfred Mann singer Paul Jones played Joseph at the Westminster Theatre at Christmas 1979 and a version featuring 60s pop star Jess Conrad ran for two successful years. But in January 1987 Lloyd Webber slipped quietly into the back of the stalls for one performance and watched the touring production in growing disbelief. He was horrified. 'I didn't believe I was listening to what I wrote,' he said. 'What I saw is light years away from what was written and intended.'

'I'm fascinated by Andrew's remarks,' retorted producer Bill Kenwright. 'Nothing, however, has been changed since the end of the last London run at Sadler's Wells six years ago.'

Lloyd Webber went away and thought long and hard. *Joseph,* like Topsy, had growed and growed. From 15 to 20 to 30 minutes and beyond. It was a staple of school, college and amateur dramatic societies on both sides of the Atlantic and provincial tours were enormously successful. Lloyd Webber summed up the situation: first, the show was perenially popular; second, it had never been a big hit on Broadway or in the West End; and third, he

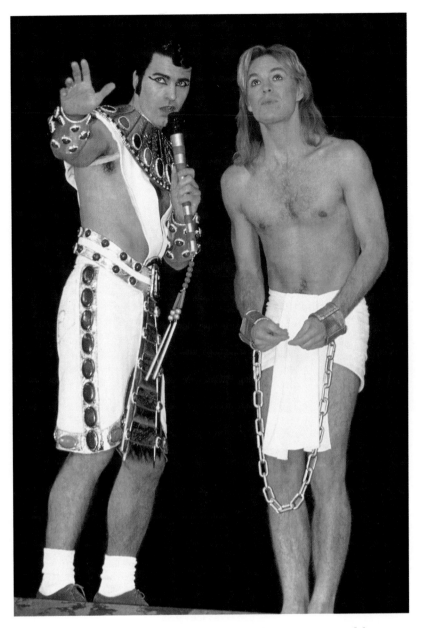

ABOVE, Jason Donovan's skimpy loincloth pleased his legion of fans; his place was taken by children's TV star Phillip Schofield (FAR RIGHT).

You would have to be a complete churl or a sourpuss of the first magnitude not to enjoy this brilliant revival of the first big musical hit for the gifted Rice-Lloyd Webber duo.

MAUREEN PATON, *DAILY EXPRESS*, 13TH JUNE 1991

But Lloyd Webber, who by now had shown as great an aptitude for understanding the bottom line of a balance sheet as he had for writing a great tune, revealed the old showman's instinct for putting on the right show with the right cast at the right time.

It was a brave but brilliant decision to pick Jason Donovan to play the title role in 1991. Brave because Donovan had never starred in a big- budget musical before and his acting experience was limited to the television studio; brilliant because his status as a teenybop idol meant house full signs were assured from the day tickets went on sale. His role as Scott Robinson in the Australian soap *Neighbours* and his subsequent career as a Stock, Aitken and Waterman pop star with hit singles like 'Too Many Broken Hearts' and 'Sealed With A Kiss' made him a pin-up on a million bedroom walls. Donovan was a bankable star. His fans wanted to see him live on stage. In the queue they rubbed shoulders with all those who had once sung in a school production of *Joseph* and with all those others who had loved *Cats, Evita* and *Starlight Express* and wanted to see the show where it all began.

The new version cost a staggering £1.5m to stage, but the Palladium took advance bookings of £2m on the strength of Donovan's name above the door. Casting him was a masterstroke. Lloyd Webber, wanting to beef up the lead role, added four new songs but Rice, upset at not being consulted, insisted he didn't want the original to be tampered with and eventually the composer backed down.

This was a very different *Joseph,* a *Joseph* with the volume pumped up. Big bass lines,

was unhappy with the current state of the touring production.

The more he pondered the problem, the more obvious the solution became. He would bring *Joseph* bang up to date with a sparkling new production, a production of which he was proud. He would dust down the show for a limited run at the London Palladium, one of the biggest and most famous theatres in Britain. It was an act of some daring. The Palladium is a venue rich in history but, with 2,400 seats, it is also a barn of a place. Performers say nothing, on a good night, beats playing to a capacity crowd. And nothing, they whisper darkly, can compare with the horror of playing in front of a few fans in the front row with the rest of the hall empty.

throbbing percussion, pulsating lights and big production numbers with sophisticated props - including coloured sheep and a Pharoah's throne which turned into a giant fruit machine - and lavish special effects. What had started as a simple fifteen-minute children's cantata for an end of term prep school concert had turned into a lavish, full blown two-hour two-act West End hit.

Donovan, wearing a long blond wig, skimpy white loin cloth and little else, much to the unmitigated ecstasy of his army of teenage fans, astounded critics with his mature melodic tones. Linzi Hateley as the narrator had a winning combination of vulnerability and vocal power and David Easter, who made his name in the Channel 4 soap *Brookside,* gave a deliciously overripe performance as Pharoah.

Lloyd Webber was with his new wife Madeleine as the first-night audience, which included Paul Nicholas, Peter Cook and Denice Lewis, rose and greeted the elaborate but exuberant new production with a five-minute standing ovation.

The London Palladium cast album went straight to number one, as did Donovan's version of 'Any Dream Will Do'. In 1968, Tim Rice and Andrew Lloyd Webber had sold the rights to *Joseph* to the Novello music publishing company for 100 guineas. In 1991 the Really Useful Company paid Novello/Film Trax £1m to buy the rights back. 'My board thought I was completely barmy,' said Lloyd Webber. But at the peak of the show's popularity, Joseph and the Amazing Money Making Machine was taking a staggering £400,000 a week at the box office. Lloyd Webber and the Really Useful Company, as composer and producers, were making £120,000 a week; Rice, as lyricist, £16,000 a week.

When Donovan, who earned £25,000 a week, left the show in 1992 he was replaced by Phillip Schofield, fresh from presenting the children's TV show *Going Live*, who beat off another former *Neighbours* star, Craig McLachlan, and Jonathon Morris from the television comedy *Bread,* for the coveted role. 'I realise my singing talents are not exactly well known,' he said at the time, 'but I'm looking forward to surprising a few people.' And he did.

Donny Osmond opened the new show in North America in Toronto but when Lloyd

Webber chose Darren Day - who looked like Donovan, acted like Schofield and sang rather better than both of them - from 3,000 hopefuls to take over at the Palladium in May 1993 it showed he had a nose for new talent as well as a gift for picking stars who would put bottoms on seats. And when *Joseph,* which was first performed three weeks before Jason Donovan was even born, finally closed in January 1994 it had become the longest-running show ever to play at the London Palladium.

That would have been hard for anyone to imagine that first night at Colet Court. Tim Rice and Andrew Lloyd Webber would work on other, more immediately successful, projects; fall out and split up; win, respectively, an Oscar and a knighthood, but although they didn't know it, those sitting there under the portrait of Sir John Colet were witnessing a performance that would change the face of musical theatre. It would take an Australian soap star to turn *Joseph* into a proper West End hit, but over the next 25 years there was always someone, somewhere, mounting a production. And although they would both move on to weightier projects, there has been little to touch the freshness and charm of this, their first venture into musical theatre together.

JESUS CHRIST SUPERSTA
THE
CAMBRI
THEAT
IS IN
EARLHAM S
OPPOSI
JESUS CHRIST SUPERSTAR
"A Supershow."
ANDREW LLOYD WEBBER

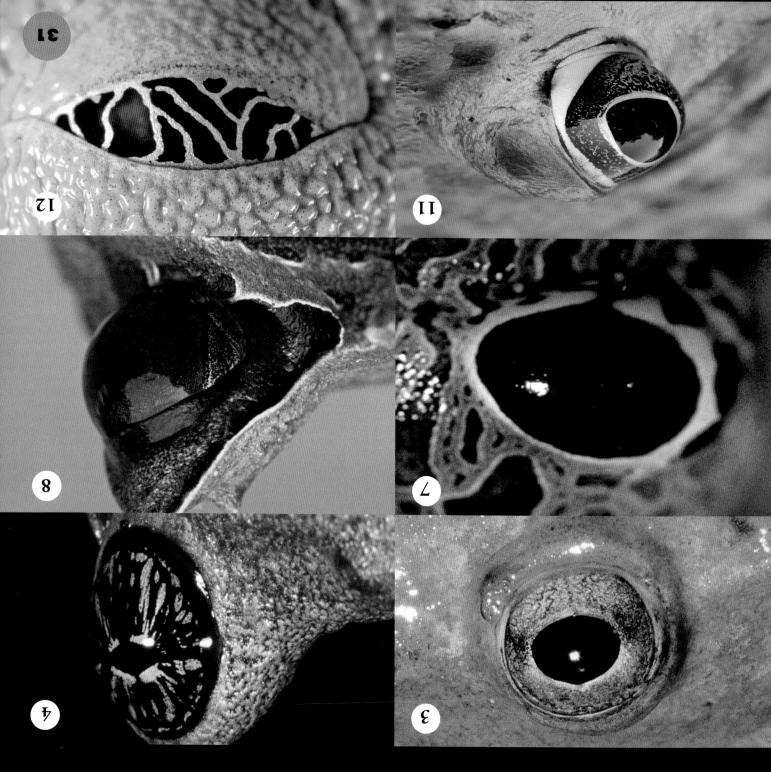

Answer: the fake eye is number 7, which is actually the back of a dwarf frog. Here are the names of the other frogs:
1. Dumeril's bright-eyed frog 2. Common big-headed frog 3. Water-holding frog 4. Poisonous tree frog 5. Smoky jungle frog 6. Mossy frog 7. Dwarf frog 8. Long-nosed horned frog 9. Red-eyed tree frog 10. Bronze frog 11. American bullfrog 12. Red-eyed tree frog

THE GLASS FROG

With its amazing see-through body, the glass frog blends in perfectly with its surroundings. This little frog hangs on to leaves with tiny, round–ended toes that seem almost to melt into the leaf surface. It lives in Central and South America.

1–3 in (3–7 cm)

MOST GLASS FROGS live high in **THE** *rainforest* **CANOPY.** At such a height, the trees are covered with **clouds** all year round and the **frogs' skin** is kept nice and *moist.* They come down from the canopy to lay eggs.

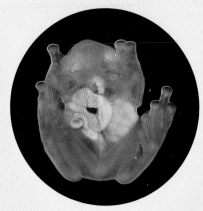

Glass frogs are more transparent from beneath. You can even see their hearts beating busily in their chests.

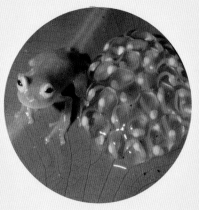

Glass frogs lay their eggs on leaves that overhang running water. The male frog stands guard and protects the eggs from parasitic flies.

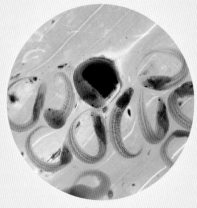

When the tadpoles hatch, they drop down into the water. They have powerful tails and are well-adapted for life in fast-flowing forest streams.

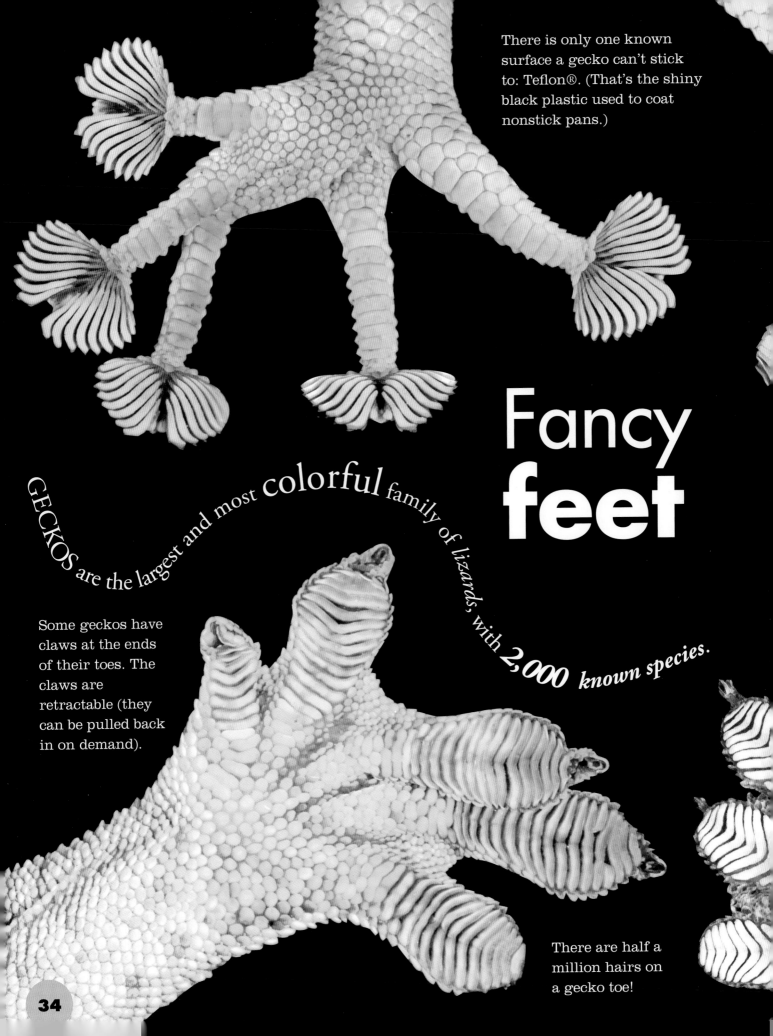

There is only one known surface a gecko can't stick to: Teflon®. (That's the shiny black plastic used to coat nonstick pans.)

Fancy feet

GECKOS are the largest and most colorful family of lizards, with 2,000 known species.

Some geckos have claws at the ends of their toes. The claws are retractable (they can be pulled back in on demand).

There are half a million hairs on a gecko toe!

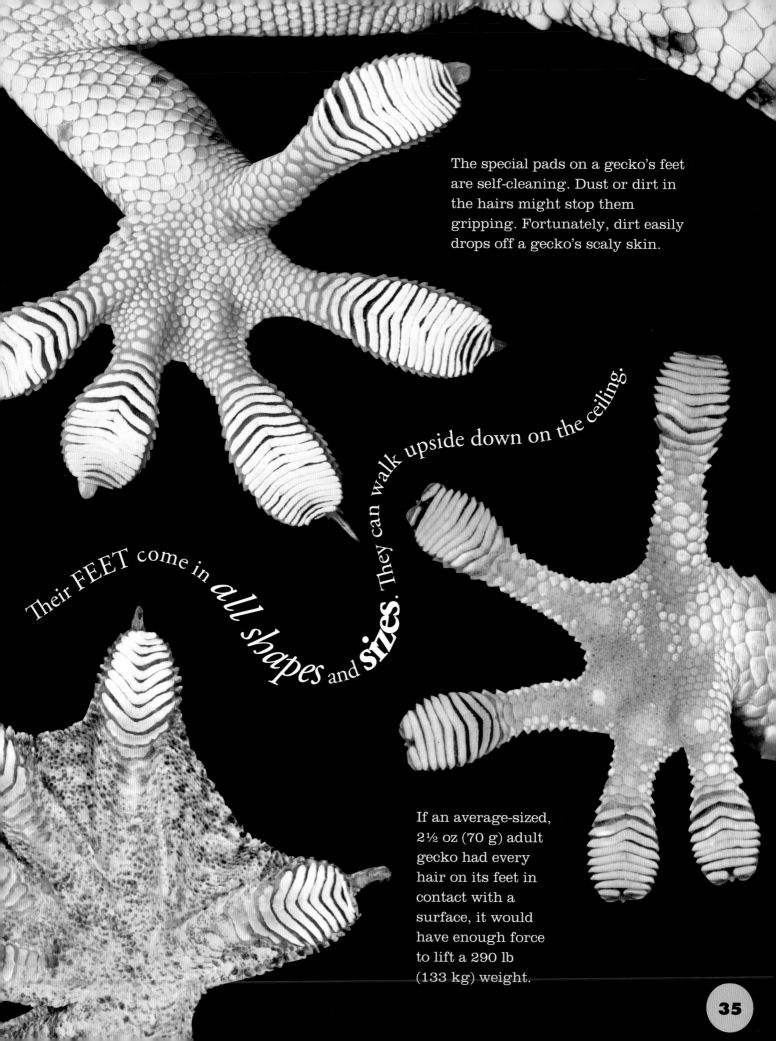

The special pads on a gecko's feet are self-cleaning. Dust or dirt in the hairs might stop them gripping. Fortunately, dirt easily drops off a gecko's scaly skin.

Their FEET come in *all shapes* and **sizes**. They can walk upside down on the ceiling.

If an average-sized, 2½ oz (70 g) adult gecko had every hair on its feet in contact with a surface, it would have enough force to lift a 290 lb (133 kg) weight.

THE WATER-HOLDING FROG

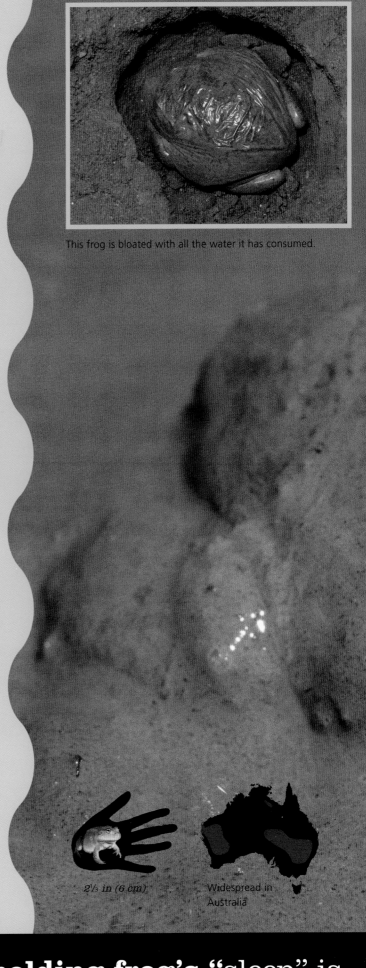

This frog is bloated with all the water it has consumed.

Where does it **LIVE?**

The **water-holding frog** (*Litoria platycephala*) lives in Australia. During the rainy season, the frog absorbs water and in doing so puts on 50 percent of its own body weight! To keep from losing this water during the dry months, it creates an underground home to stay in. Since the mud is still wet from the rainy season, its able to burrow down more than 3 ft (1 m) beneath the surface. It enters a summer hibernation and can stay underground waiting for the next rainy season. When it senses the water from heavy rains, it wakes up and starts to resurface.

STORING water

The water-holding frog stores water in its bladder and beneath its skin.

"Living **WELL**"

Aborigines used to dig up the frog to extract drinking water. They used the frog as a "living well." To gain access to the water they squeezed the frog.

FEEDING time

When active above the ground, it lives in water bodies. It feeds on other frogs, tadpoles, and small insects.

EGG laying

A female usually lays more than 500 eggs at one time! She lays her eggs and then goes into a hibernation. She enters this state in order to prevent damage from extreme dryness and heat.

2⅓ in (6 cm)

Widespread in Australia

The term for a **water-holding frog's** "sleep" is

Before...

In its normal state, a water-holding frog is just 2⅓ in (6 cm) in length.

After...

When it has consumed half its own body weight in water, its body is enlarged to 4½ in (12 cm) in length.

When active, it lives in puddles, pools, and streams.

TOP 10
DEADLIEST

Most **reptiles** and **amphibians** are perfectly *harmless* to people, but a few can inflict **lethal bites** or *kill* with a touch of their *poisonous skin*. Here are some of the **world's deadliest cold-blooded killers.**

DEADLIEST AMPHIBIAN

Poison dart **FROG**

Phyllobates terribilis of Colombia can kill you if you touch it. Just one of these tiny frogs contains enough poison to paralyze and kill 50 people. The deadly chemical in the frog's skin comes from poisonous plants, which are eaten by ants that are in turn eaten by the frog. Native peoples use the frog to make poison blowpipe darts.

Inland **TAIPAN**

The inland taipan (*Oxyuranus microlepidotus*) of Australia has the deadliest venom of any land-dwelling snake. The venom, injected by a bite, not only poisons nerves, but also causes the victim's blood to clot, blocking arteries. Before an antidote was developed, there were no known survivors of a taipan bite. Fortunately, the taipan is very shy and bites are rare.

Australian brown **SNAKE**

The eastern (or common) brown snake (*Pseudonaja textilis*) of Australia is the world's second most venomous land snake after the Taipan, based on the strength of its venom. Its bite is usually fatal, unless the victim receives an antidote. The venom contains potent nerve toxins, which paralyze the victim's muscles, and chemicals that make the blood clot.

Saltwater **CROCODILE**

The saltwater crocodile (*Crocodylus porosus*) of Australia and parts of Asia is the largest reptile on Earth, with big males weighing more than a ton. Normally seen basking lazily in the sun or wallowing in shallow water, it is capable of explosive bursts of speed when attacking. It drags its victim into the water and then rolls around to tear the body apart.

Nile **CROCODILE**

The Nile crocodile (*Crocodylus niloticus*) of Africa kills a large number of people, since locals often collect water or wash from the river. It sneaks toward victims with its body hidden in the muddy water and only its eyes above the surface. It then leaps out and snatches the victim in its jaws before dragging them in the water.

Komodo **DRAGON**

The world's largest lizard, the Komodo dragon (*Varanus komodoensis*) weighs as much as a man and can attack and devour a human being. The lizard kills prey in an especially gruesome way, biting victims with filthy teeth that are covered with disease-causing bacteria. The victim may escape, but the bite turns into a festering wound that can kill.

Eastern diamondback **RATTLESNAKE**

The bite of North America's deadliest snake can kill in a matter of hours. The Eastern diamondback rattlesnake (*Crotalus adamanteus*) venom contains hemotoxins, which attack the blood and damage a huge area of tissue, potentially leading to loss of a limb or death. Thanks to rapid treatment with antivenom, only a handful of deaths occur each year.

Puff **ADDER**

This bad-tempered African snake is called the puff adder because it hisses and puffs when approached, while curling itself into a tight S-shape, ready to strike. Get too close and it will lunge forward and sink its long fangs deep into your skin, injecting a venom that attacks the blood. The puff adder (*Bitis arietans*) causes more deaths than any other snake in Africa.

Fer-de-**LANCE**

This South American relative of the rattlesnake preys on rats and other rodents, killing them by injecting venom through its hollow teeth. The fer-de-lance's (*Bothrops atrox*) venom is packed with enzymes that destroy blood cells and body tissues, causing fits of vomiting, diarrhea, paralysis, and blackouts.

Black **MAMBA**

The bite of the black mamba (*Dendroaspis polylepis*) kills in less than an hour, and without antivenom is almost always fatal. The lethal ingredient in the venom is dendrotoxin, a chemical that paralyzes muscles and stops the lungs and heart from working. Death is usually caused by suffocation.

Bamboo pit viper

The heat pit in a python has one section. In a pit viper, it has two sections. The inner one is the temperature of the snake and the outer one heats up when the snake is near a heat source.

Sixth sense

SNAKES such as pythons, *pit vipers*, and some BOAS are able to PICK UP small *changes* in air temperature around them by using *organs* on their **faces**, called heat pits. They detect these changes as *infrared rays* (heat vision). This *sixth* SENSE allows them to locate *prey* during the night.

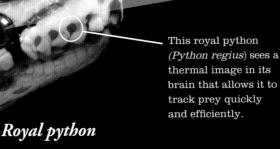

This royal python *(Python regius)* sees a thermal image in its brain that allows it to track prey quickly and efficiently.

Royal python

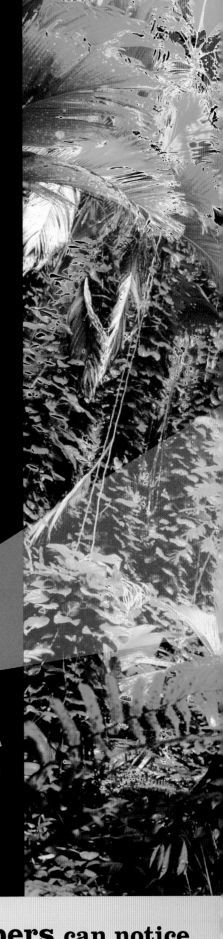

This system is so precise that pit vipers can notice

The FIVE senses

HEARING

Snakes do not have external ears. Their hearing is poor so they rely on vibrations from the ground that pass through skull bones on their lower jaws to their ears. This puff adder (*Bitis arietans*) is sticking close to the ground to sense any vibrations.

SIGHT

Snakes generally don't have great vision, although they are adept at detecting movement. The vine snake (*Ahaetulla nasuta*) is unusual in that it has forward-facing eyes that give it binocular vision and a good sense of distance.

TASTE

The Jacobson's organ enables snakes to taste and smell. The organ consists of two sensitive cavities in the roof of the snake's mouth. Their tongue gathers particles that the organ analyzes. Snakes that live in water, such as the green anaconda (*Eunectes murinus)* are able to use their tongue to gather particles underwater.

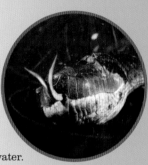

SMELL

Snakes use their sense of smell to help them locate prey. The common boa constrictor (*Boa constrictor)* detects its prey through scent and taste. Using its Jacobson's organ it is able to work out if prey is nearby. Boas wrap their coils around their victims and squeeze hard to kill them.

TOUCH

From the beginning of a snake's life, it relies on touch for guidance. It uses its tongue and pressure receptors in its skin to touch objects, move, and orientate itself. The Indian python (*Python molurus)* is using its tongue to explore its surroundings.

changes in temperature that are less than a degree.

Gecko FEET

Nothing GOES like a *gecko's toes.* They even inspire *science.*

GECKOS are *small lizards* but they've set humans a **BIG** challenge: to mimic their *amazing ability* to walk up *WALLS*. Their *secret*? **BILLIONS** of tiny hairs (called *setae*), and long toes to help a lizard grasp the *bumps*.

There's more to a gecko's feet than hair. Their toes bend backward (compared to ours), and they must "peel" them off a surface a bit at a time. It's like Velcro—it won't slip!

The toe-pads on fan-fingered geckos are split into two parts. This gives them extra grip, even compared with other geckos.

Fan-fingered gecko

There are 14,000 hairs in 1 mm² of a gecko's foot. Each hair has between 100 and 1,000 filaments that grip onto the wall as it climbs.

When SCIENCE copies *nature,* it's called **biomimetics.**

STICKYBOT is a **robot** that can **climb** *SMOOTH SURFACES* such as **glass. HOW?**

Stickybot

Stickybot's feet have rows of stiff, yet flexible "gecko tape" on them. This material produces a sticky force that allows the robot to climb up windows and whiteboards.

STICKYBOT uses **12 motors** to mimic *one animal.*

43

The newt that

This captive-bred axolotl looks like an albino—with no pigment in its skin—but since it has pigment in its eyes it's called "leucistic," which means reduced pigment.

"Wild-type" axolotls are usually dark.

Wild axolotls are only found in the canal systems of Mexico's Lake Xochimilco. Located close to Mexico City, these canals are threatened by pollution and increased development.

Axolotl means "water-dog" in

never grows UP

The axolotl is the Peter Pan of the animal world. It doesn't undergo metamorphosis like many other amphibians. Instead, it spends its entire life in a juvenile form, keeping it gills and fins, and living in water. The axolotl grows steadily bigger until it is old enough to reproduce.

Though their numbers are falling in the wild, many axolotls are kept in captivity. Axolotls are popular pets, but they are also studied by scientists because of their interesting life cycles and their powers of regeneration—axolotls can regrow entire limbs. In captivity it is sometimes possible to make the axolotls metamorphose by injecting them with special hormones that trigger growth and development. In their adult form, they look very like their near-relatives, the tiger salamanders.

the ancient language of the Aztecs.

What's for dinner?

The Gila monster stores fat in its thick, stumpy tail. It is this energy store that allows it to survive for months without food.

Lizards for starters

Most lizards are insect-eaters (insectivores), but some have special diets. Some big lizards are carnivores and eat animals such as birds, rodents, or other lizards. A few lizards are plant-eaters (herbivores).

The binge-eater

The Gila monster (*Heloderma suspectum*) only eats between 5–10 times a year, but when it does, this lizard can consume the equivalent of over half of its body weight. It mainly eats the eggs of birds or other reptiles.

The insectivore

The Sinai agama (*Pseudotrapelus sinaitus*) is a slender lizard. It has long, thin limbs, which make it good at running over the hot sand when it hunts in the heat of the day. It feeds on ants and other insects, but it also eats sand!

The vegetarian

One plant-eating lizard is the **green iguana** (*Iguana iguana*), which survives on a complex diet of leaves, shoots, flowers, and fruit. It can't digest animal protein well, although it may sometimes accidentally eat small insects and other invertebrates that are attached to vegetation.

Frog food that moves

Most frogs are carnivorous. Nearly all of them eat insects and other invertebrates like worms, spiders, and centipedes, but some of the bigger frogs take on larger prey, such as mice, birds, or other frogs.

The cannibal

The American bullfrog (*Rana catesbeiana*) is the largest of the North American frogs, growing up to 8 in (20 cm) in length. These frogs are voracious eaters and will eat anything they can fit into their exceedingly large mouths. This includes insects and other invertebrates, rodents, birds, snakes, and even other bullfrogs.

The jelly-eater

Leatherback turtles (*Dermochelys coriacea*) are the biggest turtles in the world. They live on a diet of jellyfish and comb jellies, both of which are made up mostly of water. To get enough energy and nutrients to grow so big, leatherbacks eat huge quantities of food—they sometimes eat their own weight in jellyfish each day.

Sea turtles

The diet of sea turtles varies between species. Some eat a wide range of foods, both plant and animal, but others have special diets, with adaptations that make it easier to eat particular things.

The cruncher

Loggerhead turtles (*Caretta caretta*) mainly eat hard-shelled creatures such as crabs, conchs, and clams. Their big heads and strong jaws help them to crush the shells and they can hold their breath for up to 20 minutes on their dives down to the sea floor.

The fruitivore

Izecksohn's Brazilian tree frog (*Xenohyla truncata*) is one of the very few plant-eating (herbivorous) frogs. Living in bromeliads in the Brazilian coastal moist forest, it eats brightly colored berries from arum plants and fruit from the cocoa tree. The frog helps to disperse plant seeds in its poop.

The sponge muncher

Hawksbill turtles (*Eretmochelys imbricata*) live around coral reefs, rich in marine life. They can eat a range of prey, but they mainly live on a diet of primitive, plantlike animals called sponges. The turtles are named after their sharp, birdlike beaks that make it easier for them to reach sponges growing in crevices between rocks and corals.

The mite-y eater

Poison dart frogs use poisons in their skin to deter potential predators. They get their poisons from their food. The strawberry poison-dart frog (*Oophaga pumilio*) gets its toxins from a mite that lives in the soil in Central and South America. The frog also eats other small invertebrates. As the frog eats its food, the toxic chemicals build up in its body, which makes it more poisonous.

LIVING FOSSILS

The giant salamanders of China and Japan are the world's largest amphibians. While most salamanders would fit in the palm of your hand, giant salamanders grow bigger than your arm—and some longer than the length of your entire body. NO ONE KNOWS how long giant salamanders live in the wild, but the oldest captive salamander lived for 52 years.

GIANT salamanders have changed *very little* in the last **30 million**

The Chinese giant salamander (*Andrias davidianus*) is the world's largest amphibian, growing up to 6 ft (1.8 m) in length in captivity. It is heavily built, with a flat head and a wide mouth. Like its Japanese cousin, it lives a completely aquatic existence and its short legs cannot support its body weight when it is out of the water.

Chinese giant salamander

Giant salamanders are paler on their undersides.

Skeleton of a Chinese giant salamander

Stressed-out salamanders can produce a thick, smelly mucous that makes them very unpleasant to handle.

Giant salamanders live in hollows in the banks of streams and rivers. At night, they walk slowly along the bottom, feeding on fish and crustaceans. They have a powerful bite and they catch their food with a quick sideways snap of their wide, many-toothed mouths.

What a stink!

years, which is why *they* are described as *"living fossils."*

The Japanese giant salamander (*Andrias japonicus*) is the second-largest amphibian, growing up to 5 ft (1.5 m) in length. The Japanese and Chinese salamanders breathe through their skin. Their skin has folds and wrinkles that increase the surface area, allowing more oxygen in. They like to live in clean, fast-flowing streams but numbers of both species have dropped owing to pollution and dam building.

Japanese giant salamander

Snakes & Ladders

Are you feeling LUCKY? Challenge a friend to a game of **snakes and ladders** and see who gets to the top first. BE CAREFUL not to step on a **snake**—the ones in this game all have *deadly bites!*

You will **need:**

* One or more friends to play with
* A small object to use as a counter for each person
* A die

How to **play:**

To decide who starts, everyone rolls the die and the person with the highest number goes first. When it's your turn, roll the die and move your counter along by the number. If you land on the bottom of a ladder, climb to the top of the ladder. If you land on the top of a snake, slither down to the square at its bottom. If you roll a six, take another turn. The first person to pass 100 wins. Good luck!

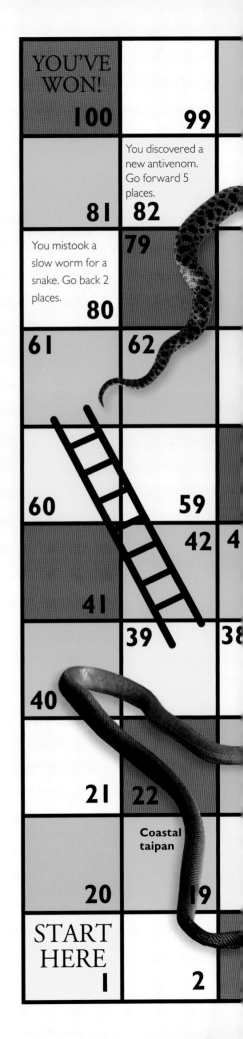

YOU'VE WON! 100

99

You discovered a new antivenom. Go forward 5 places.
81   82

You mistook a slow worm for a snake. Go back 2 places.
79
80

61   62

60   59
42   4

41
39   38

40

21   22

Coastal taipan

20   19

START HERE
1   2

Snakes and Ladders Board

	Hog nose viper					A spitting cobra spat in your eye. Go back two places.	**91**
98	**97**	**96**	**95**	**94**	**93**	**92**	
83		Black tiger snake		**87**	Death adder	**89**	
	84	**85**	**86**		**88**		**90**
			75			**72**	**71**
78	**77**	**76**		**74**	**73**		
			66	**67**	**68**	**69**	**70**
63	**64**	**65**					
			55	Beaked sea snake **54**	**53**	**52**	**51**
58	**57**	**56**		**47**			You got rattled by a rattlesnake. Go back one place.
Death adder	**44**	**45**	**46**		**48**	**49**	**50**
				33			
	37	**36**	**35**	**34**	**28**	**32**	**31**
24				**27**	Inland taipan		You wrestled an anaconda and won. Go forward 3 places.
23		**25**	**26**		**29**	**30**	
				13		**12**	
18	**17**	**16**	**15**	**14**			**11**
			You got squeezed by a boa constrictor. Go back 3 places.				
3	**4**	**5**	**6**	**7**	**8**	**9**	**10**

51

Horned lizard

Built like miniature armored tanks, horned lizards move ponderously along the baking ground of their dry desert habitats; stopping to sunbathe, dig burrows, and snack on ants. They have evolved a range of adaptations to help them survive.

5½ in (14 cm)

Found in northern Mexico and southwestern US

Bloody **DEFENSE**

Horned lizards use the spines on their backs in self-defense. In addition, they also exhibit a startling form of defense. A network of weakened blood vessels allow them to spray a stream of blood out from their eyes toward attackers. This blood tastes horrible to potential predators.

Dew **DRINK**

Living in dry, desert conditions, horned lizards have evolved to get as much water from their environment as possible. The tiny grooves between the lizard's scales channel moisture from dew that has gathered on its body toward the lizard's mouth, providing a refreshing morning drink.

Body **BEAUTIFUL**

Another adaptation to its desert environment, is the horned lizard's wide, flat body. This allows it to catch rainwater during infrequent desert showers. The lizard raises its tail and channels droplets down to its mouth. Its bumpy, mottled appearance helps it blend into its surroundings and avoid detection by predators flying above.

Sticky **TONGUES**

This ant contain lots of chitin, which is indigestible to a horned lizard. That means the lizard must eat an awful lot of ants to get enough nutrients to survive. Thankfully, the lizard has a secret weapon—a long sticky tongue, which it flicks out like a whip to gather lots of ants.

Horny **HEADS**

The lizards are named for their distinctive horns. These shapes break up the outline of the lizards' heads—making them harder to spot in among the rocks and stones of the desert. Their raised brow bumps help to shield their eyes from the strong desert sun, while thick eyelids protect their eyes from stings of their ant prey.

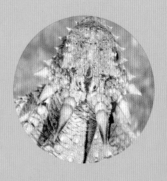

Why did this woman turn people INTO STONE?

In Greek mythology, Medusa was a fearsome, snake-headed monster. Once a beautiful woman, she was transformed by the goddess Athena as punishment for meeting the sea god Poseidon in Athena's temple. In some tales, not only was her hair turned into a twisting mass of hissing snakes, but her teeth also became tusks and her skin was made green and scaly. Anyone who looked at her hideous form turned to stone. Medusa was eventually slain by Perseus, the mortal son of Zeus, king of the gods. He did not look at Medusa directly, but watched her reflection in his metal shield before beheading her.

Even after she was slain, the head of Medusa still had the power to turn anyone who looked at it into stone. Perseus returned it to the goddess Athena, who attached it to her shield and used it to scare her enemies.

THE MEDUSA MYTH

WHEN SHE ANGERED THE GODS, MEDUSA WAS TURNED INTO A SNAKE-HEADED MONSTER.

Perseus holding the head of Medusa.

In search of the flapping FROG

The LAKE TITICACA FROG is the **largest aquatic frog** in the world. The lake it lives in is *12,500* feet (3,800 m) above sea level, making it a very *COLD* environment to reside in.

Brrr, it's chilly!

The air is thin and freezing cold so the **Lake Titicaca frog** survives by living *permanently* at the lake's bottom. The water here never rises above 50°F (10°C).

The frog doesn't usually need to surface for air, since it absorbs oxygen through its skin. It has a lot of skin with plenty of flaps and a big surface area, enabling it to breathe underwater.

The Lake Titicaca frog can measure up to 20 in (50 cm) long and weigh up to 2¼ lb (1 kg).

It does push-ups in order to circulate the water surrounding its body. This keeps its skin folds in contact with oxygenated water.

Lake Titicaca is located on the border of Bolivia and Peru.

The Lake Titicaca frog **breeds** in shallow

Why does
this frog
exercise?

waters, where it lays about **500** eggs.

Fearsome FRILLS

The frilled lizard (*Chlamydosaurus kingii*) has a loose ruff of skin around its neck. Most of the time it sits flat, like a cape around the lizard's shoulders, but when the lizard is threatened, the ruff expands and the lizard lunges forward, attempting to startle its attacker for just long enough to make its escape.

Tail TRICKERY

Some lizards have developed a startling form of defense, dropping their tails and leaving them wriggling on the ground to distract predators. Skinks, geckos, and slow worms can all detach their tails. Some can grow new tails, but these are never as long as the original.

Clever DISGUISE

The best way to keep from being eaten is not to be noticed. The pygmy leaf-dropping frog (*Afrixalus pygmaeus*) has a very unglamorous way to merge in with its surroundings—by looking like a bird dropping. It sits on leaves in full view and tries to escape attention by sitting very still.

Playing DEAD

Many predators do not eat animals that are already dead, so pretending to be dead can be an excellent way to stay alive. Some snakes have very dramatic mock deaths where they writhe erratically, bite themselves, and fall back to lie still. Sometimes blood trickles from their open mouths.

Toxic to the TOUCH

Some frogs protect themselves by making themselves poisonous to the touch. When this marbled milk frog (*Trachycephalus venulosus*) feels threatened, the poison glands that line its back and neck start to release a toxic milky secretion.

Warning RATTLE

The rattlesnake warns off predators by making an intimidating rattling sound with its tail. Its rattle is made of hollow sections that clash against each other when the snake shakes its tail.

Spitting VENOM

Some cobras spray or spit venom at a threat. The Mozambique spitting cobra (*Naja mossambica*) can target its venom with pinpoint accuracy. This spitting behavior is so instinctive that young snakes will spit even as they are hatching from their eggs.

Big and SCARY

To convince a predator that it is too big to handle, the black rain frog (*Breviceps fuscus*) puffs itself up to twice its original size. This sudden growth spurt also makes it harder to dig the frog out from its tunnel.

REPTILES and AMPHIBIANS use a variety of ways to **defend** themselves against their enemies. They **spit, rattle, trick, and scare** their way to safety.

travel blog

The LEATHERBACK sea turtle loves

Travel **FACTS**

Leatherback sea turtles are big travelers. One leatherback was tracked over an epic voyage of more than 12,500 miles (20,000 km). Leatherbacks travel these long distances to feed their appetite for jellyfish.

User **PROFILE**

Leatherback sea turtle
(Dermochelys coriacea)
Leatherbacks are the largest species of sea turtle, and one of the largest reptiles on Earth. An adult leatherback can weigh more than 1,000 lb (450 kg).

Size: 4–8 ft (1.2–2.4 m)

Departure time

Adult sea turtles spend their lives in the world's oceans. They roam large distances in search of food and mates. Adult females also make long excursions to breeding beaches, usually where they were born, to lay their eggs. Experts are still researching how sea turtles find their way back, but they believe sea turtles use Earth's magnetic field, the sea's chemistry, and their memories.

A built-in swimsuit
The leatherback's shell (known as a carapace) is made of a tough, leathery, cartilage material, which gives the sea turtle its Latin name.

Life's a beach
Once the female leatherback has found a beach, she digs a small hole in the sand using her back flippers. She then lays about 100 eggs and covers them with sand. Sea turtles usually nest at night when it is safer.

Once a sea turtle hatchling makes it past any beach predators and into the

to travel and swims from warm tropical seas to cold, temperate waters.

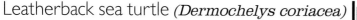

A new journey

The eggs take about two months to incubate in the sand. The baby sea turtles, known as hatchlings, can take days to dig their way out. Hatchlings normally emerge at night and make the long journey across the beach to the lapping waves. This is a dangerous time for a hatchling, because they are vulnerable to predators such as birds and crabs. About 90 percent of hatchlings never make it to adulthood.

Where to go?

The hatchlings use their flippers to travel to the sea. Experts believe they know the right way to go because of the light reflected from the water (even at night) and the slope of the beach.

Sea turtle **SPECIES**

● Hawksbill

● Green

● Loggerhead

● Olive Ridley

● Kemp's Ridley

● Flatback

ocean, it sets out on a swimming frenzy. It will keep paddling for up to 48 hours.

LOST &FOUND

WANTED

The Southern gastric-brooding frog (*Rheobatrachus silus*) has not been seen in the wild since 1981. After mating, the female swallowed her eggs, switching off her digestive system to allow the larvae to develop. After 6–7 weeks, the female regurgitated her young.

WANTED

The golden toad (*Incilius periglenes*) fell prey to climate change, with rising temperatures and erratic rainfall. Fewer breeding pools meant that frogs gathered in greater numbers and this allowed disease to pass quickly through the population.

WANTED

The Darwin's frog (*Rhinoderma darwinii*) has an unusual snout. The male uses his vocal sac to hold the tadpoles until they turn into young frogs. Numbers are declining because the frog's habitat is being destroyed through drought and deforestation.

WANTED

Last seen in 1955, the Hula painted frog (*Discoglossus nigriventer*) was once found along the eastern shore of Israel's Lake Hula. When the Hula marshes were drained in an attempt to reduce the incidence of malaria and make way for agricultural land, it also wiped out the species.

Certain AMPHIBIANS and REPTILES are declining in numbers or being lost altogether. However, lots of **new species** are being *found* every year. Although they can't replace the lost animals that become extinct, they can give scientists hope for the future.

FOUND

In 2009, a survey found that 200 possible new species of frog were living on the island of Madagascar. Statistics like these are *exciting*, since they give scientists promise of finding **new populations of other animals**. Earth contains so many surprises—scientists have to be willing to explore remote places to find and identify new species, although every now and then they'll find them in places that have already been explored.

Occasionally, species new to scientists have been known to locals for years. The **bitatawa monitor lizard** (*Varanus bitatawa*) was found by scientists who were walking across a field in the Philippines in 2010. However, the locals had been hunting it for a long time. Scientists missed it because it doesn't come down from the trees very often.

Discovered in Indonesia's Foja Mountains during an expedition in 2008, this little frog has a long, **Pinocchio-like** inflatable nose that expands when the male is calling out. He was seen sitting on a bag of rice in the scientist's campsite and is thought to be one of about 150 species of Australasian tree frogs.

Is it a bird? Is it a plane?

The Wallace's flying frog *(Rhacophorus nigropalmatus)* is also known as the "parachute frog" and is one of the few aerial amphibians. The membranes between its toes and the loose skin on its sides help it to glide through the air, although it doesn't actually fly.

Found in Malaysia and Borneo

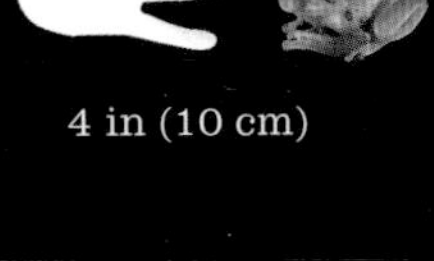

4 in (10 cm)

When I'm resting on a tree, I often face head-down. This allows me to take off quickly if I need to, I'm always ready to jump and glide.

Kuhl's flying gecko is a reptile that lives in tropical forests. It's one of several lizards that "fly" through the forest and jump from trees when escaping danger.

I am a Kuhl's flying gecko (*Ptychozoon kuhli*) and I love jumping from trees! My strong, webbed feet help me glide through the air. The flaps of skin along my flanks and my flattened, frilly tail also help to control my descent.

7–8 in (18–20 cm)

Southeast Asia

I'm a nocturnal creature so I remain still during the day. I rely on my brown skin with barklike markings to allow me to blend in with the trees. My ability to camouflage myself means I can remain undetected.

Don't LOOK UP

The **paradise tree snake** is capable of *gliding among high trees* in tropical forests. It dangles from the end of a branch and decides on its direction of travel. It then *pushes its body* away from the tree, **pulls in its stomach**, and flares out its ribs so that it is twice as flat as normal. It glides through the air in a motion of **lateral undulation** (wavelike movements that propel it forward) in line with the ground so that it can land safely. It can glide distances of up to 330 ft (100 m). It's considered to be the **most adept** of the flying snakes.

Watch out for that snake. It's flying!

The PARADISE TREE SNAKE has a slender body and a long tail. It can MEASURE up to *3 ft (0.9 m)*.

It's a daytime **hunter** and lives on a *diet* of lizards, frogs, bats, and birds. Its TOXICITY is not dangerous to humans.

How did **frogs'** legs shock SCIENCE?

In 1771, a chance discovery on professor Luigi Galvani's experiment table led, eventually, to the invention of the first battery—without which our lives today would be very different. **So how did one small hop for an amphibian become a giant leap for science?**

In further experiments, Galvani made the legs hop right across the table!

Luigi Galvani was a biologist at the University of Bologna, Italy. He was experimenting with frogs' legs and static electricity when his metal scalpel touched the brass hook that held the legs. Suddenly, the legs twitched!

Volta termed Galvani's discovery **Galvanism.**

Luigi **Galvani**

Galvani realized that electricity had made the legs twitch, but where did it come from? He mistakenly concluded that the frog's bodily fluids must have been a source of electricity, which he called "animal electricity."

A **shocking** discovery

Just after Galvani's accidental discovery, it happened again. In a separate experiment, Galvani's assistant touched the frog's sciatic (spinal cord) nerve with his scalpel while he was taking a spark of static electricity from a storage jar. Galvani wrote, "Suddenly all the muscles of its limbs were seen to be so contracted that they seemed to have fallen into tonic convulsions."

Science owes a lot to Galvani, including the study of bioelectricity (electricity in a body's nervous system) and the process of "galvanizing" (or coating) metal to protect it.

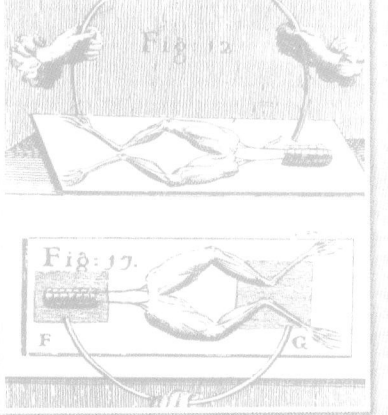

One thing **leads to another**

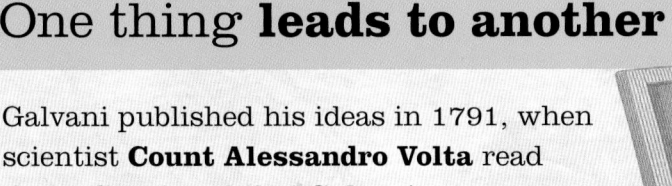

Galvani published his ideas in 1791, when scientist **Count Alessandro Volta** read them. Convinced that Galvani was wrong, Volta repeated the experiments and found that electricity did not come *from* the frog—but that wet tissue in the legs *allowed electricity to flow* between the metal instruments holding the legs. This gave Volta an idea: a pile of copper and zinc disks with layers of wet cardboard between them would not only conduct electricity, but could also store it. This "Voltaic pile" was the first battery.

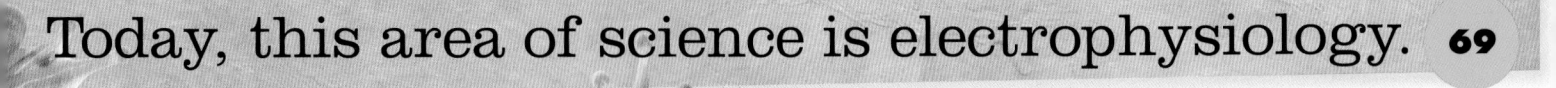

Today, this area of science is electrophysiology.

How to survive an encounter with a crocodile or an alligator

The **jaws** of **CROCODILIANS** are so **strong**

1. Do your research and keep an eye out!
Swim in designated areas only. Alligators and crocodiles tend to hunt at dusk or at night so don't go swimming at those times. Crocodilians often only show their eyes and nostrils above the water, so you probably won't spot them easily.

2. Give them space!
You should not get too close to crocodiles and alligators—15 ft (4.5 m) is usually enough room to keep between you and them.

3. Catch me if you can!
The average adult can outrun a crocodile or alligator on land. The fastest land speed for a crocodilian is only 10 mph (17 kph).

4. Don't scare them!
Steer clear of the riverbank if you're on a boat coming around a bend. Crocodilians like to bask on the banks and will react in self-defense if you scare them. If you spot a crocodile or alligator, try to let them know you're there by slapping the water with your oars or by blowing a whistle.

5. Get help as soon as you can
If a crocodilian is defending its young or its territory it might bite its opponent quickly and then let go. However, it is more likely to bite its prey and not release it. If you manage to get away from its grip then you should seek medical help immediately.

they can **CRUSH** bones when they close!

WORKING WITH
amphibians and reptiles

Animal **KEEPER**

Animal keepers are responsible for looking after animals in zoos and wildlife parks. The amphibian and reptile keepers must be expert herpetologists. They need to know about how these animals live in the wild, what they eat, how much exercise they need, and what temperature and light conditions they need to live.

Exotic animal **BREEDER**

Reptiles and amphibians are fascinating animals and many people like keeping them as pets. Taking animals from the wild can be bad for wild populations, so specialized breeders supply the pet trade by rearing animals like frogs, snakes, and lizards in captivity.

PHOTOGRAPHER

Successful animal photographers get to travel the world and have to know an awful lot about their subject to track it down and get the perfect photo. It's also not always a comfortable job—carrying heavy equipment in difficult terrain and camping in remote locations are all part of the challenge.

You want to be a what?

A **HERPETOLOGIST**

Zoology is the name given to the *study of animals*.
Herpetology is a branch of zoology and is the study of **reptiles and amphibians**. A herpetologist is an expert on these animals.

Veterinary **SURGEON**

Some vets are specially trained to deal with animals such as reptiles and amphibians. They know lots about the health and lifestyles of these creatures and how to care for them in the wild or in captivity. Working with large reptiles can be a hazardous profession, since a bite from an alligator is more serious than one from a dog.

Snake **HANDLER**

If you've got a snake problem, who are you going to call? Professional or volunteer snake handlers can be called in to remove snakes from houses and other places where they can come into contact with people. These may be escaped pets or wild snakes living where they shouldn't be—looking for shade in the summer months.

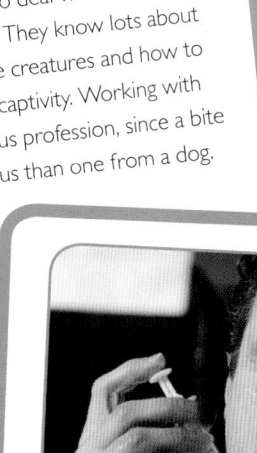

Biomedical **RESEARCHER**

Some species of amphibian and reptile produce toxins and poisons. Biomedical researchers study these chemicals and look at ways in which they can be of use to humans. More than 200 chemicals produced by amphibians and reptiles have been found to be of use in human medicines.

How does this **lizard** walk on **water?**

The **green basilisk lizard** is often referred to as the "*Jesus Christ lizard*" because it appears to walk on water. How it actually manages this **"miracle"** is by running short distances using its hindlegs. Its toes have fringes of skin that open out to create more surface area.

"These **curious** and strange-looking lizards gain their name from Greek mythology. Made up of parts of a snake, rooster, and lion, the **basilisk** was able to kill a man just from one look. The name basilisk means *"little king"* in Greek, which seems appropriate considering the crests on its head, back, and tail."

23-30 in (60-75 cm)

Found in Central America

RECORD BREAKERS

Most POISONOUS

The Colombian golden poison frog (*Phyllobates terribilis*) is the most poisonous frog, and the most poisonous vertebrate, in the world. It holds enough poison to kill 20 humans or 20,000 mice.

BIGGEST Snake

The Asian reticulated python (*Python reticulatus*), which can grow to 31½ ft (9.6 m), is the longest. The heaviest snake is the green anaconda, weighing up to 550 lb (227 kg).

SMALLEST Reptile

This title is shared by two geckos, both measuring just over ½ in (1.6 cm) as full-grown adults: the Virgin Gorda least gecko (*Sphaerodactylus parthenopion*) and the dwarf gecko (*Sphaerodactylus ariasae*).

LONGEST FANGS

The Gaboon viper (*Bitis gabonica*) is a venomous snake found in sub-Saharan Africa. The largest of the vipers, it can reach over 7 ft (2 m) in length and has huge fangs, measuring up to 2 in (5 cm) long.

FASTEST

The black spiny-tailed iguana (*Ctenosaura similis*) can run at a top speed of 22 mph (35 kph)—making it the world's fastest reptile. The fastest snake, the black mamba, can move at 12 mph (19 kph).

MOST EYES

Tuataras and many of the lizards have three eyes. The third eye is made up of light sensitive cells just under the skin on the top of the head. This "eye" can detect light and dark but can't make out shapes.

RECORD SPIT

Spitting cobras have a special type of fang with a small hole through which the venom is injected at high pressure. The Mozambique cobra can spray its venom over distances of 5½–8¼ ft (2–3 m).

BIGGEST clutch of eggs

Hawksbill turtles (*Eretmochelys imbricata*) can lay over 200 eggs in a single clutch. During the turtles' breeding season, which runs from July to October, female turtles may create 3–5 nests, each with a separate clutch of eggs.

STRANGEST life cycle

One contender for this title has to be Labord's chameleon (*Furcifer labordi*). This reptile spends most of its life (up to 7 months) as an egg, weathering the desert droughts. It lives for only a few months after hatching.

The LOUDEST

The couqui frog (*Eletherodactlus*) is a small Puerto Rican tree frog, measuring just 1½ in (4 cm) in length. For something so small, it is incredibly loud, and its distinctive "co-kee" call has been measured at over 100 decibels.

The MOST TEETH

American alligators have between 70 and 80 teeth. The teeth are long and pointed but gradually wear down, to be replaced by new teeth. An alligator can go through 2,000 to 3,000 teeth during its lifetime.

The OLDEST

The oldest vertebrate (animal with a backbone) is thought to be a Seychelles giant tortoise nicknamed Jonathan. Historians believe that he is now at least 178 years old.

Best SENSE OF SMELL

Komodo dragons (*Varanus komodoensis*) will readily feed on rotting meat. They smell with chemical detectors on their tongues and can sense dead animals up to 6 miles (10 km) away. Komodo dragons are the world's largest lizard.

Biggest LEAPS

Most frogs can leap over distances of 10 times their own body length and some species can jump up to 50 times their body length. The largest frog in the world, the Goliath frog (*Conraua goliath*), can jump almost 10 ft (3 m).

LONGEST TONGUE

Chameleons can have tongues that are as long, or even longer, than their bodies. It takes them less than a second to shoot their tongues out, and the sticky saliva on the tongue's clublike tip traps its insect prey.

MOST DIFFICULT to eat

One contender for this title must be the armadillo girdled lizard (*Cordylus cataphractus*). This lizard is covered in thick and spiked, armorlike scales. It can roll up into a ball, making itself even more unappealing to potential predators.

LARGEST REPTILE

The saltwater crocodile (*Crocodylus porosus*) is the world's largest reptile, growing to more than 23 ft (7 m) in length. Not only the largest, but also the heaviest, saltwater crocodiles can weigh over a ton.

MOST POISONOUS Snake

Sea snakes are the most poisonous snakes in the world. The beaked sea snake (*Enhydrina schistosa*) can produce enough venom in a single bite to kill 50 people.

GLOSSARY

adapt to change, becoming suited to a new place or a new use.

amphisbaenian wormlike, legless reptile found in tropical climates.

animal breeder someone who organizes the birth of baby animals in captivity and looks after them until they find a new home.

animal keeper someone who looks after animals in a zoo or wildlife park.

antidote a remedy that counteracts the effects of a poison.

antivenom a medicine that treats poisoning from a snake, spider, or insect.

aquatic describes anything growing or living in water.

bask to lie resting in the sunshine.

biomimetics science that copies nature.

captivity when animals are kept confined and looked after by people.

carnivore an animal that eats meat.

cold-blooded describes animals whose body temperature is controlled by the temperature around them.

coma a state of deep unconsciousness.

crocodilian one of the order of reptiles that includes crocodiles, alligators, caimans, etc.

endangered species animals that are at risk of extinction (no longer existing on Earth).

electrophysiology the study of the electrical properties of living tissues and cells.

estivation a kind of deep sleep that animals fall into, sometimes called "summer sleep."

evolve to change gradually.

extinct a species that has declined and disappeared entirely from the planet.

eyespot skin marking that looks like the eye of another animal. Eyespots are there to fool predators or prey.

fertilize when male and female cells join together to produce a new life.

fins flat projections on fish or mammals that help them propel or guide their bodies through water.

gills organs used to breathe underwater.

hatch when a new animal breaks out of an egg or pupa.

herbivore an animal that eats plants.

hibernate to go into a deep sleep for long periods.

incubation to keep eggs warm so they develop properly.

insectivore an animal that eats insects.

invertebrate an animal without a backbone.

lateral undulation wavelike body movements that move an animal (such as a snake) along.

life cycle the pattern of changes that occur in each generation of a species.

markings areas of color on an animal's skin or fur.

mate when male and female animals come together during reproduction.

membrane thin, flexible sheet or layer that covers, lines, or connects animal organs or cells.

metamorphosis major change in an animal's body during its life cycle, as when a tadpole changes into a frog.

nervous system the network of nerve cells in an animal's body.

predator an animal that kills and eats other animals.

prey an animal that is hunted, killed, and eaten by another animal.

retract to draw in or back. Retractable claws can be pulled back into an animal's feet.

scales small, overlapping plates that protect the skin of reptiles or fish.

sixth sense the five senses are hearing, touch, smell, sight, and taste. A "sixth sense" refers to anything in addition to the five senses.

snake handler someone who is familiar with snakes and knows a lot about them.

species a group of living things that can breed together in the wild.

static electricity a still electrical charge as opposed to a current, which moves.

thermal relating to temperature, especially warmth.

toxic poisonous.

transparent clear; see-through.

tropical describes anything that comes from (or is like) the hot region of the Earth near the equator.

vertebra a small bone in the spine, or backbone.

vertebrate an animal with a backbone.

veterinarian (sometimes called a vet) a doctor who is specially trained to care for animals instead of people.

warm-blooded describes animals that can control their body temperature.

INDEX

CREDITS

CHAPTER

1

WHAT
MAKES A
GARDEN?

THE POSSIBILITIES

The objective of this book is to explain the mystery that is the planning and planting of a garden—to show that it is really no mystery at all. There are certain rules and procedures that guide the process, and while with practice they can become quite sophisticated, they are basically simple.

The problem is that these rules are seldom remarked upon, or perhaps good and experienced gardeners are not even aware of the rules they are following, having naturally adopted certain procedures in the course of making a garden.

My hope is to speed up the process a little and help the reader avoid a lot of trial and error in making a garden. Having built a few gardens of my own, and having seen hundreds more, I have noticed that all good gardens follow similar principles, and I have attempted to organize these observations into the sections making up this book.

There are also special sections—Garden Visits and Plant Portraits—that show both the results of putting these rules into practice and some particular plants that work well.

Quite frankly, I wish I could have learned this information a little earlier in my own gardening career. It would have saved a lot of casting about—and a lot of work. There are more than a few plants in my garden that also might wish that I had discovered these rules a little sooner; many had to go because they were the wrong plant or in the wrong place.

At the very beginning I must add that results are not guaranteed—that is not in the nature of gardens and gardening. It would not be such a lively exercise and art if gardens could so easily be made perfect. Intrinsically,

they are living, growing things—quite different from the oils on an artist's canvas or the furniture in the house.

The kind of garden I have in mind is not cluttered with things. The garden I am thinking of is a simple but extremely satisfying place, devoted to plants and the experience of being outdoors, and a person's enjoyment of both. Only that person can finally plan such a garden.

If you are such a person, you should do the planting as well as the planning so you know what is going on in your garden. Planting something, then watching it grow in a richly prepared soil of your own concoction is the basic charm of gardening. Framing the plant or tree or shrub so it sits in the garden like a sparkling jewel in an exquisite setting is the challenge of planning, or garden design.

Perhaps the hardest part of planning a garden is simply recognizing all the possibilities. There are so many, yet they are so seldom fully employed. Here we have a whole box of crayons to play with, but when it comes time to begin the planning, we take out only the black. What crayons never got out of the box?

The purpose of this book is also to look at some of the possibilities in a garden—the play of light, the warmth of the sun, the sense of surprise, the drama that is possible. These ingredients are often overlooked perhaps because, as adults, we are wary of making mistakes and prefer the safe approach. Given a big box of crayons, most of us would stick to the safe colors, while a child wouldn't hesitate to use every crayon in the box. Neither should we. And if there is one absolute rule in gardening it is that almost everything takes its own time. The best plants grow slowly, and so do the best plans.

Garden Visit

THE SECRET GARDEN

The centerpiece of this garden in Santa Monica is a secret. It cannot be seen from the street, even though it is in front of the house and abuts the sidewalk. You do not get to it in a direct line, but must work your way up a wide walk into a small courtyard and through narrow passageways. You may not even see it until you are inside the house since the entrance to this secret garden is situated obliquely. But along the way you will discover some of the possibilities inherent in a garden.

The entry walk (page 15) only hints at what is to come. It is wide, expansive, and wonderfully planted. The designer, Nancy Goslee Power, sees it as a transitional space. She believes in "good, generous entrances" and favors a straight line to the door, or in this

case to the front gate. There is no leisurely curve or tricky paving to trip you up, but this is not a boulevard either. Mounding, chaparral-like plants (but from other Mediterranean climates), including a huge silvery licorice plant, *Helichrysum petiolatum*, and billowy lavender, creep onto the paving, softening the severity of a straight path.

The colors of the walk, walls, and gate in front of you are muted and earthy but colorful nonetheless. These are not "grayed" but "umbered" colors, a touch of that muddy brown pigment having been added to the paint. The plants are gray and glaucous green, the flowers subtle, and the foliage scented. Even the normally boisterous bougainvillea that covers the entry area is a soft, pale pinkish-white variety. Inside the gate the colors become a shade brighter until they reach a burnt-orange bougainvillea draped over the front door. This is 'Orange King,' which in time will mix with a bougainvillea named 'California Gold' still struggling to grow out of the shadow of the house.

In the center of this inner courtyard, tucked into the space left by the L-shaped house, is a Spanish-style pool in keeping with the architecture. It is kept full to the brim, a perfect mirror for the bougainvillea that you see as you enter or for the huge chimney above the outdoor fireplace at the left. The pool, so full and wet it has water on its rim and puddles at its feet, makes the courtyard feel cool on hot days, while the fireplace, aglow after sundown, warms those chilly coastal nights. The courtyard was designed to be the center of the house—a true outdoor room—since the house is quite small.

But, wait, you've walked right past the entrance to the secret garden. You

Just past the entry garden and foyer is this secluded patio, with a fireplace to warm the chilly Santa Monica nights, and a small pool filled to overflowing to cool the warm summer days. A bougainvillea named 'Orange King' spills from the veranda roof and a climbing rose named 'Mermaid' covers the wall. They are the wallpaper in this outdoor room.

Ordinary Palos Verdes stone is used elegantly for the steps and walls that were laid up dry without mortar. Alchemilla pectinata, with its crinkled foliage, creeps through the cracks. The cloud of pink flowers belongs to a Mexican evening primrose.

Separating the inner patio from the street is this wall, nearly obscured by luxuriant plantings of a dark purple lavender, the gray stems and white flowers of a lychnis, and tiny white Santa Barbara daisies. A variegated New Zealand flax stands guard at the gate.

can see it through a little window in the courtyard wall, so you know it's there, but you must back up a few feet and go through the gate just to the left of the entrance gate to get to it. When one gate is open, the other is hidden; that's how you missed it.

Now you come out under a stunning subtropical shrub with smoky purple flowers, *Iochroma cyaneum*, and, surprise, this garden is sunken as well as secret. This is one reason you do not notice it from the street, for it is actually lower than the sidewalk, even though the house is considerably higher. That garden is so low that the pool in the bottom does not drain but floods the sunken section. When this

happens (after a hard rain), the fish sneak out and nibble at the plants growing between the paving stones, and then retreat back to their pool when the water eventually recedes and soaks into the soil.

The front yard remained unimproved for quite a while until the idea of sinking it came to Nancy Power. It promised to liven up a potentially monotonous area that is quite small and was as flat as the proverbial pancake. The garden could have felt cramped because of the hedges surrounding it, but sinking it changed "cramped" to "cozy."

"It doesn't take much—step down two feet and it is surprising how dif-

ferent the space feels," observes Power. "You forget where it is (right next to the street) and the whole sense of scale changes."

The retaining wall is of Palos Verdes stone, often undistinguished, but looking surprisingly fine in this garden, perhaps because of the way the wall is built. It is laid up dry, without mortar, and steps back steeply. Despite lectures by masons to the effect that this is not how to build a wall, Power insisted it be done this way, pointing out drawings in a Gertrude Jekyll folio showing fine English walls. The wall works admirably at holding the soil in place and, as a bonus, makes a stage or perch for some of her favorite plants.

Because this is her own garden, Power broke one of her strict planting design rules—never use just one plant. Other designers call it "the rule of three's and five's," believing that three or five of anything looks better than one. But here "there are lots of one's," Power confesses.

This secret garden is, in fact, a plant person's paradise, chock-full of fascinating candidates for a garden. The most subtle of these, and one of Power's better discoveries on a nursery-shopping adventure, was found at the elegant Western Hills Nursery in Northern California. It's an *Alchemilla,* which has rooted into the mortarless joints of the wall next to the steps

leading into the garden, with exquisitely crinkled leaves and coloring a near match for the stone. This is the way much of the garden holds itself together—colors are controlled and build on a theme.

The inspiration for a secret garden came from the children's classic of the same name by Frances Hodgson Burnett, and the idea of creating one was hatched during a stay in England. The primary purpose was to improve the view from the house. As in many houses of this style and vintage, the largest window looked out onto the street, which wasn't much of a view. Now that window frames the secret garden and its still, moss-green pool.

A garden notebook should be the beginning of your garden as well as its permanent record. Anything that might help with the planning or planting should be included so it can be quickly found. In the author's own notebook, dried flowers and a photograph are reminders of a favorite color scheme. Rather than draw plans, build a three-dimensional model like the one shown here. These walls are made of foam-core, readily available at art supply stores. A scale ruler is a big help when making models or drawing plans.

WHERE TO BEGIN: THE NOTEBOOK

So, where does one begin to plan a garden? On paper, by taking note of what you have, what you would like, and what you may have seen somewhere else that pleases you.

These notes will be the beginning of a garden notebook, scrapbook, and diary that will direct your efforts. Most good gardeners keep one, and some have turned into literature, but what you want to accumulate are ideas, not just words. Take snapshots of the garden as it looks now, from vantage points that are important to you and your life—out the kitchen window for instance. Take photographs of plants you admire in other gardens, or in botanic gardens, and make a note of when they are in flower and how large they are (an important consideration as we'll see later). If you don't know what the plant is, you can show the photographs to a nurseryman later when it's time to purchase these furnishings for the garden.

When you see a picture of a garden you like in a magazine, cut the photograph out and paste it in this notebook; make notes of garden pictures seen in books, or photocopy the pages. Samples of wood stains, paving, and pieces of gravel can also find their way into your files. In fact, it is a good idea to start a little collection of these manmade things in some corner of the garden so you can refer to them and live with them for a while, to see if the color or texture is as pleasing as you first thought.

Live With It Living with it for a while is a very important part of planning your garden. Many expert designers suggest that you first live in a garden for at least a year so you can observe the seasons change and can discover where the most important parts of the garden for you actually are.

If you simply can't wait to get started, garden for a year with annuals and other short-lived plants. This will give you a feel for the weather and the soil, but you won't be committed to any long-term projects. I can guarantee that after living in a garden for a year you will feel differently about it.

Plans Are for the Birds What you do not want to do is draw plans on paper. Plans are only two-dimensional, and a case can be made that gardens have become a lot less interesting since professional designers started drawing plans. Most of the world's great gardens were never planned on paper. Their designers conceived them by walking about and deciding where in the earth this or that should go. Plans drawn on paper show a design that only the birds can see, from above. Instead, keep your feet on the ground and learn to envision a garden from ground level, as you might see it when walking through it.

Gardens are three-dimensional creations, but put them on a flat piece of paper and that all-important third dimension is lost. How can you tell on a plan if a tree is so low it must be ducked under, or if a shrub is tall enough to hide something? You want to be able to get a sense of what being in the garden is actually like, but you can't experience it on a paper plan.

For example, paths that are fun to follow often look awkward from a bird's view; they can only be designed by laying them out on the ground and then trying them out. Because of perspective, even formal paths that are as straight as an arrow look very different on the ground than on a plan. On the ground, the lines seem to converge in the distance; they do not on a plan.

Make a Model Instead If you want to test your ideas before you actually begin the work, try building a model of the garden. Use scraps of cardboard or the much fancier foam-core board used by architects. Make a base, complete with slope if your garden is on rolling terrain, then add the fences and the walls of the house. Be sure to put doors and windows in your walls so you can actually look out onto the garden from inside your model house. Foam-core (available at art supply stores) is especially easy to work with because it can be cut quickly with a single-edged razor blade and a steel rule, is rigid enough to stand on its own, and can be glued in a snap with ordinary white glue. Cardboard is cheaper (use an old box) but is hard to cut and glue.

You will find this model very helpful because it takes much less imagination to see what the garden will look like in three dimensions. You can make little trees and bushes and move them around until they create a vista you like. You can even plant little beds of flowers and, more than that, you can take this model outdoors and see just what will be in shade and what will be in sun at various times of the year.

Plans on paper do have their use, but they should be the last thing you do. They are, in effect, a big notepad that you can refer to during construction, covered with important dimen-

sions and names of plants. But your master plan had better be a model.

CLIMATE AND LOCATION

Location determines what can be grown in a garden and what creature comforts may be necessary. Most people are aware of their climate—is it hot or cold, or both, or not especially either—but they may not be aware of what can be grown in their climate. Though part of the fun of gardening is trying to do what oughtn't to be possible, these adventures should be the exception and, in general, a garden should reflect its climate. The United States Department of Agriculture pub-

A. *On a hillside a fence or wall acts like a dam, trapping cold air behind it.*

B. *Cold air rolls off a roof, while plants tucked under the eaves are protected.*

C. *The north side of the house is always cool and shady; the south side hot and sunny. There are plants that will be happiest in either extreme.*

D. *Cold air runs down hills and collects in valley bottoms; thus hillsides are often warmer than valleys in winter and may be considered "banana belts."*

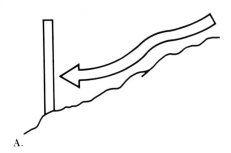

A.

B.

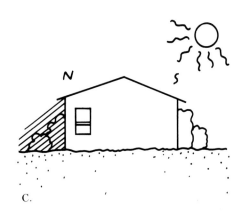

C.

D.

lishes a map that divides the country into ten climate zones, which take into account how cold it gets in winter. But the heat of summer is just as limiting a factor, as is the amount of moisture in the air. This information is not as readily available.

In California, the climate is complex enough to have prompted the state to further subdivide this unique area into twenty-four distinct climatic zones, from seashore to mountaintop to desert. California gardeners can find these zones listed on the excellent maps in the *Sunset Western Garden Book*, and in this dictionary of gardening the description of each plant includes a note indicating in which of these zones it does best.

Take Notes on Your Garden's Climate
Your garden notebook can help if you begin to write down what you observe about your climate, and what you hear from others on the subject. Gardeners, more than most people, like to talk about the weather and its peculiarities. There are a few things in particular to look for. Gardens contain microclimates that can affect plant and human happiness. Cold air tends to settle, to flow to the lowest point. It behaves much like water and can even become entrapped behind a wall. Atriums, surrounded on all four sides by walls, tend to become filled with cold air much like a bathtub with water. Fences that are built too solid dam cold air moving down a slope. Eaves on a house and trees with overhanging branches tend to protect plants from cold by insulating them from the sky.

Plants close to the ground are most likely to be blackened by frost because cold air collects near the ground. This is why small tender saplings are more likely to succumb to winter cold than taller, older trees.

Microclimates Look for pockets of warmth or cold early in the morning and in the middle of the day, and on a rough plan of your garden make a note of their location. In this way, you may find the perfect place for a certain plant that needs more or less warmth. Or you may find the places to avoid. You may also discover the spot in all your garden that you would most enjoy —the future home of a patio or deck.

Perhaps the most obvious differences, or microclimates, in a garden are the north and south sides of a house, the one being cold even in summer, the other hot. Many gardeners have observed that some plants will grow in such a cool or warm spot, whereas they will not grow out in the garden, away from the house. Citrus, for example, needs extra warmth, camellias need a little extra coolness or shade.

This north-south difference is also marked on sloping ground, the north side of a hill being much cooler than the south. In California, this is apparent because most of the trees and shrubs tend to grow on north-facing slopes, while south-facing slopes tend to have grasses or the toughest of shrubs that can withstand the hot, dry summer sun.

Banana Belts Be aware that gardens planted on the sides of hills are in an environment drained of cold air and therefore they experience milder winter temperatures. These hillsides are often called "banana belts" because they are just enough warmer to grow tender plants, though maybe not warm enough actually to grow bananas. The cold air flows down to the valley bottoms, where it collects. In Southern California, valleys became the home of deciduous fruit-tree orchards that needed more winter cold, while citrus and avocados that thrive in warm, dry climates took to the hillsides.

Breezes, Santa Anas, and Other Seasonal Winds Wind also plays a part in the garden's location and should be taken into account. Prevailing winds that cool a garden and help circulate the air should be encouraged to enter. Do not inadvertently block these with tall plantings or solid walls. Good air movement in a garden is surprisingly important to the health of plants—as well as to the comfort of people. Still air fosters plant diseases, while breezes discourage them. For this reason it is often difficult to grow things in small or enclosed places, or in corners. Plants particularly susceptible to disease, such as roses, should be out in the open where air circulates freely, in the best of light.

Ferocious seasonal winds, such as Southern California's notorious Santa Ana or devil wind, are another matter and should be excluded from the garden as much as possible by plantings or structures. Typically, these winds come from an entirely different direction than is normal. In the case of a Santa Ana, the wind comes from the north or east, while the prevailing wind is from the west. So plan your walls and tall plantings accordingly.

LIGHT

Light is perhaps the most important influence on a garden, not just because it is so necessary for plant growth, but because the garden's very appearance depends upon it. Think of these various kinds of light and how different the mood is of each:

The soft morning sun, skimming low across the garden, distinctly rosy col-

ored as it adds a pink highlight to just the tips of plants.

The warm glow of the late afternoon sun that turns even pink flowers a shade of orange.

The cool, colorless light of an overcast day, or the dark gray-blue light just before rain.

The midday summer sun that makes almost no shadows and bleaches all but the brightest colors.

Each of these lighting conditions is remarkably different and each will give the garden a remarkably different look, even if nothing else changed. If no leaves fell in winter and no flowers bloomed in spring, you could probably tell by the light what time of year it was, and what time of day. If you think these are givens and not something to remember when planning a garden, consider these points:

Flower beds can be designed to catch either the morning or the afternoon light, whichever is your favorite or coincides with your time at home and out in the garden.

Pink and blue flowers seem to glow on overcast days, but are almost invisible in the bright light of noon on a clear summer's day; yellow and orange blooms, on the other hand, look their best on a sunny day when the sun is high overhead, but look oddly out of place on a cool, cloudy day.

There is almost no point planting pink or blue flowers for midsummer, when they will not show to advantage. Perhaps that is why so many bloom in spring, when the light is low and cool and days overcast, so they can look their best.

Summer's flowers naturally tend toward yellow or orange, taking full advantage of that bright yellow sun and deep blue sky.

Most discoveries about garden light

Tulips especially, but also ranunculus, love to grow in just a smattering of shade, as do these plantings beneath the birch trees. Bare in winter when the spring bulbs are growing, the trees leaf out just as the bulbs come into bloom, protecting them from a spring sun that sometimes becomes too hot. In summer, when the bulbs are dormant, the fully leafed out birches keep them cool.

are made by accident—you happen to notice that something you planted looks great right now because the sun is where it is. Make a note about which plants look best in each lighting situation. Some flowers are prettiest when lit from above, but many more take on a special glow when lit from behind or from the side. Write down which look especially dramatic with the sun coming through the petals or which look extra rich in the ruddy light of a setting sun. If you are on an early morning walk and notice that the Iceland poppies in a neighbor's yard look wonderfully dramatic because the low sun is lighting every petal as if it were a piece of stained glass, make a note of this, and next time, plant your poppies to stand between you and the morning sun.

Look for pools of sun that might spotlight certain plants; try some beds facing east, some west, and some south. A variety of lighting situations will make the garden change throughout the day and throughout the year, as stage lighting can make changes in the same scene.

Painters and photographers have noticed that the light in various parts of the world can be remarkably different, and gardeners who have toted their cameras along on garden tours to other climates have probably seen the same thing. Using the same film and techniques employed at home often results in poor garden photographs when the light is different. To make your garden look its best, take advantage of your climate's unique light.

SHADOWS AND SHADE

If at all possible, one does not want to garden in the shade. Most plants do not like it, though some may tolerate it. There are enough challenges in gardening without taking on this one.

There are degrees of shadow—the deep shade under a big, dense tree may make it impossible for plants to grow, but the dappled shade found under a tree with a more open canopy may be just right. Many bulbs seem to do best in the lightest of shade, and many flowers (even roses) exhibited at shows are grown in some shade. It makes the colors brighter and the flowers larger, though the plants may produce fewer flowers and they will certainly grow taller and looser, their stems floppier, and leaves spaced further apart.

In general, however, most plants crave all the sun they can get, while people would just as soon stay out of it. This suggests that it might be better to put your patio in the shade of a tree or house, and leave the sunny spots for plants. Very shady places are also good for a toolshed, a woodpile, or anything that does not need sun to grow.

A Shade Map Before going much further with your planning, you should map the shadows in your garden, so you know precisely where they fall. This is easily done during one sunny day. On a rough drawing of your garden, color the areas that are in shadow at about 10 A.M., then with a different colored pencil at noon, and again, with yet another color at 3 P.M. You will now see clearly where the sunniest spots in the garden are (they will not be colored at all on your plan) and where the shadiest places are (they will have the most colors).

Lengthening Shadows You may want to make a map for summer and one for winter because the sun does not stay in the same place. In Southern California, in the middle of summer, the sun is 79 degrees above the horizon at high

While most plants don't like to grow in shade, a few thrive if the shade does not become too dark. The avocado is one of the most difficult trees to garden under, but prune some lower branches, thus raising the canopy, and enough light sneaks through for impatiens. Shady areas are also good choices for paving and places to sit.

SHADE MAP

A. *Drawing lines with colored pencils, map the shadows in your garden at different times of the day so you know which areas are shady and which are not. Here we see the shadows at 10 a.m., noon, and 3 p.m. Where the lines overlap most densely there will be deepest shade, the most difficult places to grow things in the garden.*

B. *In summer, when the sun is high, shadows fall directly beneath the object casting them.*

C. *In winter the shadows lengthen and an object may cast its shadow well out in the garden; but the sun also slants under the object—a tree in this case—so normally shaded areas are suddenly in sunlight, though it is the weak sun of winter. It's a good idea to make a shade map for both winter and summer.*

A.

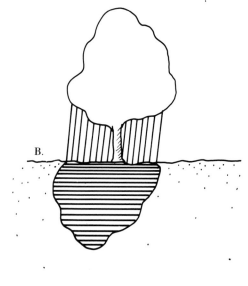

B.

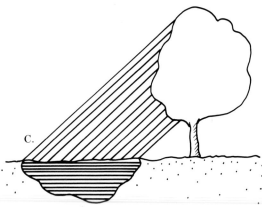

C.

noon, nearly overhead; in winter, at the same time of day, it is only 33 degrees above the horizon, half as high in the sky. This means that shadows are more than six times longer in winter. Your house's shadow may only extend three feet into the garden in summer, but it stretches about eighteen feet in winter. Plants that grow in sun all summer are suddenly in shade all winter. This can pose a few problems for the gardener because most plants that can grow in the shade do not want suddenly to find themselves in the sun, and vice versa. You can avoid this drastic change of conditions by using plants that do their growing and flowering in summer, when they can be in full sun, and are dormant or resting in winter, when they will have to be in shadow.

Roses are dormant in winter, but by the time they begin to leaf out, the sun has climbed higher in the sky and they are in sunlight. *Pittosporum tobira* 'Wheeler's Dwarf' is a slightly different example: While it does not go dormant in winter, it only grows in late spring when the sun is high enough not to effect the new growth.

A Secret Spot The reverse occurs under trees or overhead structures such as a patio covering. Plants that grow in the shade, when the summer sun is high overhead, are bathed in soft light all winter as the sun sneaks under the canopy of foliage or the patio roof. In fact, a favorite place for tulips is under the very edge of a tree's leafy canopy. They grow in the sun during winter and spring, but flower in increasing shade, which helps the flowers last longer and bloom more brightly. When this area is completely shaded in summer, the tulips are finished, and their place is taken by plants that can grow in shade. Impatiens often are volunteers for the job.

CHAPTER

2

FROM
THE GROUND
UP

Paths are absolutely essential to the design of a garden; they define its very style. The path on page 27 sets a casual, informal tone for its garden and begs for further exploration. What's around the corner? The bright golden coreopsis is a focal point when in flower, while a comfortable garden bench is inviting at all seasons.

In this chapter, you will also discover some intriguing alternatives to a lawn, such as the checkerboard hedge on pages 24–25. It provides open space (and considerable interest) in a small, urban garden. The gray squares are Santolina chamaecyparissus *and the green* S. virens.

THE IMPORTANCE OF PATHS

The paths through a garden are too often an afterthought, when they should be considered first. But before we plan our paths, let's start fresh. Try to block out all previous ideas of what a path should or should not be. Do not see a path as a narrow band of concrete that gets you to the front door or down the side yard. Do not see the lawn as a path. True, it gets you almost anywhere in the garden, but you are going to get your feet wet or muddy walking across it, the wheelbarrow is going to bog down, and, more to the point, the lawn lacks any direction or focus so the eye tends to wander nervously looking for something to settle on.

Try instead to see a path as "the tracks the eye rides upon," as Hugh Johnson has so neatly put it, because this is precisely what a path does more than anything else—it guides the eye through the garden as if it were riding on steel rails, and only later do the feet follow. Paths certainly have their utilitarian purposes, but in most gardens it isn't too important if they lead you somewhere or not because you can't wander very far afield on the average piece of property. The important thing is that a path must appear to lead somewhere. And, the further away it seems to lead, the better.

In garden design, the shortest distance between two points is not always the best place for a path. It is better to draw out the experience, to prolong that all-too-short journey through the garden, which, while you're taking it, makes the garden seem much larger than it is, satisfying a craving shared by nearly every gardener for a little more acreage. Japanese gardens often contain tortuous paths—they seem designed to trip you up—but no one really wants you to fall on your face,

just slow down and notice what is around you.

While a path can twist and turn in its routing, it should not be too narrow. In fact, a path can never be too wide. A four-foot-wide path is about the minimum. It will barely accommodate two people walking side-by-side—or a wheelbarrow. Visually, anything narrower makes a garden seem cramped and the gardener a little stingy with his paving materials. Paths give a garden focus and structure. A strong path tells you where to look, and along the way you discover the other parts of a garden. First, decide where the path is to go, and the other elements of a garden will begin to fall into place.

Formal or Informal? It could be said that a formal path makes a formal garden, an informal path, an informal garden. A formal garden is one that looks distinctly man-made, where most of the lines are straight; an informal plan is more natural in appearance, with most of the lines curved, though it may be just as contrived. Classical gardens were formal in plan until the eighteenth century, when the English began making them more natural in appearance. Formal gardens did not disappear overnight, and they are still very much with us. But from the late eighteenth century until today, most gardens have depended on curving lines and curving paths to achieve a natural look.

In today's small, enclosed gardens, where no distant view or vista is available, formal plans once again make a great deal of sense. Where the garden area is almost roomlike, a rectilinear arrangement of the spaces—paths, flower beds, patios—looks less contrived than a plan that seeks to imitate nature, which is seldom forced to work on such a small canvas. In a formal

A formal path needs a focal point at its destination. At the end of this ample path of decomposed granite (better known as "d.g."), ivy spilling from an antique urn makes an elegant center of attention. Note how this path's thoroughly compacted, gritty soil is mounded, the better to shed water.

A distant pool of light is the focal point for the formal brick path on page 29, beckoning one to explore further. Foxgloves and dainty coral bells line the way.

garden plan, one path dominates the scene and leads somewhere within sight. It might run from the back door to the back fence, in a straight line, and at its end is a distinct focal point. In classical gardens, this was often a statue or fountain, and these are still good candidates for the job. Whatever the focal point, it must stand out from its surroundings.

A Focal Point for a Formal Garden   In a smallish garden, the focal point is very important and some time should be spent to find just the perfect object. It should be complicated enough so that every detail is not visible from the other end of the path—you want visitors to come out into the garden curious to see just what this thing is. In my own garden I used a very large pot

The formal and informal garden plans on this page illustrate in a nutshell how the key differences are determined by the paths. One curves and disappears around a corner, the other is straight and focused, in this case, on a small fountain set off to one side.

In a turnabout from conventional planning, the spa and pool on page 31 were pushed into a corner and the rose garden was planted next to the house. The plan for this garden is classically formal—paths are at right angles and as straight as arrows.

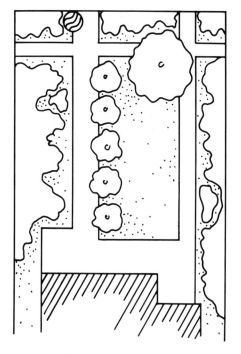

A FORMAL PLAN

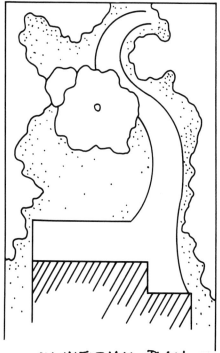

AN INFORMAL PLAN

filled with water, fish, and aquatic plants. The container is simple enough to stand out from its surroundings without being an obvious eyesore, and the plants and fish are of sufficient interest to coax even nongardeners to go and see what's blooming or how the fish are faring. Visitors are always drawn to the far end of the garden.

In large formal gardens, the focal point is often the distant horizon. The focal point at Vaux-le-Vicomte—the most famous formal French garden that led Louis XIV to appropriate the landscape designer André Le Nôtre for his own gardens at Versailles—is a perfectly proportioned opening in the trees framing the vista of a distant hill. A later owner added a huge statue of Hercules, which overstates the point.

In a plan for a formal garden, there may be other paths leading off in other directions; the main path may be set anywhere in the garden (even running from one side to the other if that is the longest dimension and main axis of the garden), but that path should be the first thing the visitor discovers so it can immediately organize the garden for the eye. There should be no doubt where to look and at what.

No End in Sight In an informal plan, the path should not have an obvious end, any more than a trail through the woods has an obvious end. It should appear to go on and on and simply disappear around a corner, with no end in sight. The object of our attention at the end of an informal path is not so much a focal point as a vanishing point—we are attracted to that point when our view is obscured. Like a trail through the woods, this path must also make some sense. There must be a reason for those curves, something that is overlooked in many plans for an informal garden. On a trail, curves

exist so the trail can go around trees or boulders, or follow contours of the land.

In gardens, paths often curve for no reason, and they end up looking quite unnatural because there is no organic purpose for their behavior, and the ever-questioning mind wonders—even unconsciously—"why do these paths wander all over the place?" It is easy enough to invent some *raison d'être* for this meandering: Mound up the soil in the beds that border the path so it seems to be following the low ground, as a stream will do; or place boulders in the way, so it must curve around them, or trees, or a mass of flowers.

To make a path without end requires some space, so formal plans are perhaps to be favored in tight places, though it is possible to fool the eye that your meandering path goes on and on. Simply let it curve around a corner or some tall shrubs, and out of sight. Hide its end and few will be the wiser.

The Draw Both kinds of path tend to draw one out into the garden—the formal plan has that fascinating object at its end, urging one to investigate, and the informal plan teases one into trying to discover what's around the corner—precisely what you want and one good reason for a strong path. Visit a garden that has only a large lawn area in back, and no distinct path, and most people end up standing by the back door, never venturing further. Visit a garden with a bold path, and most people spend only seconds by the back door before heading off on their adventure through the garden. Of course, there is much more to garden design, but a strong path is a great start. Once it has drawn you into the garden, you must make sure that something else is out there that makes the trip worthwhile. And that is the rest of garden design.

Garden Visit

A FORMAL PLAN FOR ROSES

One could say that roses have not been treated right by us gardeners. In recent years they have been relegated to their own barren corner of the yard, like royalty in exile. Though rose bushes have the grandest flowers and bloom most of the year, though they have colors more vibrant and varied than other flowers, and though they have not fallen from popularity in the least, they are most often forced to grow alone—away from the other lovely lords and ladies of the garden—in the humblest of surroundings. There they are kept for cutting, while the hoi polloi of marigolds and the like are planted in the best places. Never mind that the gardener might lavish attention on his roses, planting them with great care, pruning and primping them in the proper season, and pam-

pering them in general—they deserve to be given pride of place. And lately there are a few rose fanciers who are seeking to do just that.

Landscape architect Mark Berry of Pasadena and Aptos, California, was fortunate enough to find one such rose fancier as a client, fortunate because the client sought a formal solution to the problem of where to put roses, and Berry favors formal gardens. This formal garden is small, located behind a typical ranch-style house. The garden boasts a delightful collection of thirty-four rose bushes, and they are not crowded together in a corner of the yard. Instead, the swimming pool that the client also fancied was put in the corner, so what you see from the living room windows is a garden of roses.

The garden is still quite young in these photographs but that points out a seldom-considered benefit of a formal

To soften the hard edges of the paths in the garden below, the designer used the delicate shapes of star jasmine for the low hedges that form the borders. At path's end (just out of camera range) a bench attracts the eye.

The informal garden at the right has nary a hard edge in sight. The path curves around the house and disappears, but it is enticing and the wisteria-covered arch at the end only makes it more so. To the left of the path are a mix of tall cannas, statice, salvia, and annual phlox.

plan: The straight lines and precise edges give formal gardens a finished look right from the start, even before the plants grow up or the hedges fill in.

The plan is as linear as you can get, and it has the opposite effect of what one might expect—it makes the garden look larger than life. At the end of the major path is a humble garden bench, which serves well as an inviting focal point. To add some complexity and interest, benches are set in little alcoves along the paths. The garden is surrounded by tall leafy shrubs that screen out neighboring yards and is crisscrossed with low hedges of star jasmine. Berry likes the jasmine hedges because they are a gentle, billowy contrast to the very linear, rigid paths; and he points out that, though the plan is very sharp and formal, the materials are all soft, even the paving —a 3½-inch-deep layer of decomposed granite. The low hedges have another benefit: while the tops of rose bushes are something to admire, the bottoms beg to be hidden, which the hedges do admirably. Hedges might be considered formal attire for roses.

Garden Visit

AN INFORMAL PLAN

Gardens are often called living canvasses upon which the gardener paints with plants. If that is so, most of us are content with fairly simple compositions—a few bold strokes of color against a background of uniform green—simple but satisfying, until one sees what are the other possibilities.

Here, for instance, is a garden sure to inspire greater flights of horticultural fancy. This is the Poway, California, garden of professional illustrator Karen Kees, who increasingly spends time away from her paints and palette, devoting it instead to garden design. The artist shows in the fearless, almost brazen, combinations of colors that one might not expect to make such good companions—such as pink with orange—and in the sheer exuberance of it all. The Kees garden is also an excellent example of an informal plan. The paths go nowhere in particular,

but they enticingly disappear around corners so you can't help but follow them. At the far end of one path is an additional tease, a tipsy trellis smothered with vines that looks like a gateway into yet another, surely wonderful, part of the garden, though actually the garden doesn't extend much further.

This is, in fact, an average-size yard in the middle of a housing tract; it's not as rural as it appears. The walls and roofs in the background belong to other houses, but most of that view is screened by dense plantings so you are hardly aware of the neighbors' existence. And the foreground is so convincingly rustic that you don't question its location in the country. The paths are gravel with stones and boulders that look as though they have been washed up along its sides, suggesting a stream-bed rather than a garden path.

Everywhere the plants threaten to overgrow, if not overwhelm, the garden. They creep onto the paths, sometimes growing right in the middle of them, climb every wall, scamper across the roof, and reach for the sky. The reason you can't see around the corners, and the reason the paths wander, is that they are following the low ground between mounds of soil, which also provide excellent drainage for the flowers and a platform so they are better viewed. If the plants look richly satisfied, it has to do with the soil preparation: The beds are half organic amendment and half soil, a luxurious mix for a luxuriant paint-box planting.

PAVING POSSIBILITIES

Probably no other material used in a garden is as important as the paving you walk on, because it is so visually dominating. The texture and color establishes a look for the garden—a rough texture and earthy colors make the garden appear natural; smooth textures and brighter colors indicate that the garden is man-made. The best way to choose a paving material is to buy some samples and leave them lying about in the garden while you continue your planning. Generally, the best paving is not laid as a solid mass but is made up of individual pieces, such as bricks, large tiles, and stepping stones. Don't overlook compacted earth as a paving material, such as the decomposed granite used a lot in California, and do be aware that the glare of the sun off some materials (concrete in particular) can be bothersome.

A good method of paving is to put the material on top of a base of sand, with sand filling the gaps between pavers so rain can run through to the

Where does an informal path go? The idea is not to let anyone find out—it should appear to go on forever. Here it flows like a dry stream through a bed of daylilies and a wild mix of flowers. Gravel makes an appropriate paving.

Even the decidedly rectangular shape of common bricks can make an informal path, like the meandering beauty on this page. This classic paving pattern flows through the garden. The bricks are laid on sand and plants grow in the cracks, further softening the composition.

Grass is not always the appropriate choice, aesthetically or environmentally, for covering ground. On a sunny hillside in the Santa Monica Mountains, two pads of decomposed granite provide open space and a warm, dry place to sun. The strong row of Italian cypress in the background adds to the Mediterranean mood.

When drought-resistant plantings are called for, something other than lawn grasses must be used. In the garden on page 37 a combination of gravel and tiles was successfully employed. Sedum spectabile is the pink-flowered accent.

roots, which are inevitably underneath. Should those roots begin to lift the paving, or should the ground settle, individual pavers set on sand will not crack or break, and they can be lifted up and relaid.

LAWNS, PATIOS, AND OTHER OPEN SPACES

When you have mentally laid out your paths—and perhaps plotted them on paper—it is time to think about the other low, open spaces in the garden, the meadows, if you will, that border our trail through the woods. I like this analogy because it helps put lawns, and even patios, in perspective. So often lawns are laid down as if they were carpeting, from wall to wall. But if you think of them as meadow areas, they become much more flexible. They can then be large or small, long, narrow, or wide-spreading, regular or

irregular in shape. They don't have to be contiguous but can be scattered through the garden like the little glades discovered on a hike through the woods.

Your Personal Park Lawns are open areas, which keep a space from feeling cramped, personal parks, or meadows that can be walked on, played on, laid on. They take surprisingly little care; weeds that invade get mowed along with the grass and become part of the lawn. Dead patches are easily replaced and the entire lawn can be watered automatically without a great deal of precision—too much or too little water is not likely to be fatal, as it is with so many other plants. A really good lawn, green, healthy, and weed-free, is no small achievement, but if you are willing to settle for something less than perfection, as are most gardeners, there is nothing as easy to grow as a lawn. Without a doubt, that is why they cover such a large part of so many gardens.

A Real Luxury Some gardeners feel that there is nothing quite as elegant as a rich green carpet of grass. Landscape architect Bill Evans, who designed several of the Disney theme parks and who has a passion for plants, concedes: "One of the real luxuries of garden design is a great sweep of lawn. There is just no substitute for lawn." People with children also know that a lawn saves wear and tear on the house, since children can do their roughhousing outdoors on the soft grass. A strong case could be made that lawns are a necessary part of any garden visited by children.

But are they the only option?

The Shrinking Lawn Lawns are the consummate consumers of water, and so they are coming under close scrutiny in many parts of the country where water must be husbanded. Thriftier lawn grasses are on the way. The thirstiest—bluegrass—is already being replaced by a group of deep-rooted grasses called tall fescues; and in the sunbelt Bermudagrass, St. Augustine, and hybrid zoysias are gaining popularity because they need so little water. New varieties of these subtropical grasses have a much shortened dormant season in winter and finer leaves.

But smaller areas of lawn are likely to replace the lavish spreads of grass in the near future just because styles and ideas about what makes a good garden are changing. Gardeners across the country are already busy digging out sections of lawn to make way for more flowers or vegetables. (Less lawn may even be mandated as some communities consider limiting how much of a garden can be planted to turf.)

Plans A and B For the last hundred years or so gardens have been designed around their lawns. First the largest lawn possible for your space was laid out, then the perimeter planted with flowers or shrubs, and then other features were added. Let's call this Plan A. If you now begin to see lawns as a smaller part of the landscape, or as no part of it at all, the whole balance of the garden begins to change. Let's call this Plan B, which begins with paths and then adds other open spaces. This is exactly how the newer gardens are designed: First the paths are decided on, then the areas on either side—some are lawns, but some are other kinds of paving, including patios.

Patios As far as the design of a garden is concerned, patios can be treated just

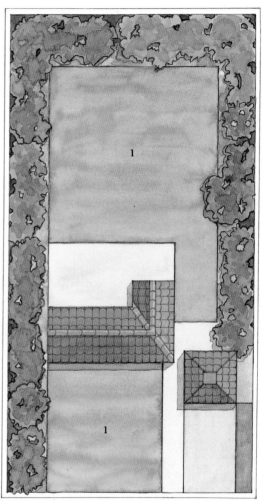

PLAN A

1. Lots of lawn

PLAN B

1. Water feature
2. Small, shaded patio
3. Decomposed granite paths
4. Smaller lawn
5. Smaller patio, now shaded
6. Flowers or ground-covering shrubs
7. Perimeter planting of drought-tolerant shrubs
8. Kitchen garden
9. Paving shaded by tree
10. Ground-covering shrubs

like lawns—they are still simply open spaces, with a harder surface. Patios are generally put right next to the house. They are handy there, functioning like an additional room, and they also help to catch some of the dirt that might get tracked into the house. Patios are often made quite large in the hope that they will be used for entertaining. But as any observer of parties can tell you, people like to congregate in smaller clusters, and when the party takes place in the house, some guests end up in the kitchen, some in the dining room, and only some remain in the living room (where they are all supposed to be).

When the party takes place outdoors, in the garden, the same holds true. So there is good reason to divide one large patio into several smaller, more intimate, areas, as shown in Plan B. When you are alone on one of these smaller patios, it is a cozy experience. And because there are several, each patio can have its own personality, allowing you to pick and choose where you would most like to sit.

No Lost Space Large expanses of paving are avoided in Plan B, but if you make each path wider and scatter several small patios through the garden, you will have the same amount of open, usable, outdoor space as you did with a lawn, while avoiding that parking lot look. Because paving can increase the amount of reflected heat in the garden, in Plan B much of it is shaded by trees or man-made structures. This also cuts down on the glare from paved surfaces. In Plan B, decomposed granite was the choice of paving material for the paths because it has a soft, natural color and feel. Patios are covered with hard materials such as paving stones to make a firm support for furniture.

Plants—any kind of plants other than grasses—cover the rest of the ground, and because the area taken up by lawn is now much smaller, there is room for more interesting plantings, from flowers to vegetables. In Plan B any of these is preferred, because almost any plant uses less water than lawn grasses. Once the balance has been shifted away from the lawn, the garden as a whole is a lot more fun— to walk through, to sit or to work in. There is still enough lawn for rough-and-tumble play, or even a game of catch, but it no longer dominates the landscape.

GROUND COVERS AND OTHER OPTIONS

Instead of a lawn in her Santa Monica garden, landscape designer Nancy Goslee Power planted the delightful checkerboard hedge on pages 24-25. It is a bold solution to providing open space in a little town or city garden. A lawn this small would not make much sense, nor would it be very interesting. Two kinds of the drought-tolerant Mediterranean herb santolina make the alternating pattern: the gray is *Santolina chamaecyparissus* and the green is *S. virens.*

Ground Covers Not a Cure-All Ground covers of various kinds are frequently sold as lawn substitutes and they make handsome little meadows if used sparingly. But having too much of the same ground cover is the surest way to make a garden monotonous—and don't think for a minute it has the advantage of being carefree. A ground cover's undoing is the lowly weed, which finds most low-growing plants easy to invade. Once a weed has taken hold, it is almost impossible to get it out of a ground-cover planting. When ground

covers are used in small patches, it is easier to keep an eye on weeds and get into the beds to remove them.

A Case for Ground Covers Ground covers use much less water than a lawn, and a few can do completely without it. In areas where water is precious, tall, spreading, shrubby ground covers are a good choice, especially where there is a great deal of ground to be covered. Landscape architect Robert Fletcher suggests "large, simple drifts of the same plant" for extensive areas, and he is not talking about the traditional ground covers but of shrubby plants that shade the ground and make invasion by weeds difficult. In test plantings at the University of Arizona, this scheme has been found to be one of the best ways to save water without adding to the heat load of a garden—far more economical with water than a lawn, and much better than paving or gravel mulches for absorbing the sun's heat. These low-growing (two-to-four-feet tall) ground-covering shrubs are planted very far apart, with a thick organic mulch temporarily spread over the ground until the plants fill in. They are planted far apart so they will not grow together too quickly and then mound up higher than they are supposed to be, thus becoming a monstrous maintenance headache. This kind of planting can create a very elegant look while using very little water since each plant can be efficiently irrigated by little drip emitters.

In the Shade One of the best places to plant certain kinds of ground covers is in the shade, where lawns would be difficult to grow. Lawns should always be in sunny spaces, as should most ground covers, but there are a few that will grow happily in shade.

Sometimes it's appropriate to use every kind of ground cover in combination. The lawn is a somewhat drought-resistant tall fescue. Blue star creeper (Laurentia fluviatilis), *thyme, and other creepers fill in between the stone pavers.*

Garden Visit

NO LAWN AT ALL

Sometimes a garden is so small that it is best to plan it with no lawn at all, as is the case with this garden in Southern California's San Fernando Valley. The owners wanted flowers and other interesting plants, and since there was just so much space, they opted to omit the conventional lawn.

Garden designer Chris Rosmini couldn't have been more delighted with this request because her gardens are well known for the exuberance of their plant materials, and she "hasn't left anyone with a lawn in years." Her plan for the garden is almost medieval, with the paths that connect all the parts looking remarkably like the oddly angled streets in a medieval town. The main path sets off from the house at an angle, and you must jog over a few feet to get onto it, but the garden is otherwise formal in plan with a definite end and focal point—a gazebo covered with curving copper pipes. Other lesser focal points anchor the ends of less important paths—

small fountains, quiet pools of water in large containers, or plants spilling fountainlike from large pots.

The areas between the paths are planted with all sorts of wonderful growing things, and the beds are raised to make them easier to enjoy, easier to weed, and—because many of these plants are finicky—to provide the best of soil and drainage. Many ornamental grasses provide graceful accents along the paths and in the beds. Note how plants grow at the foot of the raised beds to soften the paths' edges.

To one side of this grid of pathways is a covered patio, just off a greenhouse room, and there are several other turnouts along the paths where you can stop to enjoy views of the garden (all of the raised beds are enclosed by walls, tall and wide enough to sit on). At the center of the garden the paths converge and provide a central piazza. Another garden ornament yet to be decided on (these things take time) will grace this central bed. For the moment, it is full of flowers, with nary a lawn in sight.

Some gardeners wonder why they should waste space with lawns when there are so many prettier plants. Such was the case in this San Fernando Valley garden, where paths provide the open space and carry you between raised beds that are simply stuffed with fascinating plants, including some grasses—though not the kind you mow. The reddish grass so prominent in the beds is a fountain grass, Pennisetum setaceum 'Rubrum.'

CHAPTER

3
BUILDING THE BACKGROUND

On pages 44–45, the autumn gold of a majestic old ginkgo, with the brilliant red patch of annual bedding salvia behind it, looks most dramatic against the rather plain background of green.

A sketch of the garden will quickly show where background is needed. Note how a neighbor's shrub was "borrowed" to deepen the view in the top sketch.

Rather than wall your garden in with shrubs and trees, as in the sketch at the left, try irregular planting schemes, like the one at the right, with bulges and gaps for a more varied and open look.

A FRAME FOR THE GARDEN

Paths tell us where to look in a garden, but once the eye has followed a path to its conclusion it is free to roam, so the next step in planning a garden is to gently guide the eye to what we might most like to look at next. The background helps decide this by obscuring what could be objectionable—a telephone pole or a neighbor's toolshed for instance—and by emphasizing what is attractive. The background itself, be it fence or foliage, is not what you should be looking at. It is there simply to make other things look good, to focus attention on the flowers or on a fish pond—to make them stand out.

The best backgrounds are rather plain. They might be fences, walls, shrubs, or even trees, if something tall needs to be concealed, and they are often a combination of these. Fences and walls take up the least space but make a rather abrupt boundary for the garden. Planting shrubs in front of them, at least in some places, helps soften this boundary. Shrubs by themselves are perhaps the best background for a garden because they don't look so much like an end as an edge. They do not emphatically state "this is the end of the garden," but actually hint that there might be more beyond. This illusion loses its power if they are planted in a rigid row at the very edge of the garden; then they are too much like a wall themselves.

Take Inventory and Borrow Views
Before building this background, take inventory of the view. Decide what you want to see beyond the garden and what you do not. Try not to find everything objectionable on the other side of your property line or you will box yourself in with shrubbery or walls. Does your neighbor have an especially

handsome tree or shrub? Do not plant in front of it, but take advantage of the gift. This is what designers call a "borrowed landscape," though they usually borrow more than just one plant. You may find more to borrow, too. There may be a nice view across your neighbor's garden that you can borrow by planting so that it becomes part of your view and appears to become part of your garden. Even in the most cramped garden there are probably distant trees or mountains that you can borrow, and you should emphasize these by framing them with your background. If a mountaintop juts up in the distance, let your background dip to take it in.

What you do not want to see will determine where the background must be the deepest or tallest. Telephone poles are a modern curse and are particularly difficult to hide; while only a tree will do the job, it can't be planted too close to the telephone lines or the utility company will be pruning it for you, and they are not going to care what it looks like when they leave. One way to hide a utility pole is to plant far enough in front of it so that, thanks to perspective, even a smallish tree will hide it. In fact, the background for the garden does not have to be as far back as is physically possible. Lining up shrubs along the property line may enclose the garden so abruptly that it feels smaller than it is. Let the background weave in and out along the property line so it makes a soft edge for the garden, and you will be less aware that there is an edge.

It Takes Room Admittedly, this takes room—most shrubs need at least six to eight feet of width to grow in—but the background is so important to the garden's look and feel that space should be found, even if you must sacrifice some of the lawn. To get some idea of what needs hiding and what doesn't, sketch the view of the garden, perhaps from the back door, or photograph it, have prints made, then draw right on the prints with a grease pencil. Hide what you do not like with sketchy trees or shrubs, thereby emphasizing what you do like—what remains.

Remember, try not to box yourself in by hiding everything. Even if only a blank wall stares back at you from the other side of the property line, it is a few feet further away than anything in your garden and therefore will make your garden seem deeper or wider than it really is. Even a few feet of borrowed scenery let the eye escape from the garden's confines. If the garden space becomes roomlike of necessity, it's nice to have a few windows to look out of.

When you have sketched what the view from the back of the house will look like, walk out into the garden, look back at the house, and see if that view can be improved. Gardens do not have just one view, though one may be the most important because it is the one most seen (the view from the kitchen window, for instance).

The garden can frame the house as well as the view, thereby making the house more a part of the garden. If the walls of the house are too bright or too plain, they can be hidden with tall shrubs or covered with vines. A vine running along the eaves can soften the outline of the house. A small tree can break up the straight line of the roof.

Whatever you do, do not completely ring the house with shrubs. This is called "foundation planting" and is deadly to any design. Let the grass, ground covers, or paving come right up to the walls of the house in some spots and the garden will seem larger because you can see further.

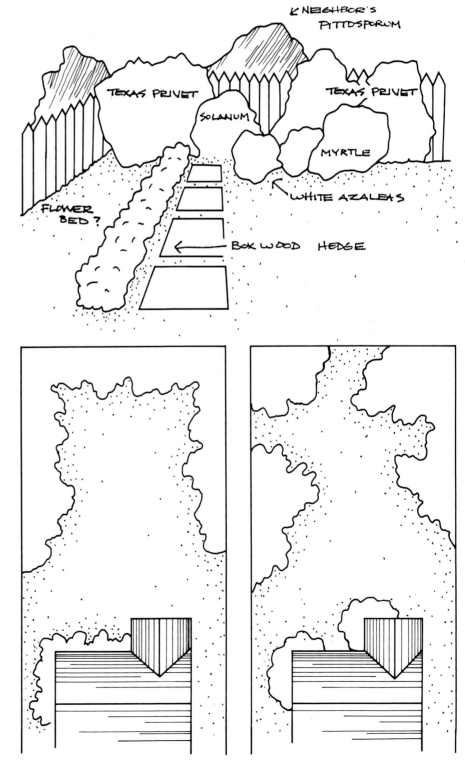

Garden Visit

ALL THE INGREDIENTS

This average-sized backyard has all the ingredients of a good garden. There is a strong path down one side, wide, ample, and as straight as an arrow. A meadowlike lawn flows roughly in the same direction as the garden walk and augments the path as another way to get to the various corners of the garden (though the most heavily worked section can be reached by the path). The lawn, edged by the path and a patio, grows in full sun, so it is healthy and happy. It is just large enough to open up the garden, but not so large that it overwhelms it. There are strong focal points, in this case the mushroom-like straddlestones brought from the Cotswolds in England (where they were used inside piles of hay so air could circulate and keep the stacks

The view from the living room on this page, framed by an umbrella of ivy, encourages the eye to dart to a focal point, the mushroom-shaped straddlestone, purchased in England and now comfortably at home in Pasadena. Tall, bearded iris make a dramatic foil for the stone.

Every nook and cranny is planted, and where there is no soil there are containers brimming with primroses and a white streptocarpus.

The view from the garden back to the house is framed by roses and a red bottlebrush tree. In the distance, a climbing Lady Banks rose helps the arbor harmonize with the rest of the garden. The handsome reddish foliage still further in the background is the neighbor's purple-leaf plum, borrowed to good effect by the gardener. The straddlestones are cleverly used to carry the eye across the garden as lily pads do a frog across a pond.

from rotting). Surrounded by creeping ranunculus, the interesting stones give the eye something to look at right away, while the general profusion of the garden sinks in.

The substantial background of leafy green plants makes the flowers stand out and screens out the neighbors without making the garden feel cramped. A purple-leaf plum in one corner keeps this background from becoming monotonous, and it is worth noting how it adds to the apparent depth of the background planting; it seems much further away than the other property-line shrubs. Though this is a garden for someone who loves flowers and interesting foliage (and uses them in grand bouquets in the house), there is a place to sit in the garden, even room to entertain.

The paving materials have a texture and color that go with the earthy look of the place—decomposed granite (or "d.g." for short) covering the path, and rough bricks making the patio. A clever planting of ivy trained over an old umbrella frame helps the patio look a little special and neatly crops the view of the garden from the house. Seen from the patio, the ivy planting helps to hide part of the two-story house.

The flowers grow in beds that are large enough for them to develop luxuriantly and with a wide variety of heights and textures, greatly adding to the beds' interest. And when one has exhausted the obvious visual treats, there is yet another level of detail— pretty plants tucked here and there, or in pots, waiting to be discovered on second look. This is a gardener's garden (it belongs to Joan Banning), in a gardener's town (Pasadena), where even the humble garden hose has an honored place and looks completely at home.

For colors to come alive, they need to be viewed against a simple background. Here, citrus and other plain green shrubs make the colors in this border pop out. The flowers include tall delphiniums, bright yellow coreopsis, and red penstemon. This border is typical of many in California in the way in which it mixes annuals with perennials to good effect.

KEEP IT SIMPLE AND LEAVE ENOUGH ROOM

The background for a garden should not distract from the garden's features, nor should it be too obvious. If it is too strong, it will tend to constrict the space; if too complicated, it will compete with the things that you really want to look at, be they flowers or a splashing fountain. The importance of a background is obvious in photographs. The next time you look at a garden picture in a magazine or book, take note of the background and see how plain it is. Photographers speak of "separation." The plants they are photographing must "separate" from their background—they must stand out— or the whole composition becomes a hodgepodge. What works for the camera usually works for the eye.

Shrubs Are Best Shrubs are the best possible background because their green color makes them a part of the garden and harmonizes with other plantings. The best background shrubs should be dark green with leaves of medium size, neither too big and bold, nor too small and delicate. If they flower, those flowers should be small and inconspicuous; most shrubs used for background plantings have simple little white flowers.

Although it is tempting to use shrubs that are colorful, remember that as a background they tend to draw too much attention to themselves. It is far more dramatic to let the plants in front steal the show. Flowers seen against a simple, dark green background seem to have colors that glow, and the various textures of other plants are more dramatic against the simple texture of the background plantings. If you want to use flowering shrubs, put them in front of plainer shrubs, but this brings up another rule of background plantings—give them enough room.

Shrubs Grow Big If a shrub is going to grow tall enough to be a backdrop, it is also going to spread laterally. Though a few shrubs do grow taller than they are wide, most need room to grow naturally into a rounded shape. Too often we don't give them this room and end up having to take them out a few years later, or we have to take out the pruning shears. As soon as we start pruning, we no longer have naturally graceful shrubs for a background, but clipped hedges, not a harmonious setting for flowers that show best in a more casual environment.

Of course you want to have as much open space in the garden as possible, but it isn't necessary to have a great deal and the sacrifices made to get it outweigh any benefits. Do we really need all that empty space, which is usually planted to lawn? Yet in most gardens, plants are pushed as close to the property lines as is physically possible, as if we were clearing the floor of furniture for a dance.

Give Plants Their Place Instead, vow to give plants their place and enough space to grow without constraint. Start thinking of an eight-foot-wide swath as just about the minimum for the background shrubs, and later be prepared to give flowers and other plants equally generous quarters. If you simply haven't the room for this graceful background of unclipped shrubs, then plant shrubs that can be pruned as hedges; but even these need at least three to four feet of garden space. If all else fails to fit, resort to walls and fences, which should also be simple and plain when used as a backdrop for the garden. Elaborate designs have their place, but not in the background.

"I Didn't Know It Would Grow that Big" In my garden you often hear, "it wasn't supposed to grow that big," a lament all too common, I suspect. In my grandfather's day (he was a landscape architect), plants were spaced far apart, and it took years for them to grow together. There was a lot of empty space between the circles that represented plants on his plans. That is one reason old gardens—especially estate gardens—often look more majestic than modern ones. Plants weren't crowded and could grow to their natural size, without unnatural pruning. Trees could become monumental in size because enough room was allowed. Shrubs could grow and spread, making an elegant and dense green backdrop for the rest of the garden. There was plenty of time.

In this impatient age, we plant everything too closely together because we want a garden to look finished within a reasonable amount of time (next week is not too soon). Trees get crowded and have to be taken out long before their time. Shrubs planted close to one another grow together so they become more like a hedge and need constant pruning. Most of us don't even know what some of the most common shrubs really look like, because they are never given the room to assume their natural shape. I don't think we modern gardeners are completely to blame. Circumstances do force us to keep moving on, and few of us can expect to spend more than five or ten years in one place, yet that is the time it takes for a plant to reach a reasonable size.

Landscape designers have a way around this: plant twice what you will eventually need, and when the flowers or shrubs have grown and begin to touch, take out every other one. Don't wait too long or they will begin to

shade each other and lose their lower leaves and branches. When you take out the temporary plants, you will again have holes in your scheme, but now the remaining plants can continue to grow and fill in. There is also this rare thing called patience. Sometimes, for the sake of privacy, a fence or wall can be a better choice, with some of the best slow-growing shrubs or trees in front of it. You just need to wait a little. Something can also be said for a little air between plants. They tend to look better, get more sun on their lower branches, and are healthier because good air circulation is important to plants.

Knowing just how large something will become can be a problem. When a garden book says, "grows to six or ten feet," figure on ten. Since I am always trying to fit a few more plants in the garden, I accept the lower number, but the plant often reaches that size in a year or two. The description of the ordinary *Pittosporum tobira* in the *Sunset Western Garden Book* shows how vague the published size of a plant can be: "Broad, dense shrub or small tree, 6–15 feet tall, rarely 30 ft." Before I learned better, I would have counted on six feet, but what would have happened to my garden if it had grown to thirty?

So it seems that plants that grow too big are a part of modern gardening, but there is help on its way. Nurseries are busy developing and introducing smaller, more compact, plants, from annuals to trees, but especially shrubs. A good example is a new dwarf variegated *Pittosporum tobira*, named Turner's Variegated Dwarf. Most people give the regular variegated pittosporum about six feet to grow in because at least one garden book says it grows to "about 5 ft. high and as broad," but mine grew that tall and

wide in two years. In one garden, I saw it about eight feet tall and a good fifteen feet across. It took up most of the backyard. This shrub is always planted in too little space, but let's hope Turner's Variegated Dwarf lives up to its billing and is a lot smaller!

Plants that grow bigger than the space I have allowed them have caused me a lot of hard work. Each time I take something out, I have to start all over again in that spot, but I'm learning. I now look up the size of each plant and then write the size on the plant label, where it stares me right in the face so I can't ignore it at planting time. I also get out a tape measure and see if the plant will really fit. I still cheat some, but I am getting better and a little more patient. And patience is one of gardening's gentle lessons.

PERSPECTIVE, PROPORTION, BALANCE, AND THE RULE OF THREE'S AND FIVE'S

Some basic rules of design make the planning of any garden planting a whole lot easier. You can use these rules when planting trees or shrubs for the background, for flowers, bulbs, and ground covers. The easiest to explain is what I call "the rule of three's and five's"—three of anything look better than one or two, and five look even better. The temptation is to plant just one of everything because at the nursery one tends to buy just one of this and one of that; or, to go the opposite route and plant a field full from nursery flats, because it's easier than trying to plan a planting scheme in advance.

The first extreme makes for a lot of odd fellows, and the other gets boring pretty quickly. Instead, try buying three or five of everything, or similar odd-numbered combinations. You can

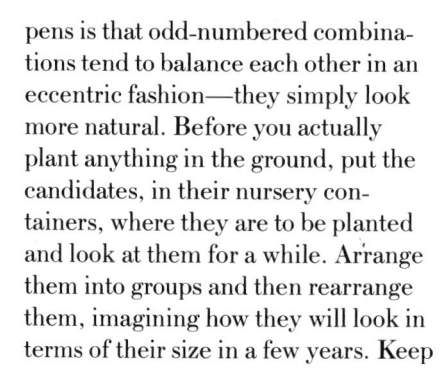

There is nothing like practice to hone a technique. To practice some of the rules of composition, purchase a variety of foam balls at a florist's supply store and arrange them this way and that. Here, a pair of balls is contrasted with three of a kind, the pair looking stiff and formal, the three more natural.

Small in front of large (lower photos) is not nearly as dramatic an arrangement as large in front of small; note how far away the small ball looks when placed behind a large one.

practice this rule with any object: I've even used foam balls to illustrate this point; or on a piece of paper, draw circles to represent plants. But in a sketch you lose the third dimension that makes gardens such a rich experience.

Try Some Combinations Make up combinations of three's and five's and see how pleasing they appear. What hap-

pens is that odd-numbered combinations tend to balance each other in an eccentric fashion—they simply look more natural. Before you actually plant anything in the ground, put the candidates, in their nursery containers, where they are to be planted and look at them for a while. Arrange them into groups and then rearrange them, imagining how they will look in terms of their size in a few years. Keep moving them around until they look pleasing. It's a lot easier to rearrange them at this point than it is after they are in the ground, so take your time and wait a few days to see if you still feel the same about their relationship.

For a Formal Look If you are not after a natural look, then balance your plantings precisely. For a distinctly formal walk put one plant on one side, and an identical plant on the other—instant formality. But I suspect you'll be happier with plantings that look informal and natural, even if the path is not. One trick is to make most of the plantings informal, but where you want to emphasize something—a gate perhaps —suddenly use a formally arranged pair of plants.

Balance Balance is a little trickier to explain, but if you think of any plant of a given size as having weight, you will begin to see how plants might balance one another. If you plant three shrubs that are each going to grow to three feet across, they will be in balance with two shrubs that each grow to about five feet across. Both groups of plants have about the same visual weight and are in balance. If you think I just broke the rule of three's and five's by suggesting that you plant two shrubs, I sort of did, but by balancing the two against the three, I came up with a total of five, so you can see that balance modifies this rule and makes it more versatile. Try it with the foam balls and see if it doesn't look right.

Perhaps the reason such planting looks right is that in nature plants tend to grow in colonies: one plant gets its start and then spreads underground or drops seed around itself—soon it's a colony of plants. However, seldom do they so get the upper hand on other plants that they completely dominate

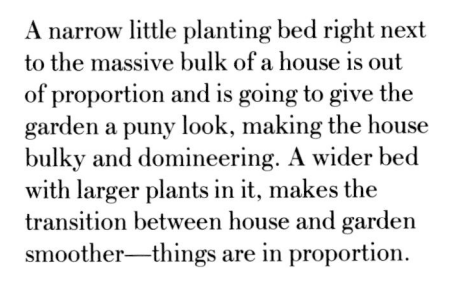

an area. They learn to share, and what you see in nature is one colony growing next to another, then another next to that, and so on, in a well-balanced fashion. The rule of three's and five's seeks to imitate this look.

Scale and Proportion Scale and proportion enter into garden planning, specifically when the natural parts of a garden are close to the man-made.

A narrow little planting bed right next to the massive bulk of a house is out of proportion and is going to give the garden a puny look, making the house bulky and domineering. A wider bed with larger plants in it, makes the transition between house and garden smoother—things are in proportion.

Perspective Perspective can be tinkered with and should be considered.

A small object in front of a large object looks as if it is close; put it behind the large object and it looks further away than it actually is and since it appears further away, the garden seems larger. This is called "forcing the perspective," and it's a particularly useful trick along a path or sight line, yet most of us tend to do the opposite. We put the smallest plants in the foreground and the largest way in back, thinking that we get privacy at the property line. So keep an eye open for someplace where you can force that perspective—the illusion of space is as good as having those few extra feet.

You can also force the perspective by using just the foliage of plants. Put large-leaved plants in the foreground and small-leaved plants in the background. Those little leaves will look a lot further away from the large leaves than they actually are.

ACCENT AND SURPRISE

Sometimes you should break the rule of three's and five's outright and plant just one plant—it's going to stick out like a sore thumb so it had better be special. But this is a great way to emphasize a favorite plant. It would not be possible without the rule of three's and five's, which makes a foil for that favorite plant—that one must be the exception, not the rule. Designers call these special plantings "accents," and they are important to the garden's design because they are supplementary focal points. In any given part of the garden, accents are the first thing you look at and they help to establish an order: First you look down your path and see the focal point at its end; as the eye begins to wander over the rest of the garden, these accent plants catch your attention and hold it momentarily.

Spires and Steeples Sometimes accent plants are not single specimens. They may be a group of plants that are quite different in shape but tend to be viewed as one object. The most obvious distinctive shape is one that is tall and lean, that towers above the generally rounded shape of other plants—spires and steeples in the village of more ordinary plants. Italian cypress are often used this way on a large scale, hollyhocks and delphiniums on a smaller scale. Their sheer verticality draws the necessary attention, delphiniums so dramatically it is difficult for me to imagine a garden without them.

Accent plants have an element of surprise to them, which makes them and the garden they grace more delightful. They may be surprisingly beautiful, or tall, or graceful, or an astonishing color.

Surprise Surprise can be an important part of any garden, but it is often lacking. A large expanse of unrelieved lawn holds no surprise. It may be elegant and lush, yet everyone knows that there is nothing unexpected out there. But let it curve around a clump of shrubs, and the possibility exists that something surprising is around the corner, just out of sight—perhaps a planting of those delphiniums waiting to be discovered, a garden pool, a pleasant bench under a tree, or an inviting swing hanging from that tree. Whatever it is, it shouldn't be immediately visible or it won't come as a surprise.

Even in formal garden plans, there is a way to create surprise. The path, just wide enough to allow passage, could disappear through a hedge just tall enough to block the view of what is beyond, and the surprise would be waiting on the other side.

More garden composition practice: Three and five are magic numbers in the design of plantings. In the upper left two large plants harmonize with three smaller ones, for a total of five.

Add a sixth plant that is decidedly different in color or size and it becomes the star, what is called an "accent."

Rather than line shrubs up stiffly, like soldiers guarding the walls of the house (or along a fence), use a variety of sizes.

At the lower right, small shrubs are placed beneath the windows, while a larger one is planted in front of the blank portion of the wall.

Two tall foam tubes add an element of surprise and excitement to the foam ball composition. A jet of water, a tall thin plant or tree, a sculpture, can add similar excitement to the plantings in the garden.

In Hortense Miller's garden in Laguna Beach, tall, old-fashioned hollyhocks prove they are still among the most surprising and delightful plants. Their companions are pink Mexican evening primrose and golden coreopsis.

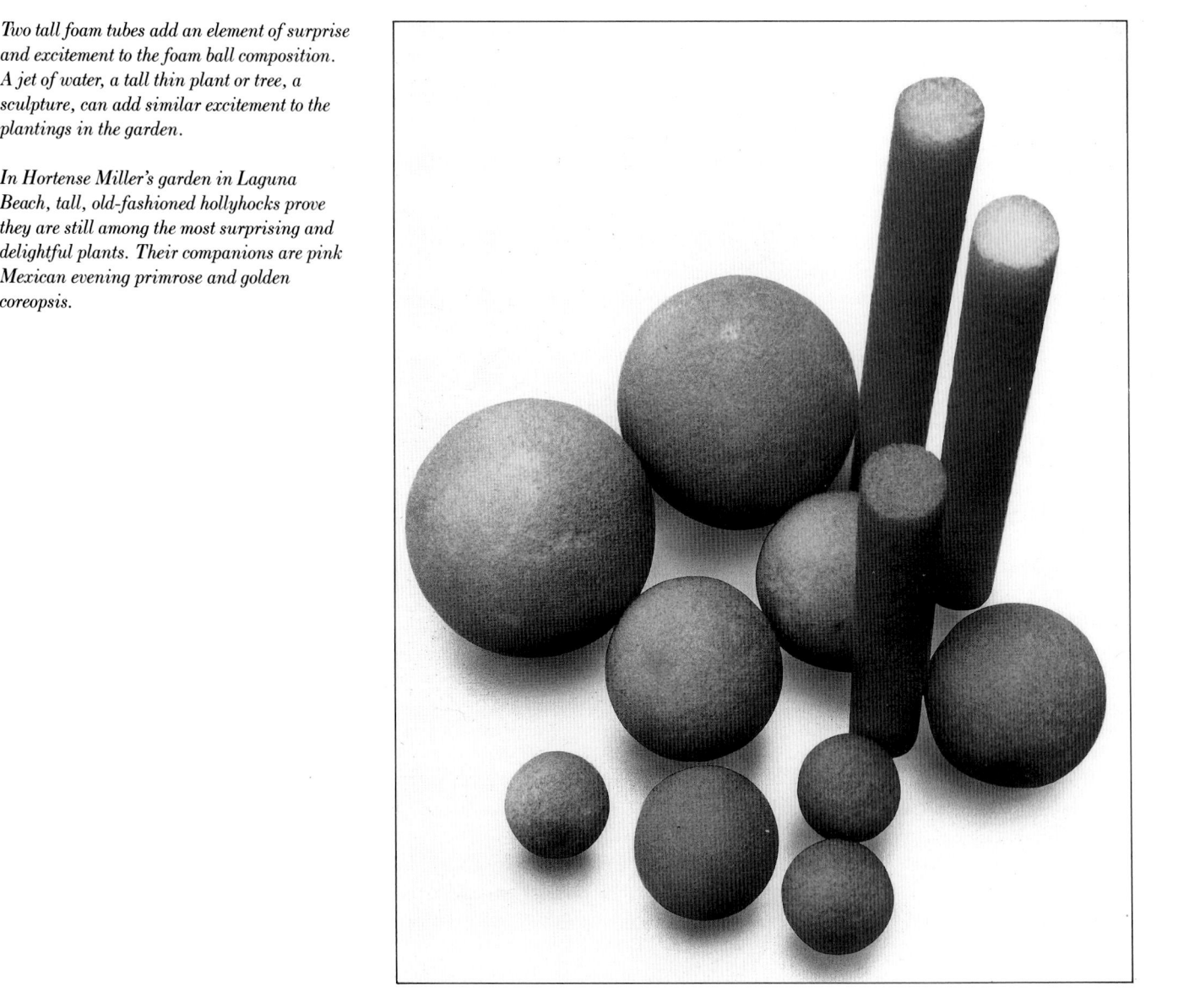

Too Much of a Good Thing Classical gardens made good use of surprise, often employing hedges and little passages, though sometimes the surprise was a little too much. The Italians loved to put hidden jets of water here and there that came on all of a sudden and soaked visitors. Even the normally restrained English overdid surprise in their gracious, quiet gardens, building ludicrous structures called "follies" that one stumbles upon on a tour of the garden—lacquer-red Chinese towers or carefully built castle ruins. Today, some of these follies still catch a visitor by surprise—perhaps "shock" better describes one's astonishment.

"Surprise" can quickly become "sore thumb" so restraint is called for. At the least, limit the surprises to one per garden area.

Plant Portrait

THOSE TOWERING DELPHINIUMS

My grandfather, a pioneer landscape architect in the San Francisco area, might not have been impressed, but he certainly would have been pleased to see my delphiniums. His delphiniums, like his rhododendrons, tuberous begonias, and fuchsias, were the kind beside which you could proudly pose. In his fading Kodachromes, the rhododendron trusses are as large as Louis Smaus's hatted head, the tuberous begonias not much smaller. And the delphiniums? They tower above everything like New England church steeples, brilliantly colored, as though painted by Portuguese fishermen.

My grandfather was a close friend of Frank Reinelt, the creator of modern delphiniums. Both were schooled in horticulture in the European tradition, in Czechoslovakia, and both apprenticed in the gardens of queens—in Reinelt's case Queen Marie of Rumania. Lured by the feats of the legendary Luther Burbank, Reinelt and my grandfather came to California in the early 1900s. My grandfather designed landscapes for the Spreckels and other San Francisco families; Reinelt designed flowers by hybridizing and selecting, creating the first dinner-plate-size tuberous begonias, the Pacific strain of primroses, and the Pacific strain of delphiniums—all of which are still the standard of perfection.

These delphiniums were the first to rival the developments of the great European hybridizers, primarily because they encompassed so many blues—brilliant blue, sky blue, robin's egg blue, blue as dark and clear as sapphires. Many had a contrasting "bee" at their center, either as black as a carpenter bee (which was neatly concealed, to my occasional surprise)

or pure white. There was nothing purplish about these flowers. They were *blue*.

The Pacific series, sometimes called Pacific Giants, is a "strain," and although the concept of a seed strain is a little confusing, it distinguishes how we in California grow delphiniums from the way they are grown in Europe. There, delphiniums are almost permanent plants. Named kinds are propagated from divisions and persist in the garden for years, becoming ever larger clumps until they must be divided and then replanted. In California, Reinelt discovered, delphiniums don't persist, even though they are perennial plants. So he developed strains that could be grown almost like annuals—sow the seed, move the young plants into the garden, and they bloom. When they're finished, pull them out and start over again. A strain is born after much crossing, when the progenies of each generation become enough alike to be called similar. Plants grown from a seed strain are not identical, but they are supposed to be nearly so. In Reinelt's case, the Pacific strains were near perfect—identical in height, color, and form. Developed between 1938 and 1940, these strains received Best of Show gold medal at the 1939 Oakland Spring Flower Show, the premier West Coast show of its time—a measure of their importance and popularity. Most of his strains are still with us, although they have deteriorated somewhat through the years. It is the nature of strains that they must be carefully and laboriously recrossed periodically to keep them strong and uniform, and that has been difficult.

The true blue strains are the Bluejay series and Summer Skies series. Other less blue or outright purple strains have names chosen from Alfred Tennyson's "Idylls of the King,"

Delphiniums, such as this towering member of the Pacific Giant strain, bring instant drama to a garden.

including the King Arthur series, Guinevere, Galahad, Lancelot, Black Knight, and the Round Table series (all of the colors from some 300 crosses).

The Pacific strains grow to a height of at least six feet, and it is not difficult to find photographs of Pacific Giants growing eight feet tall. They are usually used in a big way. I have a fading blueprint of my grandfather's design for a Hillsborough estate in Northern California which contains a delightful double border on either side of an ample path leading to a formal rose garden. These borders contain a brilliant mix of flowers and fruit trees that I plan to copy someday. But the borders are big—the reason for my delay in duplicating them. They are each 100 feet in length and eight feet wide, and there is a separate foot-wide border of ageratum, aubrieta, iberis, and petunia 'Rosey Morn' in front of the main border. The borders are so big that there is a tiny paved path behind each for access. The delphiniums are toward the back, and each of the five plantings occupies an area of about four by seven feet.

In this grand scheme, the importance of a big, strapping strain of delphiniums is evident. The delphiniums are planted in pockets between flowering fruit trees, which are "underplanted" with daffodils for spring bloom, and then with chrysanthemums, "grown on and transplanted" for fall bloom. The beds of tall delphiniums balance the weight of the fruit trees. Behind the delphiniums are plantings of watsonia, which bloom while the delphiniums are still small— just a bushy foreground. As the bulbs fade, the growing delphiniums hide the drying watsonia foliage.

To either side of the delphiniums in one planting are nicotiana and a phlox named 'Elizabeth Campbell'; nearby

are plantings of scabiosa—another fine blue flower—and iris, presumably blue. In another planting, the companions are *Salvia pitcheri*, trachelium, and *Penstemon barbatus*. In another, it is the carmine-flowered *Lilium speciosum* 'Rubrum' and phlox 'Miss Lingard' beside a flowering peach; and in still another, anthemis, doronicum, and daylilies.

The colors of the delphiniums were not specified, nor how many were to be planted, but a dozen plants in each pocket was probably close, and each planting probably contained but one color, since mad mixes were not the fashion. A clever gardener could probably guess the color of the delphiniums by the colors of the plants nearby, but, in general, it seems that most were blue contrasting with pink and red, or purple next to soft yellows.

That is how my grandfather used delphiniums professionally, but in his own modest bungalow garden in Burlingame he grew them in narrow beds just outside a sunny breakfast nook, where I remember having toast with apricot jam. There the delphiniums and other plants were not so much a composition as they were a display, like the exhibitions at the flower shows he judged. He didn't care that they were out of scale with the house, but was more concerned with size and perfection. He grew everything big and without blemish.

In my garden the delphiniums don't exactly tower. For many years my modern sensibilities kept me from growing delphiniums at all, because they simply seemed too big for the space at hand—until the advent of the Blue Fountains. This strain of short delphiniums was depicted as uniform, about three to four feet tall, and, of course, the blue-flowered sorts were prominently pictured in seed cata-

In a Santa Monica garden a colorful mixture of fall-planted annuals and perennials blooms in April. Annuals include nemesia, petunias, Shirley poppies, snapdragons, Sweet William, and anemones. Shasta daisies, Canterbury bells, columbines, and delphiniums are some of the perennials, though it is the delphiniums that steal the show. The spotted foliage belongs to Abutilon pictum *'Thompsonii.' Believe it or not, this flower bed is only seven months old.*

logues. I suppose that I should have known better than to believe the catalogue pictures, for so far they have been anything but uniform. Every plant is a complete surprise. Some grow two feet tall, some six feet. Some have stems as thick as a giant sequoia; some are as delicate as the wild *Delphinium cardinale* that grows in our chaparral. Some have fat spikes of closely set flowers; others are airy, much like the annual larkspurs.

They are not at all formal flowers, but give more the effect of a country-cottage garden; nor would they have won anything but a polite nod from the judges of the 1939 Oakland Show. I don't believe it's my fault; it's just not a very good strain by Reinelt's standards. Still, I'm delighted with my delphiniums. Passersby compliment me on my garden, even though I know that they are staring only at the delphiniums. And my English neighbors call it an English garden, simply, I suspect, because the delphiniums are there.

Blue Fountains, although far from perfect, is a useful strain because the plants fit into a modern, small flower bed. I can squeeze a dozen Blue Fountains between the roses and my modest collection of perennials. Although very few have turned out to be a true blue, they are blue enough, and the many purples are quite handsome with the purple *Salvia farinacea* and the lilac-colored veronica. The few blues make for a dramatic background for the pink dianthus and the pink and red roses.

I've grown the Blue Fountains strain of delphiniums for several years and have developed a method. I plant them only a foot apart in clusters of several. The soil is laboriously prepared in advance, dug to a foot or more, with peat moss and Gromulch mixed in so that a handful of soil, after being squeezed in a fist, crumbles apart on its own. A small fistful of Osmocote fertilizer is thrown into the bottom of each hole. That fertilizer, which looks like fish eggs, releases nutrients slowly so that the plants are fed for most of spring and summer.

Planted in that fashion, plants simply shoot up—the results are stupendous. If you had the time, you could probably sit and watch them grow. They seem to bloom within days of planting, although my garden notebook says they were planted in late January and that the first buds opened on April 5. After the main spikes flower, secondary spikes last into summer. The main spikes catch the blooming of the roses, veronicas, dianthus, and other spring flowers, and the secondary spikes bloom along with the early summer flowers, including agapanthus and Shasta daisies.

I plant my delphiniums from four-inch pots (gallon-can-sized plants bloom poorly). I do not grow them from seed, although that is the best way to start delphiniums. In the cultural directions in the Vetterle & Reinelt catalogue of 1940, it is suggested that seed sown from June into September will produce early spring flowers; seed sown in December and January, midsummer flowers; and seed sown from February to April, fall flowers. That would make an interesting experiment if you wanted delphiniums nearly year round.

The cultural description in the catalogue continues with how to get a second set of blooms, and there is no mystery here much to my disappointment. I thought I had discovered a trick, a bit of garden sorcery, in an old book on delphiniums from that golden era of California gardening before World War II. It suggested cutting back the flower spikes so that only a single leaf remained at the base. Aha!—just a single leaf—so that's the trick. I tried it and within two months the delphiniums were again in full bloom—in late summer.

A year or two later and in a lazier mood, I simply cut the spikes off above the leaves so that quite a few leaves remained and, of course, the plants rebloomed just as well—maybe even better. Reinelt's catalogue suggests to simply cut off the spikes, leaving all the leaves at the base, and then keep the plants on the dry side for two to three weeks, so they are forced to rest. When new shoots appear above ground, cut off the remainder of the old spike. Then sprinkle a teaspoon of ammonium phosphate around the base of each plant, rake it into the soil, and water thoroughly. Further, remove all but two or three of the strongest new shoots from each clump so that they will grow stronger, but I have found that an impossible task, and I rather like the airy quality of the many-spiked second bloom.

Outside of California, where these delphiniums have a better than even chance of returning in following years, the spikes should be cut after flowering and all but four or five of the new sprouts should be removed at the base. Grown as perennials, they should be spaced further apart—24 to 30 inches.

The Pacific types are usually planted from four-inch pots in the fall so they have all winter to gather the strength required for their spectacular growth. In other respects their culture is the same as for the smaller Blue Fountains that are in my garden, except that they almost always need a supporting wooden stake.

Although my grandfather and Frank Reinelt are gone, the Pacific strain survives. One of these days, I will find the room to grow them.

A SHRUB PALETTE

At this point in the planning process it's time to develop a palette of background plants. It is surprising how few gardeners know their shrubs, but it is easy enough to learn, and the learning process is pretty much the same for other plants you will need later on. A walk around the block and a trip to the nursery are good ways to start.

A Walk Around the Block On the walk around the block, you'll see what others have used for shrubs. Take note of their situation—are they growing in sun or shade, or in something in between? Are they on the south, north, or maybe west side of the house? Especially note their size, their width in particular, and, of course, whether they indeed make good backgrounds. It doesn't matter that you don't know what these shrubs are called, because you can next head to a nursery and simply look for the same plant. Find the plant tag, and now that you know its name jot it down in your garden notebook along with your observations, and you have the beginnings of a shrub palette.

If your neighborhood offers slim pickings, try another, or go to a botanic garden and see what they use, but the closer to home you find the examples, the more likely they will work well in your garden. You're not looking for outstanding specimens at this time, so it doesn't matter that you and your neighbors are all growing the same plants. There aren't that many background shrubs to choose from—plain and deep green in color with medium-sized leaves and inconspicuous flowers.

Notoriously Optimistic If you ask someone for recommendations, or begin looking through a book, be aware that any plant that is said to grow fast and thereby sounds ideal for the job is probably ill-suited. Speedy plants are seldom good in any other way. They tend to become trees in a short time, have aggressive root systems that can make growing anything else near them impossible, and often are not dense enough to make a good backdrop or provide the privacy you seek. The shrubs may make spectacular growth, but they don't do anything else well. Also, be aware that books notoriously, or perhaps optimistically, underestimate the eventual size of plants.

Four for Your Notebook They are simply shrubs. There is nothing colorful, unusual, or spectacular about their foliage, while their flowers are plain basic white. But what the four shrubs pictured on pages 66 and 67 do well is form that dark green background you need for other plants. If the flowers in your garden lack a certain punch, it is probably because they don't have the correct background. Roses, perennials, and annual flowers will appear more dramatic against this background of deep green foliage. Light green, gray green, or reddish or bronze-green won't do. These shrubs draw attention to themselves and no longer serve as a backdrop. What we're talking about is an unobtrusive—but substantial—green shrub.

Not surprisingly, several of these simple green shrubs have long been appreciated. They have been favored since Roman times for the cooling effect that their dark green foliage brings to the sunbaked gardens of the Mediterranean, though all four shrubs can tolerate a fair amount of shade. But where they excel is in sunny locations.

These shrubs can also be pruned to shape and they make fine hedges. All are easy to grow and readily available. However, nursery plants are often root-bound from sitting unnoticed in a corner too long, and it is sometimes best to order fresh plants.

PRIVETS The privet of Italian Renaissance and Roman gardens was *Ligustrum vulgare*. More often planted in California is the Japanese privet, *L. japonicum*, especially the cultivar 'Texanum', which is a low grower (six to eight feet). 'Rotundifolium' is another even lower (to five feet) cultivar, and 'Suwannee River' is supposedly lower still (to four feet).

MYRTLES Another Mediterranean plant with a long history. *Myrtus communis* has glossy, green leaves with a most pleasant scent. It grows to about six feet and is most often seen as a hedge, though it makes a handsome, small background shrub. Cultivars such as 'Boetica' and 'Compacta' are smaller, with slightly different foliage.

VIBURNUM Laurustinus, *Viburnum tinus*, also dates from Roman days. It grows to six or ten feet, in time maybe even taller. In winter, the tiny white flowers are deliciously fragrant, though subtle. In appearance, it is a slightly less formal shrub.

PRUNUS An American native, the Carolina laurel cherry, *Prunus caroliniana*, grows fast and is exceptionally neat and regular from day one—particularly the cultivars 'Compacta' and 'Bright 'n Tight'. The eventual height is between ten feet—if it's pruned as a hedge—to twenty feet when left alone. This one does best near the ocean or in partial shade far inland.

Your Own List These four shrubs were most recommended by landscape designers for use in California gardens; some also work well in other parts of the country, and there are certainly other candidates for other climates.

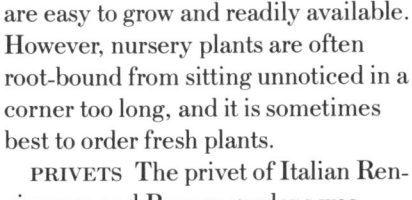

Landscape designers like simple shrubs for background plantings and these are some of their choices for California: sweet-smelling lauristinus (upper left), Japanese privet (upper right), Carolina laurel cherry (lower left), and the old favorite, myrtle (lower right), with its fragrant foliage. Other areas have their own preferences, but background shrubs should always be plain.

Viburnum tinus

Myrtus

Plant Portrait

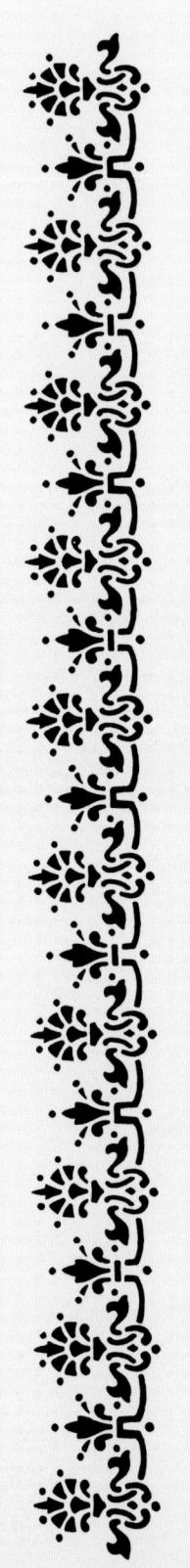

EARLY CAMELLIAS

You've probably observed in your own garden that some camellias bloom earlier than others—and these are an especially valuable lot simply because they bloom before the big spring rush when so much else does, and they are more noticeable. In California the peak of the season comes during March, but the camellias pictured here bloom in January and early February, the middle of winter. The sasanqua camellias bloom even earlier, but their blooms are generally smaller and decidedly less fancy, and the bushes are a trifle stiff and sticklike. The camellias shown here are all japonica types, with full-blown, full-size flowers on neat, dense bushes. Only the japonicas are capable of such variation—from the unusual tulip-shaped flowers of 'Tulip Time' to the complex geometry of 'Donnan's Dream'. In between are all sorts of camellia forms—semi-doubles, anemone or peony forms, variegated, and picotees.

It is the nature of early camellias to begin flowering a month or more before they reach their peak—slowly opening blooms that tend to last, thus making a more consistent showing in the garden. In comparison, midseason camellias (most are classified as such) open all at once, and though they make more of a splash, it is short-lived. The early varieties are often the prettiest and most perfect because they open when the weather is cool and mild, and therefore most camellia shows are held early in the season. These early camellias are ideal candidates for the backs of flower borders, where they can be in the shade of taller shrubs and trees, and are first-class background shrubs.

For this purpose, their colors couldn't be more suitable. The soft pinks and whites are perfect for the season and complement many spring flowers as they start to bloom. Imagine them behind the tall spikes of larkspur, Canterbury bells, bachelor's buttons, dianthus, or stock. By the time your summer garden is in bloom, camellia bushes are a glossy, deep-green backdrop for that season's warmer colors.

Camellias like shade, though not too much of it. They are one of the few shrubs that can thrive in a garden where they will have winter shade and summer sun. The north side of most California houses would be bare were it not for camellias. There they can be planted as a background for primroses and cinerarias, or they can stand alone with ferns and other shady plants at their feet.

A nice thing about camellias is that they should be planted during their season of bloom, so you can actually see what you are getting. Prepare the soil thoroughly by digging in quantities of organic matter. Camellias do most of their growing immediately after flowering, so be sure to add some fertilizer to the bottom of the planting holes. Also, take care to plant the camellia bush a bit high so that the top of the root ball sits about a half-inch above the soil level. The after-planting regimen calls for fertilizing every other month from right after flowering until early fall, when the buds are formed for next season's blossoms.

Camellia petal blight is a fairly common disease on camellias, though not as common as some suspect. Many other problems are called petal blight, but true petal blight is easily recognized because the petals become watery and soft. The only cure is cultural: rake up all fallen petals after bloom and dispose of them. The idea is to try to prevent the disease from returning or spreading, and it usually takes several years of effort.

Plant Portrait

NOT YOUR ORDINARY AZALEA

Every flower is a surprise on certain Satsuki azaleas. Some varieties have flowers that are rimmed in a contrasting color or have a collar of white, others have flowers that are solid or variously striped, deep or softly colored, or tipped in a contrasting color—all on the same plant. Satsuki azaleas are not your ordinary azaleas. The sampling pictured here merely hints at the possibilities.

Satsuki azaleas are complex, age-old hybrids of several azaleas native to the mountains of Japan, and they have been trickling into the United States by following what could be called the "bonsai pipeline," since Satsukis are mostly grown by bonsai enthusiasts. But what began as a trickle may soon become a flood as more people discover Satsukis for their gardens. They make good bonsai subjects, because they are naturally compact plants. A five-year-old Satsuki will have grown only about two-and-one-half feet tall and three feet wide, a nearly perfect size for today's gardens. Satsuki means "fifth month," which is when they bloom—in May and early June—a whole month or more after other kinds of azaleas have finished. Already Nuccio's Nurseries, the camellia and azalea specialists in Altadena, California, offers several pages of Satsukis in the catalogue, including several of their own hybrids as well as those

shown here. And there are hundreds more grown in Japan, where Satsukis have a devoted following.

The more you learn of Satsukis, the better they sound. Because of their compact size, they are unusually dense and rounded. The foliage is a dark green, sometimes flushed with bronze. The leaves of many varieties turn as brilliant as Japanese maples in fall (some bloom again at that time), though since the plants are not deciduous only the older leaves drop off. The leaves are leathery and tough; Satsukis can stand quite a bit of sun. At Nuccio's, where the summer temperatures soar and the sun bakes the surrounding chaparral, many Satsukis are grown in the open. The best situation

is one with morning or filtered sun.

Like other azaleas, however, they need a richly prepared, acidic soil and ample moisture, yet they must have the best drainage. Add lots of organic matter (peat moss is preferred, but commercial azalea planting mixes are available also). A six-inch layer tilled into the top foot of soil is not excessive. Some gardeners go even further, planting in soil that is almost entirely amendment and in raised beds.

The unusually colored and marked blooms are the result of "sporting"— when branches that appear seemingly out of nowhere grow flowers not seen elsewhere on the plant. Those are propagated to produce new varieties. Some branches may even "sport" on

your own plant—they do so easily. Once in a while, however, branches, especially those having flowers with contrasting borders, revert after planting, so what you see is not necessarily what you get. There is an element of chance.

The most spectacular Satsukis are those casually called "multicolored". Like the variety shown here named 'Shinsen', they may have some flowers of a solid color, others of a lighter shade of the same color, many striped or speckled with both shades plus white, and some almost entirely white. And as we said, each flower is a surprise, because you never know what will open or where it will show up on the bush.

One of the new, smaller shrubs is Pittosporum tobira *'Wheeler's Dwarf,' on page 72. There is an even newer variegated variety with cream-striped leaves.*

The pure red abutilon on page 73 is one of the best shrubs for shady gardens, growing to about six feet around with large bell-like flowers that bloom all winter and spring. It, unfortunately, has no specific name.

Hydrangeas, too, are great in the shade. The one on the far right is a so-called lace-cap. The lacy center never opens any further, which gives the shrub an airy look when in flower.

A FEW MORE PLANTS FOR THE SHADE

Shady parts of the garden pose their own problems and require their own palette of plants. In particular, the north side of the house presents difficulties: while it is in shadow all winter, it is likely to be bathed in sun during the hottest time of the year, as the sun climbs higher in the summer months. Camellias and to a lesser extent azaleas excel on the north side of the house and can be the backbone of any shady garden, though neither of them will bloom well in deep shade. The north side of the house is not in what gardeners term "dense shade" because that side is open to the sky overhead so though there is plenty of light, there is just no direct sun.

Hydrangeas, another candidate for a shady garden, are especially valu-able because they flower after the camellias and azaleas, carrying the show of color into summer. If you want a blue hydrangea, you had better buy it in flower. Hydrangeas must be turned blue in California because that color results from acid soil—ours is at best neutral and at worst alkaline. In New Zealand and in Seattle, where the soils are quite acid, hydrangeas naturally turn a bright—even brilliant—blue. If you scatter aluminum sulfate (sold at nurseries) around the base of a hydrangea before it makes buds, and then once again when the buds are about half-size, you might make the flowers turn blue.

In my experience, however, not all hydrangeas will become blue in acid soil, so it is best to buy one that is blue to begin with. Otherwise, you will have pink hydrangeas—unfortunately not a soft baby pink but a rather unpleasant

Wheelers
dwarf
pittosporum

shade of the color. You can also take the safe route and plant a white-flowered hydrangea.

Camellias, azaleas, and hydrangeas, as do most shade plants, like a rich, porous soil similar to what you find on a forest floor. Before planting, mix into your bed bags of organic soil amendment such as redwood or ground bark. I usually till in a six-inch layer of amendment, that has been spread on top, to a depth of about a foot; this is a lot of bags.

Abutilons are also nearly perfect shrubs for a shady location, but, unlike the hydrangeas, they can withstand a direct blast of sun during the day without wilting. They broaden the garden palette by blooming primarily in late summer and winter. No other plant in my garden flowers as long—ten months by my count—and it is one of the few plants that grows quickly to its appointed size and then seems to stop. My abutilons grow to a height of about six or eight feet and then remain there, reaching that size in about nine months with the help of lots of water and fertilizer. The best have smallish leaves and large bell-like flowers, and in winter and spring they are smothered with them. Look around and you'll find all sorts of colors, shading from yellow into red with a warm apricot in between, and a pretty white that sparkles in the shade.

Another champion shrub for the shade—even deep shade—is the dark, glossy-green Japanese aucuba. The gold-splattered variegated varieties are the most popular but I have always found them difficult to grow; not so the plain green *Serratifolia*. Aucubas are as slow as a freight train, so don't expect a big shrub for many years.

If you need one more big shrub to round out your shade planting, try *Pittosporum tobira* 'Variegata,' a two-

toned shrub that is tough as nails; in two years it will grow to six feet across and can grow to fifteen feet. It doesn't grow very tall, however, and pruning can keep the shrub smaller. The cream-splashed leaves look as if shafts of sunlight were striking through the shade. 'Wheeler's Dwarf' is a green-leaved pittosporum that also does well in the shade, growing to about six or eight feet across, but only four or five feet tall.

HEDGES, FENCES, AND WALLS

Hedges are one way to build a background and create privacy without taking up too much space. All too often, however, they are a solution to quite another problem—a plant that has grown too large for its space. These mutilated plants do not add to a garden; instead of a leafy wall of green, you see cut and ragged leaves, stubs of branches, and lots of dead, twiggy wood. Some shrubs simply do not like being sheared.

To make a good hedge, a plant must have smallish leaves. Large hedges in the background can have medium-sized leaves (three inches long); hedges in the foreground must have small leaves (an inch long) or you will see too

many cut leaves and the brown scars that appear as the leaf heals. A shrub to be used as a hedge must also grow slowly or you will never stay ahead of the shearing. Even then, the plant must be pruned before it makes more than a few inches of new growth or the older leaves will be shaded by the new and will die out. At that point, it is too late to prune the hedge back to its original size. Even with frequent shearing, a hedge is slowly going to get larger with age, so be sure to allow it a little room to spread. Hedges often lose their lower leaves in time because the growth above shades them, but you can avoid this by pruning on an angle —even a slight angle—so the base of the hedge is always wider than the top and thus receives enough light.

A good hedge can create real drama in the garden if you play with it a little. Leave a passage through it, cut windows in it, add architectural elements —an arched top or finials, perhaps. Hedges and other clipped forms can contrast sharply with more casual plantings, to create special places or focal points in the garden.

Fences, the Ultimate Space-savers, But . . . Fences and masonry walls are the ultimate space-savers, but they

work best if they are softened by plantings in front of or behind them. Plantings in back of a fence or wall tend to suggest that the enclosed area is only a part of the garden and that there is more beyond the wall. Or take another tack and try to make the fence or wall disappear. Designers often paint fences and walls a shade of deep green or gray green so they blend with the shrubbery planted in front of them. Fences and walls intended to be an unobtrusive background should be as plain as possible.

A fence can be a divider, separating parts of the garden. Dividing a garden with hedges or fences sometimes makes it seem more expansive, since there are other places to go.

Leave Gaps All fences should be built to let air pass through them—the advantage they have over solid walls. Even narrow slits between the boards will allow for air circulation, which makes the garden pleasanter to be in for plants and people. Spaces between the boards also help relieve the pressure of a strong wind and reduce the chance of odd currents and eddies that occur when winds are high. Most city dwellers notice that there are great gusts of wind at the base of tall buildings; a similar phenomenon occurs behind fences—an intensifying of the wind—unless there are gaps that let some of the wind through.

DON'T FORGET VINES

Vines strike some people as being just a little scary and it is easy to see why. Some vines are house-gobblers, tree-totalers, and fence-wreckers. Turn your back on them and they are out of control. They have been known to grow into an attic, to cover windows completely, to rip off shingles. They

Fences can be fun as well as functional, though they should also be simple if their role is to act as background. This fence mimics the cloud shapes overhead; a jigsaw did the job. It is made of pressure-treated wood that achieves the light green color as a result of being treated with a protective process that prevents rot.

can even smother a tree. Undoing their damage is hard and heavy work; extricating their victims from the tentacles painfully slow.

But vines have their place. It's the surest way to make a fence attractive or to cover the walls of a house where there is no room for anything wider. Vines can be two-dimensional plants. Because they have no natural shape, they bring a casual air to a garden, a random note. In Mediterranean gardens vines are often trained up into olive trees and other open trees. Only certain vines will do: they must be spare themselves, not too lush, and have a graceful airiness so they are like trimmings on a Christmas tree.

Some of the most commonly used vines are not well-behaved. I would think twice about planting any ivy, even Boston ivy. I have spent weeks trying to remove Algerian ivy from a fence only to discover that the fence had rotted. The builder of my house spent little to embellish the back, so I covered it with Boston ivy, which grows in shade and clings to anything with its little suckerlike pads. Though it makes a handsome green background for the garden, keeping it off the window screens is a monotonous task.

Beware of Wisteria and Other Vines I would be careful about using wisteria, which starts out sweetly enough but in time becomes a monstrous and extremely heavy vine. I am convinced it could cover an entire acre given the chance. If you want those wistful, grapelike flowers, be prepared to prune hard, and often. I would not give a creeping fig a hand-hold. This little vine looks so small and innocent in the nursery container, but at maturity its leaves triple in size and it has the grasp of a green giant. Still nursing

my wounds from the curved, sickle-sharp thorns that are designed to pierce and hold, I would never again plant a 'Belle of Portugal' climbing rose, except perhaps to cover a concrete battlement. It is much too large and quite capable of defending itself from gardeners who have only pruning shears in their holster.

All of these vines undoubtedly have a place, but it probably isn't in the average garden. They need too much room and attention.

Certain Vines for Certain Places But not all vines behave so malevolently. There are others that grow to manageable sizes and are the very models of restraint—their discovery by gardeners is overdue. This is especially true in Southern California because we can grow dozens of demure subtropical vines that flower exuberantly. Their usefulness increases each year because they can grow in those spaces, increasingly common, that are too narrow for anything else. Around new or remodeled homes, and in condominium and apartment courtyards, sliver-sized planting strips are the perfect home for a few well-mannered vines. Here are several worthy of consideration:

Currently at the top of my list is *Stephanotis floribunda*, also known as Madagascar jasmine. This vine is subtropical, reputedly growing only in a narrow frost-free band near the coast, though I have it in my garden which is well back from the beach and I am sure I have seen it much further inland; perhaps it was growing under the protection of eaves. It is a well-mannered vine that can grow in sun or complete shade, as I discovered when I removed an aging shelter from my own garden. The stephanotis had been growing in the dark under an alumi-

The wonderfully fragrant Stephanotis flori-bunda, *a very slow-growing subtropical vine, clings to a ready-made redwood trellis, bolted to a stucco wall.*

num roof and suddenly it found itself growing in full sun against a south-facing wall. I was prepared to take it out, but an experienced landscape contractor and friend told me it would adjust, and it did, without so much as a yellowed leaf.

Basking in the warmth of the summer sun, the stephanotis began flowering and in short order was covered with the white, waxy flowers that are often used in bridal bouquets, each blossom sweetly fragrant. In the shade it had bloomed once or twice, and the blossoms were a delight, but in the sun it completely covered itself with flowers. It grows to a very restrained eight to ten feet, but the price you pay for this restraint is patience. It grows very slowly. When I gave neighbors some of it for their new garden, their contractor looked at it and muttered, "slowest plant in the world." Like most vines, it attaches by twining, which means that a support of some kind is required.

Perhaps my next favorite subtropical vine goes by the not very glamorous name of potato vine, not because it looks anything like a potato but because it is a *Solanum*, which is in the potato family. *Solanum jasminoides* is what I prefer to call it because the reference to jasmine is more romantic if not apt. The flowers are white but not fragrant, and the vine is a little scraggly, the foliage sparse. I have one on the front of my house, growing on two four-by-eight lattice panels. It grew very quickly to cover these panels, then hardly at all, but it is always in flower.

Clematis, and there are many kinds, is another handsome, well-mannered vine that can be grown just about anywhere in the country. And there are more. Keep vines in mind when you need a plant that will grow in almost no space at all.

Support Needed It is even easier to grow vines on fences, the best support of all being the ubiquitous chain link fence. One of the best fence-coverers is *Mandevilla* 'Alice du Pont.' This subtropical vine grows just large enough to cover an eight-foot section of chain link fence. It grows almost as slowly as the stephanotis, but it flowers much more. The pure pink flowers begin in late spring and keep coming through summer and into fall, completely hiding the foliage. This vine needs sun but apparently likes its roots in the shade, which is also said to be true of stephanotis.

I have found it easiest to construct a support using ready-made redwood trellis panels that measure four by eight feet. The plant tendrils can then be woven into the lattice, or simply tied to it. The panels are attached with screws to eight-foot redwood two-by-two's, two at either side and one in the middle, and these are fastened to the wall. On a wooden wall, they can be attached with screws; on stucco, the screws must be driven into plastic anchors that are inserted into holes drilled with a masonry bit. These panels can also be attached to ten-foot, four-by-four posts so they are free-standing. This last method makes it easier to paint the wall behind the trellis, though the other method allows you to unscrew the whole construction and tilt it outward. I cannot attest to the longevity of these panels but I would guess that they will last at least ten years.

TREES

We don't often get the chance to plant a tree—they usually come with the place—but when we do, the choice should be carefully considered. Nothing you plant can become such a

monument (even a national treasure) or such a menace.

Trees are not only backgrounds for your garden but for the whole neighborhood. Of course, they have other functions in the garden, but above all they provide height and scale. A tree can so dominate its site that it makes all human endeavors, even the house, look temporary and of passing importance. Standing next to a tree, we do not feel so big ourselves. Some do not find this particularly comfortable while others find it reassuring, so we see certain neighborhoods full of large trees and others that are completely devoid of them. Not everyone wants to be bothered with the work or expense of caring for a large tree, and there is no doubt that trees involve one or the other—or both!

The Choice Choosing a tree is much like screening a candidate for a job.

Rather than compiling a great list to work from, look for a particular tree for the job in mind. Perhaps the two most important points to consider are large surface root systems and brittle branches, both of which can cause serious structural damage to your grounds. Trees with aggressive surface roots, such as evergreen magnolias, are impossible to garden under, and they can make short work of paving; trees with brittle branches are plain dangerous. But a solution can often be found when siting a tree. A magnolia placed in the background, away from paving, sewer lines, and other plantings, is a pleasure to contemplate and one of the most handsome of backdrops. Even trees that tend to let branches fall are not a problem if they have nothing to fall on. Then think of the eventual height and—as important—the spread. Though people shy away from a big tree, there is nothing

more majestic and lasting, and its height is of no dire consequence if it is otherwise well-behaved.

Its Shadow But do think of the tree's shadow. Some trees cast a dense shade under which it is impossible to garden; others barely freckle the ground. A dense tree shouldn't be anywhere near where you hope to garden, or want to sit, but it is perfect off in the background. Consider if it is deciduous or evergreen: there are places for both. Its nature and shadow will determine what you can grow under it. But don't forget that the ground under a tree is also the perfect place for a patio, especially one that is made of permeable paving—something that water can work its way through and that can be redone should the roots play with it.

Messy Trees People talk about how "messy" a tree is, but it is an unavoid-

Trees are the most important plants in the garden, dominating their surroundings, so they should be carefully chosen. In this garden, a California pepper (that actually comes from Peru), with a botanic name that sounds like a sneeze followed by a polite apology, Schinus molle, *commands the front of the house. Nearby companions include giant bird-of-paradise, pygmy date palms, and a crowd of azaleas. All of the other plantings are kept well away from the sensitive base of the tree.*

able attribute because the leaves and flowers are not permanently attached. Some trees drop their leaves all at once and overwhelm the gardener (but then it is finished), while others drop them a few at a time so it is easy to keep up with the work (though you are never done). Certainly, a tree that has flowers or fruit capable of staining the finish on an automobile or sidewalk is not a good choice to plant with its branches overhanging either; but another site would suit it fine.

Large or Small Leaves? The size of the leaves, flowers, and fruit that a tree bears needs to be considered, but again there is no ideal. Small leaves may be perfect for a tree growing above other plants; when dropped, they will simply disappear. But small leaves falling on a lawn can be a chore to rake up. In general, trees and lawns do not get along well. Trees don't like the frequent watering necessary for growing grass, and a lawn doesn't thrive in the tree's shade, so it is better not to plant them together, though gardeners and designers stubbornly do so despite the horticultural consequences.

Some trees drop leaves that are toxic to other plants and this may make it impossible to garden under them. This toxicity may exist to suppress competition, but it could be the perfect characteristic for a tree that will grow where you don't want anything else—over a patio or in a back corner of the prop-

erty, perhaps. Under a eucalyptus, or avocado for instance, you will find few weeds to hoe.

At Your Arboretum There are many factors to ponder when choosing a tree for your property; the worst possible way to go about it is to buy the first one that appeals to you at the nursery. Instead, in your garden diary set up a chart that lists the necessary characteristics, and as you find trees that you like, do your homework and fill it in. It might look like the chart below.

Don't be in a hurry to plant a tree, but don't put it off too long either. Do some research and discover what you need to know, then plant as soon as possible because trees take a long time to achieve maturity. You want to give your tree an early start so it can begin growing. Consider also that as the tree grows, what grows around it will have to be changed because the nearby plants will find themselves in increasing shade. Be especially aware that most fast-growing trees have serious drawbacks, so be wary.

For all these reasons it is better to keep a tree that is already on the property, even if it is not in the ideal place or is not the ideal tree. Save the tree and work around it, redesigning the garden if need be, then there's no need to start from scratch.

Trees No Bigger than a Bush Though they lack arboreal majesty, there are many small trees that may not be large

enough to create an impressive background, but still serve a useful function. Deciduous magnolias, for instance, have the small scale and showy flowers that make a decided contribution to the garden. Using small trees up close in the landscape is another way to add to the garden's depth and drama; placed in front of other trees, or planted in the middle of the garden, they become a strong foreground forcing the background to recede.

Some small trees will grow under taller trees, a sensible arrangement where another tree has grown so tall that it no longer can function as a backdrop, and you can see right under it. Eastern redbuds are an example of this relationship—they are "understory" trees—and one named 'Forest Pansy' is particularly pretty with its burgundy-colored leaves. It will grow under another taller tree that has a fairly open canopy.

Small trees might also be just the ticket for the background of a small garden. Many new small trees are being introduced by arboretums and nurseries because of this increasing demand, but don't overlook some of the shrubs that grow as large as small trees. Many do.

Sometimes the tree you need is already in place, but it is growing as a large, old shrub. In this case, take out the pruning saw and the loppers, and trim off the lower branches to reveal the tree hidden in its bushy shape.

TREES TO CONSIDER:						
NAME	ROOTS?	SHADE?	MESSY?	WHAT GROWS UNDER IT?	HEIGHT X WIDTH	MISC.
AMERICAN SWEET GUM	ON SURFACE, WRECKING SIDEWALKS	FAIRLY DARK, BUT IT'S DECIDUOUS	DROPS PRICKLY FRUIT— LOTS OF IT!	HAVE SEEN SHRUBS + LAWN	VERY TALL BUT NARROW	BEAUTIFUL FALL COLOR, HANDSOME SHAPE.

Plant Portrait

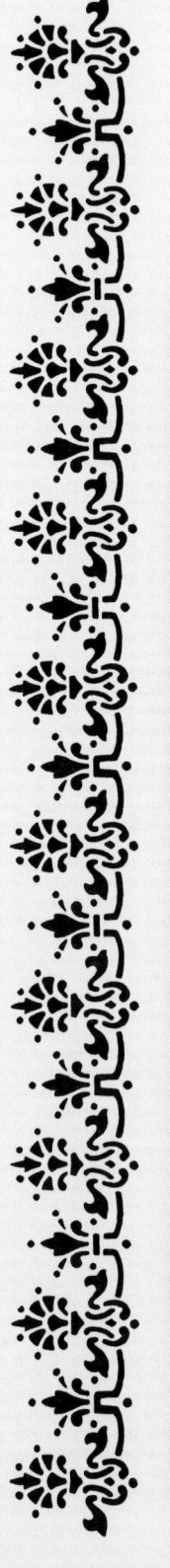

FOSSIL FALL COLOR

About 250 million years ago big changes occurred on this planet. The climate became drier, and the swamps that had nurtured the beginnings of life disappeared gradually. Plants that grew on this soggy ground—bizarre tree-sized horsetails, club mosses, and giant ferns, simple plants that were to become the earth's coal deposits— were replaced by more sophisticated flora. These were the earliest ancestors of modern plant life and, amazingly, two of these prehistoric vegetables somehow survived into

How many garden plants also exist as living fossils? Not many, but here are two: the dawn redwood, an even more ancient ancestor of the already ancient redwood, and the ginkgo, whose spectacular photograph on pages 44–45 opens this chapter. The dawn redwood, pictured on page 80, is the oddest of the pair—a conifer that loses its needles for winter—a deciduous "evergreen."

The ginkgo leaves are living fossils, shown above an actual fossil leaf of a dawn redwood.

modern times, though one almost didn't make it.

For years it was believed that all of the many *Metasequoias*, the first conifers that dominated the ancient forests (even in California) were extinct. But in a discovery that for paleobotanists must have rivaled the finding of a clutch of dinosaur eggs, a stand of *Metasequoia* was found in 1944 in a remote section of Sichuan, China. Much like California's giant sequoias, these trees were the last of their kind, having been hidden for ages in mist-shrouded mountains, and they were quickly given the popular name of dawn redwood.

Growing side by side (as they do in Southern California's Descanso Gardens), a California redwood and a dawn redwood are difficult to tell apart—until winter. Then the dawn redwood loses its leaves—it is a deciduous conifer, an oddity in the plant world (thus conifer and evergreen are not synonymous). In colder climates the leaves turn a presentable yellow before falling, though in California they turn brown or bronze at best. In compensation, the new spring foliage is the most brilliant green, as fresh as spring itself. Fortunately for gardeners, dawn redwoods never reach the heights of California redwoods. Though they grow fast at first, a mature specimen of a dawn redwood is not much taller than a liquidambar at about eighty feet, and they are naturally narrow.

Our other fossil tree, which was also preserved in China, is the ginkgo. It is almost a conifer, but its large flat leaves place it in its own family, *Ginkgoaceae*, of which it is the sole surviving member. Thought to be extinct in the wild, it apparently has survived in ancient temple gardens. Though the ginkgo is kin to the conifers, its seeds are not housed in cones but are inside plumlike fruits that can be quite odiferous once they fall to the ground. As a result, most ginkgoes are grafted male trees that don't produce fruit. Despite the unpleasant smell of the fruit, the seeds inside are a traditional ingredient in several Oriental dishes, including a Japanese mustard called *Chawan Mushi*.

Ginkgoes are among the most reliable sources of fall color; the leaves turn a clear, brilliant yellow and make a golden carpet that lasts on the ground for weeks after the tree has become bare. It is such a pretty sight that one ginkgo fancier gives his gardener a vacation so the leaves can lie undisturbed in all their golden glory on the bright green lawn. Press a leaf between the pages of a telephone book and the leaf will retain its color for years.

The ginkgo is an excellent garden tree, tolerant of just about anything, though it is painfully slow to get started and appears to grow only inches the first few years, looking awkward all the time. Gardens would probably be full of ginkgoes if the trees didn't require such patience in their first years on the part of their keepers. In time, ginkgoes become tall, slightly spreading trees, and no tree grows more elegant with age. Most attain a height of about forty feet, but some can grow even taller. There is also a stiffly upright variety named 'Fairmount' that is a good candidate to fill those tight places in a garden, and the variety named 'Autumn Gold' is distinguished by its molten color.

Ginkgoes and dawn redwoods are both excellent lawn trees, tolerating—even appreciating—the constant moisture necessary for the grasses that grow at their feet. Cool-season grasses are probably the best choice for lawns under these trees since they will do much of their growing while the trees are leafless and will appreciate the protection from the hot summer sun. I am probably not going too far out on a limb when I say that there are no better trees for a lawn, and, to top it off, these two have 250 million years of service behind them.

CHAPTER

4

**FLOWER BEDS
AND
BORDERS**

THE CENTER OF ATTENTION

At different times, different elements have been the center of interest in a garden. In Renaissance Italy, sculpture lined the garden paths and terminated every vista. In Moorish Spain, watercourses followed the paths or were channeled down their center, and splashing fountains or quiet pools were the main focus. In Tudor England, intricate knot gardens were the rage, while landscape designers of a later age used broad sweeps of lawn to capture attention. Finally, at the turn of this century, flowers got their turn.

Flowers have always been a part of gardens, but only in the more humble creations of the Italian peasants, Spanish campesinos, or English country people did flowers take center stage. It was the charm of that rustic creation, the English cottage garden, that influenced innovative gardeners such as William Robinson and Gertrude Jekyll to try flowers on a grander scale in breathtaking borders on large estates.

Pick and Choose Today's garden planner is free to pick and choose from all of these elements, but with flowers growing less and less abundantly in the natural landscape, they are bound to become more precious inside the garden's boundaries. Flowers are without question one of nature's most delightful creations, and their colorful presence is increasingly treasured.

There are other good reasons to make flowers important in a garden. Gazebos, patios, swimming pools, spas, and other man-made elements may be central to the design of a garden, but these creations are short-lived as attention-getters. One look usually suffices. Flowers, on the other hand, change with each hour, each season. They come in every con-

ceivable color and texture, and the possibilities of how and where they might be used are limitless. They can be planted and replanted, dug up and moved around, mixed and matched. One can never see all there is to see or learn all there is to know about flowers; since there is always something new to search for and acquire, the shopper in all of us can be satisfied.

Not everyone shares this affinity for flowers. Some want nothing to do with the hard work; some find flowers untidy and would prefer neat paving, a pool, or perhaps a lawn where something large and more exciting could be grown—trees or shrubbery. But this is what separates true gardeners from people who own a piece of land: Gardeners are those who believe that a garden without flowers is simply a yard. This does not mean that the other garden elements need be ignored or tucked away in some forgotten corner, only that they should be secondary to the play of nature. Water in a garden is certainly as decorative today as it was in Moorish times, and sculpture can look very much at home, but flowers will prove to be a more satisfying center of attention for a gardener or for anyone who longs for an antidote to the hectic life that is bustling just outside the garden walls.

Where We Are and Where They Might Be At this point in our planning we have carefully orchestrated the rest of the garden so the eye has a path to follow and that path leads to the flower beds, though not necessarily in a straight line. Flower beds or borders can be placed almost anywhere, but in your planning you are bound to discover that some places are better than others.

If you have mapped the hourly movement of shadows across your gar-

While there are many interesting and dramatic things that could be the center of attention in a garden, the most satisfying is a bed of flowers. White 'Iceberg' roses are the anchors in the bed on pages 82–83 and 84. Roses ought to be in every flower bed because they are in bloom for so much of the year, but there are other plants that glorify this garden, including a cloud of the tiny cream flowers of coral bells, lavender, and rosemary, dianthus, and a low-growing pink sun rose. The entry is framed by Solanum jasminoides, *and the path is flanked by compact eugenias.*

This is how big a flower bed ought to be, allowing plenty of room for a great variety— different heights, textures, and colors. It is nine feet deep, with a narrow work path just against the fence behind it, allowing access from the back. Growing here are bulbs, annuals, perennials, roses (mostly miniatures), and even a few vegetables.

den, you now know where the sunniest spots are. Following the advice in chapter three, you have created a background against which flowers can be viewed. You should also have a pretty good idea of where you are going to be sitting in your garden or where you are most likely to be when viewing it. With any luck at all, you should now be able to point with assurance to particular spots on your plans or models and say, "that's where the flowers are going to look best and grow best."

THE BIG BED

What this garden bed has that others do not is room to grow flowers—many flowers. There is sufficient space to hold a great variety—annuals and bulbs in their season, perennials, even small shrubs such as roses and azaleas, grown mostly for their flowers. Size and scale produce drama not found in smaller plots. The depth of the large bed gives the drama a chance to build, with smaller spreading plants in the foreground framed by taller and taller plants toward the back, one showcasing the other in theater-like staging.

Nine Feet It's a common mistake, not allowing enough room for flowers, but one that can easily be avoided or remedied. The typical suburban flower bed is about three feet deep, but the one pictured here is three times that size—nine ample feet between the path and the fence just for flowers. And this is not an especially large yard; its owner simply has dedicated more of it to flowers.

If there is a familiar look to this garden bed, it is owing to its English heritage, for it was in England that grand borders were first used. This is not the traditional English herbaceous

border, however, but a casual California equivalent. It relies heavily on a strong backbone of perennial plants (it's nice about these more permanent plantings that they keep the stage from looking too empty between the major acts), but it also makes use of seasonal bulbs and annuals, replanted in fall or spring, then pulled out at season's end.

If a composition as complicated as this looks hopeless for an amateur gardener, realize that this big bed was not planted all at once but evolved slowly, with plants and flowers going in as they were discovered at nurseries or at neighbors (many of them were started as divisions or cuttings from other gardens). There is always a necessary awkward period during which one discovers that this doesn't go with that— or when plants grow taller, wider, or shorter than anticipated—but constant fiddling and readjustment is part of the gardening process.

Hoick Them Out Victoria Sackville-West, who popularized informal flower borders on a grand scale at Sissinghurst, England, said, "Gardening is largely a question of mixing one sort of plant with another sort of plant, and of seeing how they marry happily together; and if you see that they don't marry happily together, then you must hoick one of them out and be quite ruthless about it. That is the only way to garden."

If that sounds like a lot of work, it is, but all that yanking out does not happen all at once as it does with beds of annuals or mass plantings of bulbs. Rather, it requires regular care—a little here and a little there; this is a garden to putter in.

When the weather is nice there is always something to do in a large flower bed, with room to try something new. You can even let things slide a bit;

Here is another big bed with a tremendous variety of plants, lower in profile to show the stone wall behind them. The wall is topped by climbing roses, two old varieties, 'Lady Forteviat' and 'Inspiration.' Clumps of daylilies and bearded iris are the anchors in this bed; perennials include columbine, coral bells, English daisy, and candytuft. Among the annuals are nasturtiums, lobelia, Iceland poppies, and also a great many bulbs.

plants past their prime, or even a few weeds, will hardly be noticed in the crowd, and other plants will draw the eye away or hide the offenders' untidiness. This is a definite advantage of a bed that is large enough to hold a great variety.

Room for Everybody In a big bed there's room for everybody, and this variety of plants is the fun of it. Freshly opened flowers greet you every morning, with always a surprise in store—colors that are unusually good together, or textures that seem just right; something blooming that you had forgotten about or something flowering for the first time. As with life in a big family, there is never a dull moment.

HOW BIG IS BIG ENOUGH?

One is tempted to say that flower beds or borders can't be too big, but there are limits, one being how far you can reach. The average person can just grab hold of a weed three feet away from where he is kneeling, and that's probably why the typical garden bed is only three feet wide. But you can easily step a little way into the front of a garden bed because the plants growing there are low enough to allow it, so now the bed can be six feet wide. If you are concerned that stepping into the bed will ruin your shoes, or worse yet, compact the soil, try putting flat stones or small pavers here and there in the front of the flower bed, giving you places to step.

You can also reach the bed from the back, for behind many large borders there is another small path for access. It is usually unseen because the flowers in front of it hide it completely, but they're not so tall that they prevent your stepping into the bed from the

back. So now you can reach six feet from front and three from the back, and your garden bed can be nine feet across. A nine-foot-wide bed is a nice size to shoot for, with an extra foot or so in back for that access path. Nine feet allows you to grow several three-foot-wide plants from front to back, enough to build some drama.

Three-foot Plants Conveniently, many flowering plants—perennials and roses in particular—grow to be about three feet across, and this is where many gardeners get in trouble. A dainty dianthus looks full and bushy in a gallon nursery can when it is only a foot across, but a few years later it will have easily spread to three feet in width. When you plant it, be sure to allow room for lateral growth.

Most annual flowers and bulbs are considerably smaller than perennials and they can be used in the foreground of a flower bed to add even more variety. They tend to look better planted in groups that seem about the right size when they measure three feet across. Be forewarned that when a bed is big and the flowers are spaced with room for future expansion, it is going to look pretty empty at first. Here is where annual flowers and some bulbs can help, temporarily filling the spaces until the perennials and more shrubby flowers fill out and fill in.

Another Trick Empty ground is nothing to be ashamed of and, in fact, it is necessary while you are waiting for plants to grow. Most gardeners like to avoid seeing these garden "bald spots," so here's another trick: Design the garden beds so they are usually viewed from a slight distance. In other words, don't put them directly below where you are to be standing or right next to where you and your visitors sit. This

way you will not be looking down on the beds, nor staring at the bare ground that is inevitably between plants. Instead, you will be looking across the bed, with plants screening the spots of bare earth. Weeds and plants' untidy parts will also be less noticeable so their presence will not disturb your enjoyment of the garden —you will not feel compelled to jump up and take care of them this instant or to plant more, when you should be happily anticipating the plants that will soon be filling in.

THINK OF FOLIAGE FIRST, BUT BEGIN WITH ROSES

When you start to plan a flower bed, one way to begin is with roses. Roses are often planted off by themselves, but they are an almost perfect anchor for a mixed flower bed. Modern roses flower often, more often than just about any other plant, so even when other flowers are not in bloom, roses are likely to be. Furthermore, you can find roses in a variety of of colors: reds, pinks, yellows, or oranges, so they will

fit into any color scheme.

However, there is a trade-off when you plant roses in a bed of other flowers—the roses won't grow as big as they do when planted by themselves. (This could be seen as an advantage in California where roses sometimes grow too tall to show well.) Because of the competition from other plants, there will be fewer rose flowers and they will be slightly smaller, but most gardeners will hardly notice this decrease in performance.

Planning a flower bed that will

include roses gives you a good opportunity to use the rule of three's and five's. Make a drawing of the bed and draw circles indicating where roses might go. Give each bush at least three feet of space and place the rose bushes about three feet back from the edge of the bed so you can plant other flowers in front of them. Don't set them too far into the bed or you won't be able to reach the plants easily, and roses need frequent care, such as cutting off dead flowers.

Roses also work well as anchors because they have handsome foliage.

Foliage as Important as Flowers A plant's foliage—in the case of roses, glossy burgundy leaves that change to dark green as they mature—is as important as its flowers; when there are no flowers, the foliage must carry the show. Modern English gardeners are especially expert at using foliage in a flower bed. Look at their gardens and note how different kinds of leaves play an important role. Plants with large leaves and plants with small ones are used, as well as burgundy-colored leaves, leaves streaked with gold, and frequently subtle gray or silver foliage. Study photos of fine English gardens and you will see the masterful use of fine textures—the ferny foliage of yarrow, for instance—and of coarse textures—the leaves of cardoon or acanthus. English gardeners are very fond of spiky leaves.

Too often flower beds rely mostly on flower color, while the foliage is a uniform green, frequently with leaves or similar sizes and textures. Beds of annuals are particularly prone to this leafy blandness since most have foliage colored a medium green.

Time to Go Window Shopping The only way to find out what the possibilities

really are is to do a little window shopping at nurseries. Look for interesting foliage. Perhaps buy a few plants, take them home, and begin experimenting. Arrange them (still in their nursery cans), rearrange them, and see what you like. Be bold and try groups that you might not normally consider. If your local nursery doesn't have much variety, try another, or ask a good gardener where he buys his plants. There are many specialty nurseries, most of them backyard businesses, that carry unusual plants. You will find that just a few extraordinary plants can bring excitement and life to the design of a garden bed.

THANK GOODNESS FOR PERENNIALS

When you begin looking for plants that will add interest to your flower bed, you will soon find yourself saying, "Thank goodness for perennials." What's so special about perennials? The great thing they offer is variety—there is no end to their numbers, no color they don't come in, no limitation on size or shape. As an added advantage, they will grow in your garden for quite a while. You can't plant them and forget them, but you can count on their lasting several years without much attention other than keeping up with the weeding, watering, and, on occasion, a little tidying up.

Sophisticates With perennials you can make a more sophisticated and somewhat more subtle composition. Instead of replanting the whole garden every six months, you can add to it, subtract when necessary, or move things about. It is easy to move perennials; in fact, a change of locale is required after a few years. Most perennials are not as brilliantly colored as annuals (annuals

must be seen by bees if they are to be pollinated and make seed for survival for another year, so they wear the wildest outfits). Perennials are just dressed in foliage for much of the year. For compensation, many perennials have beautiful foliage, which few annuals can boast of. Some are even grown just for their foliage, such as the silvery lamb's ears or the bronze ajuga.

Herbaceous and Other Perennials The traditional perennial is the herbaceous perennial—it dies completely to the ground every winter, or nearly so, springing back from the roots the following year. In California and in other Sunbelt gardens, we grow many plants that are called perennials but that are technically something else. Many are actually "subshrubs," if you look them up in a botanical reference book—short-lived, smallish shrubs. Some of these do not go dormant but actually bloom in the dead of winter. Some perennials, such as delphiniums in California, are grown as if they were annuals—you plant them each year and pull them out at the end of their season. In general, another benefit of adding perennials to a flower border is that they lengthen the flowering season, especially in mild climates.

Not Really Hard to Grow Many perennials are easy to grow, actually easier than annuals, although some require a bit of gardening skill. They often differ remarkably in their culture, but learning how to grow them is perhaps the most satisfying part of the adventure. But don't let it scare you away. A lot of gardeners have been intimidated by phrases such as "when to cut back" or "how to divide," but these techniques can be learned simply by trial and error—most perennials are very forgiving.

Perennials such as the tall blue delphiniums, the yellow and red columbine, the deep red coral bells, and the soft magenta nicotiana are important elements of this flower bed, not simply for their brilliance of color, but because they add a variety of heights and textures. A white 'Iceberg' rose also grows here with an assortment of annuals that includes stock and Iceland poppies. The tall foxgloves in the background are neither annuals nor perennials; they are biennials, growing one year, blooming the next, then dying. But in California, they grow and flower in just one season.

Plant Portrait

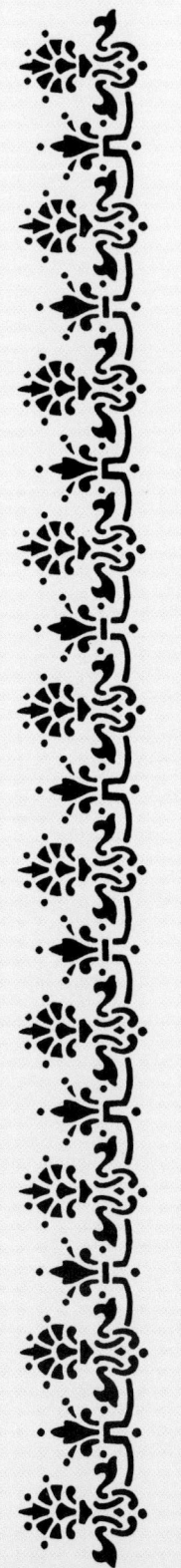

THE DAINTY DIANTHUS

Garden pinks, or dianthus, are the baby sisters of the carnation clan. They have the delicate ruffled beauty and delightful scent of carnations, but their flowers are simpler and they are on shorter stems (six to ten inches) that do not need staking to stay upright. Pinks and carnations are botanically *Dianthus* and are "perhaps native to the Mediterranean region," according to the best authorities. That's a good guess, because they do have the gray foliage of plants accustomed to a lot of sun. It may even be the best guess, because pinks have been grown in gardens since antiquity, and their true origins are hidden in the haze of the past.

If there were garden "ancient worthies," dianthus would be included in their ranks. They are ancient indeed, having adorned garlands and coronets in Greece and Rome, survived the Middle Ages in cloistered monastery gardens where their flowers flavored wines and graced illuminated manuscripts, and were transported to England, either by Norman monks or possibly attached to the stones that were imported for Norman watchtowers (depending on which account you read).

As early as 1578, an herbal distinguished between "coronations" and the "small feathered Gillofers, known as Pynkes, Soppes-in-wine, and small Honesties." In Shakespeare's time, the smaller dianthus was commonly called gillyflower, and before that, Chaucer knew it as "gilofre," until pink became the popular name.

They became popular flowers in Elizabethan times and, later, at their zenith, several hundred varieties of pinks and carnations were offered by English nurseries, though few of those

made it to our own shores. Because the best kinds must be grown from cuttings, they were difficult to import because of strict plant quarantines, but enough did emigrate to brighten our gardens with their dainty flowers and silvery foliage.

History alone gives them charm.

with blossoms in April and May. In summer, the plants are a low mound of gray, but by fall some of the leaves turn brown and the plants are less than tidy. Shearing flowering stems as they fade in summer helps encourage new growth and may prompt them to flower again. No need to be too careful—just get out the hedge shears, cut off the old flower stalks, and don't worry if you trim a little off the leaves.

Different varieties of dianthus are surprisingly different horticulturally as well. I have grown a variety called Penny that blooms all year and seems likely to live forever. It is now five years old and is a four-foot-wide patch of gray in the garden, usually covered with flowers. Other varieties I have tried are not nearly as long-lived and tend to flower at certain definite times. I will take a guess and say that the simpler the flower—those with single rather than double petals—the sturdier the plant. But most are not what I would call permanent plants in the garden, eventually dying out in sections, so I always keep a few cuttings going to make sure I don't lose them.

In England, they have naturalized on lofty castle walls, which hints at their soil preference—gritty or porous with the speediest of drainage. But this doesn't mean they like drought. On the contrary, they seem to need as much water as any other plant; they just don't want to sit in puddles of it.

Dianthus are started anew from "slips" (a garden word that existed in Shakespeare's time)—short shoots that do not terminate in a flower or bud. These should be gently pulled off the plant so that a small "heel" of the parent stem remains, then rooted in damp sand. The shoots are easy to root; simply strip off some of the lower leaves, plunge them partway into pure sand, and keep moist.

Their scent is heavenly, and the gray foliage offers welcome relief in a too-green garden. Low and sturdy, they make an elegant, nearly perfect, edge for a flower border and are especially attractive next to paths, spreading onto the pavement.

Dianthus make a delightful addition to the late spring and summer garden, where they thrive in a sunny spot, although they may be difficult at other times of the year. Typically, they grow wonderfully the first year, spreading into a dense, gray mound several inches high and a foot or two across, then in California covering themselves

Garden Visit

ONE BIG BORDER

In many respects it would be difficult to find a less typical California garden than the one pictured here. True, there is a swimming pool and a patio, but this garden is devoted to plants not to outdoor living, as are so many gardens in this sunny climate.

It is the garden of Ruth Borun, an avid gardener who was not too proud to call in a little help when faced with bringing order to her burgeoning collection of remarkable plants. Like many a gardener's garden, it had grown joyfully but haphazardly over the years. Garden designer Chris Rosmini was asked to help with its reorganization; the huge raised bed that sweeps the length of the garden was her solution.

The bed is so broad that there has to be a path behind it, without which the plants in the center would be completely out of reach. As it is, one must step gingerly through the lush growth to reach the remote interior. It is wide enough to hold a great variety of plants. Though most are perennials of one kind or another, the most obvious exceptions at this time of the year are the watsonias, annuals whose tall pink and white bulbs are in bloom. This bed is wide enough to accommodate truly tall plants. Near the pool you can see a profusion of perennials grown mostly for their foliage, especially those with gray leaves. This rich array entices you to spend a great deal of time looking at the plantings—this is what most pleases avid gardeners.

The work that went into the Borun border was phenomenal. Ruth Borun is always stopping to pull this weed or nip that bud. That is what gardening is all about and yet another reason why perennials are so popular with people who love to grow things.

There is ample room for really big flowers in this curving raised bed that borders a lawn on one side and has a path on the other for easy access. The tallest plants are watsonias, South African bulbs that are completely at home in this Los Angeles garden. Columbines and penstemon also stand tall, while Verbena rigida stand out—they are the pure purple flowers in the foreground. Tufts of blue fescue, an ornamental grass, can be seen in the front row, perched atop the wall of broken concrete.

DIVISION AND DORMANCY

In time, most true perennials need to be cut back and divided. They originated in cooler climates, where they had to die to the ground to survive winter. In the garden, we cut them back instead, because it's neater and in mild climates, like California's, we need to force them to rest. The champion tool for cutting back perennials is actually made for edging the lawn—the Corona No. 5 shear—long and hefty enough to cut a bunch of stems at once.

Be aware that not all perennials sold as such should be cut back to the ground. Remember that some are not true herbaceous perennials and they should usually just be tidied up. If you're in doubt, leave the plant alone and see if the stems die back or not. If a perennial flowers early in the season, cut it back then and it may flower again. Later in the season, hold off until the onset of winter and enjoy the seed stalks produced after the flowers.

Ideally, in California's mild climate, you will never have a garden of perennials that are all cut back and dormant. There are plenty of plants sold as perennials that look good at all times of the year. But there is a definite down time in November and December when there are few or no flowers and many plants are producing only seed stalks. This is the time of year to "rework the border," which usually means digging and dividing.

Simple Division Division is necessary because most true perennials grow as spreading clumps. If you look closely at a true perennial, you will see that what appears to be one plant is actually a number of smaller plants growing together. As they grow ever wider, they deplete the soil beneath them so totally that the center of the clump begins to fail. At this point, dig it up and either pull the clump apart or slice it apart with a sharp spade. Most serious perennial gardeners keep a flat-bladed spade, sharpened with a coarse file, just for this purpose.

Dig the entire clump out of the ground so you can see what you're dealing with and then split it apart. These clumps can get pretty heavy, so this might not be feasible if yours has grown very large—one reason you want to attend to this every few years. The old center of the clump is usually discarded, and the vigorous younger outer growth divided into small pieces and replanted. Extra divisions can be given away and most gardeners get pretty shrewd about swapping their extras for some perennial they don't have. Most of this dividing (and swapping) is done during winter.

Renew the Soil Because perennials use a soil so heavily, it is very important to prepare the soil thoroughly before planting. The idea is to make it as rich as possible by adding fertilizer and organic amendments (the kind sold by the bag at nurseries—usually a mix of specially treated barks and sawdust). These are mixed in with a spade, spading fork, or tiller, and the result is a fluffy, rich soil that will sustain a perennial for a number of years. When it is time to dig and divide, the soil can be renewed by adding still more organic material, especially fertilizer. Any complete granular fertilizer will do.

A well-prepared soil is also a lot easier to dig in, so the perennials are easier to dig up, divide, or move. This is one advantage of using perennials. If you don't like the way they look where they are growing, or if they grow too tall or wide for their spot, it is no big problem to move them elsewhere.

Dividing perennials is not the mystery it is often made out to be. Very simply, many perennials grow as clumps of individual plants and in time the inside of the clump deteriorates. Then the idea is to dig it from the soil, split the clump apart, discard the old center and replant the fresh outer growth. Two examples are pictured here. A big clump of agapanthus at the upper left and right, and a clump of a classic herbaceous perennial, veronica, at the lower left and right. Note the individual plants of the veronica—one stem with roots.

Garden Visit

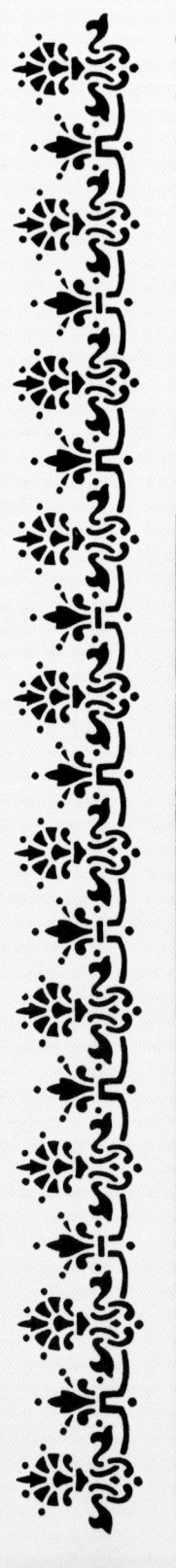

GRANDSTAND GARDENING

There is something to be said for grandstanding in the garden—arranging all of the plants with the shortest in front, the tallest in back and the in-betweens in between, as if all the flowers were sitting neatly on bleachers. This classic arrangement still gets the most applause, especially when the flowers are in the front yard, as the two borders pictured here happen to be. Barely a leaf or stem is visible, with the shorter plants hiding all the foliage of the others, so only the flowers can be seen.

Notice the other classic staging devices used in these two beds. Wisely, they have been set back a little from the street or sidewalk. This not only keeps the flowers from being trampled, but it allows that narrow strip of lawn between street and garden to make a nice green foreground for the colorful blooms. At the same time, it prevents the glare of the adjacent concrete from intruding. If the sidewalk were a more handsome or elegant path in the back of the garden, this strip of lawn wouldn't be necessary. There are good reasons not to have it, but instead to

The two summer gardens on these pages are striking examples of bleacher-like staging. White vinca and perennial candytuft (not yet in bloom) comprise the lowest front row in the garden on page 98. Behind them come marigolds and marguerites, spikes of purple salvia. Taller zinnias and roses occupy the back.

Lobelia and sweet alyssum have front-row seats. Pink and red annual phlox, pansies, and Chrysanthemum paludosum are behind them, with zinnias in back. Overlooking all is still another row, of roses.

let the flowers spill over into the strip. However, necessity sometimes forces compromises in the garden plan. Backing up the flowers are substantial walls of brick or stone—natural materials that complement the flowers. They complete the picture, acting as one side of the frame, the lawn being the other.

The beds are not too narrow; one is about five feet broad, the other has undulations that vary from four to eight feet. To grandstand like this requires a variety of heights and a wide enough area. Both beds are filled with summer flowers. Zinnias are the major players, but perhaps more important are the smaller flowers in the foregrounds since they are the very foundations of the planting compositions and must look the tidiest. In one bed, a low hedge of perennial candytuft, *Iberis* (out of flower at the time of the photograph), does the job year round. In the other bed the front row is occupied by old-reliable sweet alyssum and lobelia in two shades, a dark violet and a lighter lavender. These spill right onto the lawn, so the grass must be edged by hand.

The second row has two tiny chrysanthemums, neither of which has a proper common name: *Chrysanthemum paludosum* has white blooms that look like Shasta daisies, and the *C. multicaule* has buttery-yellow flowers, partially closed on this overcast day. Perennials of various sorts, including the blue bedder *Salvia farinacea*, dwarf agapanthus, and even an ice plant also grow there. In the other bed, summer's favorite annual, miscalled *Vinca rosea* (it's really *Catharanthus*) provides a cooling white influence.

Note that both garden beds use roses at the very back of the borders, where you can see their flowers but not their scraggly bases—a neat trick.

Annuals have the brightest and splashiest colors of all, zinnias being the perfect example. The strain called California Giants on page 100 is one of the best and most vivid.

Mary Ellen Guffey, pictured on page 101, tends a garden planted mostly with annuals on a hillside in Malibu. This is the spring garden, put in during the fall, a favorite time to plant in California.

There is no reason not to mix annuals, bulbs, perennials, or any other plant, in the same bed. The spring garden on page 102 by Sassafras Nursery & Landscaping uses yellow tulips and a pink double tulip named 'Angelique' with anemones, cineraria, primroses and forget-me-nots, all happy under the light shade of an old olive.

A PLACE FOR ANNUALS

Though perennial flowers offer more variety and more interesting foliage, annual flowers such as zinnias and marigolds are by far the brightest and the most floriferous. Every garden, including the most subdued, should have a place for them, even if it is only in pots. True annuals grow, flower, and die in the course of a single year. This probably accounts for their flamboyant colors and huge flowers—they have only a short time in which to attract bees and other pollinators if their race is to survive into another year.

Many of the most colorful annuals originated in Mexico—zinnias and marigolds are among the best known— and they flower during the warmest weather in sunny colors. They are native to an area in Mexico where win-

ters are so dry that most plants cannot survive the season, so these annuals die in winter. Summers are, by contrast, wet and warm, and this is when they sprout and grow. In California, we call these the warm-season annuals, because they are planted in spring for summer bloom.

The Cool-Season Crop We also grow annuals that come from climates much like California's (some do come from this state, including California poppies and godetia or farewell-to-spring). In these climates, the summers are dry but the winters are wet, so these flowers grow during the cool, rainy season and we call them cool-season annuals. In other parts of the country, these cool-season annuals are usually planted very early in spring, before those that need warmer weather. Most

of these cool-season annuals can tolerate a little frost.

Interestingly, these annuals tend also to have cooler colors, though there are some very bright exceptions. Canterbury bells, cineraria, English daisy, foxglove, larkspur, linaria, and stock are some cool-season annuals (or plants grown like annuals) with cool colors; calendulas, iceland poppies, and pansies are some with much warmer colors.

Not Actually Annuals Some plants grown as annuals actually aren't. They may be biennials (such as Canterbury bells or foxglove) or perennials (such as English daisies), but through the years gardeners have discovered that these plants are most successful when planted every year, then taken out at the end of their season. In Southern California, the popular impatiens will last more than a year, but they look their best if they are replanted every spring.

Bays, Plots, and Pots If you use shrubs and perennials to form the backbone of your flower bed, create some bays in which to plant the annuals. Most annuals are fairly short-stemmed compared to perennials, so little bays cut out of the front edge of the flower bed make perfect homes for them.

To the very sensitive perfectionist, the strong colors of many annuals are inharmonious with the more muted colors of perennials. If this is an objection, try planting annuals in their own little plots in another part of the garden. You might even plant your annuals in beds in the front yard and perennials in the back to make the best of both worlds. Or plant some of the vivid annuals in pots. Annuals do particularly well in containers because they grow fast, can take a lot of water, and thrive on fertilizer. Pots filled with bright annuals bring color close to the sides of the house where patios or paving preclude planting in the ground.

That Summer Sun-Winter Shade Problem Annuals are also a solution for that summer sun-winter shade problem. There are parts of the garden that get drenched in sunlight in summer, but are bathed in shade all winter when the shadows lengthen. In winter, use cool-season flowers such as primroses or cinerarias that tolerate shade, replanting these beds in spring to give the garden summer color with those flowers that like the sun.

Plant Portrait

PANSIES IN PARTICULAR

The most enduring and perhaps endearing of fall-planted, cool-season flowers are the pansies and violas, pansies being the flowers with the charming, contrasting faces, and violas the ones that are plain-faced but just as pretty.

In California, if they are planted in October they will flower within weeks and keep on flowering until the first hot days of summer, maybe longer. Even if they get straggly after a few months, there is a way to bring them back. And if you are one of the unlucky few who have had pansies die suddenly for no apparent reason, there is a solution for this as well.

Pansies have been an important part of California gardening for a long time. In 1908 John McLaren, creator of San Francisco's Golden Gate Park and author of one of the earliest books on California gardening, said of the pansy: "This popular plant is a favorite of rich and poor alike, everyone who has a garden growing a few pansies. This is deservedly so, in view of its wonderful variety of color and its free-flowering habit together with the ease with which it may be grown."

At that time, much attention was being given to hybridizing and crossing, with the goal being bigger and bigger flowers. In 1915, E. J. Wickson noted in *California Garden Flowers:* "Pansies are a great delight if well grown from choice strains of seed, of which a number of seedsmen are making a specialty. A pansy specialist is coming to be regarded as a very high-class horticulturist."

Bigger and Better By 1928 choice strains made the cover of at least one seed catalogue, that of the Los Angeles firm of Aggeleler & Musser, a consider-able feat considering the competition from other flowers and vegetables. These strains had names such as Mammoth Wonder, A&M Super Maximum, and Mastodon, the names indicating that size was of utmost importance. About the same time plants as well as seed began to be sold, but not in plastic pots as they are today. You dug your own from fields and loaded them into wooden boxes. At Paul J. Howard's Flowerland nursery on La Brea, plants were sold for fifty cents a dozen or three dollars per 100. By 1949 Better Gardens nursery in San Marino was offering Genuine Imported Rogglie Swiss Giants, Steele's, and a mix named Santa Anita Jumbo, which shows how far back the tradition of pansies blooming at the Santa Anita racetrack goes.

The culmination of all this breeding was a strain called Majestic Giants which won the first All-America award for pansies. According to Lew Whitney of Roger's Gardens in Corona del Mar, who has planted thousands of these flowers in gardens, they are still the best of the big-flowered, long-stemmed, pretty-faced pansies and the most popular at nurseries.

Those long stems, by the way, were developed so pansies could be cut and arranged, a problem modern gardeners have not had to contend with. Lew remembers his mother having a special shallow bowl just for pansies, and old seed catalogues make quite a point of long-stemmed pansies for cutting. One contemporary seed catalogue from the English firm of Thompson & Morgan still carries two cut-flower strains—Violet Queen and Yellow Queen—and the catalogue photos of these pansies, neatly tied into little bundles, ought to tempt one to try pansies as cut flowers. But for attractive cut flowers you really needn't look further than

Violas and pansies are perfect in pots, especially if the containers are set up on a ledge so you can look into those little flower faces. This bowl is filled with a strain named Beaconsfield.

the Majestic Giants.

There are other strains of large-flowered pansies, and there are even some called Steele's, presumably descended from that old-time strain now valued for their smaller, but softer-colored flowers. There is also a mix called Race Track, which honors the huge field planted every year in the center of the Santa Anita racetrack.

Violas As pendulums have a way of doing, this one is now swinging back and the smaller-flowered violas are returning to fashion. One good reason is that the ancestor of all violas is a perennial, and as a result violas or viola-flowered pansies bloom the longest of the lot. They can even live over from year to year.

Violas are descended from *Viola cornuta*, but so much crossing has gone on that most violas are now a mix of pansy and viola, which is why some seed catalogues invented the term viola-flowered pansies. But you are pretty safe if you call any plain-faced pansy a viola. The best of these is a strain called Crystal Bowl, which is the common plain-faced pansy at nurseries, sold either as a mix or as separate colors. It is the longest-flowering of its kind, and it blooms for what seems forever. You are likely to tire of it long before it gives up. Clear Crystal is a similar strain. You will also find some other small-flowered violas that are always one color, such as a strain called Ruby or Ruby Queen, whose deep red blooms are more the color of a garnet and are among the most velvety of violas.

Just What Are They? It is a little harder to figure out what to call some of the pansies or violas that fall somewhere between the two categories. One of these is called Bambini, and it has the

cutest of all pansy faces with distinct eyes and a smile but small, viola-sized blossoms. Beaconsfield is an interesting pansy with the three lower petals a deep purple and the uppermost pure white. Moody Blues is striking with the upper petals colored purple and a purple face on the lower white petals. Imperial Blue and Imperial Orange Prince have only faint faces, but they are two of the prettiest violas or pansies, whichever they are.

You may also find some small-flowered pansies or violas that have extremely deep color and complicated markings. These are sold only in small pots, when they are in flower, and they are seldom named, but I suspect that they are descendants of what used to be called Shakespeare's pansies—violas with some Johnny-jump-up in them.

The Johnny-jump-up is the least civilized of the viola clan and grows so easily it will naturalize in gardens. Some even consider it a weed. It has its own botanical name of *Viola tricolor*, a reference to the lilac, purple, and yellow petals. A fancier Johnny-jump-up, which is a deep, velvety purple, is named 'King Henry' two more charming flowers would be hard to find.

This by no means exhausts the list, but it should help with the shopping because the best way to buy pansies or violas—if you want to plant them by the dozens in the ground—is when they are small and compact, well before they have flowered.

Pansy Problems One reader wrote in early spring, "Some of my violas are already giving up the ghost, the stalk seemingly severed right at the soil line." Another, "I lose lots of pansies each year. Have tried everything—putting them on mounds, cutting back watering, more watering, etc. And they

Pansies and violas are a little hard to tell apart; Azure Blue at upper left is a pansy, and Crystal Bowl, just below, is a viola. 'King George' at upper right is a Johnny-jump-up.

still die. Healthy plants seem to just rot away." The problem is a fungus, one of the many named *Rhizoctonia*. It attacks the very base of the plant and literally severs it from the roots. It may be brought on by too much water, but some readers suggested that even cutting down on the watering didn't help.

The solution was suggested by Lew Whitney at Roger's Gardens. They spray the plants with Ortho Multipurpose Fungicide, which contains the active ingredient Daconil, emphasizing that this will not bring back plants already infected, but—in their experience—will prevent the fungus from attacking nearby pansies or violas. It can be used preventively by spraying new plantings as soon as they go into the ground, then following up with a second spraying a few weeks later. The fungus lives only on the soil's surface so there is no need to soak or drench the soil; just get the surface good and wet, especially around the base of the plants.

Cut Them Back All pansies, but in particular the smaller, viola-flowered strains, will bloom from January into early summer. This was known back in Wickson's time, and a report from Mr. W. M. Bristol of San Bernadino, in the 1915 edition of *California Garden Flowers*, states: "Probably there is no place better adapted to the production of magnificent pansies than southern California. The weather from January to July is more or less cool and moist, conditions favorable to the growth of the pansy, and with proper management the plants will produce an immense crop of blossoms of large size."

Since they last such a long time in the garden, it is common for pansies and violas eventually to get long, leggy, and straggly, and you certainly want to avoid buying them when they already look like that. At the nursery, find tight, compact plants that have not begun to lean or topple. Should they become leggy in the ground, try another trick passed along by Lew Whitney. Even though it sounds drastic, cut pansies and violas back to within an inch of the ground; fertilize and water them and watch them come back! If only a few stems become leggy, these can be pinched back. The reason stems become long is most often lack of light. Heed Mr. Bristol's advice from 1915: "Don't believe the threadbare and absurd statement that 'pansies like a shady place.' Set them where they will receive full sun but no reflected heat from buildings."

Not for Shade Though pansies will tolerate some shade, they prefer sun; therefore the information found on some plant labels at a nursery, "plant in part shade or shade," is dead wrong.

"Remove all blossoms as they wilt," continues Mr. Bristol and this advice is seconded by Mr. Whitney. If pansies and violas are allowed to go to seed, they will not last nearly as long as they should. Lew Whitney goes so far as to let his thumbnail grow a little longer in winter so he can use it in true nurseryman fashion to nip off the pansy flowers as they fade.

What pansies and violas like best is a cool and moist soil, so it is worth the effort to add organic amendments before planting and to mulch after planting. Their beds must never be allowed to dry out. These plants like moisture, but Mr. Bristol's advice is again as appropriate today as when he wrote it: "Don't give them a shower-bath with the hose every day or two. It is folly. It hardens and packs the ground while the roots may be suffering for moisture. Once a week or two

make holes or furrows among the plants and keep water therein until the ground is thoroughly soaked."

You may not want to irrigate with furrows, but when you water, do so thoroughly. Old books make quite a point of never letting pansies go completely dry and of mulching with some organic material. Full sun for the tops, cool and moist for the roots.

A Place for Pansies The traditional place to plant pansies has always been along the front walk so their cheery faces can welcome visitors. A plan in the 1908 edition of *California Gardening* shows pansies on either side of the walk and flanking the front door against the house, at the base of the rose bushes. Because they are neat and long-lasting, pansies and violas are among the best choices to plant in the front of the flower bed or the front row of a perennial border.

Pansies, and especially violas, are the perfect companions for spring bulbs. After you plant the bulbs, plant pansies on top. They will flower both before and after the bulbs and the fading bulb foliage can be bent over and hidden beneath the pansy foliage. A favorite combination mixes yellow daffodils, which can be planted in the fall, with blue violas, or the pansy strain labeled Azure Blue, or one of the blues from the Crystal strain.

A less obvious place for pansies is about five or six feet in the air, in hanging baskets or in window boxes, simply because you can then enjoy them face-to-face. It would be tempting to make a window box just for pansies because they are so cute when viewed at eye-level. Seen up close, their faces resemble cats', with the streaks being the whiskers, and this is borne out in the name of one old-time pansy strain—Felix.

A mass planting of ranunculus shows the power of bulbs, especially if just one color is planted, though the few orange flowers in the field of yellow are a deft way of adding interest. These tender bulbs that are actually tubers shaped like a clump of bananas are planted in the fall in California, for joyful spring bloom.

A PLACE FOR BULBS

Bulbs are similar to annuals in that they are not permanent elements of the garden—at least not those parts that grow above ground. In California some bulbs must be replanted each year, while many others will apparently disappear for the summer. Those return the following fall or spring after spending part of the year underground where they must not be disturbed or overwatered.

Many daffodils, for example, will live from year to year, but not if the bulbs get too wet in summer. Therefore, you can't simply plant something else on top of daffodil bulbs, especially not other plants that need a lot of water. One solution is to plant something that needs little water—a low-growing herb or perennial, or a ground cover—at the time the bulbs are planted.

This gardening strategy also solves the problem of what to do with that withering foliage. After a bulb flowers the leaves must be left on until they naturally dry up (the plant needs time to move the food stored in its leaves to the bulb). If the bulbs are planted under something else, the browning bulb foliage can be tucked under the other plant's leaves.

Tied in Knots Another age-old way to deal with withered foliage is to tie it in a simple knot, which makes it appear that the gardener knows what he or she is doing, while it doesn't much improve the appearance of the garden bed. Yet another solution is to plant the bulbs behind other plants that are still growing so that as the bulbs wither, they are hidden by plants growing up in front of them. These are rather sophisticated ways of dealing with bulbs and require a good deal of gardening savvy, but a garden notebook can help. Make a note of when the bulbs bloom and how long the foliage lasts.

Simpler Solutions Yet another way of dealing with the fading bulb foliage is to plant the bulbs off by themselves. A favorite spot for early spring bulbs is under a deciduous tree. There they get all the light they need in winter and early spring and protection from the sun in summer. Leaf litter provides an attractive mulch in summer and holds down weeds.

Or you can do what so many gardeners end up doing: Dig up the bulbs—after the foliage yellows—and store them in a cool, dry place. You can even move them out of the garden before the foliage fades if you dig them up and temporarily plant them somewhere in the back, then store them away when the leaves are brown. The final solution is the simplest—just toss this year's bulbs out and buy new ones next year. In this case, be sure to dig up the bulbs right after flowering, while the stems are still strong enough to give you a handle for lifting the bulbs out of the ground. At the least, be sure to get the bulbs out while the foliage is still visible or you'll have the devil's own time finding them in the garden bed.

Plant Portrait

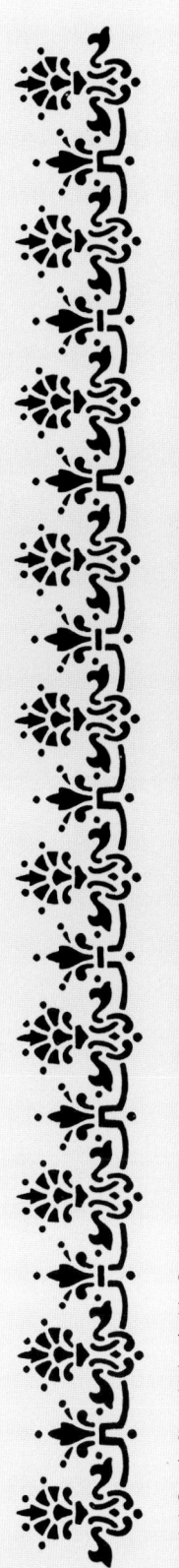

TRICKS WITH TULIPS

Before you decide that bulb planting will become an annual affair, be aware that it can be a lot of work. George de Gennaro, who is known for his beautiful food photography, plants some 15,000 bulbs each year and we asked him for this self-portrait at planting time so others could see just what is involved. Amazingly, he doesn't even look tired. Then he photographed this same spot in spring and you can see that it was worth all the effort.

Planting bulbs is no small task. Huge piles of earth are dug from the beds and piled to one side, after which wheelbarrows of sand and soil amendments are brought in. Compared to other garden chores, this is more like a military operation, but the result is spectacular. Twelve months later there are masses of bulbs blooming with dress parade precision at a regimented height—a spring so glorious that it is difficult to conceive of having such beauty in your own backyard.

What happens to these traditional Dutch bulbs is quite different in most Southern California gardens. Tulips, and especially hyacinths, tend to bloom at various heights and at different times, sometimes when they are barely out of the ground. Daffodils are less difficult to regiment, but we seldom see displays as picture-perfect as those in the de Gennaro garden.

The problem with tulip bulbs is their Dutch heritage. Bred in a bleak northern European climate, these bulbs do not expect January days with temperatures in the 80s. Though we cannot provide a mantle of snow, we can buffer them better against the occasional heat of a California winter and the strong sun of spring. Note the depth of the trench in the picture. Bulbs are not merely planted, they are buried. At least six inches of soil cover the bulbs, which means that the planting holes must be at least eight inches deep. The bulbs are safe from any hot winter weather beneath that blanket of soil—although it might be more apt to compare the insulating soil to a down quilt, since it is fluffy and light, more like potting soil than garden soil. Each year the de Gennaro bed is amended with organic matter while the sand cushioning the bed of bulbs gets mixed in each time the bed is prepared for planting. There is now a twenty-year accumulation of sand and organic soil amendments. The result is a soil so light and airy that it quickly drains away excess moisture and makes it easy for the bulbs to push their way upward to the surface.

The inch-thick layer of washed builders' sand added to the bottom of the planting hole is extra protection from a too-wet soil and helps hold the bulbs upright when the soil is shoveled back into the hole. Bulbs are spaced four to five inches apart atop this sand, with the exception of hyacinths, which are spaced five to six inches apart to allow room for their fat flower heads. Another clue for the sharp-eyed: Note when the bulbs are planted. This photo was taken on January 22, and some bulbs are already starting to sprout. De Gennaro plants late, very late, usually in January.

Before being planted, the tulip and hyacinth bulbs are refrigerated for a month or more in large coolers that are used by de Gennaro in the course of his food photography. It's a necessary step because these two bulb types need a simulated winter dormancy to bloom properly. Keep yours in the fridge.

This thirty-foot-long bed is only one of twelve such beds devoted to bulbs, all of them being in partial shade provided by flowering peach and nectarine trees, dogwoods, birches, magnolias, and other deciduous trees that are only partially leafed out when the bulbs bloom. This slight shading undoubtedly helps the tulips develop the long stems they properly should have, but often cannot achieve in Southern California.

Anchoring the bulb beds are plantings of perennials such as coral bells and columbine, and when the bulbs are finished, more perennials are put in. These later perennials include masses of delphiniums, coreopsis, veronica, and marguerites; sometimes summer annuals are added, to last through the summer and fall. The bushy marguerites are a particular favorite as a summer filler since they grow incredibly fast in the late spring. Because these plants must be watered in summer, all of the bulbs are taken out after blooming; the tulips are thrown away because they will not flower a second year.

The timing of bulbs, perennials, and annuals—when they should be planted and when they bloom—works out surprisingly well. The permanent plantings of perennials—coral bells are the favorite—are dug up and divided when the bulb beds are prepared in January. That works out neatly since January is a good time for that chore and perennials bloom better when restarted in that fashion. January is such a favorable time to divide the practically dormant perennials that de Gennaro is often able to leave huge clumps of them sitting out of the ground for days, with no ill effects, while other work progresses.

The perennials planted after the bulbs bloom are usually kept for only one season, as though they were summer annuals. A good time to plant perennials is when the bulbs finish in May. De Gennaro plants most of his

from gallon cans, but our experience indicates that even when planted from four-inch pots in early May, perennials will put on quite a show in June and July, then carry a few flowers into fall.

May is also a good time to plant summer annuals, and the bulb beds usually can accommodate some zinnias or impatiens as well. De Gennaro used to plant chrysanthemums after the bulbs were finished since the mums, in turn, would be finished blooming in the fall, before it was time to plant bulbs again. But now de Gennaro

reserves the fall as a time to rest from garden chores.

A permanent "planting" of rocks also helps define the beds and somehow makes the bare earth of late fall and midwinter (after the annuals and some of the perennials have come out) look quite natural while the garden awaits bulbs. Once the bulbs are in, it doesn't take long to see green shoots begin to poke through the ground followed by buds and flowers—a benefit of planting late.

In bloom at this point in the season

Planting bulbs can be big work, as you can see in the picture on page 110. Photographer George de Gennaro plants thousands each winter, digging huge trenches with an inch-thick layer of sand in the bottom to cradle the bulbs. The soil that goes back into the hole is thoroughly amended.

In spring, all the work pays off. On page 111 you see the same bed four months later, with 'Apricot Beauty' tulips in the foreground, mixed with Dutch iris and 'Soleil d'Or' narcissus. The deeper-colored tulips in the background are the variety 'Gudoshnik.'

(April) are the orange and red, 'Gudoshnik' tulips, a tulip named 'Apricot Beauty' the narcissus 'Soleil d'Or' mixed with a few Dutch irises and, in the path, a few crocuses planted with primroses. In this same bed, under a deciduous magnolia and several birches, are many other tulips and daffodils backed up by tall lilies, which bloom at different times.

Will this grand scheme work in a smaller garden? Absolutely. It will even work in containers; the big display of bulbs nearer the de Gennaro house is grown in containers. In a small garden, the principles of how deep to plant, when to plant, and how to prepare the soil still hold true. The only difference is the number of bulbs to plant. Just remember that a dramatic show of flowers depends on having a lot of one variety, so it's more effective to plant fewer kinds but more of them. Believe it or not, even the de Gennaros pass up different varieties of bulbs that they would like to try in favor of having a mass display. But as you can see, it works wonderfully.

Plant Portrait

MORE BULB STORIES

Bulbs needn't always be a lot of work. There are bulbs that can be planted in small holes and ways to use them that require fewer bulbs. Since bulbs are one of gardening's great mysteries, beginning as one thing—a pulpy mass in a papery husk—but developing into quite another, it seems only natural to describe their planting and flowering as if it were a mystery story recounted by a gumshoe gardener. Here are three intriguing cases to consider. They really happened this way.

A Classy Bulb October 25. Picking through a cardboard box at the nursery in Bay City, it looked too late for these bulbs. I could find only some that had sprouted and seemed ready to bloom. If they had been garlic or onions I would have left them there, but they were saffron, a classy bulb if there ever was one. I bought myself a dozen at forty-five cents.

October 26. I found the ideal spot for them, a narrow alley of soil between two concrete stepping stones. Under a hot October sun, I planted the bulbs just below the surface, with the sprouts above ground. I left no room between the bulbs, and in that skinny slit of soil they looked uncomfortable, like sardines in a can. They were a long way from their ancient Mediterranean home, but so are a lot of us in the City of Angels.

November 4. Nothing happened for eight days. A patient man would wait. I wasn't one. I dug up a bulb. It was making progress. In the last few days it had grown a dozen roots, each about three inches long. I carefully planted it again and went back to waiting.

November 11. It was one of those days that was already hot and dry and starting to fray the nerves—everything was too bright, the sky too blue. I stepped outside and through the glare of the early morning sun saw the saffron crocus in full flower. It was going to be a pretty day after all.

Around the Mediterranean, saffron is grown as a cash crop, like lima beans. I tried to imagine what a field full of saffron would look like. I couldn't. Even these few flowers were a spectacle. From the back door I could see the brilliant red saffron styles which yield that precious spice that sells for an arm and a leg and turns everything it touches a golden orange. Out in the garden, on hands and knees, I observed the light veining in the lilac petals that made the flowers look like feathers with the styles lying languidly across them, a fortune in saffron there for the picking. But I couldn't do it. Fortune would have to wait for another day.

November 12. Next morning the flowers were still there, and I found a lot of good reasons to walk by them during the day. But by night the show was over. Another round of flowers could be seen pushing their way through the dense bundle of leaves so there would be other days like this. Now it was time to harvest the styles. I picked them from between the wilted petals and set them aside to dry. Paella was their future and I made a note to plant more next year, though I managed to fill a tiny brown vial with this year's crop. Maybe I'd buy an acre down in Escondido. With saffron at eight dollars a bottle, I could see easy street right around the corner.

March 15. Months had passed since the last saffron flowers had faded, but I could still see them glowing in that too-bright October sun. Their leaves are just beginning to yellow now, and since they are long enough to trip over, I cut them back to about four inches so they would look like little tufts of grass. I

didn't want to trim them any further because they still needed to manufacture enough food to carry them through the long, hot Los Angeles summer. I look forward to their return—they're one of the few bulbs that come back every year.

Not a Weed October 21. They were the ugliest bulbs I had ever seen, dark and crusty like some rough loaf of bread you'd find on a monk's table. Labeled *Oxalis purpurea* Grand Duchess, they came in a plastic package filled with sawdust that the grower probably hoped would hide their ugliness. I bought some anyway. The picture on the package looked pretty, and they

were called Grand Duchess. I liked that. At home I gave them a hurried burial, covering them with just an inch of soil, spacing them about two inches apart, pointy part up. They lay between the stepping stones just outside the front door.

November 5. I had almost forgotten about those ugly little bulbs, but this morning there were a few clover-like leaves in that narrow space between the stepping stones. They were staying low as if they knew they could get stepped on.

November 11. Leaves are starting to fall from the trees, but the gap between the stepping stones is now a field of bright green shamrocks.

November 16. I got up late and went out into the bright morning, squinting, to fetch the paper. I never made it. There at my feet were dozens of tiny, white flowers glistening in the midday sun like miniature china set out for field mice. I went back in, poured a cup of coffee, and came out again to sit on the front steps. I could see why they were named Grand Duchess. This oxalis didn't look anything like the weedy variety that strangled parts of my garden. This one had elegant glove-white flowers.

January 1. The new year found the oxalis still in flower. They close up every night and only open when the sun is bright overhead, and if you spend too much time at the office you never see them. I make a point of not spending too much time at the office.

March 30. There are still a few flowers on the oxalis, but the foliage is beginning to yellow and collapse in the warming weather. This was one tough plant. It flowered for four-and-a-half months, got stepped on, and went without water at times. It might be a Grand Duchess, but no pansy.

Postscript. While the oxalis planted between the stepping stones has stayed and bloomed for three years, others planted in the best soil, in garden beds, have spread all over the place, becoming almost as weedy as the genuine oxalis. I now know to keep them confined and not to pamper them in the least.

Freesias Are Fragrant October 21. Freesias are pretty bulbs, long, slender, and covered with a fine mesh like a lady's stockings. It was hard not to buy a lot, but there was just one spot beside the path where, with a little shoehorning, I could fit some in. I bought a variety called Matterhorn. I had heard that the white varieties did best the second and third year and that they came close to being as permanent in the garden as any bulb. I filled a small, brown paper bag with them and brought them home.

November 25. I found the paper bag with the freesia bulbs under some seed catalogues on the workbench. What can I say? I had forgotten about them. But they didn't look any the worse for wear; I planted them, so close together that they were almost touching, and covered them with about two inches of soil. Now all I had to do was water and wait. In this bulb business there is a lot of waiting.

December 5. I didn't have to wait long. Slender green leaves are pushing

out of the ground so quickly you can hear them shove the soil aside.

March 6. The leaves have been up and ready for a long time and today the flowers make an appearance. They are not white like the 'Matterhorn Mountain', but creamy with a touch of yellow at their base. At night, in the still moist air, their fragrance is memorable, even from a distance recognizable as freesia. Like good perfume, it is neither overpowering nor too crisp.

March 30. Some flowers stand out in a crowd. Even though there are all sorts of flowers blooming at this time of year, the freesias hold their own. Flowers keep opening along their arching stems, like swans lifting off from a lake; the spent flowers can be pulled off to keep things tidy. I tidied up my few freesias, sat back on my haunches, and looked around to see where I could plant more next year. The garden looked swell.

WHAT ABOUT WILDFLOWERS?

There are wildflowers and then there are "wildflowers." Genuine wildflowers are native to the area. Other flowers, native to other places, are often called "wildflowers" either because they grow so easily or because they are relatively "unimproved," that is, they haven't been turned into true garden flowers through hybridization or selection.

Pictured on these pages are examples of each and they illustrate two distinct ways to treat wildflowers. The spectacular field—what one expects— is full of "wildflowers." This is one of the seed fields of Environmental Seed Producers, the leading supplier of seed used in most wildflower mixes found at general nurseries. Though these mixes often contain California natives, such as the ubiquitous California poppy, they also contain many other flowers from all over the globe that have been found to grow with ease and have the simple look of a wildflower.

Real wildflowers—the genuine article—grow on a hillside overlooking the San Fernando Valley at the Theodore Payne Foundation in Sun Valley, California. The Foundation's purpose is to encourage the planting of California natives, and it is one of the primary suppliers of seed, most of it collected by volunteers from wild fields. This planting, put in by volunteer Kevin Connelly, grows with no supplemental irrigation. Rains germinate the seed and keep it going, so in some dry years the crop is a little meager. The planting was photographed during one of the drought years.

But even in a good year, it is a far cry from the other field of "wildflowers," and it is not what one usually imagines a field of wildflowers to look like. But climb to the top of this hill, and it looks right and smells right. You can step among the flowers as you can in the mountains or high desert. The colors are pure and bright—clear yellow, pure orange, bright blue—and the flowers are familiar to a day-hiker —California poppy, chia, tidy-tips, and thistle sage.

Growing Your Own Anyone who has grown *real* California wildflowers can tell you that growing these dainty wildlings, some of which are endangered in their natural areas, is somehow holier than other garden pursuits. There is no denying the impact of that waist-high field of "wildflowers" from a nursery mix. Which way to go?

Where you live, on what soil you garden, and on what scale you attempt to grow wildflowers should help you decide. If you live on flat land, with a clayey soil, most real California wildflowers will be difficult to grow. A better choice would be the mix "wildflowers," which undoubtedly will contain some true ones. Note that the "wildflowers" in the photograph are growing on prime agricultural land, with irrigation, a situation much more akin to the typical garden than the hilltop site at the Payne Foundation. Where wildflowers grew at one time, wildflowers will probably grow again. Here the soil and the site favor the natives.

Weeding Is the Chore You can probably grow either kind of wildflower in small garden beds, where it is not difficult to look after them. But if you expect to grow even a small meadowful, you should be prepared for a lot of work though you might be lucky and have the right combination of soil and location. And no weeds.

It is weeding that makes growing wildflowers such hard work. Though it might seem that nothing could be

There are wildflowers and then there are "wildflowers." The real thing is grown by Kevin Connelly on a hilltop at the Theodore Payne Foundation in Sun Valley, California. The other kind of "wildflowers" aren't necessarily native to the area (or even to the U.S.) but grow as if they were, with little help from man. Were they not so pretty, they might be called weeds. On page 117 a field of "wildflowers" is being grown for its seed. European red poppies and bachelor's buttons make a dazzling combination.

easier than growing flowers that ought to grow there naturally, once the soil has been disturbed, by gardening or by clearing, weeds quickly get the upper hand; they are successful invaders and have displaced many native plants. Even Kevin Connelly, who has planted many meadows of wildflowers, tackles only a small area at a time (as pictured here) when weeds are present or their seeds lie in wait.

Should you decide to give wildflowers a try, begin in the fall, before the rainy season arrives. First you

must clear the ground, being careful to disturb it as little as possible so you don't bury any weed seed (you'll see why). Then water thoroughly for several days to sprout the weed seed or bring persistent perennial weeds back to life. Once the weeds are up and growing (it takes several weeks), the easiest way to eliminate them is by spraying with a short-lived herbicide called Roundup or Kleenup. This will kill everything above ground and, since it's systemic, the roots as well, though a few perennial weeds might

survive even this. To be certain your land is entirely weed-free, water again after everything appears dead and wait to see if anything returns.

Time to Sow This should take you into December, the first month in which we can usually count on rains in Southern California. Now the wildflower seed can be sown and perhaps protected with bird netting so a few seeds remain to germinate. Rain or irrigation will bring up the wildflowers—also more weeds. As soon as you can tell one

from another, it's time to get down on hands and knees and begin separating the wheat from the tares.

There is no need to sow seed thickly, because, as Kevin Connelly puts it, "if one seed germinates, they all will." In fact, sowing thickly only makes weeding more difficult. Weeds that grow too close to a wildflower shouldn't be yanked out but should instead be cut off with small scissors. And don't think that all the weeds will have sprouted with the first rain; that's not their nature. To assure survival some seeds

germinate with each rain, in case others were routed by drought.

In defense of all this weeding, Kevin points out that people have to spend hours in the hot August sun weeding a dichondra lawn, but that with wild-flowers you can do your weeding in the cool of winter and spend August at the beach. Either way you go, with real wildflowers or their look-alikes, they can be the prettiest things you have ever planted. Just be prepared for some hard work if a meadowful is what you have in mind.

Garden Visit

A WILDFLOWER SUCCESS STORY

Perhaps the most unlikely place in the world to find wildflowers, or any native plant, is beside a spa. Think of it—drought-toughened California plants, valued because they need so little water, growing right next to it. For that matter, one does not expect to find a meadow of delicate wildflowers growing in the confines of an ordinary suburban backyard, but much about the garden pictured here is astonishing.

The big surprise is seeing the spa in the middle of a field of flowers. The next surprise is noting how well it blends into the overall picture. Except perhaps for the color of the water, it could be a puddle, or an isolated pool left behind at the end of the rainy season, for the spa has been worked into a natural-looking stream bed that runs diagonally across the garden. This was the inspired idea of the late Steven Dyer, with the actual design worked out and drafted by Richard Borkovetz. This man-made stream is no rushing cascade. Most of its length merely suggests water, since the only water is to be found in the spa. It is refreshingly subtle, content with being a simple, small stream bed, gone dry for the summer—marked only by its rocky bottom, a perfectly believable phenomenon.

The rocks that define the bed were all gathered in the Claremont area and are used most adroitly. They are all rather small, small enough to have been pushed down the mountainside by a stream this size, and there are not too many. The bed of the stream uses still smaller rock and loose gravel, and it doubles as a path across the garden, augmented near the patio's edge by a few concrete pavers. It follows the natural slope of the land and seeks the low ground as a stream naturally

would. Its origins are hidden behind the garage and by shrubbery; its destination is also out of sight, in the side yard.

The plantings, including the wildflowers, are the work of Janet Dyer. Janet is a regular visitor to nearby Rancho Santa Ana Botanic Garden, the premier native plant garden in the state, and the influences of that magnificent public garden can be seen in this much smaller private one. Most of the plants are California natives, and all are drought-resistant because this garden gets by on natural rainfall with only a little supplemental irrigation in summer. There are other flowers from similar climates around the spa—the orange ice-plant and annual African daisy being the most conspicuous. But the flowers that make up the meadow are the genuine article—California poppy, bird's eyes gilia, blue thimble-flower, tidytips—wildflowers that could once very easily have grown on this gentle slope before it was reshaped into a tract of houses.

Originally, this area was a lawn, and after it was removed wildflower seed was sown and simply raked into the soil. Fall and winter rains brought the flowers up and nourished them. Surprisingly, nothing was done to the soil in preparation for planting, but Janet has been blessed with good fortune and an appropriate soil.

The soil is decomposed granite, a gritty, loose soil that drains excess water quickly. Each summer after the wildflowers finish up, Janet waits for them to scatter their seed, then cuts them to the ground, leaving the litter where it lies. In summer the ground is left dry and the shrubs and succulents in the garden carry the show, but with the first rains of autumn, up come the colorful wildflowers, all on their own.

Resembling a quiet pool in an otherwise dry Southwest streambed, a spa is surrounded by wildflowers. California poppies are the light orange brushstrokes (the deep orange are the flowers of an ice plant) and they are easy to grow. More trying are the dainty lavender bird's eyes gilia in the background and the yellow tidytips. The rocks and gravel that make up the dry streambed are also used for a diagonal path across the garden so the wildflowers don't get stepped on.

CHAPTER

5

COLOR,
HARMONY, AND
CONTRAST

Sometimes a simple scheme is the best color scheme of all, especially for a beginning gardener on the first few tries. The cream flowers of a Pacific Coast iris named 'Chimes' harmonize nicely with an old white picket fence in the picture on pages 120–121.

Pink flowers and gray foliage are a classic and very simple color scheme. The pink is a spreading and somewhat rambunctious Mexican evening primrose. The gray foliage belongs to an artemisia.

SIMPLE SCHEMES

Have you ever picked a flower and carried it, like a paint chip, to another plant to see if the colors go together? One would not dare to paint a room and put curtains, rugs, and sofas in it without carefully evaluating the compatibility of their colors, yet in the garden color schemes seldom get such consideration. Perhaps this is because flowers are pretty no matter what their color, or perhaps because the colors of flowers are so much more complex than the colors on a fabric or a paint chip; on the one hand we are delighted with flowers, but at the same time we are not too sure why. Sometimes we are not even sure what color they are. Some flower colors are particularly tricky. What is a "blue" flower, for instance? Few are truly blue.

Observation gives us something concrete to work with. If we take a thoughtful second look we might note what colors we like and which ones harmonize or go together. And perhaps we might make special note of those that do not. What we like is no small part of this decision-making process because different people have very different likes and dislikes and most find that their ideas change as they develop as gardeners.

Change Colors change too. Another reason to keep your own garden notes is that colors look very different in different parts of the world and under different skies. California, for instance, has intense contrast of light and dark, the shadows being so much blacker, the sunny spots, so much more glaring. It is almost impossible to look at both at the same time. The eye just can't handle the difference, and the camera cannot accommodate it, which is why so many gardens are photographed on overcast days.

Under England's often cloudy skies, the light is much softer and the contrast between shady and open areas hardly noticeable. In Southern California, coastal gardeners also live with overcast skies almost every day, while inland gardeners hardly ever see a cloud. These two situations call for a very different selection of colors. Color changes with the time of day as well as with the seasons, hues appearing warmer and darker when the sun is rising or setting, brighter in summer, and cooler in winter.

Impossible? If the question of color in the garden sounds impossibly complicated, especially for men, who have much less experience with color than women do, there are simple ways to approach it. Even if you have only learned that a red tie looks good with a blue blazer, you can be on your way because it's possible to create very simple color schemes in the garden, which can then develop with your knowledge and ability into something far more complex and challenging.

Finding satisfying color schemes can become a gardener's lifework, along with learning how to grow the particular plants one needs to create these schemes. In modern times, in our smaller gardens, this often becomes the main point of garden planning. Once those paths are in, the background planted, and the beds for flowers in place, we could sit back and happily watch things grow—if it weren't for the fact that we will probably never get the colors quite right. We might not even recognize the possibilities at first. Most of us are thrilled when a bed of mixed flowers first comes into bloom, but after a year or two of growing them, we begin to see that there is work to be done.

Hot colors are sometimes hard to use in a garden, but one solution is to put them all together. Deep red dianthus, hot red penstemon, and bright red roses grow in colorful harmony with the blue-gray foliage of a grass named Festuca ovina glauca *and the "blue" of lobelia.*

HOT, COOL, AND TRUE BLUE

Gardeners have discovered that you can divide nearly all flowers into two groups—those that are colored red through blue, and those that are yellow through orange. If at first you only plant flowers from one or the other group, you will have simplified things greatly without limiting yourself, because the colors within each group are most likely going to harmonize.

The red-through-blue group is particularly easy and pleasing because, even though red is a member, these colors are cool and comfortable to look at. They look best in cool light, under overcast skies in winter or early spring. There is one condition—the red must be pure red, without a hint of orange, perhaps just a hint of blue.

An orange cast makes red hot and moves it into the other group. Be particularly careful with roses, since the red of roses can go either way, toward orange or toward pink. Pink is probably the most common color in the red-through-blue group, and it is a very easy color to live with in the garden. There are hundreds of pink flowers, and you can even have flowers that shade toward salmon without upsetting the color cart.

Blue? True blue flowers are practically nonexistent, though hundreds are called that. Agapanthus, campanulas, pansies, salvias, veronicas, and a hundred other plants are called "blue," but in reality they are violet or purple. While violet or purple flowers harmonize with pink and true red, they contrast with yellow, in a striking way. The so-called blue-bedder salvia, for instance, blends nicely with pink flowers, but it makes yellow flowers seem absolutely dazzling.

Yellow and Orange Yellow and orange are much hotter colors, and consequently such flowers are harder to handle. But they are invaluable in summer when paler, more pastel colors almost disappear in the brilliant sunlight. Bright yellows and oranges do not mix easily with other colors, so they are often used alone; the exceptions are the most subtle shades, which will blend with other flowers if they are kept in the minority. However, yellow and orange flowers can make an exciting accent in a red-blue scheme. With time and some experimenting you can discover how to use both groups of colors in the same bed, remembering that one group should always be decidedly dominant.

The Simplest Scheme Using only one color is the simplest scheme of all, and yellow is the first color to come to mind because so many flowers are yellow, or what gardeners call "gold." For instance, use tall golden gloriosa daisies for a background, with tall American or African marigolds in front of them. In front of these can go the shorter, smaller-flowered French marigolds, and in front of them the short golden fleece *(Dyssodia).* Don't worry if they are lemon yellow, orange, or somewhere in between—they all are variations of yellow and will blend beautifully.

WHITE, GRAY, AND GREEN

It has been said that white is the peacemaker in the garden. Wherever one suspects that two colors might not go together, separate them with white flowers and harmony will be restored. White flowers have the gift of bringing a delightful airiness with them and keeping a garden from seeming congested. They seem to glow in the distance, and at dusk they have a

certain magic when other colors all but disappear. Like shafts of sunlight, they add luminosity to the plantings.

In a garden using flowers of only a single hot color try adding white flowers to cool things down. Leave a few open spots in the front row for the low-growing *Chrysanthemum paludosum*, which looks like a miniature Shasta daisy, and back between the marigolds plant the real Shasta daisy and maybe a few plants of feverfew. All of these have white flowers and they will bring a little peace to this hot composition.

A crafty gardener always has a few white-flowered plants standing by at planting time.

Gray Foliage Gray or silvery leaves act much like white flowers. They too can mediate differences between other colors, but they are especially valuable when more light is wanted in the garden because they reflect it so well. Planted in a garden bed that is becoming too green and dark, they add airiness and open up the composition.

Gray-leaved plants make a garden appear sunnier simply because we associate gray-leaved plants with sunny climates, which is where most of them originate. Because gray-foliaged plants reflect light, they are best put off in the distance, though the temptation is to use them up close because their foliage is so interesting. But they attract the eye when they are at a remove, becoming a misty gray, and seeming to make the garden much deeper than it really is.

Green Flowers With so much green foliage in the garden, green flowers might seem to be redundant. But they act like white flowers and help separate conflicting colors in the garden, adding openness. Green flowers have a certain

fascination and are a fine conversation piece. There are not many kinds, but one is especially useful and easy to find, if only in seed catalogs. It is the pale green-flowered form of the common bedding nicotiana, a native American plant that blooms for months with a nice growth to boot.

Getting Started Though entire books could be devoted to color in the garden—or to the subject of color alone—there is nothing quite like plunging in and finding out what works. Pick a garden bed and decide on the basic scheme, be it the red-pink-blue colors, or the yellows and

oranges. Begin collecting plants with these colors and then try sketching a color plan. Draw blobs of color and see how one looks next to the other. There is no need to get the colors absolutely right. Try contrasting dark and light shades of the same color for emphasis. The dark shades often look like shad-ows of the lighter colors, and this contrast gives depth to the planting. Now add white, gray, and green wherever airiness is needed, or peace-making between two colors.

A surprisingly sophisticated flower garden can be constructed in this fashion, with surprisingly little expertise.

White flowers and gray foliage act like shafts of light in the garden, and they can also work as peacemakers, settling disputes between other warring colors. On page 126, three of the best perennials with gray foliage are lamb's ears, snow-in-summer, and dusty miller. Blue star creeper is the ground cover between the stepping stones in this garden designed by Robert Fletcher.

Coral bells, on page 127, is one of the best of the white flowers and will grow in some shade. This is the native California species, Heuchera maxima.

Plant Portrait

A PORTFOLIO OF WHITE FLOWERS

Warm summer evenings are the best time to appreciate the magical appeal of white flowers. Their cool presence lingers long after the sun has set, their pale petals glowing in the twilight. Many perfume the air with sweet summery fragrances; in the garden, scent is somehow associated with the color white. The vining jasmine and stephanotis, common gardenia and citrus blossoms, and the not-so-common white heliotrope are some of the sultriest.

Many white flowers need no introduction, but there are others deserving of more recognition. The white heliotrope, for instance. It is uncommon at nurseries and actually began as an indoor plant offered by Logee's Greenhouses in Danielson, Connecticut. In much of the country it can be grown outdoors as an annual because it develops so quickly, but in California it becomes a long-lasting vining shrub, thriving in partial shade or full sun. It is very easy to grow, rambling at first among its neighbors until it mounds up to become a small haystack of a shrub about four feet tall and eight feet across. Or it can be trained to climb a trellis. It has a delicious, sort of candy-store scent.

Two more summer bloomers are the white *Scabiosa caucasica*, with flowers growing atop twenty-four-inch stems while the foliage occupies but a square foot of ground, and the white yarrow—*Achillea millefolium*—also a fine flower for cutting and about the same height. *Achillea millefolium*, which lives up to the thousand leaves in its Latin name, spreads on underground roots to make quite a patch. It shouldn't be planted where it might overwhelm lesser plants.

The tall spires in the garden pictured here belong to *Verbascum chaixii*,

Two examples of white flowers for the garden are shown on page 128. Top, the popular double Shasta daisy named 'Esther Read,' and below, the rare but rambunctious white heliotrope.

Designer Christine Rosmini planted one whole section of her garden white. The tall spires belong to the rare Verbascum chaixii; *each has a royal purple center. At their base is a white scabiosa, and just behind it is a white lantana. In the background are white 'Iceberg' roses and yarrow.*

one of my favorite plants, a garden gem waiting to be discovered by more plant prospectors. It develops a two-foot-wide clump of large green leaves and sends up spire after spire of glistening white flowers, each with a dazzling royal purple center that can only be discerned on close inspection. It is a perennial arising from big carrot-like roots and its tall white shafts add

drama to the flower bed or border.

White flowers are so cool and pleasing that they can become a gardener's addiction, leading to all-white schemes such as the one pictured here in a Los Angeles garden. Inspired by the all-white garden of Victoria Sackville-West at Sissinghurst Castle in Kent, designer Chris Rosmini set aside one corner of her garden exclusively for

white flowers. All of the flowers mentioned in this chapter are in it, plus white lantana that surrounds the verbascum, and white delphiniums that tower in the background. The best white rose for landscaping is 'Iceberg,' used by many designers as peacemaker and anchor in garden beds. Other white or near-white roses are 'Honor,' 'Pristine,' and 'Sweet Afton.'

Plant Portrait

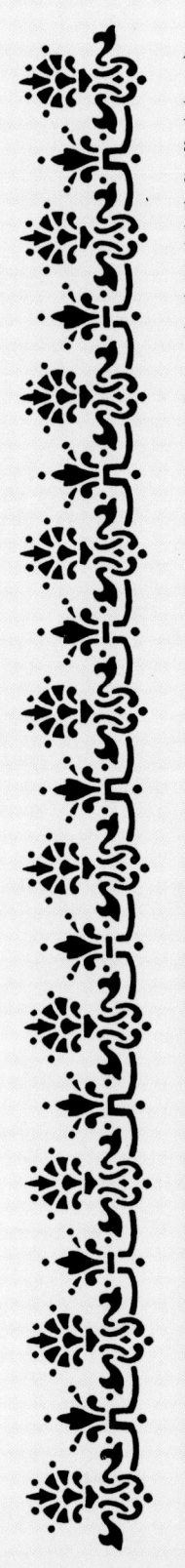

A PORTFOLIO OF GRAY FOLIAGE

Most gray-leaved plants developed in sun-drenched climates, where they adopted this coloration as a defense; the tiny white hairs that cover the leaves, or the white, waxy coating—glaucousness—reflect the heat and trap a tiny bit of cooling moisture near the leaf's surface.

Gray-leaved plants may be bluish, greenish, or silvery; in the garden each shade can be used to a particular advantage. Silvery plants are the boldest. They stand out among the other flowers, as if illuminated by their own personal shaft of sunlight. Blue-gray plants are the coolest looking and are best mixed with green plants that have a hint of blue in their leaves, or with lavender and purple flowers. Gray-green plants are the most common and offer an image of softness and subtlety when mixed with other plant-ings. Gray-green plants are especially attractive mixed with pink flowers.

Purple, pink, and white are the colors traditionally thought to go best with gray-leaved plants, but the possibilities go beyond the traditional. The brilliant cherry red of a rose named 'Double Delight' is close to perfection when planted near the gray foliage of lamb's-ears. Soft yellows that are not too golden are also delightful near gray foliage and, in fact, many gray-leaved plants do have yellow flowers.

Lamb's ears and lychnis are two of the prettiest and most useful gray-greens. Lamb's ears (*Stachys byzantina,* formerly *S. lanata*) is aptly named; the leaves are soft and silky—one is almost tempted to say cute and cuddly. It is probably the most useful of the gray-leaved plants—a favorite of the English gardener Gertrude Jekyll, who knew so well how to use plants in the garden. At the front of a flower

Gray color schemes at work: A ground covering of blue fescue in front of the taller dusty miller on page 130, photographed in the parking lot of the Huntington Botanical Garden.

Landscape architect Isabelle Greene used shades of gray foliage to carry the eye far into the distance. The silver of Senecio leucostachys *in the foreground gives way to the steely gray of St. Catherine's lace, then to the gray green of English lavender's foliage and the gray carpeting of yellow-flowered gazanias.*

border it is unsurpassed; in England we find it a traditional choice for planting in front of roses, and a good many rose plantings in America would be immensely improved placed behind a row of lamb's ears to hide their bare bases. The plant is equally effective bordering a concrete walk or drive, where its gray leaves are so harmonious with the color of the concrete that they lend elegance to this otherwise drab material.

A perennial, lamb's ears spreads rapidly in good soil and warm weather to become a six-inch-tall mat measuring several feet across and dense enough to discourage weeds. Should it spread too far, you can cut it back; it is not invasive and is easy to pull out. In winter, older leaves shrivel, but enough remain to keep the planting presentable. It flowers in spring with small pink blossoms too modest to be noteworthy. Old clumps eventually deteriorate, but it is easy to start a new planting from pieces that have rooted.

Lychnis coronaria 'Alba' is a white-flowered form of the common perennial magenta-flowered Maltese cross. Its flowers, which occur only occasionally, are graceful! and airy, but the dense crisp clump of leaves is unusually handsome—each leaf a shimmering gray-green edged with silver hairs. The plant grows slowly to make a six-inch-tall clump about eighteen to twenty-four inches across.

An example of the blue-gray coloration is blue fescue *(Festuca ovina glauca)*. Most often seen as a ground cover in California, it is even more effective used more sparingly, planted here and there in natural-looking clumps—small ten-inch-tall tufts of grass among the flowers—in meadow-like fashion. *Festuca* 'Bronzeglanz' is an even wispier gray-green grass. Silvery-gray plants are the most

striking because of the way they reflect the light. One of the prettiest is a yarrow *(Achillea)* named 'Moonshine'. The ferny leaves make a low, handsome clump that slowly spreads until it measures several feet across. This yarrow does not seem weedy as so many

do. The distinctive flat-topped flower spikes, a clear, clean lemon-yellow color, grow about eighteen inches tall. Planted in front of blue agapanthus, they offer a fine spectacle. The foliage has a soothing fragrance.

Perhaps the most silvery plant is the

A dianthus named 'Jealousy,' on page 132, not only has gray foliage but white flowers. A small green eye in the center of each flower inspired the flower's intriguing name.

Lamb's ears, on page 133, is the perfect plant for the foreground with soft, velvety-gray foliage and a low, tidy habit of growth, at least for the first year. It is a traditional choice for planting in front of roses, as it hides the bare base of the bush and harmonizes with the rose's reddish foliage.

common dusty miller *(Senecio cineraria)*, a shrubby perennial with leaves that are nearly white. Often sold as a bedding plant, it will grow to about two feet around, eventually needing a bit of pruning (or replacing) to stay neat. The flowers are most often cut off before they bloom because, being a rather plain yellow, they aren't harmonious with the rest of the plant. But if there is a place in the garden where you want foliage to pop right out of its surroundings, the senecios can't be beat.

Plant Portrait

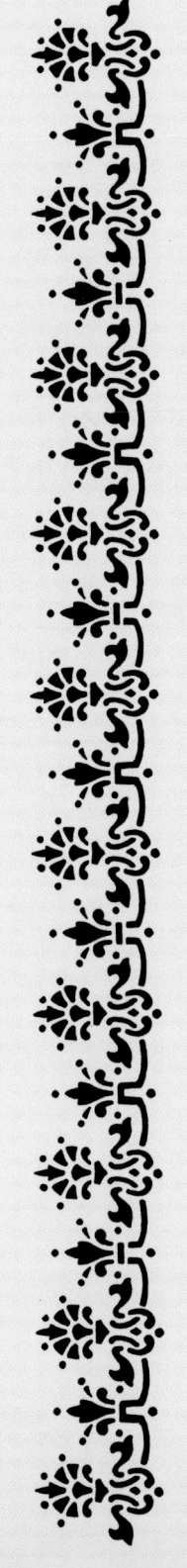

A PORTFOLIO OF GREEN FLOWERS

Avid gardeners sometimes find themselves heading down some curious avenues. Take, for example, plants with green flowers. Grass is green; flowers are supposed to be colorful. However, once you've discovered green flowers, they become plants that you simply must have. Beyond their surprising coloration, green flowers are similar to white flowers in that they can be planted anywhere in the garden without causing a ruckus; they won't compete with other colors and they soften harsh contrasts.

Corsican hellebore *(Helleborus lividus corsicus)* is an unusually bold and handsome plant. It grows as clumps of stems in true perennial fashion, usually attaining a height of two feet and growing to several feet across after a few years. The apple-green flowers begin to appear in late fall and, in California, last well into summer. What makes this hellebore so useful is its ability, once it becomes established, to survive in shade with merely a spattering of sunlight and with little care. It will even compete successfully with tree roots or grow on the north side of a house.

Several euphorbias have greenish flowers, but *Euphorbia wulfenii* has shocking shamrock-green flowers that begin in January and last into June. It grows as a slowly spreading clump of three-foot-tall stems. As with many euphorbias, this one can tolerate less than ideal irrigation and some shade, though the flowers are greener in good light. For a yearly restart, cut the entire clump to the ground in the early fall.

'Green Goddess' is an absolutely elegant calla lily that is treated somewhat like a weed at the Huntington Botanical Gardens in San Marino,

and a fad at florists. It is tough and tall, growing to a height of four or five feet. Flowers begin in February and keep blooming through spring. It will grow in sun or shade and is, therefore, another candidate for the difficult north side of a house. It gets along with infrequent watering but thrives with lots.

The chartreuse-flowered form of the common shrimp plant *(Justicia brandegeana,* formerly *Beloperone guttata)* makes a showy four-foot-tall shrub that seems forever in flower. It prefers partial shade where its color becomes less yellow, although if there is not enough light the growth might be a bit lax. An eastern exposure is ideal. It likes water but can get by with little.

Green may seem an odd color for a flower, but it is actually quite useful, working much like gray foliage or white flowers—as a break between more brightly colored flowers. Here are some of the best: Corsican hellebore on page 134, and on page 135, a nicotiana named 'Really Green,' top left, the shrubby Justicia brandegeana 'Chartreuse,' top right, Euphorbia wulfenii, bottom left, and a calla lily named 'Green Goddess,' bottom right.

CHAPTER
6
**DETAILS
MAKE THE
DIFFERENCE**

An old cart filled with impatiens, bedding begonias, ivy, and grape ivy is the finishing touch for the shady corner of a patio, seen on pages 136–137.

Other finishing touches are much smaller—a few rocks and pebbles at the base of a container, and some very small plants to its right can do the trick. The little fern is the tough sun-loving Cheilanthes fendleri, *normally found in rock gardens; the pink flowers belong to a true geranium.*

THOSE LITTLE PLACES

Pebbles, pools of water, plants tucked here and there and similar elements are the finishing touches for a garden—the embroideries, the details you see on second look that keep you fascinated. Adding these embellishments is relatively easy, but the idea often does not occur to gardeners until they have gardened for a great many years. That's perhaps just as well, because these little touches cannot be planned in advance. The spots where they work best—the small places in the garden—do not exist until the basic bones of the garden are established and have perhaps fleshed out and grown a bit.

Plants—smaller than those found in the flower bed—are the most fascinating details because no matter how often you visit the garden, they will always look different, changing day by day, or even hourly, and certainly with the seasons and the years.

Little Plants Small bulbs are an excellent example. The crocus pictured in this chapter, a rare species named *Crocus goulimyi,* only discovered in 1955 growing wild in southern Greece, has its own little place beside a path in my garden. Anywhere else it might be overwhelmed, but here, protected on one side by the path and on another by a large rock and a very dwarf eugenia, it holds its own. It flowers in the fall when this particular spot happens to be bathed in the low sunlight of the autumn months. It is the perfect place for this plant, but I could not have planned for it, even though I was on the lookout. In good time, as the garden evolved, the spot simply appeared. I also made sure that such little places would occur by not filling the garden chock-full at first, and by

making paths and flower beds somewhat irregular in shape so there would be nooks and crannies in which to tuck treasures.

Little plants such as this *Crocus goulimyi* often turn out to be the most delightful in the garden; I always look forward to the month of October when this crocus is in bloom. When finished, it is a trifle untidy for the entire winter; in summer, it is completely dormant, so its season is just one short month. But when it is not flowering it does not leave a gaping sore in the side of the garden since it occupies such a small space.

Many plants make equally suitable details, or finishing touches, for a garden. A number of plants sold as ground covers (such as ajuga) actually work better planted in little places, and many plants sold as alpine or rock garden treasures are perfect candidates for the nooks and crannies in the garden.

And Pebbles Mulches of pebbles, such as those surrounding crocus bulbs, are another kind of finishing touch, though their contribution is not so much to add interest as to neatly hem the garden— where the rough edges show, where the soil is too obvious, or where little plants need a setting and some protection from hard rain. They also add another texture, one halfway between the smooth, hard surface of paving and the soft, rumpled velvet of plants.

ACCESSORIES FOR THE GARDEN

While little plants and pebbles could be considered finishing touches, other details in the garden might be compared to the furnishings and accessories in a room. Boulders, rocks, pebbles, and stones are the most natural accessories. Used with restraint, they become solid anchors for the garden and foils for special plants, but there is a danger of overdoing their presence, especially in areas where rocks are not found naturally.

A Place for Boulders, Rocks, Stones, and Pebbles For a rock to look at home in the garden there must be some logic in its placement. Large rocks, for instance, are best buried with only a third of their bulk showing, rather like an iceberg at sea. This is an old rule of landscaping but one hard to follow if you have just spent money commensurate to its size for a large rock or have expended energy lugging it into the back yard. Refined rocks, like refined people, do not display everything they've got.

In nature, rocks are seldom found just lying about at random, unless they are at the base of a hill or in a gully where water or gravity may have carried them. Used as if they were in a dry stream bed, you can leave most of the rock exposed above ground, but other smaller stones should also be evident. The best way to see how rocks should be used in the garden is to imitate nature: large boulders are usually buried up to their necks; smaller rocks are always in the company of stones and pebbles and are usually gradated by the stream that deposited them, not randomly mixed.

Or you might use rocks like sculpture, selecting a particularly interesting specimen and displaying it in a special place.

Sculpture Plants that are either naturally sculptural or are made so, such as topiary—plants trimmed to a shape they would not have in nature, perhaps a pyramid or a rabbit—are accessories for the garden, not unlike a small sculpture set on the mantle. Sculpture

itself can be used as a detail, though it is difficult to keep a piece of sculpture from stealing the show and becoming a focal point of the garden. Plants growing in containers are somewhat sculptural and extremely versatile as garden accessories because they can be moved around until just the right place is found for them.

Birds and butterflies—the real thing, that is—could even be considered finishing touches, and you can add plants such as butterfly weed to the garden that will attract these lively and colorful visitors.

Furniture Outdoor furniture is certainly another finishing touch, one that should be considered early on but only in the sense that you must leave enough room and a suitable place for it. What furniture will look best and, for that matter, which way it will face, is best decided after the structure of the garden is built. Besides a location for the obvious table and chairs, you will want to keep an eye open for places where a bench might be welcome, though your feet and legs may suggest this location before your eyes do. Where would you like to sit down and rest, and what view might you like to contemplate while catching your breath between garden chores?

No one place in the garden is perfect so a variety of seating choices is called for. Put seating where it is bathed in morning sun, a bench that is in shade in the middle of the day, and maybe one that is lit at night. Is one flower bed especially pretty when back-lit by the sun? Then put a place to sit in front of it. There is really no way to plan for this, and these places must be discovered after the garden is in. Don't overlook frivolous furnishings such as a swing hanging from the largest tree in the yard. Imagine how wonderful that would be to come upon unexpectedly.

On Second Look These details are what you see on second look and shouldn't detract from the overall picture of the garden, which means they must be used with subtlety and be scaled appropriately. The garden's path should still command the situation, and the focal point should not have strong competition. The background should carry the most weight and the flower beds be the prettiest elements. But once these things are taken care of, it's time to add the details, one by one, as they occur to you, and as spots for them open up.

Garden Visit

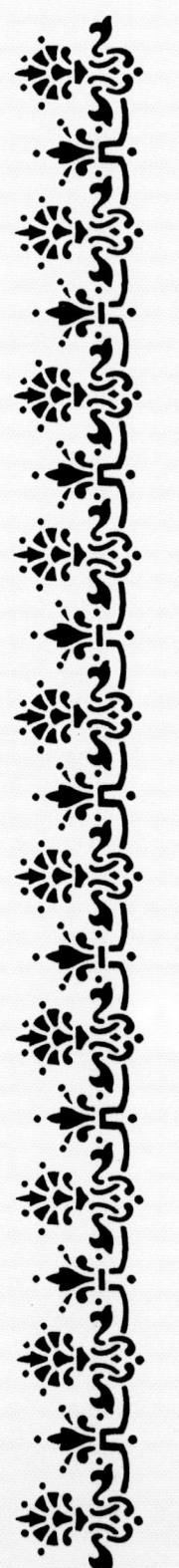

A COMPACT CITY GARDEN WITH BRILLIANT TOUCHES

This little garden depends heavily on small details. There is more to look at, more to discover here than in most large gardens. Every square inch has been thought out and carefully planted or ornamented in such a way that no matter where you look you will see something of interest. Los Angeles landscape designer Chris Rosmini used even the walls that shield the garden from the busy street as places to plant. Succulents grow in little balconies and make a living mural that is the unquestioned focal point for the garden.

Most of the paving blocks are spaced far enough apart for plants to grow between them, and where plants might get stepped on, shiny little pebbles take their place. Very tiny plants grow in tall flue-tile planters where they are safe from all the dangers that beset small flora—feet, competition from other plants, and flooding—everything except snails. Most of these minuscule plants are gem-like alpines ordered from rock-garden specialty nurseries, and they need the best of drainage.

Other details, while not miniature, are smaller than they usually are: a fountain, for example, contained within a large concrete pot, or outdoor lights that make the garden useful at night. But more than any other elements, plants are used as the details in this garden—a great variety of leaf and flower colors, shapes, and textures, delightful every time they are rediscovered. There is even a small sculpture sitting inside the fountain, a secondary focal point after the first overwhelming sight of the wall of succulents. The sound of the fountain is also a detail of sorts.

On the other side of the fence on this page is a street; the wall of succulents hides the view while a small fountain masks the noise.

Sedums and other succulents grow in the wall's planting pockets. Water runs from one pocket to the next through drainage slits.

Pre-colored concrete flue tiles provide homes for rock-garden plants that might otherwise be lost or trampled underfoot. The gray mat and almost white leaves belong to two species of the Raoulia.

Plant Portrait

PLANTS BETWEEN PAVING STONES

One of the first things visitors notice about my garden is that I grow plants within the paths. They can scarcely fail to notice since one could literally trip over the plants, though nobody has yet. My paths are made of pavers roughly two-by-two feet in size. These are set on a two-inch-deep base of tamped sand with approximately a two-inch space between pavers, and this gap is wide enough to plant in.

The plants are a welcome respite from all that paving, which, while it may be practical, is still a lot of hard surface. The plants that overgrow it help diminish the size of the path without lessening its usefulness. They also help blend the edges of the garden where it meets the path, contributing to a more natural look. The flower beds don't end abruptly, nor does the lawn, but one bleeds into the other.

The spaces between and around stepping-stones make perfect homes for many small plants including the summer bulb Zephyranthes grandiflora *on page 142 and the tiny woolly yarrow,* Achillea tomentosa, *page 143. The purple flowers belong to the wandering* Verbena rigida.

Planting in the middle of pathways is not an original idea. Vegetation springs up on its own quite naturally wherever there is a crack to grow in, and other gardeners before me have taken advantage of the little planting spaces, but plants in a path still surprise this most practical modern generation.

"Don't people trip on them?" No, because they are not in the center of the path but off to either side. "Well, what about weeds?" There is no short-age of these, to be sure, but I have modified a little weeder that fits between the pavers and makes short work of unwanted plants. It is called a "Cape Cod Weeder" and came from tool supplier Walt Nicke in Topsfield, Massachusetts. I filed off about an inch of the blade so it is precisely the width of the gap between the pavers.

"How do you plant in those narrow gaps?" I use a narrow trowel. I dig up the soil, amend it with sand and organic matter, put it back in, and plant. Then I put a mulch of small rock around the plants which also keeps feet from getting stuck in the gap. The path gets watered with the flower beds.

"Don't the plants get stepped on?" On occasion, but they are actually quite visible, framed as they are in concrete. In fact, this is where I grow some of my choicer plants, little rock-garden-sized plants and bulbs. Even the kids have learned to maneuver around them with their bikes and various other vehicles, and newcomers to the garden tend to tread lightly at first, as if they were stepping over a rattler sunning himself in the middle of the path. In effect, it works much like the zigs and zags in Japanese paths, slowing one down so there is time to observe the garden and soak up whatever is there. But when you need to get a wheelbarrow down the path, you just roll right over them. They bounce back. Plants that spread too far into the center of the path do get stepped on and learn to grow lower, to hide down in the cracks.

I have found these plants to be the toughest: a little Australian violet *(Viola hederacea)* that grows in shady sections; a tough gazania-like plant named *Drymondia* that could probably be run over by a tank; a low-growing yarrow and dianthus that would be overwhelmed by other plants if they were grown anywhere else in the garden; creeping oregano and thyme that smell good when they get stepped on; and the creeping, but fairly tall (for a path), *Verbena rigida* that brings a most casual air to the planting when it is in full flower.

This informality is perhaps what I like most about planting in paths—it's short of looking weedy, but does look overgrown, suggesting that the gardener is not too stern a fellow.

Pots can be artful or amusing, like the one on page 144. The author built one large trough in the shape of a pig (the inspiration came from an early American weather vane) and filled it with herbs and flowers. The lattice ends hide the boards that make the actual planter box. A piece of rope serves as the tail.

A study in proportion on page 145, these pots hold sweet peas, a surprising candidate for container culture. The sweet peas climb natural bamboo poles.

A PLACE FOR POTS

Plants growing in containers are perhaps the best accessory of all because they can be changed and moved about with ease, and can be put in places where flowers might not otherwise be able to grow—on the steps leading to the back door, for instance, or against a blank wall beneath a window, and beside a driveway where there is no room for anything else.

Plants grown in containers can be dramatically sculptural—a spiny yucca, for example—or flamboyantly colorful—a potful of zinnias or the piñata-colored portulaca. They become minor focal points or strong secondary accents of interest. At the very least, a plant in a container may simply be pleasant or utilitarian—a pot of herbs for example—and helps flesh out the garden composition, adding soft color or greenery.

Band-Aids I often use potted plants as Band-Aids, to hide a scar in the garden. If something poops out before it should, or perhaps grows too tall and leggy, a potted plant on the path or

patio in front of the offending plant covers up the eyesore, just like a Band-Aid.

Potted plants can also distract the eye from parts of the garden that are not at their finest. They can even be the primary focal point, especially if you do what large public gardens often do—keep pots of colorful flowers growing in back somewhere so they can be moved out front as the contents of other pots have finished blooming.

Collectibles Many collectible plants, such as orchids and bromeliads, or rare

ferns and begonias, are best kept in containers. First, because their special needs can be looked after (primarily the need for a special kind of soil), but also because they are so unusual that they do not fit visually with the rest of the garden, and a container sets them apart.

Relatively cold-tolerant orchids, bromeliads, and staghorn ferns are particularly useful in Southern California since the plants can be mounted directly to slabs of wood or cork and hung on vertical surfaces, such as walls and fences, where nothing else could

grow. They are epiphytic plants that, in the tropics, naturally grow up from the ground and attach themselves to trees. The kinds needing some soil can be grown in small pots with special hangers that allow them to be grown on vertical surfaces. Should it get too cold, they can be taken down and temporarily moved to a warmer spot, even indoors, for the night.

Another Art Growing plants in containers is quite a different gardening technique than growing them in the ground. A potted plant would not last a week without care; it is entirely dependent upon the gardener for water and nutrients. Watering at all times is essential, but during the summer, plants in containers may need to be watered every day. Since they require regular care—even when you are on vacation—it is important that when you first plan your garden, you make sure your pots and containers can be watered easily and quickly. You should be able to reach them with a hose without knocking down other plants in the process. It's a good idea to keep a collection of watering cans scattered throughout the garden, filled at all times. If they are handsome ones, the cans become a sort of garden ornament.

The Same Rules Apply When arranging planted containers in the garden, apply the same principles you use when planning your flower beds. Flowers in containers also look elegant as formal compositions (as on the steps pictured here) or grouped in casual clusters of three's and five's. Small pots set behind large pots give the illusion of being further away, so if you put large containers in the foreground with small ones further back, you stretch the apparent length of the garden.

Garden Visit

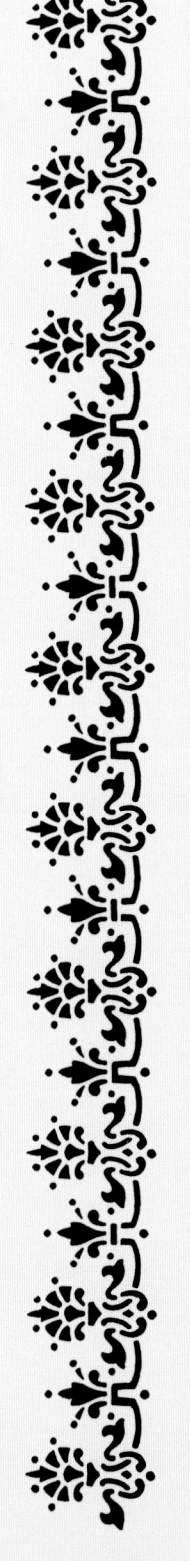

PARADISE AT PARKLABREA

At Parklabrea, the large apartment complex in the heart of downtown Los Angeles, 1,150 small concrete patios are set among the communal court-yards of the aging development. One of these seven-by-seventeen-foot slabs is as flower-filled as an English country garden. Not surprisingly, it is tended by English gardeners who cannot understand why every patio is not as pretty as theirs.

Film producer and writer Ronnie Kinnock and his wife, Beryl, brought their love of flowers—and the knack for growing them successfully—with them from their London townhouse. Confronted by the concrete, it was obvious to them that ordinary flower pots simply wouldn't do. So the Kin-nocks devised the clever containers seen here. The wooden troughs are raised above the height of the win-dowsills, on trestle-like legs, thus they can be appreciated from inside the apartment as well as from the patio. Elevated like this, they add a third dimension of height to the otherwise flat patio. The gardener doesn't have to stoop while working among the con-tainers that have still another advan-tage and asset for renters—they are portable. A few planters are double-deckers not unlike London's famous buses: plants that enjoy the sun ride on top, shade plants below.

What grows in the containers? The Kinnocks' favorite is lobelia, "as close to gentian blue" as they could find in California. They grow the Crystal Pal-ace strain, which blooms most of the year. Other favorites include phlox, sweet alyssum, ivy geranium, and a little white daisy named *Chrysanthe-mum paludosum*—all proper residents of a country garden, but thriving here in the middle of a large city.

Masses of purple lobelia, white sweet alyssum, and red geraniums spill from homemade containers that conceal the stark concrete patio of an inner-city apartment complex in Los Angeles. Some of the wooden containers are double-deckers with room downstairs for plants that can tolerate a little shade.

WATER IN THE GARDEN

Nothing brings sparkle to a garden like a bit of water. It needn't be torrents, or cascades, or even a small lake or pool. It can be as modest as a bird bath, but in the right location water will be a cool and refreshing sight in hot weather, the play of light from its surface bringing delight on all but the gloomiest of days. Even on a rainy day, water adds another element and another level of complexity to the design of a garden.

When you add a recirculating pump, water even sounds refreshing, though care must be taken because a steady splash can also become as annoying as the drip of a faucet. It takes some experimenting to find just the right combination of factors that makes splashing water sound good. The play of water must be tuned like an instrument. The music of slowly moving water is more restful than turbulent water, yet the sound should have a certain degree of complexity or it soon becomes monotonous.

More Pitfalls There are other pitfalls: in a garden water should look completely natural; if you want to use it, you must carefully consider its character. Water flows. It has a logical beginning and a logical end, the one being higher than the other. Water that suddenly appears at the top of a pile of rock is unnatural and disquieting. Is this an artesian well? A spring? A geyser like Old Faithful? A leak? Where did it come from?

Unless you live on a very steep slope, a waterfall—that landscaper's favorite—is a natural impossibility. But water needn't plummet to be dramatic. In a stream bed it can swirl and churn with only a slight drop in elevation. A natural-looking stream should

have its source and end hidden from sight so it appears just to have wandered onto the property and then meandered off again.

Fountains have no such constraints because they are obviously man-made and one does not question their source. A fountain generally looks at home in a garden, especially a small one, though it is difficult for it to be anything but a focus of attention.

Pools of water, man-made or natural, are the easiest to fit into a garden and the easiest to live with. Stocked with fish and plants to keep the water clean, they are virtually carefree; though quiet and restful, pools are far from static, sparkling in the sun or rippling when a breeze blows over their surface. However, to make a natural pool look natural is no small trick, and you will find it challenging to disguise the water's edge so it does not look contrived. The giveaway is usually a glimpse of the material lining the pool. The edge must be absolutely level or the lining is going to show above water.

A formal, obviously man-made pool is much easier to build and one tends not to question its rim or source.

Portable Pools Easier still, in fact foolproof, are portable pools. Portable is a relative term because, once filled with water, even the smallest container is too heavy to budge. But the containers are portable when empty and can be moved if the area becomes too shady or otherwise inappropriate. Large pots made of concrete or terra cotta are candidates; so are half-barrels made of oak and sold at nurseries, though these will need plastic liners or a thorough cleaning and soaking to make the staves watertight and to dispel the lingering reek of whisky—their original contents.

There is no minimum size, but

In the author's own garden, a large concrete pot alongside the path contains a fountain. The cord for the submersible pump runs out the drainage hole in the bottom of the container and the hole is sealed with roofing cement. Agapanthus are in the foreground, while a gardenia is the fragrant background. The gray foliage belongs to Jerusalem sage, Phlomis fruticosa. *Little plants are tucked everywhere possible and granite pebbles and stones dignify and harmonize with the plain concrete pavers and pot.*

Almost everything in this fall-planted garden is edible as well as decorative—an intriguingly practical idea. The most colorful plant is an ornamental kale. Other contributors to this vegetable tapestry include red and green lettuces, cabbage, parsley, Swiss chard, and even Brussels sprouts towering in the background. The ornamental kale, for all its beauty, is also edible, by the way.

something about two feet across and nearly as deep will accommodate several fish and any water plant, even water lilies. The fish are necessary to keep mosquitos from breeding in the pool, and they also help with its natural balance, consuming excess algae and plant growth and providing food for the aquatic plants. Ordinary goldfish are the best bet, though little guppy-like mosquito fish may be the only kind able to survive in very small or shallow pools.

A PLACE FOR GOOD TASTES

I confess that in my own garden vegetables have been outnumbered by flowers in an increasing ratio in recent years. I could find beautiful fresh vegetables easily enough at the market but not the flowers I now grow. Still, even in a garden designed to show off flowers in a restful landscape, a place can be found for those edible things that taste so much better homegrown.

Fresh Fruit In particular I am thinking about fruits of all kinds. Blackberries can be trained against a fence and can serve as an ornamental vine. Nothing tastes as wonderful as sun-warmed fresh blackberries. Some of the garden's trees can be fruit trees. Peaches and apricots never reach their full potential of flavor or ripeness at markets; these are fine choices for the garden because they grow on handsome small trees that set out pretty spring flowers.

Be aware that fruits of all kinds have specific climatic needs. In Southern California we are particularly cognizant of this because so many popular fruit varieties—the Elberta peach or Red Delicious apple for instance—will not thrive in our warm winters. They need more chilling (the specific num-

ber of hours when the temperature is below forty-five degrees) than we can provide; but other varieties of the same fruit—the 'Babcock' peach or 'Anna' apple—need less chilling and grow well here. Berries, grapes, and even citrus and other subtropicals have differing requirements, though the limiting factors with them may be whether it gets hot enough to ripen fruit or too cold for their survival.

The great advantage of growing fruit trees or vines is that they almost always serve two functions—as ornamentals and as edibles. Already mentioned is the flowering season of most deciduous fruit trees, because of which some are sold as dual-purpose trees. Fruiting-flowering peaches such as 'Red Baron' are an example. Citrus and many evergreen fruit trees such as loquats or guavas can be used successfully as background plants or, if they are dwarf varieties and are kept neatly clipped they can even become focal points of the garden. Lemon trees have been used as hedges; grape vines can cover trellises as decorative architectural elements.

Herbs Most herbs are decidedly ornamental and many cannot be found fresh at markets. Others are used in the kitchen so often that it is handy to have them growing nearby. Mix them right in with the rest of the flowers and plants in the garden, though it is wise to avoid putting them where insecticides will be sprayed, next to roses, for example.

And Vegetables Most vegetables are a little harder to work into the garden scheme. Though they are, for the most part, ornamental, they are also annuals, large annuals at that, and while they may look great at certain times of the year, at other times they

are too young and small, or past their prime, or their space is empty while you wait for the seasons to change.

Some particularly clever gardeners manage to incorporate vegetables and fruits into the garden nonetheless, though I have managed to find a home in my beds only for strawberries, artichokes, and cardoons, all of which happen to be perennials. The rest of my fruits and vegetables are grown in containers, out of the way while they are coming on but in full view when they are fruiting. Because they are such a sorry sight at markets, hard as rocks and about as tasty, tomatoes always find a home in the garden, though usually in pots.

But see what the designer of the garden pictured here did with vegetables!

A KITCHEN GARDEN

Perhaps the best way of all to use edible plants in the garden is also the oldest: set aside a kitchen garden where fruits, herbs, and vegetables can be grown to perfection. This special place allows you to give them the care and the room they require.

There is no need for the kitchen garden to look any less like a garden than other parts, but because its plants are subject to marked seasonal changes, it is best kept separate. The traditional way to set it apart is with a hedge or low wall as seen in gardens at least since medieval times. Neat raised beds are often used to organize the garden as well as to make the soil warmer and better drained. There is no need to truck in extra soil; the beds will become higher after all the amendments are added that make the earth rich enough for vegetables.

There is only one logical place for a kitchen garden and that is right outside the kitchen. Too often, though, the garden ends up in the back forty where the cook or cook's helper is not likely to make many trips. It is much better, for the sake of your table, to have all the delicious foods you grow as handy to the cook as possible. Kitchen gardens that need daily watching—for pests, for signs of needed water or fertilizer, for exact time of harvest— should be conveniently located.

During their growing period almost all edible plants need a full day of sun, and some could even use a little reflected heat from a wall, so when you plan your kitchen garden, pick a sunny, warm spot. Many vegetables are susceptible to diseases that can be diminished with good air circulation, so pick a spot that is breezy.

Room to Grow Each plant needs a specific amount of space, and one way to plan a kitchen garden is to look up the size of each vegetable (or fruit or herb) and simply draw circles to scale. Cut these out and arrange them as you like, making sure one plant doesn't shade another. To start you on your way, we have drawn some of summer's favorite vegetables. Copy them on stiff paper or cardboard, cut them out, assemble them (they will stand upright like vegetable chess pieces), and then arrange them on a plan of your kitchen garden. The plan should be drawn to a scale of three-quarters inch on paper equals one foot in the garden, the same scale as the vegetable cutouts.

If you want to try growing vegetables mixed in with flowers, or elsewhere in the garden, use these cutouts to experiment with locations. There is even a cutout of a half-barrel container in case you can't find any other place to plant vegetables. It's the perfect size for growing them and can go anywhere in the garden, even on the patio.

Deciduous fruit trees are highly ornamental when in flower, productive when laden with fruit. Some are especially beautiful, such as this 'Red Baron' peach, a special kind of peach called a "fruiting-flowering" variety putting out many more flowers than most. In this case each flower is double with many more petals than normal. The peaches aren't bad either and there is no shortage of them.

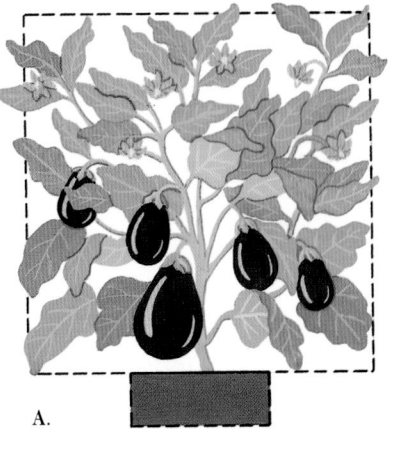

A.

KITCHEN GARDEN PLANNER

To make a vegetable garden in miniature, xerox pages 154–157. Glue sheets to stiff paper and cut pictures out along broken lines. Some need bases to stand on, with a slot cut for the tab. The scale is 3/4 inch to 1 foot. Make a plan of your garden to the same scale, place your cutout models on it, moving them about until the garden layout pleases you.

On pages 154–155:
A) For the eggplant, make a base 1½ inches in diameter.

B) The sunflower requires a circular base 1½ inches in diameter.

C) Two pumpkin plants can grow in a 6-foot diameter circular plot (4½ inches on model) if you weave their stems together. Slit semicircles along dotted lines and hook one over the other.

D) For the red bell pepper, make circular base 3/4 inch in diameter.

E) The row of corn should be folded vertically down the center into a free-standing L shape. It holds 16 plants.

On pages 156–157:
F) Cut out the bed of melons and lay it flat on your plan. Five plants will grow in this 3 x 12 foot bed.

G) The 12-foot-long trellis made of welded wire accommodates 11 bean plants and 5 cucumber vines.

H) A half-barrel planter can hold all sorts of vegetables. Assemble the model using tabs provided.

I) Tomatoes grow very well in a circular cage. Roll the tomato drawing into a cylinder, fastening with tabs and slots; insert bottom tabs into a circular base 2¼ inches in diameter.

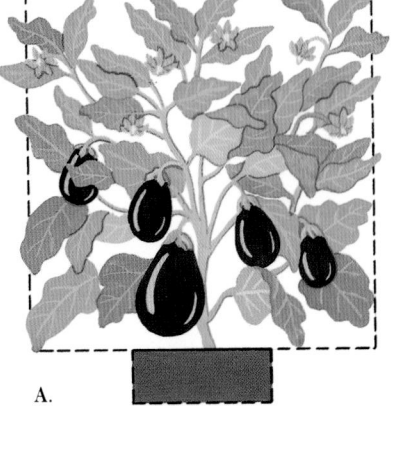

B.

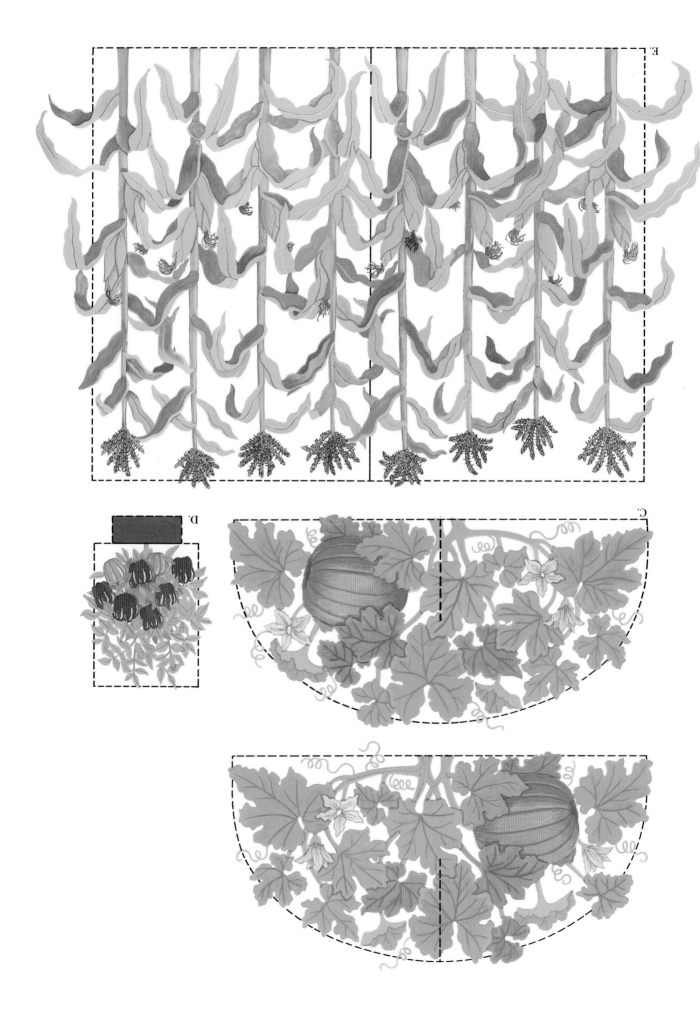

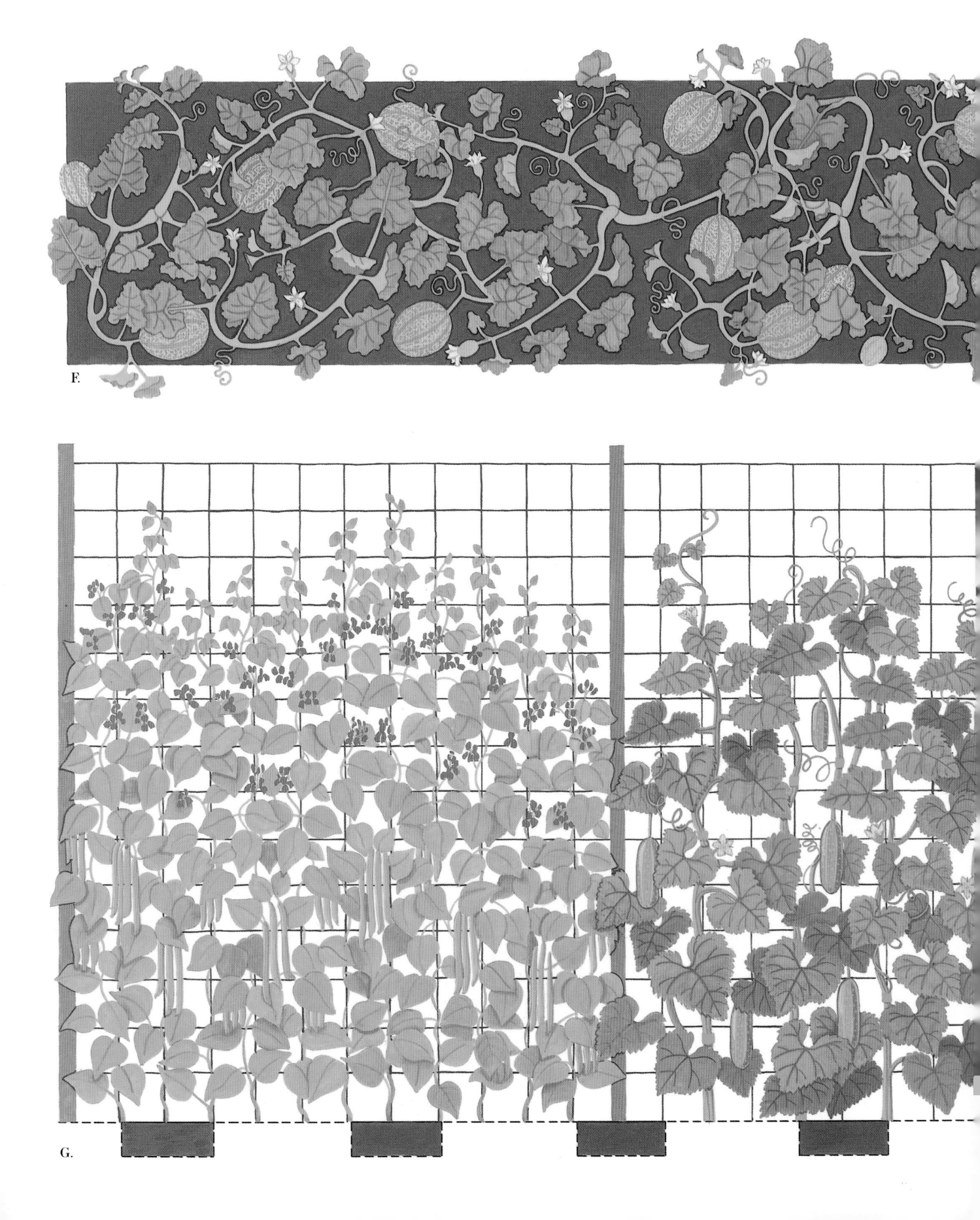

F.

G.

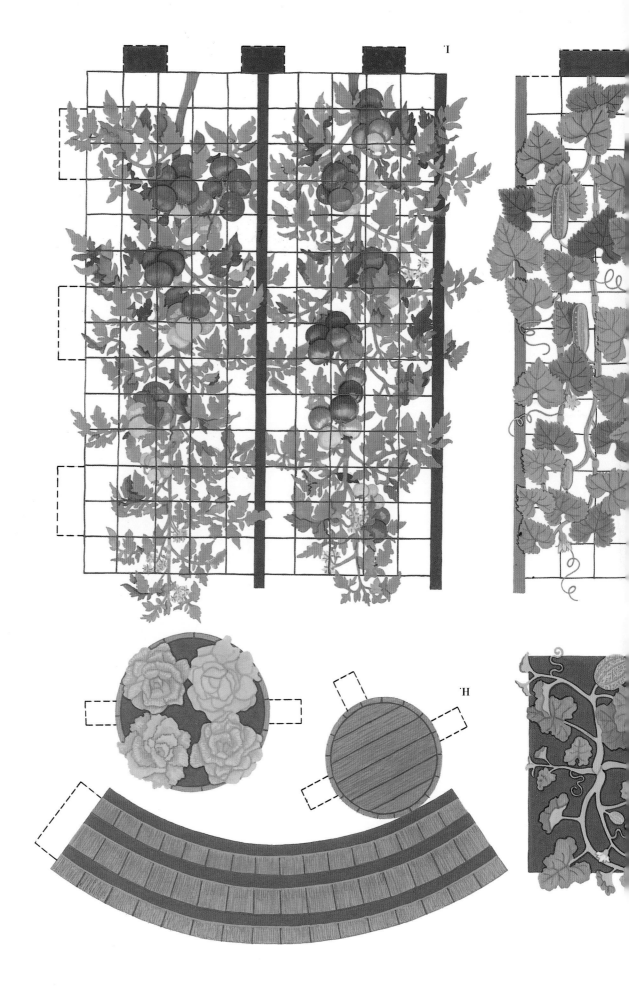

THE IMPORTANCE OF
SOIL PREPARATION

Good gardens have good soil; you need look no further for the secret to their success. And there are no shortcuts. Good soil takes work and time to build, but it is crucial to the successful growing of some of the showier plants.

In planning the garden, we have segregated plants so they grow in special beds, or in borders for flowers and vegetables, or in areas devoted to lawn or ground covers, or as background. Thinking of these areas one at a time, as separate places, helps with the planning process but it also aids with the planting because not all plants need the same kind of soil preparation: some need a great deal, others, somewhat surprisingly, do best without.

Plants That Need Soil Preparation
Flowers (especially perennials) and vegetables, but also lawn grasses and small ground covers—highly productive small plants whose roots grow mostly in the top foot or so of soil—need the most soil preparation. Typically, they grow wild in rich or well-drained soils, and their root systems are not designed to forage far and wide for moisture or nutrients. Another group of plants that need soil preparation are those that might be found growing wild in the woods, including most shade plants such as azaleas and camellias. These expect a soil that is porous and rich with organic matter, such as the leafy soils that make up the forest floor.

Plants That Don't But there is no need to prepare all the soil in a garden. Recent research tends to indicate that trees, shrubs, and shrubby ground covers actually seem to do better when the soil is not tampered with too much.

Their roots are very different from those of smaller plants, being designed to plumb the depths of the earth in search of moisture and nutrients. The roots of a tree can extend a distance four times the spread of its branches, while shrub roots can grow twenty or more feet deep into the ground.

They Need Air Even experienced gardeners sometimes forget the importance of air for roots. They talk about "good drainage," knowing that many plants need a soil that drains excess moisture so it will not become soggy. But what they are really speaking of is air at the roots. A plant's roots need air, just as the leaves do, and as do the soil organisms that help a plant convert raw nutrients into the form it can use. These microorganisms are what makes a soil smell good and seem healthy.

"Good drainage" simply means that there is not so much water in the soil that it excludes air. Water can actually bring air right behind it, if it keeps on moving down through the soil and doesn't rest. You can see in the bathtub what happens in the soil: water running down the drain sucks air in behind it, making that gurgling sound that tells you the tub is empty.

Making "Good Drainage" Rocky and sandy soils are naturally airy, but clay and loam soils are less so, in some cases having no air at all. It's easy enough to test for air—simply dig a hole, fill it with water, and see how long it takes to drain away. If it disappears quickly, you have an airy soil; if it sits for an hour or two you do not.

To make a soil airy you must open up the spaces between the soil particles. Rocky soils and sandy soils are composed of large particles with lots of air spaces already between them, but loam soils have much smaller parti-

The coiled hose, the trowel, the weeding fork, and pruning shears, these homely tools on pages 158–159 symbolize the work and craft of gardening.

A garden begins with the preparation of the soil which is composed of tiny particles. The smallest are the particles in a clay soil, the largest, the particles in a sandy soil. The tiny particles pack closely together, excluding air and water, so a gardener's job is to separate them chemically or physically. A rough turning over of the soil with a spade begins the process.

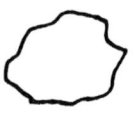

SAND PARTICLE

LOAM PARTICLE

CLAY PARTICLE

CHEMICAL SEPARATION

PHYSICAL SEPARATION

cles, while clay soils have particles that are essentially invisible with correspondingly little air space between.

You can open up these "heavy" soils chemically or physically, the latter being the most common way because physical amendments solve other problems at the same time. Soil gypsum (sold at nurseries) is a chemical amendment used in California to open up a soil; it chemically binds the particles into larger chunks. But it is only useful in certain soils that are alkaline and made of a heavy clay found in the Southwest. (In other parts of the country, lime is sometimes used instead of gypsum, but never in California because lime is for acid soils in generally high-rainfall areas; California soils are neutral or alkaline.) Soil amendments, such as ground bark or peat moss, have the physical means of separating soil particles; they simply shove aside the particles, providing airy spaces.

Preparing the Soil for Trees and Shrubs
Because the roots of trees and shrubs extend over so much territory, it is nearly impossible to effect much change in the soil where they grow. It is best to choose trees and shrubs that grow in your particular kind of soil. If a plant description says it "needs good drainage" and you garden on clay, forget it. Even if you do prepare the soil, the initial success will probably end in eventual failure with the plant dying after it has grown to be quite large.

Instead, plant something that likes the kind of soil you have and do little in the way of preparation. Dig the hole and pile the soil to one side. After planting, put the same soil back in the hole, but pulverize it thoroughly, making sure that there are no large chunks. The fluffed-up soil will improve drain-

age for those first few critical months. A year later the tree or shrub will not be able to distinguish the soil in the hole from the soil surrounding it so the roots will grow far and wide with no impediment.

Research has shown that roots want to stay in a well-prepared soil and not venture out, like someone under warm covers in a cold house. Since this well-prepared soil is also probably quite rich, the plant grows quickly at first but then falters when the roots become trapped in the planting hole. A tree or shrub planted in soil with little or no preparation, though it might get off to a slower start, will overtake its pampered brother within two years of planting.

A Fluffy Soil for Flowers In nature, flowers tend to grow in the best spots and the best soils, as do grasses and plants used as small ground covers in the garden. These all need the best soil in the garden, one that can be described as being "fluffy."

Flowers need good drainage and a soil that holds moisture near the surface and nutrients. The way to achieve these needs is to add organic matter to the soil. Organic matter may be home-made compost—well-rotted horse or dairy manure (not steer manure), specially treated sawdusts (nitrogen must be added or the organic amendment will steal it from the soil), or peat moss. At first it is best to use something that is available in large quantities; in California, that is usually some mixture of specially treated ground barks and sawdusts, often called RSA for "redwood soil amendment" since they contain redwood sawdust. Later, you can be more creative and find things like mushroom compost (left over from the growing of mushrooms) to further enrich a soil.

Soil preparation is an ongoing task since the original work gets undone in time. Thoroughly prepare a soil for flowers or vegetables and it makes everything else easier, from weeding to watering.

PREPARING A GARDEN BED

Flowers and vegetables need the best soil, and preparing their beds requires the most time and effort. Lawns and areas of ground cover have to have almost as much work done on their soil, but grass and small plants are neither as demanding or productive as flowers and vegetables. Think of what those last two produce in just a single

season! Where do they get the building materials or the energy but from the soil? Because organic matter, such as ground bark and peat moss, acts like little sponges, while also separating the soil particles, they are the preferred amendment (amendment being anything added to the soil). Sand can also separate soil particles and is used for that purpose in potting mixes, but it does not hold onto nutrients or keep moisture in the soil.

Sand Sand can have the reverse of the desired effect as a soil amendment —adding sand to some soils is like adding gravel to cement: it turns it into concrete. Sand can be useful as a soil

amendment where you do not want to increase the water- or nutrient-holding ability of a soil—in areas where herbs are to grow "lean" so their oils are more potent, for example. But proceed with caution and experiment first.

Moisture and Nutrients While it may seem odd that we want soil to retain moisture, while at the same time encouraging it to drain quickly, there is really no contradiction. We are just looking for optimum levels of moisture—enough to sustain plant growth for a week or more, but not so much that it excludes air or that the plant drowns. The best soil amendments maintain an optimum balance,

acting as reservoirs and soil separators. They also retain nutrients, those essential plant foods added to the soil as fertilizer. For this reason, amendments are even mixed with sandy soils because sandy soils have little ability of their own to hold onto moisture or nutrients. For all practical purposes, *any* soil that is going to be asked to grow flowers, vegetables, or lawn grasses should be improved with organic amendments.

A Test There is a simple test to see how your soil shapes up, before and after amending it. Squeeze a handful of moist—not wet—soil. If it remains a tight ball, it is a clay that needs amending to increase its airiness. If it crumbles into small chunks you have a good soil, at least as far as its structure is concerned. If it disintegrates into grains, you have a soil with too loose a texture—a sandy or rocky soil—and need to add amendments to increase its ability to hold onto nutrients and moisture.

After you have amended the soil, try the same test and see if it seems better. The best soil for flowers, vegetables, and lawn should crumble into small chunks and feel moist but not sticky or grainy.

And a Formula How much amendment should one add to a garden bed? Probably a truck full, and though it is sold by the bag, it can be ordered more economically by the truckload. Have the amendment piled to one side of the driveway and use a wheelbarrow to add it to the garden as you need it. You will want to add 25 to 50 percent amendment to the soil. If you plan to dig to a depth of a foot, this means adding a four-to-six-inch layer of amendment on top, then mixing it in. That's a lot.

Here is a recipe for preparing a 100-square-foot garden bed—a handy way to figure this all out. Divide all the garden beds into 100-square-foot sections—4 by 25 feet, 10 by 10 feet, 6 by 16½ feet, and so on—so you know how much of each ingredient to buy. Add the following amounts to each 100 square feet of garden bed:

Four three-cubic-foot sacks (a common size) of amendment, or about one-half a cubic yard (truckloads come by the cubic yard).

Two pounds of a complete, all-purpose fertilizer (a one-pound coffee can holds about two pounds of fertilizer).

Ten pounds of gypsum (only in alkaline soils, like California's, that are like a heavy clay).

Mix It In Now comes the work. All the amendment must be mixed smoothly into the soil the way a cook mixes flour and water—there should be no clumps or chunks. The best way is to dig up the garden with a spade after having watered it several days before. The soil should now be moist—not dry or wet—which is the best way to work it. The spade should have a long (eighteen-inch) blade and the blade should be straight. Work across the bed, turning over one row at a time, but don't completely flip the soil over, just turn it on its side. Don't be neat—you are trying to break the soil into big clods that will later be pulverized, and you want to leave a jagged bottom in your trench.

You do not use a rotary tiller at first. That tool digs to a uniform depth and it actually can polish the soil just beneath where it is working. This forms an interface between the soil that is being improved and the untouched, native soil just below, an interface that can block the movement of roots and water.

With the bed dug and rough, spread

Soil preparation in progress. After the soil has been turned with a spade, a small rototiller does an excellent job of mixing in the various amendments. Don't think this is a one-time job. Every few years flower beds such as this, and vegetable gardens as well, require rejuvenation because these prodigious producers use up a soil. At the same time you have the ideal opportunity to divide perennials or move plants to better locations. This is work best done during the cooler times of the year.

Even though there are many new watering devices, it is hard to beat the accuracy and efficiency of the old-fashioned watering basin. That collar of mounded-up soil funnels water directly to the roots of the plants. Here watering basins surround newly planted or recently pruned roses. Watering basins also let you water new plants more often than nearby established plants (which might suffer from too much watering). You simply fill the new plants' basins more often.

the amendments and fertilizer (and gypsum if you are using it) on top of the clods of earth, but note the previous precaution about gypsum. The fertilizer can be any inexpensive brand that contains all three essential nutrients—nitrogen, phosphorus, and potassium—in about equal amounts. It will have numbers like 8-8-8 on the label, or 12-10-10, or something similar. Unless you know what you are doing, avoid fertilizers with a large first number. That first number indicates the amount of nitrogen; too much of it can give plants a chemical burn.

Time for a Tiller Now you can use a rotary tiller (available where gardening equipment is rented) to do the final mixing. You don't need a big unmanageable tiller because the ground has already been roughened and loosened by spading. The nice thing about the tiller is that it is going to thoroughly pulverize the soil and thoroughly mix the ingredients, as an eggbeater would blend flour and water. If you wish, you can do this final mixing with a spade or spading fork, but it will be difficult to break up all the clods completely or to mix the ingredients thoroughly. It will also be more work than you can imagine.

STOMP IT DOWN, WATER, AND WATCH OUT FOR WEEDS

When you have finished adding amendments to the soil, the ground is going to be a lot higher than when you began. By amending, tilling, and digging, you have fluffed up the soil like an eiderdown quilt. This is an advantage because plants are most sensitive to too much water at their crowns— where the roots join the trunk or stem of the plant—and it is impossible for the crowns to get too wet if they are a

few inches above the ground level.

Most likely, however, the bed when amended will be more than a few inches above ground, so you are going to have to stomp it down. It may seem crazy to fluff up the soil and add all those air spaces only to stomp it back down, but you must recompress it or the air spaces are going to be so big and the soil so porous that water will simply run right through and barely dampen the new plants—a soil can be *too* airy. Actually "stomp" may be too strong a word. On lawns, this is done with a big, water-filled roller, but on a garden bed it is enough simply to walk firmly all over the fluffy soil. In time, the soil will settle of its own accord and you can expect it to settle even further after you have stomped it down.

Now Water and Wait Watering will help settle the soil additionally, and rain will do even more. Put a sprinkler on the bed and water it thoroughly; water it several times, in fact, to bring up the weeds whose seeds may be lying in wait. The way to germinate seed is to keep it constantly moist, so for a week or more don't let the bed dry out.

You really want to wait for the weeds to sprout *before you plant*. (This may be the best advice you ever get.) The nearly constant watering is going to sprout the weeds; but because of the muddy ground, it is going to be difficult to enter the bed and get them out if you have already planted flowers.

If before planting you wait two weeks, watering all the time, the weeds will sprout and you can hoe them out in a jiffy. Or spray them with a short-lived herbicide such as Roundup or Kleenup. These work best in warm weather, killing roots and tops. Because these herbicides are short lived, you can plant as soon as the weeds are dead.

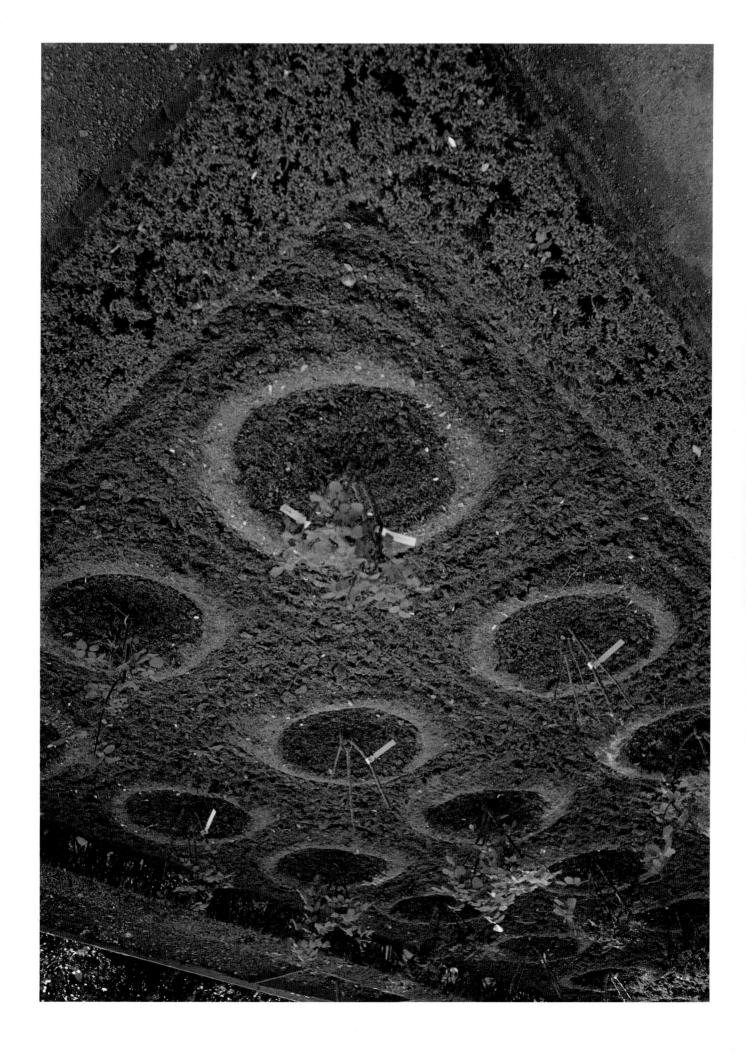

Lots of Weeds? If you are starting a garden bed or lawn in an area where a great many weeds grew or are still growing, it's better to back up a little and take care of them before preparing the soil. Again, Roundup or Kleenup are the most frequently used herbicides, but you must follow the directions carefully since they work only under some conditions and in certain

kinds of weather. In heavily weed-infested areas, where there are no tree or shrub roots, you might want to invest in having the ground fumigated professionally. That will kill everything, though you must wait to plant for about a month after fumigation. Only fumigation wipes out all the seeds and roots of perennial weeds (such as Bermuda or devil grass). Because it is the nature of weeds to be survivors, they can withstand the most vigorous watering and hoeing; even after such treatment some weeds still remain hidden and waiting for the right time to spring up again.

You will never be completely rid of weeds, but a good start goes a long way toward keeping them in check.

Not the End of It Soil preparation is never finished. It is an ongoing job. Every time an area is replanted, it must be amended again because previous amendments are used up by the plants, or they simply lose their efficacy. You needn't add as much after the original amendment, but at every opportunity you should continue to add to the soil of a flower bed or vegetable garden.

Lawns and ground-cover plantings are another matter. Once they are planted there is little you can do to further improve the soil, other than fertilize. They too will eventually need to be dug up and replanted, though that might take as long as twenty years.

A Possible Exception There is one instance where you might not want to prepare a flower bed in the manner just described: if you are going to grow plants that are native to your area or similar in their demands to native ones. In California, there are many plants that we can grow with little or no

water beyond the regular rainfall. For these plants the beds are perhaps best left with little or no soil preparation other than digging and tilling it. Adding organic amendments would increase the drainage of the soil, but that would also mean you must water more often because amended soil is more porous than natural soil and the water runs right through it—this is true, at least, in the case of clay soils, our most common kind.

The catch is: You must be very careful about watering in summer because if you do the soil will be unnaturally damp for that time of the year. Native and other drought-tolerant plants should be watered their first year in the ground while they are becoming established, but then irrigation should be as infrequent as once a month. Avoid watering in August altogether, or you will encourage root rots that thrive in moist, warm soil.

DIGGING A HOLE AND OTHER PERTINENT PLANTING INFORMATION

Trees and shrubs are the easiest to plant because they require the least soil preparation, even though the hole you plant them in must be big. Some new research suggests that you dig this hole in a new fashion: to avoid any kind of "interface" where two different kinds of soil come together like a solid wall. You do not want the hole to be neat, but rather to have a jagged surface so the roots cannot become confused and begin circling round and round as they often do inside a nursery container.

The hole need not be deep. Dig it just deep enough so the plant can rest on a pedestal of solid ground after planting and so it will not settle. You don't want it to settle, or in time its crown is likely to become buried, making it very susceptible to all sorts of fatal rots and diseases.

The hole should be wide, however, about three times as wide as the root ball. On either side of the solid pedestal, dig a little deeper so the roots have a place to go; in the bottom of this circular trench put a complete fertilizer. It should look something like the drawings on page 166.

Remember not to add amendments to the dirt that you shovel back into the hole, just pulverize it so there are no clods or chunks, and gently tamp it down with your foot as you fill.

Root-bound Plants Watch out for plants that are root-bound. This means that the roots have begun to circle inside the nursery container or to collect at its sides or bottom. They must be untangled and straightened out, and if they have become completely matted you may have to pull or cut some off to give them a fresh start. If this is necessary, you should also cut off some small branches in order not to overburden the remaining roots. The plant will quickly recover. After untangling the roots, drape them over the sides of the pedestal in the planting hole.

You must also watch out for root-bound plants in garden beds, but you can dig an ordinary hole because all of the soil has been prepared. Planting in your rich and fluffy new soil will be a treat. Around new plants be sure to press down the soil firmly with your hands, or it will be so loose that the water will simply flow around and past the new plants' roots.

Can't Water Too Much At first you almost can't water too much. The roots have yet to grow out into the soil, and it is hard to keep that root ball moist, but after a few weeks, as the roots begin to

spread into the new soil, the watering should begin to taper off. The first year make sure the plant has adequate water at all times, but after that it should be established well enough to get by on a minimum. After the plant has had a year in the ground, it is far more important to let the soil dry a little between irrigations or rains so it does not rot from too much moisture.

Bare-Root Planting There is another way to plant and that is "bare root." Bare-root plants are just that—they are sold while dormant with no soil around their roots. In California, it is the favored way to plant roses, deciduous fruit trees, and even some deciduous ornamental trees such as birch; the time to plant is short—January and February.

Many believe that planting bare root is the best way, although it is possible only with the few plants sold like that. A problem with planting anything grown in a container is that the roots have been restricted and are not growing in a natural fashion—they are growing around in a circle instead of spreading out. Planting bare root lets you position the roots so they can continue to reach out into the soil and you can be sure that they are not pot-bound.

It is best to buy bare-root plants that have been kept in bins filled with damp sawdust, but instead, most nurseries sell them with their roots wrapped in plastic bags. When you buy them wrapped in this fashion, you are gambling that the roots are alive and healthy, not dry, or (more likely) rotted. If the roots are the least bit dry, they should be soaked overnight in a pail of water to plump them up. If they are rotted, they will feel squishy, and if you cut the roots, the inside will not be white but off-color. Reject them!

How you dig a hole would seem to be one of those things that never change, but recent research has shown there is a better way. The idea is to dig a hole in which the plant's roots will not become trapped. So make the sides of the hole slope away from the center to encourage roots to grow out and away from the plant (upper left).

It is also important that the plant not settle into the soil after planting, so leave a pedestal of undisturbed soil for the plant to sit on (center left).

Bare-root plants go in a similar hole but their roots should be spread over a cone of soil mounded up in the bottom (lower left).

Staking is a regrettable practice because it adds little to the aesthetic quality of a garden. But staking is absolutely necessary for tall flowers such as delphiniums. Stakes should go in the ground at planting time so they do not disturb the growing roots later on. Tie the plant directly to the stake with something soft and flexible. Trees and other large plants should not be staked this way; they should be tied between two sturdy stakes placed about a foot on either side of the trunk. This allows them to sway in every breeze and develop strength. Tied tightly to a stake, they lose strength, like an arm confined in a cast.

Enough Roots? You are also gambling that there are enough roots. Many roots are lost when the plant is dug from the field, but there should still be a good number. If there aren't, consider taking the plant back to the nursery in exchange for another. A few nurseries are now potting up their bare-root plants. They see it as a compromise solution. If you plant immediately, you can simply shake the soil off the roots and plant it bare root; if you can't get around to it right away and wait too late in the bare-root season, the plant will be able to root into the potting mix in the container, and then you can plant it as if it were container-grown.

With bare-root plants, never let the roots dry out completely, but also never let them soak for longer than overnight. They should be plump with moisture before being planted, and it is best to keep them out of the sun for the first few days. Spread the roots out, then dig a hole a little wider than the spread of the roots. In the bottom of this hole mound up a cone of soil to set the plant on. This cone supports the plant and lets you arrange the roots so they are all heading in the right direction—down and out.

Sprinkle a little fertilizer in the bottom of the hole and cover it with an inch of soil. You can add soil amendments to the dirt that will be put back in the hole, or you can simply put the soil back in the hole after first pulverizing it. There is some debate about which is the better way. Do not fill the hole with soil that is wet or full of clods. Some gardeners sieve it through a quarter-inch screening to make sure it is not lumpy. It's very important that the soil be pulverized and fine and that it be firmed down as it is put back in the hole. You want to avoid any large air spaces next to the roots. After

filling the hole, mound up soil in a ring around its circumference to make a basin, then thoroughly soak the soil.

WATERING WISDOM, STAKING, AND MULCHING

Water is a precious resource in California where gardeners should use it prudently. Trees and background plantings of shrubs, large-scale ground covers, and other utilitarian plantings should be chosen for their ability to survive with little water. Water should be saved for the flower beds and the vegetable garden, and these should be watered with care.

Much of the water we put on the garden is wasted by evaporation. The trick is to wean plants from a regimen of frequent watering to watering less and less often but more thoroughly each time. Let the water run awhile so it soaks deep into the soil. There it is safe from evaporation, a waiting reservoir for plant roots.

Though many people think they must water every few days, it is quite possible to water less than once a week, even in the southern half of the state, if when you water you do so thoroughly. Then, before watering again, check with a spade or soil probe to see if the soil is dry several inches down, and water only if it is. In time, you will develop an instinct for when to water.

When you first plant, you must water often because the plants haven't tapped into the soil yet. During the first few weeks, it is almost impossible to overwater, but after that, begin the weaning process. Later in a plant's life overwatering is a definite danger and the leading cause of plant mortality.

Fertilizing Is No Mystery Feeding plants or, more properly, fertilizing them, is easy if you do not get confused by the multiplicity of products made for the job. All you really need to add to most California soils—after initially preparing the soil—is nitrogen, which is the first of the three numbers on a package of fertilizer—the 10 in the 10-8-8 formula found on the package label. The other elements should be added whenever you are planting or preparing a soil, otherwise they are of minor importance since they cannot move down in the soil, even in liquid form. They must be down where the roots are from the beginning.

But nitrogen does move in the soil. In fact, it moves right on through a soil, beyond and beneath the plant roots so it needs to be added regularly. It is the element most responsible for growth. Always use products that are high in nitrogen, fertilizers with numbers like 14-0-0, 16-8-8, 10-8-8, or something similar. Do be aware that very high nitrogen fertilizers, with numbers like 24-0-0, can burn plants if used improperly, so apply them precisely according to instructions.

If fertilizers still seem mysterious, simply buy a product labeled as an all-purpose granular fertilizer, scatter it among the plants, and use a sprinkler to water it into the soil.

Container Exceptions Plants grown in containers are the exception to many of the rules previously mentioned. They probably should be watered every few days, or even every day in hot weather, and they need to be fertilized often—every few weeks—with a fertilizer that has all the necessary elements since the plants are growing in an artificial soil. It is easiest to buy potting soil by the bag and extend it by adding one-third to one-half natural soil. You will also have to water less often with this mixture.

Staking Staking plants is something to avoid if possible—but often it is not possible. Some plants just won't stand up by themselves, delphiniums being an example. So if you plant delphiniums, foxgloves, or other tall plants, put stakes in the ground at the same time to avoid damaging the roots later.

Mulching The last step, and one that is optional, is to cover the bare ground around plants with a mulch of some kind. In the flower garden mulch keeps rain and sprinklers from splashing mud up onto the foliage, and helps keep down weeds, though it may also encourage all sorts of bugs. These include earwigs and cutworms as well as their predators, such as ground beetles or stinkbugs. Mulches also help regulate changes in soil temperature from day to day. They can be a problem if kept too moist, for plants will make roots in the mulch when they should be rooting much deeper. The ideal is a mulch of medium-sized organic matter (about the size of the pieces that come out of a compost shredder), piled about two-to-three inches deep and kept dry with infrequent watering. Plastic and other artificial mulches are best to use in the vegetable garden where appearance isn't so important. What does matter is not to encourage bugs: there is nothing worse than finding a head of lettuce full of earwigs.

THE ZIGS AND ZAGS OF GARDENING

Many people have the idea that the road to a good garden is straight—you come up with a plan, plant accordingly, and then wait for everything to mature. You expect to do a little weeding and tidying up from time to time, and there will be tempting new plants each spring, but otherwise you are finished—the garden is complete.

In fact, a gardener's course contains many zigs and zags. Something grows too big, or is the wrong color, or up and dies. A path is in the wrong place or a patio gets too much or too little sun. What is more, your taste is sure to change as you discover plants you didn't know about or after you see what others have done in their gardens. While my intent in telling you this is to forewarn you of these zigs and zags, I do not want to sound the least bit discouraging since the ever-changing nature of a garden is one of its most charming attributes. Gardening is an ongoing affair, changing with the seasons and the years. It is never static and you are never done. A garden is always alive and growing and so should be the gardener.

In my own garden I have moved one azalea seven times trying to find the perfect place. I have excitedly ripped up entire sections to make room for newly discovered plants. A favorite tree died but the resulting vacancy left an unexpected sunny spot for flowers. The central path has been added to and subtracted from to afford a better flow through the plantings (and to make room for a wheelbarrow at one point). After discovering how wonderful a small bed of flowers and ornamental grasses looked when back-lit by the sun, I even moved a patio and bench so they could overlook this sunny scene.

You do not want to tear up paths and patios too often, however, and the guidelines in this book should help give the garden a solid backbone to begin with. But do not be afraid to make changes when necessary. Look forward to them, because with every change comes experience, knowledge, awareness, satisfaction, and growth.

Some of the basic tools of gardening: A straight-bladed spade for turning soil and dividing plants, kept sharp with a bastard file; a small trowel and fork for planting, loosening soil, and weeding; pruning shears, including the long-bladed Corona No. 5, a favorite for cutting back perennials; a little container with a granular fertilizer to add to the soil when planting or cultivating; measuring spoons; plant tags on which to write the name of a plant and when it was planted. Without this last bit of information, you cannot really learn what you are growing and when to expect it. Names are important for the growth of the garden—and the gardener.

INDEX

PICTURE CREDITS